T0338221

EARLY PRAISE FOR

FOUNDATIONS OF INVESTMENT MANAGEMENT

"This marvelous book is thorough, rigorous, and comprehensible—an unusual combination. It is an indispensable reference for both practitioners and those interested in the investment management arena. It deserves to be on the bookshelf of every serious investor. David Linton has beaten the market of investment books!"

—**William H. Miller III,** Founder of Miller Value Partners and Former Chairman and CIO of Legg Mason Capital Management

"David Linton successfully tackles the ambitious task of providing an all-in handbook for newly minted finance professionals. The resulting volume offers extensive coverage of the theory and practice of finance, but it also avoids getting bogged down in extraneous details. Linton's remarkable command of the material makes the exposition remarkably clear and, when mixed with some lively anecdotes, even entertaining. I am confident that this book will serve in the years ahead as an essential guide for folks who are new to the industry, as well as for those who have labored on trading floors longer than they might care to admit."

—**Nathan Sheets**, former Under Secretary of the U.S. Treasury for International Affairs and Director of International Finance at the Federal Reserve Board

"David Linton is the epitome of a scholar practitioner. He understands the theory, the real world, and how the two interact. *Foundations of Investment Management* is a comprehensive examination of the process of investing, covering the key investment instruments, the markets they trade in, and their role in portfolio construction. Although detailed, it is written in a style that is accessible to non-professionals. Experienced investors will also benefit from insights on the interrelationships between macroeconomics, regulators, and markets and how the keen mind of an experienced investor thinks. This book will benefit anyone looking to improve their knowledge of, and skill at, investing."

—**Stephen G. Moyer,** CFA, Adjunct Professor, University of Southern California, Author of *Distressed Debt Analysis*

"This book gives the reader an essential inside look at the investment industry from someone whom I have had the pleasure working with 'in the trenches.' It's an accurate, timely, and very readable account of how different pieces of the financial markets, policy making, and investment community come together to create today's market ecosystem. Even more important, the book brings vividly to life the individuals, companies, and policymakers who are behind some of the most important and consequential decisions that will impact our investment future."

—**Vineer Bhansali,** PhD, Founder and CIO, LongTail Alpha, LLC. Former Managing Director and Head of Quantitative Portfolios, PIMCO

"David transforms the theoretical concepts of finance into practical investment material. In the current environment of low interest rates and record high equity markets, David's framework provides a useful guide to navigate the treacherous financial waters of passive and active portfolio management."

—**Ben Emons,** Managing Director, Medley Global Advisors, Author of *Mastering Stocks and Bonds*, *The Financial Domino Effect*, and *The End of the Risk-Free Rate*

"*Foundations of Investment Management* is an ideal balance of breadth and depth; it covers all the critical areas in which a successful asset manager must be proficient while not burying practitioners in technical details. Additionally, reader-friendly anecdotes highlight and simplify complicated principles and each chapter closes with investment implications that ensure the content is actionable. This book is perfect for both seasoned professionals as well as students of the investment management industry, and it is a must read for onboarding investment professionals entering the industry."

—**Bob Greer**, Scholar in Residence, J.P. Morgan Center for Commodities at the University of Colorado Denver Business School, Senior Advisor at Core Commodity Management, Author of *Intelligent Commodity Investing*

"*Foundations of Investment Management* is an unparalleled volume that is based on well-researched finance principles, but mixes in rich, on-the-ground knowledge from leading practitioners. This book brings in the best of both worlds. The end result is a one-stop shop of investment knowledge. You can save money and space on your bookshelf by having this one volume replace other texts. This is the new go-to book for students, academics, and seasoned professionals."

—**Dominic Garcia,** Chief Investment Officer, New Mexico PERA

"David Linton has compiled a very thorough guidebook to the asset management business in *Foundations of Investment Management*. He offers an extremely user-friendly overview for new investment professionals, those interested in pursuing an investment career, or seasoned professionals who want to better understand how capital markets operate. The book is laid out logically and each chapter stands on its own. Readers will appreciate the friendly and fun approach that David takes to effectively articulate complex subjects."

—**Michael Skillman,** Chief Executive Officer, Cadence Capital Management

"*Foundations* provides a great starting point for young professionals looking to understand both the breadth and details of investing. David does a wonderful job blending a practitioner's application with academic theory. The stories are thoughtful and bring to life so many things we hear in the financial press. Having been in the investment industry for over 20 years, resources such as this are hard to find and much needed."

—**Dominic Nolan,** Senior Managing Director, Pacific Asset Management

FOUNDATIONS OF
INVESTMENT
MANAGEMENT

MASTERING FINANCIAL MARKETS, ASSET CLASSES, AND INVESTMENT STRATEGIES

DAVID E. LINTON, CFA

Copyright © 2020 by David Linton

ISBN-13: 978-1-60427-165-2

Printed and bound in the U.S.A. Printed on acid-free paper.

10 9 8 7 6 5 4 3

Please visit the WAV section of the publisher's website at www.jrosspub
.com/wav for the Library of Congress Cataloging-in-Publication Data.

Direct all inquiries to J. Ross Publishing, Inc., 300 S. Pine Island Rd., Suite 305, Plantation, FL 33324.

Phone: (954) 727-9333
Fax: (561) 892-0700
Web: www.jrosspub.com

DEDICATIONS

First, to my beautiful wife, Laura—without whom this book would never have been written—I am immensely grateful for the support you have given me and the love and guidance you have given our children.

Second, to my amazing children, Leah, Joshua, and Matthew—without whom this book would have been written two years earlier—I wish you to be good, brave, and happy. Watching you grow has brought me immense joy, and I hope one day you might dust off this book, browse through it, and ask me about it.

Finally, to my readers—without whom this book would have no utility—I appreciate that you have decided to spend your personal time reading this work, and I hope you gain some insights that might help you further your careers and serve your clients.

CONTENTS

FOREWORD

The field of investment management is constantly evolving. From ticker tapes, to the internet, to whatever comes next, as our industry changes you must be able to change with it.

By selecting this book, you are likely relatively early in your educational journey. There is much to learn, but as you learn it's the ability to apply that information that is going to help you and your clients succeed, which is commonly distilled into concepts like generating alpha (i.e., outperforming your peers).

From that perspective, this book provides not only an excellent introduction to the field of investment management, but it also, perhaps more important, provides context on how to make this information actionable in a way that few books do (or try). While it's important to know what a stock is, for example, it's far more useful to understand how stocks or other investments come together to help clients accomplish their goals.

The "now what" is something this book constantly seeks to address . . . how do you take this new knowledge and frame it in a way that will help you generate alpha; however you define it. For example, should interest rates fall, how should the managers of a defined benefit plan respond in order to ensure the plan does not experience a shortfall in saving for their liabilities? How should investors make sense of central bank activities? If you find yourself either as an institutional investor or interacting with one, understanding their objectives and reaction functions and how they position their investments given changing market conditions is invaluable. This book provides the answers to those questions and many more, explaining in detail how to benefit from this knowledge.

Whenever you learn something, it's important to understand the qualifications of the instructor. I've had the privilege of knowing David for more than decade. He has worked in a variety of positions that provide him with a unique perspective on the fundamentals of investing, as well as how to apply these fundamentals in your career. This experience gives him insights that someone purely from academia may not appreciate and allows him to thread theory into practice.

In closing, I love this industry and I'm excited that you want to learn more about it. The more time you spend reading books like this one the better prepared you'll be for whatever the future holds. Good luck and enjoy!

David Blanchett, PhD, CFA, CFP
Head of Retirement Research
Morningstar Investment Management LLC

PREFACE

Over the years, I've had the good fortune to work with several colleagues who composed their own books and thought pieces that brought value to their readers and investors. My objective is that this work can contribute, in at least some small way, to a body of investment knowledge that further enables investment professionals to provide valuable services to their clients. A secondary objective is to help bridge the gap between what is taught at universities or can be found in a textbook, and how investment management functions from a practitioner's perspective. Therefore, I believe this work should be particularly useful to investment professionals who are generally early in their careers and are still trying to understand how their roles fit within a broader industry.

With few exceptions, my experience of working in a variety of capacities—trading, managing portfolios, and developing products—has been positive and I consider myself to be exceptionally fortunate; the professionals with whom I've worked and the opportunities they afforded to me were truly extraordinary. While my work ethic played a role in my career progression, luck was certainly a component as well. I sincerely hope that my readers will have similar opportunities and positive experiences during their careers.

While writing this book, I surveyed nearly a hundred professionals at dozens of buy-side firms and asked them (among other things): "What do younger investment professionals with whom you work generally not know or understand (that you think they should)?" and "What did you learn later in your career that you wish you had learned earlier in your career?" I sincerely appreciate the insight and feedback they provided, which no doubt contributed to this book's content and utility. Additionally, as I composed this book it became apparent that despite my best efforts, this book would benefit from one or more individuals contributing to each chapter's content. It was at that time that I contacted several friends, colleagues, former professors, and mentors—most of whom agreed to coauthor individual chapters. Each one of the coauthors is an expert in his or her respective field, and I am thrilled to have assembled this team.

Their generous donation of time and knowledge has contributed to the depth, relevance, and utility of each chapter. My sincerest thanks.

Additionally, I hope that this book will be a friendly and fun read; each chapter can be read independently and is bookended with stories and investment implications. Additionally, I've included a plethora of anecdotes, data, and primary sources in hopes of bringing to life the most valuable and relevant trends, tools, pitfalls, and best practices. For example (and my first anecdote), not long after I started a position as a repo trader at PIMCO, I was asked to compose and distribute a note discussing the LIBOR fixing scandal. This note would be sent to the firm's global traders, portfolio managers, and analysts (about 400 in total). I dutifully composed a thorough piece, complete with a detailed history and timeline, and I sent it out. About five minutes later, Bill Gross, founder and then CIO of PIMCO (and known in the press as the *Bond King*) responded (replying all): "Gee, this is a great history lesson. But, if I wanted a history lesson, I'd read a book. What are the investment implications ??!!"

At that moment, my stomach sank, but in hindsight, it was a spot-on observation. Investment management organizations should always maintain a laser-focus on ensuring everything it does is in the client's best interest. From the portfolio manager's perspective, this means that every analysis ought to have an investment implication (even if the implication is to continue to monitor until there is a future development). Otherwise, the *analysis* is just noise and functions as a distraction from the primary objective of a portfolio manager, which is generating strong, risk-adjusted returns. This is the first lesson I learned from the man who most in our industry consider to be history's greatest bond investor. With this lesson in mind, every chapter will close with a summary and investment implications.

Finally, I have been asked to state that this book does not constitute an endorsement of any of the people, products, or organizations mentioned herein. All of the opinions are my own, or those of my coauthors, and not those of any current or former employers.

Enjoy!

ACKNOWLEDGMENTS

This book has been shaped by the insight, feedback, and suggestions of countless friends and colleagues. Their contributions have added to this book's depth, accuracy, relevance, and utility. No doubt I will forget to mention someone (sorry!), but I will do my best to see that those who generously volunteered their time receive recognition. Thank you.

To begin, I would like to thank Steve Buda at J. Ross Publishing, without whom this book would have remained an aspiration and an unpublished manuscript. Steve's guidance and willingness to publish a book from a relatively unknown investment professional were paramount to this project's completion and (hopefully) success. Friend and colleague, Steve Moyer, introduced me to Steve Buda as well as reviewed early drafts of several chapters. He also kindly agreed to coauthor a chapter with me, and he and his TAs made several material edits to my chapter on fixed income. Robin Yonis, a friend and colleague, graciously provided invaluable counsel, while my manager, Matt Babcock, supported this initiative from its inception and shaped this book's outline and format.

Separately, each of my coauthors donated their time and knowledge, and in doing so, materially increased this book's value to our readers:

- Andy Ross, who was a pleasure to work with and without whom the chapter on hedge funds would have remained more elementary in content and tedious in convention.
- Ben Emons, from whom I learned much about the publishing industry as well as a thing or two about investment strategies in a zero-interest-rate environment.
- Bob Greer, whose industry experience and knowledge of commodities is second to none.
- Dan Villalon, who helped me make it through both Professor Fama's course as well as the chapter on factor investing. Both were lifts that needed a mental heavyweight of Dan's caliber.

- Di Zhou, who also helped me complete Professor Fama's course, is a fellow USC Trojan and a good friend. I hope readers benefit from her insights on stock picking because I have.
- Matt Brenner, to whom I am grateful for both connecting me with my current employer as well as elevating the discussion on institutional investors.
- Steve Moyer, without whom this book would not have come to fruition. A friend and scholar, Steve's contributions to the chapters on financial markets and fixed income were significant.

Separate from my coauthors, several friends, colleagues, and mentors reviewed draft chapters and offered both feedback and encouragement, including: Audrey Cheng, Bhanu Singh, Bill Gross, Bruce Brittain, Ivor Schucking, James Meehan, Jessie Shapiro, Nathan Sheets, Peter Bretschger, Ronit Walney, Timothy Hanlon, and Yuri Garbazov.

Next, I'd like to thank my colleagues at Pacific Life Fund Advisors, who encouraged me to advance this project and reviewed portions of the draft manuscript, namely: Carleton Muench, Howard Hirakawa, Jordan Fettman, and Matt Babcock. I would like also to thank the legal team at my former employer, PIMCO, for reviewing my manuscript for accuracy. They were professional, friendly, and thoughtful.

Additionally, I want to acknowledge the contribution from the following investment professionals. Each completed a comprehensive survey that was designed to help ensure that I would cover all topics and answer all questions pertinent to our target audience. For example, two of these questions were: (1) What did you recently learn that you wish you had known earlier? and (2) What do recently hired investment professionals not know—but should? While I couldn't incorporate every response into this work, the insight I received no doubt enhanced this book's utility, and for this I am grateful.

My thanks to: Alex Haugh, Alina Rosu, Barry Motz, Ben Emons, Bhanu Singh, Bruce Brittain, Chris Floyd, Christine Cawthon, Colleen Tycz, Dan McGee, Dan Villalon, Daniel Ong, David Blanchett, Don Vessels, Donelle Chisolm, Emanuele Bergagnini, Ivor Schucking, Jacqueline Hurley, Jay Warwick, Jordan Fettman, Keri Nuzzi, Kevin Holt, Kyle Colburn, Leo Tallon, Mani Govil, Margaret Clemons, Marshall Murphy, Matt Babcock, Matthew Cobb, Matthew Pearson, Michael Giesecke, Nick Hooten, Nikki Noriega, Peter Bretschger, Robert Lambert, Russell Shtern, Ryan Kagy, Scott Berman, Sean Barrette, Shawn Connor, Steve Moyer, Tad Young, Ted Smith, Tim Paulson, Timothy Hanlon, Tom Felago, and the seventeen people who chose to remain anonymous.

Finally, my wife, Laura, whom at the very moment at which I am writing this, is preparing dinner for three hungry children, ordering scholastic workbooks, and paying the power bill. She works far harder than I do, and her contribution to our family is far greater than I will make. She's as beautiful as the day we met, and her energy, dedication, and love for her family are inspirational. This book would not have been possible without her.

ABOUT THE AUTHOR

David E. Linton, CFA, is the Director of Portfolio Construction and Manager Research at Pacific Life Fund Advisors LLC (PLFA) and has 15 years of investment experience. He is also an Adjunct Professor of Finance and Business Economics at the USC Marshall School of Business, teaching Investment Analysis and Portfolio Management. In his current role with Pacific Life, he is responsible for the portfolio construction of the PLFA suite of asset allocation products, and he shares responsibility for the manager research and due diligence  for roughly $40 billion in sub-advisory relationships. Additionally, Mr. Linton is a member of the PLFA Investment Committee and Asset Allocation group, specializing in fixed income, and he is the lead trader for the Pacific Funds Multi-Asset Fund. Prior to joining PLFA, Mr. Linton was a Vice President and Portfolio Manager at PIMCO. While there, Mr. Linton worked in a variety of capacities and his responsibilities included comanaging PIMCO's overnight cash investing and financing book on the Short-Term Desk, working as a sovereign credit analyst on the Emerging Markets Desk, and trading investment grade nonfinancial corporate bonds on the Investment Grade Corporate Desk. Mr. Linton was also a Product Manager and member of the PIMCO Solutions Group with a focus on tail risk hedging. Mr. Linton has a BS in business administration from the University of Southern California, graduating magna cum laude, and an MBA from the University of Chicago Booth School of Business, graduating with honors.

At J. Ross Publishing we are committed to providing today's professional with practical, hands-on tools that enhance the learning experience and give readers an opportunity to apply what they have learned. That is why we offer free ancillary materials available for download on this book and all participating Web Added Value™ publications. These online resources may include interactive versions of the material that appears in the book or supplemental templates, worksheets, models, plans, case studies, proposals, spreadsheets and assessment tools, among other things. Whenever you see the WAV™ symbol in any of our publications, it means bonus materials accompany the book and are available from the Web Added Value Download Resource Center at www.jrosspub.com.

Downloads for *Foundations of Investment Management* include classroom-friendly Powerpoint slides for each chapter covering main points and investment implications, simple optimization examples, a special online-only chapter of the book, and several of the book's most insightful exhibits.

Part I

Markets, Vehicles, and Participants

1

FINANCIAL ASSETS AND CAPITAL MARKETS

Stephen G. Moyer, CFA[1]
Adjunct Professor
USC Marshall School of Business

David E. Linton, CFA[1]
Director, Portfolio Construction and Manager Research
Pacific Life Fund Advisors LLC

J. Wellington Wimpy, or just *Wimpy*, is the memorable, bumbling, and over-weight character in the comic strip *Popeye*. Desiring a hamburger to consume today, but lacking the funds to pay for the hamburger, he became known among Popeye readers for asking diner patrons to extend him a loan to pay for his dinner. The phrase, "I'll gladly pay you Tuesday for a hamburger today," was first used in 1932[i] during the Great Depression—a time when, no doubt, it was common for people to ask for loans to cover their meals. Since then, however, it has become an expression to illustrate financial irresponsibility, which Bill Gross evoked in his September 2012 *Investment Outlook*, "The Lending Lindy."[ii] The relevance here is that Wimpy unknowingly created a financial asset when someone made him a loan to purchase hamburgers. A financial asset is a non-physical asset whose value is derived from a contractual claim. Financial assets are generally more liquid than physical assets such as real estate, commodities, or any other asset that you can see and feel. In the case of Wimpy's transaction, another diner patron, or perhaps the manager of the diner, agreed to give Wimpy a hamburger in exchange for his promise to pay for that hamburger

---

[1] The authors would like to thank Tomy Duong and Amy Lin for their research support in finalizing this chapter.

in the future. Because the hamburger has value and its consumption requires repayment, this transaction includes *consideration*—meaning a contract has been created. Following Wimpy's consumption of the hamburger, the party that extended Wimpy the loan now has a claim against Wimpy, and that claim can be transferred to another person. This makes that claim to Wimpy a financial asset that can appreciate or depreciate. Finally, looking at Wimpy's stature, we may wonder if his consumption of a hamburger was necessary for nourishment or an ill-advised example of overconsumption made possible by his ability to find a willing lender of capital.

While a contractual agreement is universal among all financial assets, the sources from which financial assets derive their value, the terms of the contractual agreements, and the rights afforded its owners are highly variable. In this chapter, the focus will be on the three most common types of financial assets: bonds, stocks, and derivatives. Once a foundation has been established as to what these securities are, how they trade, and who participates in the issuance and purchase of them, the attention will then pivot to a more general discussion of capital markets. Specifically, there will be a description of both the benefits and risks inherent to modern capital markets and a discussion of how failures can occur while financial markets remain *efficient*. We will close with a summary and investment implications.

FINANCIAL ASSETS: BONDS, STOCKS, AND DERIVATIVES

Bonds—What Are They?

Bonds are securities of indebtedness or legal promises to make payments in accordance with contractually defined terms. Since the income opportunities they generate for their owners are typically *fixed*, unlike an equity dividend that varies with the economics of the company, the bond asset class is generally referred to as *fixed* income. Bonds have indentures, which are formal legal agreements that specify the terms of the bond and the obligations of the borrower. Usually bonds are structured so that the borrower agrees to make regular interest payments prior to repaying the principal balance of the loan, in full, at the maturity of the loan. The terms of these loans can vary including the frequency of the interest payment (monthly, quarterly, semi-annually, etc.), the rate of the interest payment (1%, 3%, 8%, etc.), the size of the loan ($1 million, $1 billion, etc.), and the term of the loan (overnight, 5 years, 30 years, etc.). Other aspects of bonds include seniority (if there are multiple debt holders higher or lower in a capital structure), collateral (if there are assets pledged as collateral to the bondholder), and covenants (requirements of the borrower to follow guidelines, such as limiting the future issuances of debt). Bondholders have broad legal rights that are specified in the indenture (contract) between the issuer of the debt and the purchaser of the debt, and this indenture must comply with the provisions in the Trust Indenture Act. The Trust Indenture Act of 1939 requires, among other things, the appointment of an independent trustee. The trustee has several responsibilities including monitoring the borrower's compliance with the terms of the indenture, representing the bondholders, and facilitating the ability of bondholders to take coordinated action such as making an amendment or declaring a default.

Bondholder legal rights fall into three categories including:[iii]

- *Financial terms*: these terms specify most of the economic characteristics of any given bond and its valuation. The most critical terms are the bondholder's right to receive periodic interest payments and a principal payment at the maturity of the bond. Other common terms may include call provisions (allowing the company to repay the bond early), put rights (allowing the bondholder the right to demand early repayment), mandatory partial-redemptions (requiring the company to periodically repay a portion of the bond prior to its maturity), conversion rights (allowing the bondholder to exchange bonds for corporate equity), and subordination clauses (reducing the bond's claim status to other lenders).
- *Protective covenants*: these are essentially promises by the borrower that are designed to manage the risk of the lender. They are intended to enhance the likelihood that bondholders receive contractually specified interest and principal payments by limiting certain activities of the borrower following the issuance of the debt. Common covenants include debt restrictions (limits on future debt issuances to protect against the firm becoming overleveraged), dividend restrictions (limits to ensure cash or other assets are not inappropriately distributed to equity holders to the detriment of bondholders), and a broad variety of other limitations such as restrictions on asset sales, mergers, liens, sale/leasebacks, and transactions with affiliates. All of these actions could potentially impair the bondholder's rights or status.
- *Miscellaneous provisions*: these provisions specify a variety of bondholder rights and trustee obligations and can be thought of as *housekeeping* items that don't neatly fit in the two aforementioned categories. For example, these provisions include the right to receive a notification of default or special payment.

Until the early 1980s, bonds issued pursuant to an indenture were documented via an elaborate paper certificate that was physically transferred when the bonds were traded. Additionally, if the bond made periodic interest payments, the certificate would then come with smaller *coupons* that were typically attached to the larger paper certificate, as shown in Figure 1.1. These coupons could be detached from the paper certificate and then presented to a designated bank window or mailed to a processing center following their payment dates. From this process comes the expression *clipping coupons* to describe purchasing a bond with the intention of regularly receiving interest payments.

The monitoring of each security's principal and interest date, collecting coupons, and endorsing certificates for transfer was a highly cumbersome process. To address this, and several other problems associated with physical stock and bond certificates, the Depository Trust Company (DTC) was formed to act as a centralized clearinghouse. As of July 2017, DTC was responsible for the custody of $52.4 trillion in securities issued in 131 countries and territories.[v] Beyond the

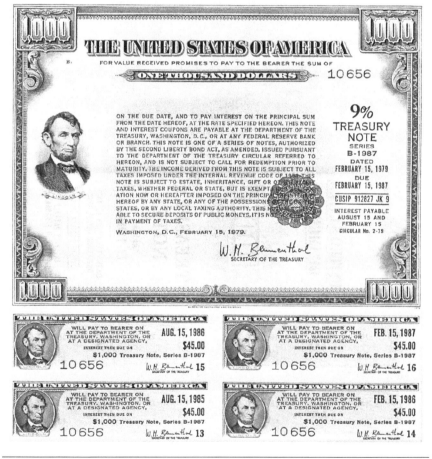

Figure 1.1   8-year, 9% U.S. Treasury Note, issued February 15, 1979. *Source*: The Joe I. Herbstman Memorial Collection of American Finance[iv]

efficiency provided by DTC, in 1982, to reduce tax evasion, the U.S. Congress passed the Tax Equity and Fiscal Responsibility Act (TEFRA) which restricts the issuance of debt instruments in bearer form.[vi] As a result, the use of paper bond certificates in the United States has mostly ceased and digital records of bond ownership have become the norm. Currently in the U.S., banks or other institutions hired to take custody of assets are responsible for maintaining electronic records of the ownership of the financial assets.

As will be discussed more fully in Chapter 7, the value or price of a bond is a function of its coupon relative to the yield to maturity[2] of other comparable risk bonds. For example, if the current 5-year Treasury note had a coupon of 3% and was trading at 100,[3] then another Treasury note with five years of remaining life that had a coupon of 4% would trade for more than 100—or above par. Why? Well if the bonds were otherwise identical except for the coupon, all investors would prefer the 4% coupon bond. Their demand for the bond would cause its price to increase to the point (approximately 104.5) where its yield to maturity was equivalent to the 3% bond.

When new bonds are issued, their coupon is typically set at a rate such that the bonds will sell for 100 or at a slight discount. To determine the appropriate coupon, investment banks and governments solicit orders from investors to determine, given the market circumstances at that moment, what coupon is required to entice investors to pay par. The reason for this is simply that if the borrower is going to issue $1 billion in bonds, it typically wants $1 billion in cash.[4] After the bond is issued, its future trading prices will remain a function of its coupon relative to the yields at which other similar risk and maturity bonds are trading in the market. If market interest rates rise, the price of the bond will fall, and vice versa. Investors have almost innumerable bonds among which to

---

[2] The concept of yield to maturity (YTM) will be developed more fully in Chapter 7. Suffice it to say here that YTM is the discount rate that causes the present value of all future coupon and principal payments to equal the bond price. As the discount rate or YTM increases, the present value of such payments declines; hence, the value of the bond will fall. When yields decrease, the opposite is true.

[3] If the current price of a bond is equal to the principal that the bond will pay at maturity, it is trading *at par*. Because the price of a bond is quoted as a percentage of par, a bond trading at 101 means the purchaser will pay 1% more for the bond today than they will receive at maturity.

[4] It should be noted that bonds are occasionally sold at nontrivial discounts. The best known of these are 0% coupon bonds that sell at significant discounts, pay no interest during their life, and then par at maturity. One might wonder why firms don't issue bonds using higher coupons that would cause them to be issued for greater than 100. This would basically represent the lenders paying more at issuance and collecting *excess* coupons over the life of the issue. While investors should be essentially indifferent, the long-standing convention in the market is that new issue bonds are sold at par or at a slight discount, but hardly ever at a premium.

choose, thus the market is in a constant state of finding an equilibrium where bonds all trade at equivalent risk-adjusted rates.

Bonds—Evolution of Investment Structures

While bonds are the most common form of debt instrument that are used to borrow money, there are two other relatively recently developed instruments that should be briefly discussed: syndicated bank loans and securitizations.

When most people think of a loan, they think of a bank loan. Loans provided by banks are still an important source of capital to companies, and loans are also the most common structure used in financing the real estate market. While there are some important legal differences between bonds and loan structures, they function similarly. Historically, a bank loan was a bilateral transaction between the bank and the borrower. The borrower, which could be either an individual or a company, could simply approach a branch and essentially fill out an application. A loan representative would ask a lot of questions and perhaps verify some financial information and thereafter a decision whether or not to make the loan would be made. If the loan was particularly large and thus represented a concentration risk to the bank, several banks might team up to share the risk. As transaction sizes grew, banks developed a new structure to distribute the risk—called *syndicated loans*. In a syndicated loan, the loan is divided into $1 million units and then those units are sold to a large number of investors, which is similar to a bond offering. During the origination of a syndicated loan, the role of the originating bank is to negotiate the loan terms and then find other investors to purchase the loan; this is in contrast to the more traditional role of a bank, which is to both underwrite and fund the loan. Because of the relatively modest unit size and a relatively large and diverse number of investors who are familiar with the loan's characteristics, syndicated loans now trade actively in the secondary market.

There are two important differences to note between syndicated loans and bonds. First, while a bond typically has a fixed interest rate over its lifetime (e.g. 8.0%), loans are structured with an interest rate that changes, or floats, depending on market interest levels. Banks adopted floating rate structures to help them manage interest rate risk. Banks partially fund themselves by borrowing funds for as little as a single night. Because a bank's funding costs are a function of interest rates on any particular day, bank funding costs are variable. A bank couldn't prudently take the risk of making a 5-year loan at a set interest rate if there was a risk that its own borrowing costs could rise above the rate it received on the loan. To mitigate this risk, banks structured loans such that the loan interest rate would adjust as short-term interest rates changed. Historically, banks used the London Interbank Offered Rate (LIBOR) as a standardized measure of short-term interest rates.[5] When a loan interest rate was specified, it would be LIBOR plus an additional interest premium, called spread, to provide the bank a profit margin and compensate it for the credit risk. For example, the loan could be priced at LIBOR + 2.5% (or 250 basis points). If LIBOR equaled 1%, the interest rate on the loan would be 3.5%, but would adjust as frequently as monthly or quarterly to reflect changes in LIBOR. The fact that loan interest rates move in tandem with the market means that the price volatility of loans (i.e., the risk that the loan will increase or decrease in price because of changes in market interest rates) is much lower than that of fixed coupon bonds.

The second important difference is that syndicated loans, particularly if they are issued with a credit rating of BB or lower (which are commonly referred to as *leveraged loans*), are almost always secured by a lien on the assets of the issuer. In contrast, most bonds, especially those of governmental entities and companies with credit ratings of BBB or higher, are unsecured. In other words, if there is a worst-case default and liquidation, the unsecured creditor has no specific assets to seize to provide a recovery and will have to share whatever money may be available with other unsecured creditors. As a result of this difference, syndicated loans generally fare much better in bankruptcy compared to unsecured bonds of the same issuer.

The other relatively new class of debt securities is called a securitization. While there are numerous forms, in general, a securitization involves bundling many relatively small loans into a large pool and then selling interests in that pool or portfolio to investors. Securitization was first developed for residential mortgages. Banks would make 30-year mortgage loans to individuals, typically at a fixed interest rate. As discussed before, a bank holding a 30-year fixed rate mortgage when it had variable funding costs resulted in substantial interest rate risk. In response to this, as well as several other problems, securitizations were developed. In a securitization, the bank holding the mortgages sells the mortgages to an independent, single purpose entity—typically called a special purpose vehicle (SPV). The SPV purchases a large pool of mortgages (e.g., $1 billion in aggregate amount) and then simultaneously sells undivided interests in the pool to investors. The cash contributed by the investors funds

---

[5] The primary regulator of LIBOR is the Financial Conduct Authority (FCA), a regulatory body in the United Kingdom. In July 2017, Andrew Bailey, chief executive of the FCA, announced plans that the FCA would attempt to phase out LIBOR, with banks no longer submitting daily fixings by year-end 2021. (*Source*: https://www.fca.org.uk/news/speeches/the-future-of-libor.) In response, in April 2018, the U.S. Federal Reserve began publishing a Secured Overnight Financing Rate (SOFR), which is based on the rate that large banks exchange overnight loans for U.S. Treasury collateral. The expectation is that this rate will eventually replace U.S. LIBOR as the floating reference rate utilized in bank loan, mortgage, and other financial contracts. (*Source*: https://www.newyorkfed.org/markets/opolicy/operating_policy_180228.)

the purchase of the mortgages. Thereafter, all monies collected on the mortgages, less certain administrative and related fees, are distributed to the securitization unit holders.

Securitization is a unique way of pooling assets and diversifying default risk. Consider an investor who wishes to include residential mortgage debt in his or her portfolio. Before securitizations, this investor would have to try to either originate or purchase single mortgages, and if the mortgage defaulted, the investor could have significant risk of loss. This exposed the investor to significant idiosyncratic risk. With securitization, because thousands of loans are pooled together, expected losses can be statistically estimated and appropriately priced by investors. Mortgages may also be aggregated from different property types and regions allowing investors to diversify geographic and other risk. Additionally, it is easier for an investor to trade an interest in a securitization in the secondary market, like a bond, which improves market efficiency. Virtually any debt instrument can be securitized. While the market began with residential mortgages, it quickly spread to other loan types—such as automobile loans and leases, credit card receivables, student loans, commercial real estate mortgages, and boat loans. There has even been a securitization based on the future royalties of David Bowie songs![vii]

The development of securitizations has revolutionized finance in many ways. First, it allows investors to easily invest in different asset classes on a diversified and credit-enhanced basis. Before securitizations, how could a non-bank ever invest in credit card receivables? From the perspective of the issuer, securitizations allowed the originators of the loans to better manage their balance sheets. Consider the challenge of GM wanting to finance the purchasers of all its cars. The more cars it sold, the more it would have to finance on its corporate balance sheet, which would quickly prove infeasible. With securitization, it now continually sells the new auto loans to new securitizations, essentially allowing it to quickly recycle its scarce capital. Finally, securitizations allow for various aspects or risks inherent in the underlying pool to be segmented and sold to investors who prefer certain security types. Consider a securitization backed by 30-year mortgages. Because mortgages pay down over time and mortgages are repaid in full when people move, the average life of a 30-year mortgage is only about 10 years,[6] but there is considerable uncertainty as to exactly when an investor will receive some of the cash flows. Securitizations can alleviate this risk

---

[6] This is a very general estimate. Many factors, including in particular the interest rate on the mortgage, influence its expected average life. For example, for mortgages originated in 2006 and 2007 when interest rates were relatively higher, their average life was as short as 4–5 years because when interest rates declined following the 2008 recession, homeowners refinanced their high-interest mortgages with new low-interest mortgages.

by creating different tranches or classes of securities and then channeling the cash flows pursuant to an agreed formula. So, for example, a mortgage securitization could contain a tranche or bond that would payoff in exactly three years. And because it could reduce a prospective investor's risk related to the timing of cash flows, the investor will require a lower return, which effectively increases the overall value of the pool's cash flows.

Bonds—Who Issues and Purchases Them?

According to the Bank of International Settlements (BIS) and the Securities Industry and Financial Markets Association (SIFMA), an industry trade group that represents banks and asset management companies, the size of the global bond market exceeded $100.1 trillion in 2017.[viii] By comparison, global total gross national product (GNP), or the value of all items produced and consumed, was $84.8 trillion at the end of 2017.[ix] As shown in Figure 1.2, the largest domicile, or country of issuance, is the United States, whose bond market was estimated at $39.3 trillion (39.3%) in 2017. The European Union collectively had the second largest bond market, at $28.2 trillion (28.1%), while Japan is the third largest bond market at $12.7 trillion (12.6%). Emerging market bonds collectively were valued at $14.0 trillion (14.0%), and this is the most rapidly growing market, driven largely by China's economic ascension. By comparison, in 2007, emerging markets bonds represented only 4.4% of the market.

Entities that sell bonds can be classified into three broad categories: governments, corporations, and securitization vehicles (which include mortgage-related

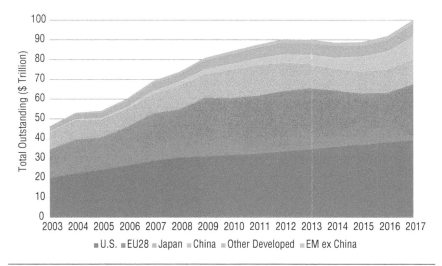

Figure 1.2 Global bonds outstanding. *Source*: BIS and SIFMA

securities). In the United States, government entities—including the U.S. Treasury, state governments, municipalities, and government agencies—are the largest bond issuers. In the third quarter of 2018, these government entities collectively issued $882 billion in debt. Most of the debt issued was used to refinance existing debt, while the balance was to fund the gap between tax receipts and expenditures, typically referred to as fiscal deficits. The second largest category is the securitization entities discussed previously. In the third quarter of 2018, $631 billion of securities were issued by securitization entities in the United States. Last but not least, corporations are the final major issuer of debt. Corporations issue debt for many reasons including: financing acquisitions, making capital investments in their own business, repurchasing their shares, or refinancing existing debt. In the third quarter of 2018, $322 billion of corporate bonds were issued in the United States.[x] As shown in Figure 1.3, in 2018 the stock of treasury securities, municipal bonds, and federal agency debt aggregated to just over $21 trillion (excluding intragovernmental holdings)—or approximately 50% of U.S. debt outstanding. Mortgage-related and securitized issues have $11.4 trillion (23%) outstanding, while corporate issuers have $9.2 trillion (21%) debt outstanding.[xi]

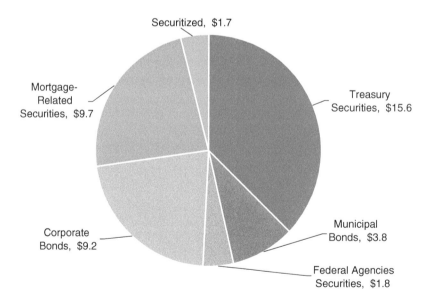

Note: Corporate equities include both listed on exchanges and closely held common and preferred shares issued by domestic corporations and U.S. purchases of shares issued by foreign corporations; mortgage-related securities include GNMA, FNMA, and FHLMC mortgage-backed-securities and CMOs and private-label MBS/CMOs; Treasury securities include only interest bearing marketable public debt.

Figure 1.3   U.S. debt outstanding ($ trillions). *Source*: SIFMA

So who are the largest buyers of bonds after they are issued? Global central banks are the single largest purchaser of U.S. bonds, who collectively own $6.3 trillion of U.S. Treasuries. One reason central banks accumulate U.S. Treasuries is that their home country has a balance of trade surplus with the United States so they choose to purchase U.S. Treasuries with their excess dollars. The alternative would be to exchange those dollars for their home currency, which would tend to increase the home currency's exchange rate and make the country's exports less competitive. As of January 2019, the largest holder of U.S. Treasuries (by country of domicile) is China, which held approximately $1.1 trillion followed closely by Japan,[xii] which held approximately just under $1.1 trillion.[7] Other large purchasers of U.S. debt are individuals, some of whom buy bonds directly into their brokerage accounts while others purchase fixed income mutual funds. According to the U.S. Federal Reserve, at the end of 2017 U.S. households held $82.3 trillion in financial assets, of which $4.1 trillion were investments in treasuries, agencies, municipal bonds, corporate bonds, and other debt securities.[xiii] Additional large purchasers of U.S. debt include foreign investors, endowments and foundations, pensions, and other corporations. See Chapter 3 for a detailed discussion of these institutions, their objectives, and their investment reaction functions.

Stocks—What Are They?

A business can be structured in several legal formats. An individual can start a business without any identifiable legal format. For example, someone can start a shoeshine business by simply setting up a stand, providing the service, and collecting the revenue. In that case, the business is essentially the individual. Alternatively, several people could team up to form a business—say several accountants to provide tax preparation services—and decide to establish a legal entity called a partnership. The governing documents of the partnership would define ownership, distributions of profits, allocations of liabilities, etc. These approaches worked for relatively small and simple businesses, but as business ventures grew more complicated and needed to raise capital from a large number of individuals, an alternative structure, *the corporation*, was developed. The corporation offered a number of economic and legal advantages. First, ownership of the corporation was represented by shares of stock, which represented fractional ownership interests in the firm. This allowed firms to raise capital

---

[7] Note: These data are sourced from both U.S. and non-U.S. based custody accounts; non-U.S. based custody accounts may not be attributed to the actual owners. However, despite this limitation, we can infer that the vast majority of treasuries held in Chinese and Japanese custody accounts are owned by their respective central banks.

from multiple sources because they could essentially sell a potentially unlimited number of shares. Second, corporations are able to legally limit the liability of their owners to the amount invested.

Relating to this latter point, consider the dilemma of somebody financing a new air transport service intended to compete with FedEx and UPS. Shares of stock are sold to buy a plane, which is then filled with precious cargo. If the plane crashes due to pilot negligence and the cargo is damaged or destroyed, no doubt the owners of the cargo will sue for damages. If investors in the shares had to worry about this potential liability being borne by them (i.e., they had to write extra damage checks), they would likely be very reluctant to invest, particularly when they likely were not involved in the management of the business and hiring of the pilot. To eliminate these risks, corporate legal entities *shield* their owners from the liabilities of the corporation. Stock investors might lose some or all the value of their investment, but they cannot be held liable for any additional amounts. This was a key advancement that allowed capital to be raised from individuals and entities that might not be involved in the business and thus have no way to mitigate their risk.

While the corporation had certain risk mitigation advantages, it raises certain governance issues. The shoeshine stand owner and the tax accountants are actively engaged in the day-to-day operation of the business and thus all have an interest in making the business be successful. However, after a corporation sells shares to many investors who are not involved in the business, how can shareholders be certain those running the business are placing the interests of the shareholders ahead of their own? To manage this risk, corporations are structured with a board of directors who are elected by the shareholders. These directors, in turn, supervise the managers of the business. If the managers don't work in the interests of the shareholders, the directors can replace them. If the directors are inept, the shareholders can elect new directors. This system is not without its problems, but it's the best that's been devised.

Thus, to return to the question with which this section started, a share of stock is a claim of partial ownership of the corporation. As a matter of accounting parlance, that ownership share is sometimes referred to as an interest in the firm's equity. A shareholder is a person or entity that owns one or more shares of equity. Like bondholders, shareholders have broad legal rights. However, unlike bondholders whose legal rights are specified in an indenture or loan agreement, shareholders' rights are specified by the laws of the state in which they are incorporated, and are further defined in the certificate of incorporation and by-laws of the corporation.[xiv] In the United States, and typically around the world, shareholder rights include:[xv]

- *Economic rights*: as owners, the shareholders benefit from any improvement in the value of the corporation. Essentially, as the value of the firm increases, the value of the stock should correspondingly increase. In addition, shareholders have the right to receive any dividends or other distributions declared or made by the corporation.

- *Control rights*: the basic control right of a shareholder is the ability to vote their shares for the election of the company's board of directors, who in turn are responsible for the day-to-day operations of the firm. As a practical matter, the relative amount of influence of any shareholder is a function of the percentage of shares they own. Typically, in large, publicly traded corporations, no shareholder owns more than 5% of the stock. As a result, a governance issue economists call the *agency problem* exists. Specifically, it may not be in any individual's best interest to invest the time to oversee the company because the individual has limited ability and economic incentive to effect change. However, most states and corporate Articles of Incorporation require a majority of shareholders to approve certain extraordinary transactions, such as mergers and acquisitions or amendments to the corporation's Articles of Incorporation.
- *Information rights*: although the amount of information that a company is required to provide pursuant to state statute is fairly limited, as a practical matter, most large companies have substantial disclosure obligations with owners either by contract or federal regulation. With respect to private companies, sophisticated angel, venture capital, and private equity investors will require extensive information disclosures as part of their investment agreements.
- *Litigation rights*: shareholders may sue on behalf of the corporation, naming the firm's officers and directors as defendants, should management or the directors breach their fiduciary duties to the shareholders.

Like bond certificates, until recently, equities owners received a stock certificate at the time of purchase. These elaborate certificates were originally issued in bearer form, meaning whoever held the certificate in their possession was entitled to corporate dividends. By the 1960s in the U.S., the use of physical stock certificates began to overwhelm the processing abilities of major exchanges. The industry solution was to *immobilize* stock certificates in a central location and note the change of ownership through book entries. By 1990, the DTC held 32 million paper stock certificates in custody.[xvi] However, like bond certificates, over the past thirty years, paper stock certificates have been rapidly eliminated and replaced with electronic records, a process known as dematerialization. As of January 2012, the DTC held only 383,400 stock certificates—down 99% since 1990. Today, stock certificates are primarily held as collectables and displayed as works of art (see Figure 1.4).

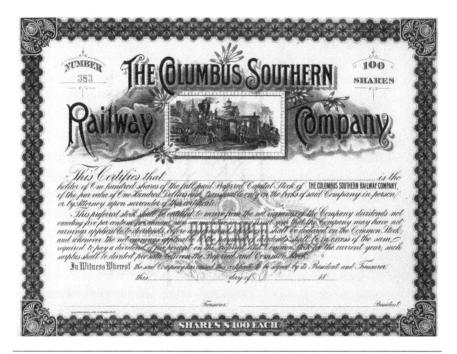

Figure 1.4   A Columbus Southern Railway Company stock certificate

Stocks—Who Issues and Purchases Them?

According to SIFMA data, the size of the global equity market reached $85.3 trillion by year-end 2017 as shown in Figure 1.5. By comparison, this is still $14.8 trillion smaller than the global bond market. The largest equity market is the U.S. equity market, whose value was estimated at $32.1 trillion (37.7%). The European Union block of 28 countries comes in second with a combined market value of $14.2 trillion (16.7%).[8] Emerging markets ex-China are collectively the third largest equity market, valued at $14.6 trillion (17.2%). The fourth largest equity market is now China, which is estimated at $8.7 trillion (10.2%). The growth in Chinese stock market value has been truly remarkable. Using 2005 as a base when its value was only $402 billion (1.0%), it has grown at an average compounded annual rate of 29% for twelve years.[xvii]

It is important to note that the statistics presented above only relate to shares of equity traded on public exchanges, usually referred to as public equity. A

---

[8] Unlike equities in the U.S., China, or emerging markets ex-China, the aggregate market value of European equities had not recovered from their pre-2008 recession peak. By comparison, in 2007 the EU equity market was valued at $15.4 trillion (25.4%), meaning its global market share has fallen by approximately 8.7% in the 10-year period ending 2017.

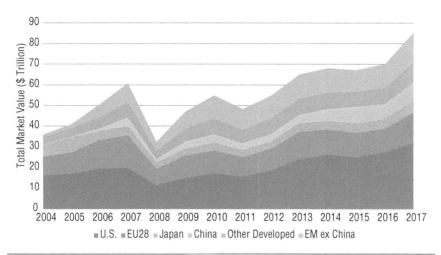

Figure 1.5 Global equity markets capitalization by country. *Source*: World Federation of Exchanges and SIFMA

significant amount of equity value is held in the form of private equity and is typically managed by either venture capital or private equity firms. These firms are often structured as limited liability entities where a professional manager identifies, executes, and manages the investments on behalf of large institutions (such as pensions, endowments, and family offices) who provide the capital. The private equity market has grown substantially in the last two decades. According to the 2018 McKinsey Global Private Markets Review, 2017 private equity deal volume reached $1.27 trillion, up from $190 billion in 2000. Meanwhile, committed but not yet deployed general partner capital reached $1 trillion, up from around $300 billion in 2000.[xviii] Despite the size and growth of this market, private equity can still be viewed as an incubator for public equities because most companies that are held by either venture capital or private equity firms will eventually be sold to firms with public equity or will become public firms themselves.

The process by which the equity of a corporation becomes *public* is called an initial public offering (IPO). In an IPO, a corporation will engage the services of an investment bank or group of banks, called the underwriters, to help organize and market the offering. As part of this process, the firm will file a registration statement with the Securities and Exchange Commission (SEC) to *register* a certain portion of its shares for public sale. The registration statement will include a detailed disclosure document, called a prospectus, that essentially explains all material aspects of the corporation and its operations to new investors. This prospectus must be approved by the SEC, which is charged with making sure that there is sufficient information for an investor to make an informed investment decision. Once the prospectus is in near-final form, the underwriters will then use it to market the stock to prospective investors (typically large institutions or various funds). For well-known companies (like Facebook, Google, or Alibaba) this is a very high-profile process that is closely watched by market participants. After the marketing is completed, feedback from prospective investors will be used to *price* the offering, which will determine the price at which the underwriters will sell the registered shares to the public investors.

While the corporation is private, there are significant limitations on how and to whom the shares in the corporation can be traded. Private company securities are commonly referred to as *restricted* and can only be sold to qualified investors. Following an IPO, the shares registered and sold in the offering can be purchased by anyone and the shares will typically trade freely on one of several exchanges. This opening up of the market to all investors often results in chaotic trading immediately following an IPO because investor demand for shares frequently exceeds the limited amount being offered.

While the IPO offers an opportunity for the corporation to raise cash from the public and provides early investors an opportunity to monetize their investment,[9] it comes with a variety of trade-offs. The prospectus, discussed earlier, requires the company to make significant disclosures about its business and strategy that it otherwise might prefer to keep secret from its competitors (and potentially customers). In addition, public companies must file periodic reports with the SEC about their operating performance and governance and they are liable to public shareholders for any material misstatements in such filings. According to SIFMA data, in the third quarter of 2018, $60.1 billion was raised by U.S. and foreign corporations in the U.S. IPO market. Secondary, or *follow-on* offerings, whereby additional shares in already public companies are sold to investors, totaled $42.1 billion.[xix] Do these equity issuance numbers seem small? Aggregating both initial and secondary offerings, in 2017 U.S. equity issuance was only $199.3 billion[xx]—less than 1% of the total U.S. equity market value. By comparison, in 2018, $7.4 trillion in bonds were issued in the U.S.[xxi]—17% of the total value of the bond market. The primary reason for this disparity is that equity doesn't mature, whereas bonds do. Equities are perpetual securities that remain outstanding until they are retired either by corporate repurchase, merger, or bankruptcy. Conversely, bonds have finite lives and therefore mature; so, a majority of bond issuance is to refinance or *roll* maturing debt, thereby requiring significant annual issuance to maintain a steady stock.

That's who issues equities; so, who owns them? Steven Rosenthal and Lydia Austin of the Tax Policy Center attempted to answer that question as of the end

---

[9] In an IPO of a venture capital-backed firm, the original investors will typically, for marketing reasons, be limited in how much stock they can sell in the offering. But, once the company is public, those investors can, over time, monetize additional portions of their holdings via secondary offerings or pursuant to other provisions of the securities laws.

of 2015. Using a variety of sources and assumptions, they estimated the single largest category of U.S. equity holders are U.S. households who held $15.3 trillion in U.S. equities (67%)—either in taxable accounts (mutual funds, ETFs, or direct holdings: see Chapter 2) or nontaxable accounts (pension plans, 401k, IRAs, etc.).[10] Foreigners collectively held $5.8 trillion (26%) of U.S. stock, while U.S. institutions, including insurance companies and nonprofits, held an additional $1.7 trillion (7%).

Derivatives—What Are They?

Derivatives are financial contracts whose value is derived from the value of another asset. These contracts have no intrinsic value themselves (unlike the way a bond or share of stock has intrinsic value); rather, its value is derived by virtue of the interrelationships specified in the contract. While there are dozens of types of derivatives, according to the BIS, the most common exchange-traded derivatives are futures and options[xxii] while the most common over-the-counter derivatives are forwards, options, and swaps.[xxiii] For more information on the types of derivatives, their definitions, how they trade, how they settle, and who uses them, please see Appendix Table 1.1 at the end of this chapter.

One of the simplest derivatives to understand is a call option on a stock. A stock call option is a contract that gives the holder the right (but not the obligation) to purchase the stock for a specified price (the strike price) on a given date in the future (e.g., 30 days in the future). Assume that when the parties begin negotiating the call option, the stock is selling for $10 and the strike price is set at $13 and the exercise date of the option is in 30 days. The value of the option in 30 days will completely depend on the then trading price of the stock. If the stock is trading for $13 or less, the holder of the option will not exercise the option and it is worth nothing. If the stock is trading above $13, its value is market price—$13. If the option costs $1, then the buyer makes a profit only if the stock price exceeds $14. Of course, the investor who buys the call option will have a view on the future stock price (why would they waste money on buying the call if they thought the stock would go down in price), but the value of the call option is completely dependent on the stock being greater than $13 on or prior to the exercise date. With an *American* call option, the holder has the right to purchase the stock at $13 at any time prior to or at the expiry of the option, whereas the holder of a *European* call option may only purchase the stock at

[10] Of note: Rosenthal and Austin found that from 1965 until today, the balance of equities held in individuals' taxable accounts such as broker accounts, had fallen from over 80% to approximately 24% in 2015. Alternatively, the percentage of equities held by individuals in retirement accounts had grown from under 10% in 1965 to approximately 43% in 2015. This shift can be largely attributed to tax policies encouraging individuals' use of retirement accounts.

$13 at expiry. This added *optionality* that is afforded to the American option raises its value relative to a European option.

One of the inherent risks to owning a derivative is the potential for a counter-party to fail to honor the terms of the contract. In the case of the call option, if the price of the stock increases from $10 to $20, will the counterparty deliver a share of stock in exchange for $13? For a derivative on the company's stock, there is no claim against the underlying company. In fact, the company is unlikely to know (or care) that the call option exists. Rather, the derivative is between two parties at arms' length from the company. The mechanisms that have been developed in order to manage counterparty default risk will be discussed shortly.

Although many derivatives are now standardized, they can take any form and cover virtually anything to which the parties agree. There are two primary motivations for investing in derivatives—speculation or risk mitigation—with the later representing the vast bulk of derivative transitions. Consider a few common risks that a company might want to mitigate or hedge. A company has borrowed $100 million using a floating rate bank loan priced at LIBOR + 4.0%, but the company has since become concerned that the LIBOR rate will increase. If the LIBOR rate should increase from, say, 2% to 10%, the borrow-ing cost of the company would increase from 6% to 14%. If this occurs, the company may not be able to pay the interest and may potentially be forced to declare bankruptcy.

In order to hedge against a rapid rise in the LIBOR reference rate, the com-pany could enter into a derivative contract called a fixed-for-float interest rate swap. If this company were to utilize this contract, the company would agree to pay a counterparty (typically a bank) a fixed rate on the $100 million (called the notional amount) and the counterparty would agree to pay LIBOR to the com-pany. Let's assume that the company and the bank agreed that the company would receive the LIBOR rate and the bank would pay a fixed rate equal to 3.5%. From the company's perspective, it has swapped a floating rate liability for a fixed rate liability. As a result, its financing rate has been transformed from LIBOR + 4.0% to 7.5% (3.5% + 4.0%). Through the utilization of this derivative, the company has ensured its financing cost will neither rise nor fall for the duration of the swap.

Alternatively, assume that the company is domiciled in Brazil, where local interest rates are high owing to elevated inflation. Rather than borrow at an el-evated local rate, the Brazilian firm chooses to borrow in the U.S. bond market where nominal rates are lower. The Brazilian company now has currency risk. If all of its revenue and income is in Brazilian reals (BRL), how many reals will it take to buy $100 million in U.S. dollars (USD) at the maturity of the loan to pay it off?[11] In this case the company might enter into a foreign exchange forward

---

[11] There, of course, is also currency exchange risk associated with each interim periodic interest payment.

purchase contract with a bank that will essentially fix the USD/BRL exchange rate on a specified date in the future.

What's the difference between a risk mitigator (hedger) and a speculator? For this discussion, the primary difference is whether the party has underlying exposure to the risk they are trying to mitigate. Imagine an airline and oil producer both enter into a contract whereby the airline is insuring against rising oil prices while the oil producer is insuring against falling oil prices. Both entities are hedging. Furthermore, in the example of the Brazilian corporation, the company borrowing the money was inherently exposed to certain risks—either interest rate risk, currency exchange rate risk, or potentially both. The counterparty on the other side of the derivative contract might also be mitigating risk or it may be speculating. For example, in the foreign currency swap, the counterparty might just have a strong conviction that the USD/BRL exchange rate will decline in the future and they'll make a profit.

Why are derivatives attractive to speculators? The basic answer is leverage. Consider the stock call option discussed earlier. If one believed that the share price was going to go from $10 to $20, then they could just buy the stock and potentially double their money. Alternatively, assume the call option cost $1. If the stock goes to $20, they will have a profit of $6—$20 minus $13 (exercise price) minus $1 option cost—and enjoy a 600% profit. Plus, if the stock falls in value to $5, the investor who bought the stock will lose $5, whereas the option investor is only out the original $1 option cost. But this sounds too easy—heads you win, tails I lose? The catch, of course, is that in many scenarios, the option will expire worthless. In the example, for the option to be profitable, the stock must appreciate 40% in 30 days—a possible, but statistically improbable, scenario. Naturally, the price of the call option (or any derivative), which professionals calculate using elaborate statistical models, will reflect the probability assessment of each party to the transaction.

The leverage aspect of derivatives exacerbates the counterparty default risk that was previously mentioned. Consider the interest rate swap on the $100 million notional amount. The terms, again, were that the bank paying LIBOR (when LIBOR is initially 2.0%) would receive a fixed rate of 3.5%. Assuming rates didn't change, this implies that in the first year the LIBOR payer would receive $3.5 million and pay $2 million. But what if some unforeseen economic disruption occurred and LIBOR rose to 7%? Now the LIBOR payer would be responsible for paying $7 million and effectively losing $3.5 million per year. If this loss[12] resulted in the default of the counterparty, this banking failure could cause a ripple effect through the broader economy. First, the borrower who was expecting to receive the 7% LIBOR payment (from the now defunct financial

---

[12] In reality, a major bank could easily have $100 billion in swap exposure, which would make this a loss of $3.5 billion per annum.

institution) is now responsible for the higher-than-expected interest payment. This unexpected increase in borrowing costs may cause this borrower to also default on its loan. The default on this loan will result in losses to the owner of the loan, and so on.

Recognizing these risks, financial market regulatory bodies have developed mechanisms that require that the parties to derivative contracts (which are generally large corporations, banks, or other financial institutions) constantly monitor the economic value of the contract, and if it becomes negative, post collateral to minimize the potential loss to the counterparty in the event of a default. The requirement to post collateral is called *margining*. How the margining mechanism works depends on which of the two ways derivatives are commonly traded. The first trade method is a bilateral negotiation and agreement of terms. This methodology is referred to as *over the counter* (OTC), and it does not involve the use of an exchange. The second method of trading involves the use of an exchange, which is an institution where standardized securities or contracts are exchanged or traded.

If two parties want to trade derivatives bilaterally, they generally first negotiate and execute an International Swaps and Derivatives Association (ISDA) master agreement. ISDA is a New York based trade organization that, among other things, works "to make global derivatives markets safer and more efficient."[xxiv] To accomplish this, the ISDA has developed a *master agreement*, which is a legal contract between two counterparties that specifies the terms and conditions relating to the purchase and sale of derivatives between institutions. In practice, most banks and institutions use the ISDA master agreement as a template and then further negotiate terms to reflect the unique circumstances of any particular transaction.

An important component of the ISDA master agreement is a credit support annex (CSA), which specifies the terms of margining. Under the standard CSA, margining is required when a derivative's price changes such that should the derivative be closed, one counterparty would incur a gain and the other counterparty would incur a loss. The CSA requires a counterparty in the loss position to post collateral (such as cash or U.S. treasuries) for the benefit of the other party. If a counterparty fails prior to the maturity of the derivative, any collateral that has been posted can be immediately seized by the other party. If all counterparties in all derivative transactions were fully margined, there would be a significantly lower probability that the failure of one participant (e.g., a large bank) would cause a domino effect that threatens the entire system.[xxv]

In practice, securities are rarely fully margined, meaning the failure of a bank will cause (albeit generally small) losses with each counterparty with exposure to the defaulted bank. Additionally, the collapse of a bank will cause a flurry of trading as counterparties attempt to reestablish positions (e.g., replace a defaulted interest rate swap), which can lead to trading costs or losses during the period when positions are in the process of being reconstituted. For these and several other reasons, since 2009, regulators have made a concerted effort to reduce the size of the OTC derivatives market and migrate derivatives trading to exchanges. Derivative exchanges utilize a central counterparty (CCP), which guarantees the financial performance of its clearing members. When a derivative trades on an exchange, the CCP becomes the buyer to the selling counterparty and the seller to the buying counterparty. As in bilateral trades, CCPs margin positions with their counterparties daily. Should a clearing member fail to margin trades to the CCP, the CCP would declare a default and the defaulting member's collateral would be seized and its positions liquidated. Any loss associated with the default would be covered by the CCP's reserves. Important to the broader financial system, no other market participants would need to reconstitute positions because the CCP would continue to guarantee the performance of all of its remaining derivative positions. Although regulators have sought to encourage migration of trading to exchanges with CCPs, they have, at best, had only modest success, as shown in Figure 1.6. According to the BIS, for the 10-year period ending on June 30, 2018, the total notional value of exchange-traded derivatives increased $20 trillion (26%), while the notional value of OTC derivatives declined $78 trillion (12%), and the market value of OTC derivatives declined by $10 trillion (49%). A major impediment to the

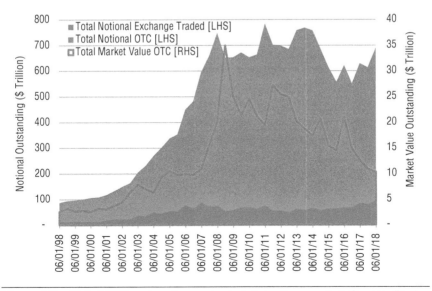

Figure 1.6 Global OTC and exchange-traded derivatives market. *Source*: Bank of International Settlements[xxvi]

shift to exchanges is that exchanges require contracts to be standardized. However, many derivatives require significant customization (such as interest rate swaps or total return swaps), such that these derivatives need to be negotiated bilaterally. As a result, most derivatives are still traded OTC—a trend likely to continue for the foreseeable future.

Derivatives—Who Issues and Purchases Them?

So how big is the derivatives market? According to the BIS, as of June 30, 2018, the global notional value of exchange-traded and OTC derivatives exceeded $689 trillion![xxvii] By way of comparison, in 2017 the global bond market was around $100 trillion, while the global equities market was around $85.3 trillion. So how is it that the derivatives market is ~3× the size of the global stock and bond markets combined? The reason has to do with how derivatives are tallied. Returning to the interest rate swap example, the contract covered a notional amount of $100 million, which is how the BIS would have *counted* the contract. But if LIBOR stays relatively stable, the economic value of the contract would be relatively small. In most cases, the market value of derivatives contracts is far below the notional value of these contracts. In fact, the BIS estimated that the OTC traded derivative notional value was $595 trillion, while the market value of those derivatives was only $10 trillion as of June 30, 2018.[xxviii]

Because of the requirement for strong creditworthiness to mitigate counterparty default risk, derivatives are largely written and purchased only by the world's largest banks and corporations. Exchanges and banks go to great lengths to evaluate and ensure the ongoing creditworthiness of their counterparties. Most individuals are insufficiently creditworthy to participate in these markets. A 2009 ISDA survey revealed 94% of the world's largest corporations use derivatives. All 78 of the world's largest banks and diversified financial institutions use derivatives, most commonly to hedge interest rate sensitivity and exposure to currency exchange rates. Insurers also commonly utilize derivatives, usually to manage exposure to interest rates, currencies, and equity prices. Finally, 93% of the 377 largest nonfinancial institutions use derivatives to regularly manage exposure to interest rates, currencies, and commodities.[xxix]

CAPITAL MARKET BENEFITS

Capital markets refer to activities related either to the transfer of funds from an entity that has excess cash to an entity that needs cash, or a transfer of risk from an entity that wants to shed it to an entity that wants to assume it. Economists generally refer to this activity as intermediation. With respect to savings and investments, the markets are constructed to match those with excess savings to those who need capital and also to improve the efficiency of that transfer so that each individual entity doesn't need to seek and find one another, create legal agreements, and transfer funds manually. With respect to transfers of risk, capital markets are constructed so that those desiring to mitigate risk and those seeking risk can find each other easily and agree to terms that are largely uniform and intelligible.

The operation of a traditional bank is a simple illustration of how capital markets work. Banks essentially match savers who have excess capital with borrowers who need capital. For example, Mary owns a furniture boutique and needs $50,000 so she can purchase inventory for the store. Joe has $50,000 that he wants to safely invest and still know that he can always recover it quickly without risk of loss. The bank will compete with other banks to entice Joe (and thousands of other savers) to deposit his savings with them by offering an attractive savings account interest rate—say 2%. Mary may have many options as to where she can get the business loan, so if the bank wants her business they will have to offer an attractive loan rate, say 5%. Theoretically, if Joe and Mary knew each other they could have arranged the loan directly, but Joe might not be skilled at assessing the credit quality of Mary's business and might worry that if she defaulted, he would lose his money or if he needed his savings for an emergency, that Mary might not be able to instantly repay him. So, the bank acts as a medium to indirectly match Joe and Mary—and the 3% interest spread (5% loan rate – 2% deposit rate) that it earns is compensation for, among other things, assessing and bearing Mary's credit risk and offering Joe liquidity and peace of mind. Thus, everyone is better off.

The stock market is another obvious form of capital market. Perhaps Mary's business has grown and she needs more permanent capital to rapidly expand her store base. She decides to sell equity in her company via an IPO. Joe has $500,000 he wants to invest in the stock market, and chooses to invest a portion of it with an investment manager that specializes in finding investment opportunities in relatively small but fast-growing retail businesses. The fund manager uses a portion of Joe's investment to buy some of Mary's stock. Again, the market works to match a saver with excess capital with someone who needs the capital.

Derivative exchanges are another important capital market. It turns out that Joe is a farmer who, among other things, grows corn. Early in the crop production cycle, Joe becomes concerned that bumper crops across the country might result in depressed corn prices when he is ready to harvest and sell his corn. To hedge this risk, he goes to the Chicago Board of Trade (CBOT) and buys a corn futures contract that effectively locks in the price he will receive for his corn when he delivers it at the end of the summer. The entity writing the future might be a frozen corn producer that doesn't want to take the risk that a late summer hail storm might wipe out corn crops and cause prices to spike. Another form of capital market, the CBOT, allows the two parties to essentially hedge each other's risk again allowing everyone to be better off.

Without capital markets it's hard to imagine how large infrastructure projects would get financed. In 2008, a syndicate of banks (again using the savings of people like Joe) agreed to extend $2.3 billion in financing to enable the first expansion of the Panama Canal since it opened in 1914.[xxx] Thanks in part to this necessary financing, in 2016 the expanded canal opened, enabling ships 1.5 times the previous Panamax size to pass through its locks, doubling the canal's capacity. As a result of the canal's expanded capacity, global shipping costs have fallen, which should result in global consumers benefiting from lower prices. Panama gets more tax revenue, the banks' shareholders benefited from a profitable loan, depositors benefited from the interest on their savings, consumers get cheaper prices—again, capital markets have dramatically improved the world economy.

CAPITAL MARKET RISKS

While capital markets have made, either directly or indirectly, substantial contributions to improvements in societal welfare, they can also cause damage when capital is misallocated. For capital markets to function properly, providers of capital must be well informed and act in their self-interest when they make a loan or buy a stock. Investors might invest in some risky ventures, but the expectation is that the potential rewards offset the risk. As the perceived risk increases, the price of the capital correspondingly increases and that price mechanism ensures that only projects with appropriate risk-adjusted returns receive the capital. Even at the individual consumer level, if the interest rate on a car loan rises from 2% to 20%, most people are likely to purchase a less expensive car or explore alternative transportation options. Like all exchanges in a free market economy, price is the primary mechanism of allocation. In this section, we will briefly discuss one instance and two potential instances where capital is misallocated, creating an unstable and potentially damaging situation. These situations are the subprime crisis in 2007–2009, the growth of the syndicated loan market, and the structural demand for U.S. government debt.

The Subprime Mortgage Crisis

Unfortunately, as the complexity of the capital markets increases and providers of capital become increasingly removed from the assessment of the risk of their investments, the risk of capital misallocation increases. A prime cause of this has been a trend for intermediaries that arrange capital investments to not bear any of the risk associated with those investments. Securitizations present a clear example of this. As previously described, in a standard securitization, an originator of loans will accumulate a large pool of those loans and then effectively sell them to the securitization SPV. That sale essentially transfers the risk of loss from making bad loans to the investors of the securitization. The securitization investors recognize this risk, and thus demand that independent third parties—in this case credit rating agencies—review the assets and other aspects of the transaction and provide an opinion on the risk, or conversely, the *safety* of the investment. The highest safety grade issued by Standard & Poor's Corporation (a major national rating agency) is the famous *AAA rating*.

While the involvement and oversight of a rating agency no doubt substantially improves the safety of these financings, the self-interest of a third party who has no capital at risk (and happens to have its fee paid by the promoter of the securitization) is inherently different than the self-interest of a provider of capital that bears the risk of loss if it makes bad lending decisions. A relatively recent example of the consequences of this separation of risk is the subprime mortgage debacle that most acknowledge was a major contributing cause of the 2008 Great Recession.

Without reviewing ancient history, home mortgages were originally made by banks or savings and loans that held the mortgage for its entire 30-year life. Not surprisingly, banks took great care in making sure that the borrower was a good credit risk and that home value substantially exceeded the mortgage amount. Fast forward to the early 2000s when subprime mortgage originations exploded. The originators of these mortgages were typically mortgage brokers who intended from the beginning to sell the mortgages to either a securitization entity or the Federal Mortgage affiliates.[13] These brokers were compensated on loan volume and not the quality of the loans originated.[14]

While the rating agencies recognized that subprime mortgages were riskier than traditional prime mortgages, the agencies had little history of how subprime mortgages performed over various economic cycles. This is because these mortgages were a relatively new asset class. Finally, the investors in the securitizations, even though they were often seasoned mortgage professionals, had little direct knowledge about the quality of the mortgages. These investors generally relied on summary statistics describing the securitization and the *AAA* or *AA* rating issued by the rating agency. While these investors bore the risk of loss,

---

[13] See Chapter 8 for a brief discussion on the requirements to sell a mortgage to a Federal Mortgage affiliate.

[14] In fact, mortgage brokers were paid both a commission as well as a *yield spread premium* (YSP) on some loans. A YSP allows the broker to share in the *extra* interest associated with higher interest rate loans made to less creditworthy borrowers, thus incentivizing brokers to originate riskier loans. Often these loans were based on *stated* incomes where there was no verification of the borrower's income, and thus no way to be sure they could afford the loan. For good reason, these came to be known pejoratively as *liar loans*.

they had no involvement in the loan-making decision process. And those who were involved in the loan-making process, bore no risk of loss and were incentivized to make as many loans as possible. Clearly, in hindsight, but probably with thoughtful foresight, this was a recipe for disaster.

At the root, this represented a basic failure of proper capital allocation. If all the risks had been properly assessed, the cost of the subprime loans either would have been substantially higher—thereby reducing the quantity of subprime loans originated—or proper due diligence would have been performed and many applicants would have been denied loans. But because there was a decoupling of risk taking (the making of the loan) and risk bearing (owning the loan), there was a breakdown in the proper operation of the market. As a result, billions of dollars of loans were made inappropriately. When the borrowers of those loans defaulted—sometimes due to an inability to pay the mortgage, other times due to a decline in the value of the property that wiped out the borrower's equity—the value of the related securitizations fell rapidly and caused investors to question the solvency of the over-leveraged investment banks that held them. This was essentially why Lehman Brothers was forced to file bankruptcy, which precipitated the financial crisis.

The Syndicated Leveraged Loan Market

The decoupling of risk taking and risk bearing also appears to be present in the syndicated leverage loan market, which is another market that has grown rapidly in the last decade and over which many market professionals have concerns. As discussed earlier, in the good old days, banks that made loans to corporate borrowers would carefully investigate or underwrite the loan to assess the probability that it would be repaid because they would hold the loan and bear the risk of loss. Syndicated loans are typically arranged by a relatively small number of money center banks (i.e., the largest in the world). These arrangers are responsible for doing the primary loan underwriting and negotiating the terms of the loan (including important protective covenants), but they then sell the loan in pieces to other investors and seldom keep a meaningful amount on their own balance sheet. The loan purchasers, who are generally sophisticated and experienced, often must rely on an analysis of fairly generic financial statements[15] and the opinion of the rating agency. This environment creates a risk

---

[15] Historically, when banks made significant loans to corporations, their due diligence investigations would include the review of far more detailed, not publicly available financial information than is generally disclosed by banks in SEC filings. This information would include, among other things, detailed loan performance and loan loss data as well as financial projections. Because syndicated loans are essentially sold publicly, this important nonpublic information is not made available to investors.

that substantial amounts of capital will be misallocated (or at least mispriced) to many borrowers.

In October 2018, former Federal Reserve Chairwoman Janet Yellen, in an interview with the *Financial Times*, spoke bluntly about what she views as troubling developments in the U.S.-leveraged loan market. In that interview, she stated: "There has been a huge deterioration in standards; covenants have been loosened in leveraged lending." She continued, "You are supposed to realize from the crisis, it is not just a question of what banks do that imperils themselves, it is what they do that can create risks to the entire financial system. That lesson, to me, seems to have been lost."[xxxi] Yellen pointed to the increase in covenant-lite loans and increasing leverage of the issuers. Specifically, as of January 2019, approximately 79% of the $1.2 trillion in outstanding syndicated loans have few or no covenants limiting the borrower's behavior.[xxxii] Meanwhile, leverage for these loans reached 6.9× in early 2019, just below the all-time high of 7.0× in Q3 2018.[xxxiii]

U.S. Government Debt

At the risk of taking on a politically controversial topic, an additional example of capital misallocation *may* be occurring in U.S. sovereign debt (i.e., U.S. Treasury bonds or USTs). Because the United States is the largest economy in the world and has been among the most politically stable of the developed nations, the USD is by far the most widely held and used currency on the planet. It is the leading reserve currency—meaning that it is the currency of choice for foreign currency reserves by foreign central banks. In addition, it is the primary currency used in many foreign transactions, including importantly, oil sales. As a result, there are a lot of USD outstanding, and the easiest way to invest a USD is in a UST. A second order consequence of this is that there is tremendous structural demand, on average, for USTs which means the borrowing cost for the federal government is relatively low (in both nominal and real terms), and the borrowing rate is likely lower than it would be if the USD did not hold its unique status as the world's reserve currency.

Because of this structural demand for U.S. government debt and the low financing cost associated with its debt, there seems to be increasingly less fiscal discipline by the federal government. As of year-end 2018, the federal debt exceeded $22 trillion, and following the 2017 Tax Cuts and Jobs Act, the U.S. Congressional Budget Office estimated that the U.S. fiscal deficit will grow from $860 billion per year in 2018 to over $1.3 trillion per year in 2028. Additionally, net interest payments are estimated to grow from $316 billion per year in 2018 to $915 billion per year in 2028.[xxxiv] Citizens seem to be rightly concerned even if policymakers are not. In a March 2018 survey by the Global Strategy Group,

74% of participants agree or strongly agree that the national debt should be among "the President and Congress's top three priorities." [xxxv]

Deficit spending is a contentious subject. Sometimes, for example in 2009 during the depths of the Great Recession, deficits were deemed important to stimulate the economy and reduce unemployment. Additionally, it was argued at the time that borrowing to fund infrastructure improvements will add to the productive capacity of the economy and benefit future generations. But borrowing to fund current consumption that does little to add to the productive capacity of the nation simply shifts a payment burden onto subsequent generations and possibly harms the potential growth rate of the economy.[16]

Why is this characterized as a problem of capital misallocation? If almost any other country ran sustained deficit to GDP ratios as high as the U.S., their cost of external debt financing would likely increase substantially. Furthermore, if U.S. deficits were being financed with debt that cost 8% instead of 3%, politicians would likely make fiscal discipline a much higher priority. Governments, like every other person or entity, respond to their cost of capital. Because the U.S. is in the unique and enviable position of holding the world's reserve currency,

---

[16] In 2009, economists Carmen Reinhart and Kenneth Rogoff published *This Time is Different: Eight Centuries of Financial Folly*. As the title suggests, this seminal piece collected global data across eight centuries, highlighting that (among other things) history is replete with examples of governments overborrowing and then defaulting, whether the default is explicit via principal reduction or implicit via high inflation. In 2010, Reinhart and Rogoff published *Growth in a Time of Debt*, in which they state, "When gross external debt reaches 60% of GDP, annual growth declines by about 2%; for levels of external debt in excess of 90% of GDP, growth rates are roughly cut in half." Unfortunately for the authors and policymakers alike, in 2013, Thomas Herndon, then a PhD candidate at the University of Massachusetts, attempted to recreate one of Reinhart and Rogoff's tables and discovered an excel error whereby only 15 of 20 countries in the 90+ debt to GDP category were included in the average growth calculation. In an interview shortly after the error was made public, Herndon and UMass Professor Michael Ash state, "What we find is that average growth is modestly diminished when countries hit the 90%—as countries approach the 90% public debt to GDP ratio. There's no cliff."

Perhaps Reinhart and Rogoff bit off more than they could chew; the growth of an economy is driven by a plethora of factors including the economy's openness, rule of law and property rights, economic conditions of trading partners, the level of citizen's education and social mobility, governmental stability, exchange rate regimes, business cycle, fiscal situation, trade balance, and much more. So, attempting to solve for economic growth using the single variable of national debt as a percentage of GDP was likely a fool's errand. But, the logic is clear and irrefutable even if the data isn't—all other things equal, a higher debt burden means more tax revenue is diverted toward interest payments and not government programs that may improve economic conditions, such as infrastructure or education. Sadly, the discrediting of the statistical link between high public-debt burdens and poor economic growth has contributed to increasing apathy among policymakers' view toward high U.S. public debt.

which results in a high demand for USTs, interest rates do not respond to normal market mechanisms and capital may be misallocated.

In summary, capital markets have the potential to create great value in society by matching capital with the best ideas and investment opportunities. As illustrated, when capital markets function properly everyone wins. However, for capital markets to function properly, the price of the capital must properly reflect the risk to which it is being deployed. When the risk pricing mechanism breaks down because *risk taking* becomes separated from *risk bearing*, capital will be mispriced and misallocations will likely occur. Usually those misallocations will not result in something as destructive as the Great Recession, but credit bubbles, another code word for misallocations, have become an increasing area of concern.

MARKET EFFICIENCY AND CAPITAL MARKET FAILURES

While University of Chicago Professor Eugene Fama was not the first economist to make the case that past stock prices are not predictive of future stock prices, he is widely credited for developing and advancing the *Efficient Market Hypothesis* (EMH). The EMH postulates that asset prices reflect all available information. Therefore, an analyst valuing stocks or bonds cannot beat the market by analyzing charts, company balance sheets, google trending searches, or any other source of information, because all of this information is already incorporated into the price of every security. It is for this reason that active stock mutual fund managers net of fees, on average, do not outperform market indexes.

One should be careful in interpreting what the EMH, or the concept of efficiency, really means or implies. First, it does not imply that there is any type of consensus that a particular asset, such as an individual stock, is properly valued. The reality of the market is that every participant probably has a slightly different view of the value of a specific stock. Every time a trade takes place, the seller implicitly thinks the buyer must be a fool for paying too much for the stock (otherwise why would the seller sell) and the buyer must think the seller is equally foolish for not realizing the stock is cheap and likely to increase in value (otherwise why would the buyer buy). So, efficiency is just the temporary equilibrium of all participants' interpretation of the available market information.

Second, the market never has *all* of the information. Investors often think they have unique information that gives them an edge. Consider the stock of a pharmaceutical company with a drug that is undergoing a clinical trial. An investor who is participating in the trial and believes the drug is effective might buy the stock, but that doesn't mean the market reflects all information. If the company sends a press release two days later announcing positive clinical results, it will lead to complete internalization of the information.[17] However, as a legal and regulatory matter, whether an investor has an unfair information advantage (i.e., trading on insider information) is a significant concern and central to the notion of whether the market is fair.

Finally, the EMH does not imply the price is correct—just that it reflects all available information. This last point is important because it rationalizes how there can be significant changes in market prices without suggesting the prior market price was *wrong*. Consider a market crash. Was the market wrong the day before a crash? No, it just means that new information likely became available that changed investors' outlooks (either for an individual stock or the entire market). For example, articulated changes in Federal Reserve policy will often have significant impacts on market prices, but that doesn't imply the market was wrong the day before the change was disclosed.

If market crashes aren't the result of investor mistakes, what does cause them? (If the authors knew this we would be too busy counting our money to write this book!) There are a number of theories, three of which will be briefly discussed here. Economist John Maynard Keynes believed that market economies were by their nature inherently unstable and prone to recessions in periods of low demand and inflation in periods of high demand and that government intervention was frequently needed to provide stability. Economist Hyman Minsky argued that humans' innate propensity to be lulled into complacency during periods of sustained stability coupled with banks' competitive desire to grow, leads to deteriorating lending standards during times of extended periods of strong growth and few defaults. This fuels asset price appreciation which further reinforces the banks' view that the risk of loss is de minimis.[xxxvi] Then one day something happens that causes everyone in the market to realize that prices are irrationally high (a *Minsky moment*[18]) and a massive correction ensues. Statistician Nassim Taleb, author of *Black Swans*, asserts that the problem is that

---

[17] This rapid internalization and repricing following a press release is in line with the semi-strong EMH, which states that all publicly available information is incorporated into a stock price. By contrast, a weak EMH states that there is no informational value in past price movements because stock prices follow a *random walk*. Finally, the strong EMH hypothesis states that all information, both public and private, is incorporated into the price of a stock. In practice, even the most die-hard of EMH enthusiasts concede that insider information is not always incorporated into a stock price, meaning the strong EMH will remain an academic hypothetical.

[18] The term *Minsky moment* was coined by economist and former PIMCO Portfolio Manager Paul McCulley when describing the Russian financial crisis of 1998, the Fed's response to the 2001 U.S. recession, and later the 2007–2009 global financial crisis.

the market improperly assesses the implications of low probability but high impact events. When such an event occurs (which is not often since they are by definition low probability), the market is essentially "surprised" and reacts dramatically.

SUMMARY AND INVESTMENT IMPLICATIONS

Summary

Modern capital markets match individuals and institutions that have excess capital or risk with those individuals and institutions that lack capital or risk but would like it. The motives of capital market participants typically include the desire to either make an investment that will lead to value creation in the future, increase or forgo current consumption, reduce risk, or increase risk if they feel they are being sufficiently compensated for that risk. Stocks and bonds are financial assets issued by capital market participants. These securities are essentially contracts documenting the transfer of cash to the issuer and specifying the holder's rights to receive cash flows in the future. Derivatives are also issued by capital market participants; however, while stocks and bonds are generally used to facilitate the transfer of capital, derivatives are primarily used to transfer risk between participants. Financial markets are where individuals and institutions go to trade stocks, bonds, and derivatives. In practice, the terms financial markets and capital markets are largely used interchangeably.

Capital markets are essential to the functioning of a modern economy. In the long run, economic output is determined by the economy's stock of capital and overall productivity. Financial markets enable both people and businesses to increase their capital, both physical and mental, more than would be the case should these markets not exist. Therefore, we are all the beneficiaries of these markets as they facilitate a more optimal allocation of capital and risk in the economy. However, for markets to work properly, the price of capital must efficiently reflect all associated risks. When the pricing mechanism breaks down, capital can be misallocated, sometimes with disastrous social and financial consequences.

Finally, markets are *efficient*, meaning the prices of assets include all publicly available information—and when new information becomes available, prices rapidly adjust. This doesn't mean that boom-bust cycles are less likely to occur owing to the financial market's efficiency. Rather, it simply means that it is very difficult to outperform the return of the broad stock and bond markets.

Investment Implications

- Capital markets exist to match entities with excess capital and those that desire additional capital as well as to match entities with an aversion to risk and those seeking risk. Individuals, corporate executives, and senior government officials should utilize these markets to borrow if and only if they are using this capital for productive means. In other words, prudent issuers of debt or equity should only deploy capital on projects that will generate future cash flows that provide appropriate risk-adjusted returns to investors.

- Debt investors should be cognizant of the borrower's motives for financing and not simply the borrower's willingness and ability to service additional debt. Additionally, investors should be leery of lending to individuals, institutions, and governments that are utilizing the capital markets to merely increase current consumption and not future productivity.

- It is wise to always have a contingency plan should the economy suddenly contract or the value of investments significantly fall. Regardless of whether Keynes, Minsky, or Talib properly diagnosed the causes of financial dislocations, periods of significant financial instability and heightened volatility are reoccurring and nearly impossible to forecast.

- As markets are efficient, investors are wise to minimize trading and management costs of their investments. In Chapter 5 we will go into greater detail regarding investment manager fees and the debate of active versus passive management.

Appendix Table 1.1 Options, futures, forwards, and swaps

Derivative	Options	Futures	Forwards	Swaps
Definition	The right (but not the obligation) to buy (call) or sell (put) a security at a given price (the strike) on or before a certain time (the contract maturity).	A legal agreement to buy or sell a specific asset at a given price (the strike) at a specified time in the future (the maturity).	A legal agreement to buy or sell a specific asset at a given price (the strike) at a specified time in the future (the maturity).	A legal agreement to exchange cash flows based upon two separate financial instruments or indexes for a given tenor. The most common swap is an interest rate swap, whereby one party pays a fixed interest rate (the fixed leg) in exchange for an interest rate that varies (the floating leg), often with another index such as 3 month USD LIBOR. The cash exchanged is the interest rate differential between the fixed and floating legs multiplied by the notional value of the swap.

Continued

Derivative	Options	Futures	Forwards	Swaps
Listed or Over-the-counter Trading	Both. Listed options trade on exchanges and are standardized contracts whereas over-the-counter options do not trade on an exchange and are not standardized (bespoke).	Listed. All futures contracts are standardized for quality and quantity of the underlying asset and are traded on an exchange.	Over-the-counter. Forwards contracts are not standardized and are not traded on an exchange.	Over-the-counter. Swap contracts are not standardized and are not traded on an exchange.
Cash or Physical Delivery Settlement	Both. Most options are physical settled, meaning the transfer of the underlying security occurs should the option be exercised by the holder of the option. Some options are cash settled, meaning a dollar value of the option is calculated, based on a predetermined formula, and transferred from one party to the other.	Both. Most futures contracts are cash settled, meaning the value of the future is debited from one account and credited to another account on the maturity of the future. A small percentage of futures are physical settled, meaning the underlying index or commodity (whether it be a stock, oil, or corn) is physically transferred from the short (seller) to the long (buyer) of the contract.	Both. Forward contracts are highly customizable between parties and are often settled through either cash or physical delivery.	Cash. However, given the bespoke nature of swaps, nothing precludes counterparties to settle with physical securities; however, this is not common.

Continued

Derivative	Options	Futures	Forwards	Swaps
Use	Speculation: Allows the holder to speculate as to whether a security, index, or commodity will rise or fall without owning the reference security or index. If a speculator anticipates the underlying security will rise (fall), she may purchase (sell) a call or sell (purchase) a put. Hedge: Allows the holder to protect themselves, in part or in whole, against a appreciation or depreciation in the value of the security, index, or commodity. If the hedger owns (is short) a security, he may hedge their exposure by purchasing (selling) a put or selling (buying) a call.	Speculation: Allows the holder to speculate as to whether an index or commodity will rise or fall without owning the reference index or commodity. If a speculator anticipates the index or commodity will rise (fall), he may purchase (sell) a futures contract. Hedge: Allows the holder to protect themselves, in part or in whole, against an appreciation or depreciation in the value of the index or commodity. If the hedger owns (is short) an index or commodity, he may hedge his exposure by selling (purchasing) a futures contract.	Speculation: Allows the holder to speculate as to whether an index or commodity will rise or fall without owning the reference index or commodity. If a speculator anticipates the index or commodity will rise (fall), he may purchase (sell) a forward contract. Hedge: Allows the holder to protect themselves, in part or in whole, against an appreciation or depreciation in the value of the index or commodity. If the hedger owns (is short) an index or commodity, he may hedge his exposure by selling (purchasing) a forward contract.	Speculation: Allows the holder to speculate as to whether an index, commodity, currency, or interest rates will rise or fall. The speculator needs to post little, if any, initial margin. If a speculator anticipates interest rates will rise, she may enter a swap whereby she receives a floating interest rate and pays the fixed interest rate. She will benefit should interest rates rise above the fixed leg. Hedge: Allows the holder to protect themselves, in part or in whole, against an appreciation or depreciation of an index, commodity, currency, or change in interest rates. If the hedger owns (is short) an index, he may hedge his exposure by selling or paying (buying) the return of that index and buying or receiving (paying) a fixed or floating cash return.

CITATIONS

i. Shapiro, Fred R. (2006). The Yale Book of Quotations.

ii. Gross, William H. (September, 2012). "The Lending Lindy." *Investment Outlook*, PIMCO.

iii. Kahan, Marcel. "Rethinking Corporate Bonds: The Tradeoff between Individual and Collective Rights." *New York University Law Review*. Vol. 77, No. 4. Available at SSRN: https://ssrn.com/abstract=304062.

iv. The Joe I. Herbstman "Memorial Collection of American Finance." https://www.theherbstmancollection.com/bonds-1933—.

v. http://www.dtcc.com/about/businesses-and-subsidiaries/dtc.

vi. IFLR. (January 2010). Morrison & Foerster LLP, "No more bearer bonds?"

vii. Espiner, Tom. (January 11, 2016). " 'Bowie bonds'—the singer's financial innovation." BBC.

viii. SIFMA "2017 Fact Book." www.sifma.org. p. 52.

ix. The World Bank. GDP (US$) All countries. https://data.worldbank .org/indicator/NY.GDP.MKTP.CD.

x. SIFMA. (3Q 2018). "Research Quarterly." https://www.sifma.org/ resources/research/research-quarterly-third-quarter-2018/.

xi. https://www.sifma.org/resources/research/bond-chart/.

xii. Department of the Treasury/Federal Reserve Board. (March 15, 2019). Major Foreign Holders of Treasury Securities.

xiii. B.101.h Balance Sheet of Households. (September 30, 2018). Federal Reserve Statistical Release. Z.1 Financial Accounts of the United States.

xiv. Kahan, Marcel. "Rethinking Corporate Bonds: The Tradeoff between Individual and Collective Rights." *New York University Law Review*. Vol. 77, No. 4. Available at SSRN: https://ssrn.com/abstract=304062.

xv. 40 University of California, Davis. Vol. 40:407 (2006–2007). The Fundamental Rights of the Shareholder.

xvi. Krantz, Matt. (May 25, 2010). "Electronic records are replacing paper stock certificates." *USA Today*.

xvii. SIFMA. "2017 Fact Book." www.sifma.org. p. 55.

xviii. "The rise and rise of private markets." (2018). *McKinsey Global Private Markets Review*.

xix. Research Quarterly. (November 2018). Third Quarter 2018. p. 24. SIFMA www.sifma.org.

xx. SIFMA "2017 Fact Book." www.sifma.org. p. 22.

xxi. https://www.sifma.org/resources/research/bond-chart/.

xxii. Bank of International Settlements. Website. (September 19, 2018). Table: D1. "Exchange-traded futures and options."

xxiii. Bank of International Settlements. Website. (February 5, 2018). Table: D5. Global OTC derivatives market.

xxiv. https://www.isda.org/about-isda/.

xxv. ISDA. Collateral Steering Committee. (March 1, 2010). Market Review of OTC Derivative Bilateral Collateralization Practices (2.0).

xxvi. BIS Statistics Explorer. stats.bis.org. Tables D1 and D5.1.

xxvii. BIS Statistics Explorer. stats.bis.org. Tables D1 and D5.1.

xxviii. BIS Statistics Explorer. stats.bis.org. Tables D1 and D5.1.

xxix. ISDA Research Notes. (2009). ISDA Derivatives Usage Survey.

xxx. "Financing deal for Panama Canal expansion signed." (December 24, 2008). *Ordons News*.

xxxi. Fleming, Sam. (October 24, 2018). "Janet Yellen sounds alarm over plunging loan standards." *Financial Times*.

xxxii. Cross, Tim. (February 20, 2019). "Leveraged Loans: Cov-Lite Activity Levels Off, Though $922B Remains Outstanding." *Forbes*.

xxxiii. Haunss, Kristen. (March 15, 2019). "Regulatory crackdown unlikely in US leveraged loan market." *Reuters*.

xxxiv. CBO's April 2018 report: "The Budget and Economic Outlook." www.cbo.gov/publication/53651. Table 4-1.

xxxv. Global Strategy Group—March Fiscal Monitor Survey 3.18. https://www.pgpf.org/sites/default/files/PGPF-Fiscal-Confidence-Index-032618.pdf.

xxxvi. Minsky, Hyman P. (1986). *Stabilizing an Unstable Economy*. New Haven, CT: Yale University Press.

2

INVESTMENT VEHICLES[1]

In 2002, I received an inheritance from my grandfather. The son of Eastern European immigrants, he grew up in a working-class community in Pittsburgh during the Great Depression, served during WWII, and became a pharmacist when he returned home. When he passed away, exactly one year following the death of my grandmother, per his will, his financial assets were divided between his children and grandchildren. While I received a small percentage of his financial assets, the amount was pro rata; so, this inheritance provided me with a near-complete picture of all his investments. There were dozens of stocks. All the companies were domiciled in the United States, and most of them were industrials with operations in Pittsburgh—or the Eastern seaboard, more broadly. The largest positions were concentrated so only four or five securities constituted 50% of his portfolio, and most of the equities paid high dividends. He owned no mutual funds, no bonds, and no international equities. Rather, he picked stocks in companies he knew and understood or were recommended to him by his broker. He was both an intelligent man and an excellent saver. "Always reinvest the dividends!" was his favorite advice he repeatedly bestowed upon me when, as a youth, I talked to him about the stock market.

When he was in his prime *saving years*, picking stocks and keeping deposits at a local bank were the two primary methods available to individuals to acquire and grow their stock of financial assets. In fact, household investments in mutual funds in 1960 were at most 1.1% of total financial assets in the U.S.[2,i,ii] It's clear now that his portfolio was largely a product of his time. It was not diversified; whether measured by geography, sector, or number of investments, his portfolio

---

[1] I would like to thank Audrey L. Cheng and Robin S. Yonis for their assistance in reviewing and composing this chapter.

[2] We say *at most* because Federal Reserve data aggregates nonprofit organizations with households in their statistics. Therefore, some nonprofit investments may be included in this figure.

was too risky given his age, and his portfolio exhibited several behavioral biases (see Chapter 11) including a *home bias*. Specifically, all the companies in which he owned stock were domiciled in the United States and they were generally headquartered on the East Coast. Despite these shortcomings, he did an excellent job supporting his family and building a comfortable nest egg; so, given the limited tools available to him and his occupation as a pharmacist (and not an investment professional), I'm leery of being overly critical. Rather, it is apparent that he, like most of his generation, could have benefited from other investment options that were not prevalent or easily accessible to everyday investors then, but are widely available to investors now.

MUTUAL FUNDS

One such investment vehicle that my grandfather lacked but is largely ubiquitous in people's portfolios today are mutual funds. Mutual funds are companies whose main purpose is the business of investing, reinvesting, and trading in securities and other investment instruments. Thus, they are companies of pooled investments, meaning multiple investors' capital is pooled into a single fund and managed by an investment adviser. Instead of shares in a company, the purchaser of a mutual fund owns shares that represent the value of that investor's proportionate ownership of the mutual fund's portfolio and the income that portfolio generates.[iii] Mutual funds are extensively regulated and must adhere to various laws, including (but not limited to): Investment Company Act of 1940 (Investment Company Act), Securities Act of 1933 (Securities Act), Securities Exchange Act of 1934 (Exchange Act), state corporate or trust laws, state blue sky laws,[iv] and if futures or swaps are used by the fund, the Commodity Exchange Act (CEA) and the National Futures Administration (NFA). In addition, the investment managers who manage the funds are subject to the Investment Advisers Act and a fund's distributor, typically a broker-dealer firm, is subject to the Exchange Act and the rules of the Financial Industry Regulatory Authority (FINRA). The Investment Company Act of 1940 defines and regulates investment companies.[3]

The term *mutual funds* typically refers to open-end investment companies that are not traded on an exchange, but whose shares can be purchased from

---

[3] There are three types of investment companies: face-amount certificates (which are rare but included here for completeness), unit investment trusts, and management companies. Management companies are further broken down into open-end and closed-end funds, some of which may be traded on a securities exchange.

and redeemed by (sold to) the issuer of the fund at the fund's net asset value calculated at the end of the day (4 p.m. eastern time), every day the U.S. markets are open. Mutual funds may be structured as corporations or trusts under state law.[4] The entity must then register with the Securities and Exchange Commission (SEC) to be a registered mutual fund (unless there is an applicable exemption from registration under the law). While state law imposes typical corporate or trust requirements on mutual funds, the 1940 Act imposes certain additional requirements, including (but not limited to): a requirement that the board be comprised of a two-thirds majority of independent directors and the review and approval of certain important fund matters, including specific agreements, by a majority of those independent directors.

Mutual funds do not typically have their own employees. Rather, they have a board of directors who are elected by the mutual fund shareholders;[5] the fund board is primarily responsible for looking after the interests of fund shareholders. The Investment Company Act and rules adopted by the SEC thus impose specific responsibilities on independent directors to monitor potential conflicts of interest between the fund and its adviser. Additionally, the fund board is responsible for approving the hiring or termination of fund service providers, which includes an investment adviser (a separate legal entity) to manage the fund's investments, as well as a distributor (or principal underwriter), a custodian, and a transfer agent. For example, if you were to purchase

---

[4] Investment companies can be organized under any state's laws, but mutual funds are most often organized under the corporate laws of the state of Maryland or the trust laws of the state of Delaware or Massachusetts. When a fund is formed under a state corporations' law, its board is composed of *directors* and is called a *board of directors*; when a fund is formed under a state's trust laws, its board is composed of *trustees* and is called a *board of trustees*. For the purposes of this chapter, reference to the board of directors of a mutual fund shall include and apply equally to a board of trustees.

[5] The initial directors/trustees of a fund must be elected by shareholders; but vacancies thereafter may be filled by appointment by the then elected directors/trustees so long as at least two-thirds of the directors/trustees of a fund have been elected by shareholders. In the event that less than a majority of directors/trustees of the fund have been elected, the board must call a shareholder meeting within sixty days for the purpose of electing directors to fill any existing vacancies. Note that until 2001, the SEC did not require that a majority of the board members be independent from the investment adviser. That meant that the investment adviser employees could hold a majority of the seats on fund boards. Recognizing this obvious conflict of interest, in 2004 the SEC began requiring that at least 75% of a fund's board be independent from the investment adviser and that a fund have an independent chair. These requirements were vacated by a court decision and as of this time have not been proposed again by the SEC; but in practice, independent directors make up 75% of board members in nearly 90% of fund complexes.

the Vanguard 500 Index Fund, its prospectus currently specifies that the board of trustees has hired The Vanguard Group, Inc. as the investment adviser. Typically, shareholders must approve a change in the investment adviser; but often, funds with sub-advisers are authorized to change sub-advisers without a vote of shareholders approving such a change subject to certain conditions.[6,v]

The U.S. mutual fund structure is complex, expensive, and is it not actually necessary to manage investments. Rather, a fund adviser could operate a fund without a fund board of directors. However, having a fund board protects investors by overseeing situations where the investment adviser may have a conflict of interest, such as with respect to its own management fees. Fund advisers want to maximize their own profits, whereas the fund boards realize every dollar in additional fees is a dollar that reduces shareholder profits. The role of the fund board is to negotiate an advisory fee that is reasonable in light of the services that the investment adviser provides. This can be a difficult situation for fund directors since the investment advisers are the entities that seed and launch mutual funds, incur legal expenses, and appoint the initial board of directors. The fund board, in turn, then hires the investment adviser.

Even if a majority or two-thirds of fund board members are independent from an investment adviser, it is still unlikely that a fund board will fire and replace a mutual fund investment adviser. However, boards have come close. In 2005, Putnam Investment Management, LLC settled with the SEC and paid a $40 million fine for failing to disclose conflicts of interest to the Putnam Fund Board of Trustees and its shareholders. Specifically, Putnam had arrangements with more than 60 broker-dealers who received brokerage commissions in exchange for providing services that promoted the sale of Putnam funds.[vi] Following this revelation, the Putnam board of trustees oversaw the hiring of a third party to conduct a compliance review, every other year, until 2013.[vii] In addition, many fund boards have significant and in-depth negotiations with the investment advisers before approving their advisory fees or they insist upon breakpoints in fees. Breakpoints are fee reductions that occur once asset sizes

---

[6] Funds with sub-advisers typically obtain an exemptive order from the U.S. SEC to permit the investment adviser, subject to oversight by the fund's board, to change sub-advisers without a shareholder vote, subject to certain conditions, including having initial shareholders approve this authorization to the investment adviser, including disclosure in the fund's prospectus advising shareholders of this method of operation, sending disclosure specified by the SEC about the change to shareholders. The investment adviser cannot change the sub-adviser to an affiliate of the investment adviser without a shareholder vote.

reach certain levels that (in the opinion of the fund board) would result in appropriate compensation to the adviser. This sort of negotiation is much more prevalent than firing an advisory firm.

So, how well does an independent board of directors perform its intended purpose of representing shareholder interests, which includes minimizing fees? A. Joseph Warburton published a paper in 2008 in the *Journal of Corporation Law* comparing the fund fees within the UK mutual fund industry between funds organized as corporations with corresponding fund boards and funds organized as unit trusts generally with a single trustee that holds limited powers. In short, mutual funds organized as corporations charge front-end loads that are an average of 0.24% lower and management fees 0.05% lower than their unit trust counterparts. Additionally, the author's estimate of mutual fund gross of fee *style-adjusted returns* did not show a statistically significant difference between the corporate and trust mutual funds. The author's conclusion is that the U.S. mutual fund corporate structure, with independent boards, does in fact benefit shareholders.[viii]

So, what are the different *types* of mutual funds? There should be a straightforward answer to this question, but the legal definition of these products and the way investment professionals describe these products is not uniform, which often leads to confusion. In the public forum, when someone describes the different types of mutual funds, they are generally referring to closed-end funds, open-end funds, unit investment trusts (UITs), and exchange-traded funds (ETFs), all of which we will review in this chapter. Conversely, the SEC[ix] and Investment Company Institute (the leading association representing investment companies, their investment advisers, and underwriters) regularly use the term mutual fund to describe only open-end funds. To further confuse the matter, the legal definition of these products is different still. The commingled investment vehicle that people are describing when they say a *mutual fund* is not an investment *product* but an investment *company*. U.S. securities law subdivides investment companies into three groups that include open-end companies (manage open-end funds or exchange-traded funds), closed-end companies (manage closed-end funds or interval funds), and UITs (manage unit investment trusts or exchange traded funds).[x] For the remainder of this chapter, all of the aforementioned products in which individual investors can invest will be referred to as mutual funds, and there will then be descriptions explaining how each of these funds is unique. A summary of each of these funds and their unique attributes can be found in Table 2.1.

Table 2.1 U.S. mutual fund similarities and differences

	Capital Contributions	Capital Redemptions	Traded on an Exchange	Price of shares	Lifespan	Tax Considerations	Active or Passive Management?	Appropriate For
Open-end Funds	Ongoing. Investors purchase shares directly from the fund. Liquidity is managed by the investment management company.	Ongoing. Investors redeem shares directly from the fund. Liquidity is managed by the investment management company.	No.	Net asset value (NAV); this is calculated daily by the fund administrator and directly corresponds to the value of the portfolio positions.	Infinite.	Shareholders generally must pay income taxes on the interest, dividends, and/or capital gains distributed to them. Additionally, when an investor sells shares he or she will realize either a taxable gain or a loss. Finally, a shareholder may incur a tax liability owing to interest, dividends, or capital gains, even if the fund has depreciated in a calendar year. This is because securities sold during the year may have been sold at a higher price than their cost basis thereby generating a capital gain.	Active or passive management. It is worth noting that even passively managed open-end funds will experience some trading during the lifetime of the fund. This is because portfolio positions will be revised to align with a benchmark.	Individual investors, generally held in qualified (tax deferred) accounts such as an IRA or 401k.

Continued

	Capital Contributions	Capital Redemptions	Traded on an Exchange	Price of shares	Lifespan	Tax Considerations	Active or Passive Management?	Appropriate For
Closed-end Funds	Severely limited. Capital is raised during an initial public offering (IPO). A closed-end fund may have additional public offerings to raise additional capital; however, this is at the discretion of the fund manager.	Severely limited. Investors generally need to sell their shares in the secondary market in order to withdraw their capital. However, capital in the fund remains unchanged until it is returned to the investors according to the fund's distribution policy.	Likely; may also trade over-the-counter.	These can drift significantly from the net asset value of the underlying instruments. This is because there is no direct mechanism that ties the fund price to that of the NAV.	Finite, but generally extended beyond their original lifespan.	Shareholders generally must pay income taxes on the interest, dividends, and/or capital gains distributed to them. Additionally, when an investor sells shares he or she will realize either a taxable gain or a loss.	Active or passive management. It is worth noting that even passively managed open-end funds will experience some trading during the lifetime of the fund. This is because portfolio positions will be revised to align with a benchmark.	Individual investors, generally held in qualified (tax deferred) accounts such as an IRA or 401k.

Continued

	Capital Contributions	Capital Redemptions	Traded on an Exchange	Price of shares	Lifespan	Tax Considerations	Active or Passive Management?	Appropriate For
Interval Fund (a type of Closed-end Fund)	Limited. Capital may be contributed at predetermined intervals, such as quarterly, semi-annually, or annually. Investors must provide the investment company notice prior to a subscription.	Limited. Capital may be withdrawn at predetermined intervals, such as quarterly, semi-annually, or annually. Investors must provide the investment company notice prior to a redemption.	Generally no.	NAV; calculated daily by the fund administrator and directly corresponds to the value of the portfolio positions.	Finite, but generally extended beyond their original lifespan.	Shareholders generally must pay income taxes on the interest, dividends, and/or capital gains distributed to them. Additionally, when an investor sells shares he or she will realize either a taxable gain or a loss. Finally, a shareholder may incur a tax liability owing to interest, dividends, or capital gains, even if the fund has depreciated in a calendar year. This is because securities sold during the year may have been sold at a higher price than their cost basis thereby generating a capital gain.	Generally active management.	Individual investors, generally held in qualified (tax deferred) accounts such as an IRA or 401k.

Continued

	Capital Contributions	Capital Redemptions	Traded on an Exchange	Price of shares	Lifespan	Tax Considerations	Active or Passive Management?	Appropriate For
Unit Investment Trusts	Severely limited. Capital is raised during an IPO. UITs generally do not have follow-on capital raises.	Ongoing. Investors redeem shares directly from the fund. Liquidity is managed by the investment management company. Some investment management companies make secondary markets by purchasing shares from shareholders who wish to redeem their shares, and then selling these shares to other buyers.	No. But, investors can obtain UIT price quotes from brokerage or investment firms, and some UITs list their prices on Nasdaq's Mutual Fund Quotation Service.	NAV; calculated daily by the fund administrator and directly corresponds to the value of the portfolio positions.	Finite. At the termination of the trust, all assets are liquidated and returned to unitholders or reinvested in another trust. Fixed income UITs generally have 20–30 year lifespans, which correspond to the tenor of bonds held in the portfolios.	Unitholders generally must pay income taxes on the interest, dividends, and/or capital gains distributed to them. Additionally, when an investor sells units, he or she will realize either a taxable gain or a loss.	Passive. Typically the portfolio is constituted following the product's IPO and remains unchanged for the life of the trust.	Individual investors, generally held in qualified (tax deferred) accounts such as an IRA or 401k.

Continued

	Capital Contributions	Capital Redemptions	Traded on an Exchange	Price of shares	Lifespan	Tax Considerations	Active or Passive Management?	Appropriate For
Exchange-Traded Fund	Ongoing. Investors purchase shares on an exchange from another investor or from an Authorized Participant (AP).	Ongoing. Investors sell shares on an exchange from another investor or from an AP.	Yes.	The value of the share transaction may differ from the fund's NAV. However, trading by the AP keeps the price close to the NAV through the process of creating and redeeming shares.	Infinite.	ETFs can be more tax efficient than other mutual funds because ETF shares are redeemable "in-kind." When an ETF fund manager needs to liquidate a portion of the portfolio, the fund manager typically delivers portfolio securities to an AP. The AP then redeems units and may choose to liquidate the portfolio securities. This process does not create a taxable gain or loss.	Generally passive management. "Smart Beta" products have elements of active management (see Chapter 11).	Individual investors, held in (qualified) tax deferred accounts, such as an IRA or 401k, or in taxable accounts such as brokerage accounts.

Open-End Funds

As mentioned previously, mutual funds are commingled investment vehicles that are available to individuals, managed by an SEC-registered investment adviser, organized as a corporation or trust, and overseen by a fund board who hires the investment adviser. Unique characteristics to open-end mutual funds include:[xi]

- *Ongoing capital contributions*: unless a fund is closed to new capital, investors may purchase new shares from the fund at any time. The investor acquires shares based upon his or her capital contribution at the NAV of the fund following the transfer agent's receipt of a subscription (purchase order); the NAV is calculated each day that the New York Stock Exchange is open. The investment adviser will then purchase additional assets (such as stocks or bonds) with the additional capital consistent with the fund's investment objectives.
- *Ongoing capital redemptions*: when an investor sells (redeems) his or her shares, the investment adviser is responsible for raising the cash by selling fund assets, if necessary, in order for the fund to be able to pay the investor for the redemption. The transfer agent is then responsible for retiring shares in exchange for cash minus any fees associated with the redemption, at the next NAV determined following the redemption order.
- *Infinite lives*: there is no maturity for the fund. The open-end fund currently holding the record for oldest surviving product in the U.S. is the MFS Massachusetts Investors Trust, which was launched in 1924.[xii]

Closed-End Funds

Closed-end funds share many commonalities with open-end funds in terms of their legal structure, availability to retail investors, government regulations, and utilization of a fund board. However, closed-end funds differ from open-end funds in several ways:[xiii]

- *Limited capital contributions*: closed-end funds raise capital during an IPO—at which time investors acquire shares and the fund raises its capital. A closed-end fund may have additional public offerings to raise additional capital; however, this is at the discretion of the fund manager. As well as additional public offerings, a closed-end fund may institute a rights offering, which allows existing shareholders the right to purchase additional shares, usually at a discount to the NAV; although, this is not common.

- *Limited capital redemptions*: with few exceptions, closed-end funds are closed to capital redemptions. Therefore, if an investor would like to liquidate his or her investment during the life of the fund, he or she generally must do so in the secondary market by selling his or her shares to another investor. As a result, the price of the closed-end fund shares may drift from the NAV of the underlying investment value. Some closed-end funds return ordinary dividends and capital gains, while others have distribution policies that include the return of capital.
- *Finite lives*: closed-end funds have a finite life after which all fund capital is returned to shareholders. However, in practice, closed-end fund lives are often extended with the consent of the shareholders.

As mentioned before, owing to the closed nature of the fund, the value of a fund share may drift meaningfully from the value of the underlying securities. When the price at which the closed-end fund is transacting is well below the value of its underlying holdings, the fund is known to be trading at a *discount* to the NAV. This offers investors a unique opportunity to purchase assets at a discount that can enhance the purchaser's yield. How? A 5% fixed income portfolio acquired at a 10% discount is the equivalent of a portfolio yielding 5.6% (5% / 0.90). However, unless the underlying fund is liquidated, the investor will not realize capital appreciation. This has enticed some activist investors to acquire meaningful stakes in closed-end funds that trade at a discount and pressure their fund boards to take actions beneficial to the investors. Most recently, this occurred on March 1, 2016, when shareholders of the AllianceBernstein Income Fund, Inc., a $1.8 billion closed-end fund (one of the world's largest) trading at a 10% discount to NAV, voted to convert the fund into an open-end fund. This process involved selling the assets of the AllianceBernstein Income Fund (closed-end) to the AB Income Fund (open-end); shareholders received newly issued shares, after which they could sell their shares at the fund NAV, which is equal to the value of the underlying assets.[xiv] This action constituted a nearly 10%, or $180 million recognized gain to the closed-end fund investors who sold their shares.[xv]

It is worth noting that interval funds are technically closed-end funds; however, they are different from closed-end funds in two unique ways. First, interval fund shares do not trade in the secondary market. Rather, the fund makes periodic repurchases of shares from investors at predetermined intervals. Investors who redeem their shares receive a value equal to the fund's NAV minus applicable fees. Second, most interval funds regularly offer investors additional shares, which is an opportunity to contribute additional capital. These dates usually correspond with the dates that investors may redeem shares. This structure was created in 1993 following an amendment to Investment Company Act Rule

23c-3,[xvi] and in response to investor complaints that closed-end fund shares often traded at a significant discount to the fund's NAV.[xvii] By making periodic redemptions and subscriptions, the interval fund's share price more closely trades around its NAV. Interval funds in the United States are a small, but growing fund product, growing from \$5.75 billion in assets under management in 2004 to \$26 billion in assets by Q3 2018.[xviii]

Unit Investment Trusts

UITs are also commingled funds that are regulated by U.S. securities law and share many similarities with both open-end and closed-end funds. However, they also have significant differences in terms of their lives, capital flows, and portfolio construction:[xix]

- *Ongoing capital contribution*: like a closed-end fund, a UIT raises capital during an IPO. However, unlike a closed-end fund that may have additional capital raises via a rights offering, UITs generally do not have follow-on capital raises.
- *Capital redemptions*: like an open-end fund (and unlike a closed-end fund), the trusts are required to allow capital redemptions by redeeming outstanding units at their NAV. In practice, some fund managers maintain a secondary market for their own UITs, which provides the managers with the opportunity to sell units to investors at a later date.
- *Finite lives*: like a closed-end fund, UITs have finite lives specified at their launch. However, unlike closed-end funds that regularly have extended lives, trust lives are not extended. Some fund managers permit unitholders to automatically reinvest distributions into a separate mutual fund that holds similar securities and has a similar investment objective.
- *Other unique features*: UITs regularly employ a *buy-and-hold* strategy whereby securities are rarely sold once purchased after the portfolio is initially constituted. With respect to fixed income UITs, as bonds mature, their principal is typically returned to investors in the form of UIT capital distributions.

Exchange-Traded Funds

First launched in 1993, ETFs are a relative newcomer to the U.S. mutual fund industry. These products are hybrids of existing structures, but they also come with the benefit of being tax efficient because share redemptions generally do not create taxable events for other shareholders.[xx] Other unique features include:

- *Ongoing capital contributions and redemptions*: like open-end funds, investors may enter or exit a fund at any time; like closed-end funds, investors enter and exit the fund by purchasing or selling shares on an exchange.

- *Infinite lives*: like open-end funds, there is no sunset or maturity of these funds.
- *Other unique features*: ETFs utilize authorized participants (APs) to create and redeem ETF shares as well as facilitate trading of ETF shares. APs are large banks and are the only investors that directly interact with the fund. When an AP would like to create ETF shares, the AP is tasked with first purchasing each of the underlying fund's holdings, known as a creation basket. The AP may then exchange the creation basket for creation units. Once this transaction is complete, the AP may then sell the newly created ETF shares at its discretion. The same process works in reverse as well if the AP would like to redeem ETF shares; it delivers those shares to the fund and receives in return a portion of each of the underlying funds' holdings.[xxi]

GROWTH OF THE MUTUAL FUND INDUSTRY

Commingled investment vehicles, which today most closely resemble closed-end funds, were originally modeled on British investment trusts. These trusts were used in the 1860s to allow individuals to invest in railroads; railroads are an illiquid investment, so a closed-end fund was an appropriate investment vehicle because the capital used to buy the railroad will not be redeemed.[xxii] The first closed-end fund in the United States, The Boston Personal Property Trust, was created in 1893.[xxiii] Early investment companies and fund managers preferred the closed-end nature of these commingled vehicles because managers did not need to raise cash to meet redemptions or deploy capital following subscriptions. Additionally, without the need for immediate liquidity, fund managers could lever their fund by posting fund collateral, raising additional cash, and reinvesting that cash by purchasing additional securities.

This type of fund continued to gain popularity until the Great Depression; by 1929, there were roughly 700 closed-end funds in the United States.[xxiv] While these funds offer significant benefits to investors, including diversification and exposure to illiquid assets, the closed nature of the funds means the value of the fund shares can meaningfully drift from the value of the fund holdings. This problem was particularly acute prior to the Great Depression when it was not uncommon for a closed-end fund to trade at a 50–100% premium to its underlying assets.[xxv] Following The Great Depression, closed-end fund prices continued to vary from their assets; Lee et al. (1990) show that from 1965–1986, the median closed-end fund generally traded between selling at a 10% premium to a 25% discount to its underlying securities.[xxvi] Separately, an additional risk to closed-end investors prior to the Great Depression was a lack of regulatory safeguards ensuring these funds were appropriate for individual investors and by extension not significantly leveraged.

The Great Depression and its fallout permanently changed the U.S. mutual fund landscape. Most closed-end funds were completely wiped out owing to their leverage. In response to the stock market crash and the financial distress this caused investors, the U.S. Congress passed the Securities Act of 1933 and Securities Exchange Act of 1934, which created the U.S. SEC and then tasked that commission with protecting investors by maintaining fair, orderly, and efficient markets and facilitating capital formation.[xxvii] In 1940, the U.S. Congress passed the Investment Company Act of 1940, which established regulations for investment companies and the mutual funds they sold to investors. Following the passage of these acts, investment manager requirements included filings with the SEC, public disclosures of the financial condition of the fund manager, and the establishment of a board of directors. Additionally, the Investment Company Act of 1940 places limits on leverage, establishes minimum liquidity balances, and includes several other investor safeguards.

The total number of fund managers, open-end funds, and closed-end funds had fallen from over 700 in 1929 to 436 by the time the 1940 Act was passed. At the time, total assets in open-end funds were around $800 million while total assets in closed-end funds were around $1.2 billion.[xxviii] Over the subsequent years, mutual funds in general and open-end funds in particular grew in popularity among investors. By 1950 the number of mutual fund assets funds had grown to around $3.2 billion, and roughly three-quarters of those assets were managed in open-end funds.[xxix,xxx] Growth in the mutual fund industry remained steady through 1980 and most of new mutual fund investments, also known as fund flows, went into open-end funds. By 1980 there were 564 open-end funds with $134.8 billion in assets.[xxxi] Then, just as the baby boomers were reaching their prime earning years and the personal savings rate for the U.S. was about 10.0%,[xxxii] industry growth went parabolic, as shown in Figure 2.1. Adoption of mutual funds became widespread, the number of households owning a mutual fund grew from 6% to 25% between 1980 and 1990,[xxxiii] and assets in open-end funds grew almost tenfold to $1.1 trillion across 3,079 funds.[xxxiv] When asked about the growth of the industry in an interview from 1990, Jon Bogle, chairman of the Vanguard Group described the 1980s as a "wonderful abnormality," while Michael Lipper, president of Lipper Analytical Services stated that he expected "the early '90s will be a struggle for mutual funds."[xxxv] Both Bogle and Lipper were wrong, and the mutual fund industry grew another

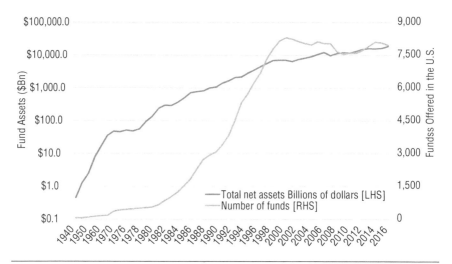

Figure 2.1   U.S. Open-end mutual fund industry. *Source:* Investment Company Institute

twelvefold from 1990 to 2007 with mutual fund assets reaching $12 trillion and the number of open-end fund offerings growing to 8,040.[xxxvi]

In 1993, State Street Global Investors launched the S&P 500 Trust ETF. The stated objective of this product is providing investment results that, before expenses, correspond generally to the price and yield performance of the S&P 500 Index. This product has low operating expenses (currently 0.0945%)[xxxvii] and is passively managed—meaning the fund manager is not attempting to outperform the benchmark by incorporating sector and security selection tilts. This fund is not a traditional open-end or closed-end fund; rather, it was the first ETF in the United States.[xxxviii]

At the end of 2017, registered investment companies in the United States managed over $22.5 trillion[xxxix] with 45.4% of U.S. households now owning at least one fund.[xl] Of those assets, $18.7 trillion or 83% were open-end funds,[xli] $275 billion or 1.2% were in closed-end funds,[xlii] $3.4 trillion or 15% were ETFs,[xliii] while a modest $85 billion or 0.4% were UITs, as shown in Figure 2.2.[xliv] Owing in part to the aforementioned advantages of ETFs, and a broader adoption of passive equity strategies (see Chapters 6 and 10), ETF assets and fund offerings have experienced stronger growth than other fund structures in the past 25 years. The ETF universe in the U.S. has grown from 19 funds in 1996 to 1,832 in 2017. ETFs now cover all major asset classes including equities (domestic and international), commodities, and fixed income.[xlv]

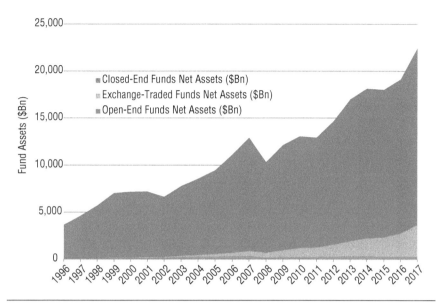

Figure 2.2 U.S. mutual fund assets. *Source:* Investment Company Institute

BENEFITS OF MUTUAL FUNDS

Mutual funds have continued to grow in popularity since the 1940s. As of 2017, there were 10,318 open-end funds, closed-end funds, and ETFs into which investors can invest.[7,xlvi] By comparison, in late 2017 there were 3,671 publicly listed companies, down from a peak of 7,322 companies in 1996.[xlvii] So, there are now about three times as many U.S. registered mutual funds as U.S. publicly listed companies. To what can we attribute this popularity of mutual funds? In addition to the passage of several laws between 1933 and 1940 aimed at protecting individual investors, there are at least four other factors that have contributed to the growth of the mutual fund industry: diversification, professional management, breadth of product offerings, and ease of transaction.

The benefits of diversification were forever enshrined in the literary world when de Cervantes wrote in Don Quixote that one should "not venture all his eggs in one basket." Good advice—and some years later mathematicians proved that financial diversification leads to better risk-adjusted returns for investors. At the 2009 Chicago Booth Investment Management conference, I sat next to Cliff Asness, founder of AQR and former PhD student of Nobel Laureate

---

[7] Figure excludes UITs.

Eugene Fama. Asness asked me, "What are you learning in Fama's class?" I told him we reviewed the mathematics behind portfolio construction and some of the early academic papers upon which today's understanding of finance is built. I admitted to him that I didn't totally understand all of the math surrounding portfolio diversification. "Simple," Asness responded, "think of it this way: on average, we all get the market return. If we each own one stock, we each experience the volatility of that one stock and, in general, individual stocks are more volatile than the market owing to the idiosyncratic risk of individual securities. The optimal solution is to diversify away idiosyncratic risk so that we all still get the market return but at a lower volatility." Simple to him, I suppose, but I think I'll stick with the adage not to place all your eggs in one basket.

The next benefit of mutual funds is that they are professionally managed. It is a daunting task to identify stocks and bonds to purchase and sell. When an individual makes that decision, chances are she is trading with a professional that is both more familiar with that security and has the tools that are necessary in order to know if the trading price is appropriate. Owing to these disadvantages, it should be no surprise that individual investors generally underperform professionals.[xlviii] In addition to being at an informational and technological disadvantage, personally managing a portfolio of investments is time consuming and few people have the necessary time to dedicate to this venture.

Additional draws to mutual funds include their breadth of product offerings and ease of transaction. This breadth of offering allows investors to gain exposure to anything from broad stock or bond markets, commodities, real estate, or a blend of those assets. Additionally, mutual funds allow investors to gain exposure to asset classes that were not accessible to small retail investors a generation ago. For example, for as little as $20, an investor can purchase a share of an ETF that has exposure to livestock, European real estate, or Brazilian equities. Furthermore, mutual funds are easy to purchase. Banks and online brokerage firms offer small savers access to these funds with relatively small commissions.

With respect to ETFs, proponents argue that over time an ETF will outperform passively managed open-end mutual funds. This anticipated outperformance can be attributed to several sources, including lower trading costs. With an ETF, the trading costs associated with an investor either entering or exiting the product are borne by that investor and not the fund, as is the case with an open-end fund. Additionally, ETFs do not meet client redemptions by liquidating underlying security holdings; therefore, the portfolio does not need to hold a cash balance, which is generally a drag on performance, and the ETF may always be fully invested.[xlix] Furthermore, because the manager of the underlying portfolio does not need to purchase or sell securities shares to invest or raise capital, there are far fewer taxable events. As a final point, ETFs typically offer lower fees than their open-end counterparts. In 2017, the average expense ratio of an index equity ETF was 0.21% while the average expense ratio fee of an actively managed equity fund was 0.78%.[1]

DISADVANTAGES OF MUTUAL FUNDS

As mentioned previously, there are now over 10,000 open-end funds, closed-end funds, and ETFs from which individual investors can choose. The growth of this industry and the proliferation of investment options speak to the benefits they confer among those who utilize them. However, should an investor choose to utilize these products in lieu of managing all investments personally, there is one primary disadvantage of which investors should be cognizant: fees. Depending on the share class, funds may charge some or all of the fees described in the following sections to its investors.

Shareholder Fees (Generally One-Time Fees)

- *Sales loads*: this is akin to a commission paid to a broker when shares are purchased or sold. A fee applied at the time of purchase is also known as a purchase fee or front-end sales load. A fee applied at the time of sale is also known as a redemption fee, deferred sales load, or back-end sales load.
- *Exchange fees*: this is incurred when an investor exchanges fund shares for the shares of another fund within the same fund group. Many funds waive this fee in order to encourage investors to stay within the fund group.
- *Account fees*: this is incurred if an account value falls below a predetermined level.

Annual Fund Operating Expenses (Generally Ongoing Fees)[li]

- *Management fees*: this is incurred and paid to the manager of the fund.
- *Distribution (and/or service) 12b-1 fees*: these are incurred and paid to the distributor of the fund to pay for the marketing or distribution of the fund.
- *Other*: these are incurred to pay for legal and accounting costs associated with the fund's management.
- *Total annual fund operating expenses*: these are expressed as a percentage of the fund's average net assets and is an aggregation of the annual operating expenses mentioned earlier.

To complicate matters, different share classes have different fees associated with them. Class-A shares generally have lower annual operating expenses but charge a front-end sales load. Class-B shares generally have no front-end sales load but may have a back-end sales load that varies depending on the length of time the shareholder has been invested in the fund. Class-B shares may convert to Class-A shares if held long enough. Class-C shares may have a front-end or back-end sales load, but the loads are generally lower than Class-A or Class-B loads. Class-I shares are sold only to institutional or high net-worth investors and typically have high minimum balances but lower management fees.[lii] That's a lot to consider when buying a mutual fund! So, what share class should an investor purchase to minimize fees? Thankfully, the FINRA, being a U.S. self-regulatory organization that works closely with the SEC, built a web-based tool to help investors make that decision. The FINRA Fund Analyzer[liii] allows investors to compare mutual fund share class fees, and by using user-driven assumptions including the holding period and fund return, the analyzer estimates fund fees between each share class. Fortunately for U.S. mutual fund investors, the average fund net expense ratio or the total annual amount as a percentage of assets that is charged to the shareholder has been steadily declining since 2003, as shown in Figure 2.3. According to the Investment Company Institute, since the

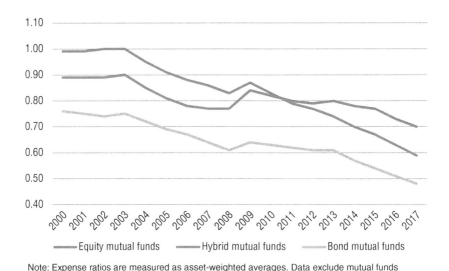

Note: Expense ratios are measured as asset-weighted averages. Data exclude mutual funds available as investment choices in variable annuities and mutual funds that invest primarily in other mutual funds.

Figure 2.3   U.S. mutual fund net expense ratios. *Source*: Investment Company Institute

year 2000, the asset-weighted average expense ratio for equity funds, hybrid funds, and bond funds have declined by 0.40%, 0.19%, and 0.26% respectively.[liv]

Other than ongoing fees paid to managers, an additional disadvantage of mutual funds is the tax liability that could be incurred by mutual fund shareholders. While an investor may buy and hold a mutual fund share, the investor will receive distributions from the fund manager, usually late in the fourth quarter of each year[lv]—and these distributions will be taxable. These distributions are the payment of principal, interest, or dividends from the underlying securities of the funds. Mutual fund investors can elect to have these distributions reinvested in more mutual fund shares or returned to the investor,[8] but regardless of the fund investor's election, these distributions will be reported on the investor's Form 1099 and will be subject to capital gains or ordinary income tax. The determination of capital gains or ordinary income for an equity security sold will be based on the length of time the fund manager held that security, and not the length of time an investor held the mutual fund share. This means that an investor who purchases a mutual fund in June and experiences a decline in the price of the mutual fund through year-end, will likely receive a taxable distribution even though the market value of his position has declined.

ETFs have gained in popularity because they largely avoid this frustrating tax liability. Specifically, ETF managers do not purchase and sell securities throughout the year; rather, the AP purchases and redeems both shares and portfolio holdings, which does not create a taxable event for the ETF holder. For this reason, it has become increasingly popular for investors to purchase ETFs in nonqualified accounts like a Schwab or TD Ameritrade brokerage account and/ or purchase traditional open-end mutual funds in qualified accounts like 401(k)s and IRAs. Critics of ETFs point out that these products are not an investing panacea and come with costs and risks unique to them. The first is that purchasing and selling ETFs includes a commission, like trading a stock or bond, which an investor may be able to avoid if they purchased a traditional open-end mutual fund. Second, a majority of these funds are passive, meaning fund managers are unlikely to outperform their benchmark; rather, the performance of these funds will likely equal that of the benchmark minus management and other fees. And last but not least, the liquidity of these products remains open to disagreement among market participants. Some fixed income ETFs, particularly those that invest heavily in illiquid high-yield bonds or bank loans, may experience heightened volatility in a *rush to the door* scenario. In such a scenario,

---

[8] Mutual fund investors typically reinvest these dividends; in 2016, investors reinvested $246.1 billion of $271.2 of dividends earned in mutual funds according to the 2018 Investment Company Fact Book, Table 29.

a significant percentage of an ETF's investors simultaneously sell the ETF to the AP, who in turn delivers shares to the investment manager in exchange for a basket of securities. This basket of securities is illiquid and difficult for the AP to sell without moving the market significantly lower. What happens next? It is uncertain because we have no empirical data to analyze since these products were not heavily utilized during the 2008–2009 financial crisis.

Returning briefly to mutual funds more broadly, a final critique of these products is that the funds do not eliminate the need for investors to perform due diligence such as identifying funds that do not have excessive fees and are appropriate given the investor's objectives. Investors need to sift through a universe of thousands of fund options to determine which managers are likely to add value to their benchmarks, which fund managers are stable organizations, and which funds charge appropriate fees. Morningstar has a suite of tools to help investors evaluate fund managers and their funds, and we recommend visiting their website. However, even if all of these issues are addressed, an investor must still ensure she is choosing a fund that is appropriate given the investor's objectives. An investor who is 30 years old has a different risk tolerance and return objective than an investor who is 65; thus, every investors' portfolio of stocks, bonds, and other investments will differ since each investor's willingness and ability to assume risk differs. But most mutual funds target specific asset classes and therefore do not offer asset class diversification. This creates a problem for fund investors because they must now pick a portfolio of mutual funds that when aggregated is appropriate given the investor's risk tolerance and investment objective. However, most individuals do not have the financial knowledge necessary to accomplish this task any more than they have the expertise necessary to build a portfolio of individual stocks and bonds. To solve this problem, investment firms developed a new kind of fund: a fund of funds!

TARGET RISK (LIFESTYLE) FUNDS

The *fund of fund* is a product that invests in other mutual funds and not individual securities, and it can trace its origin to the 1960s. In 1956, an American mutual fund salesman named Bernard Cornfeld moved to Paris to sell American mutual funds, primarily to American Army officers.[lvi] In 1962, Cornfeld launched the first fund of funds, which grew to $420 million in assets at its peak. The fund collapsed and was put into liquidation by the Supreme Court of Ontario in 1973 amid allegations of fraud.[lvii] While the initial fund of fund's legacy has been tainted, the concept behind it has withstood the test of time; in 2017 in the United States, there was over $1.5 trillion in fund of fund assets in target date and target risk funds.[lviii]

Target risk products have names that reference the riskiness of the product, such as "conservative," "moderate," or "aggressive." As the name implies: the more aggressive the product, the higher both the targeted risk and return. In practice, this leads to a higher allocation to equities vis-à-vis a lower allocation to fixed income. Most target risk funds are *closed architecture*, which means the fund companies allocate exclusively to their own products. For example, the portfolio managers of the "growth" Vanguard target risk product[lix] only allocate to Vanguard index products to gain domestic and international equity and fixed income exposure. A smaller subset of investment companies offers target risk funds that invest in third-party companies. This is known as *open architecture*. The benefit of open as opposed to closed architecture is that the manager of the target risk product is unconstrained and can select best-in-class products across the entire spectrum of fund offerings. For both open and closed products, managers typically invest in the lowest-cost share class of the underlying funds, which is often the *institutional* share class.[lx] Both open- and closed-architecture funds are often offered by retirement plan sponsors and are commonly held in tax-sheltered or qualified retirement accounts like a 401(k) or IRA. As of 2017, 44% of target risk funds were held in such accounts.[lxi]

The benefits of investing in target risk funds in lieu of purchasing individual mutual funds are similar to the benefits of investing in a mutual fund in lieu of purchasing in individual stocks and bonds: investors receive diversification, professional management, and ease of transaction. With respect to diversification, target risk managers allocate across asset classes. Depending on the product, this can include large-cap, medium-cap, small-cap, domestic, international, and emerging equities, as well as domestic, international, emerging market, investment-grade, high-yield, and low-duration fixed income. Some target risk products also have an allocation to *alternatives* including real estate, currency, and other nontraditional asset classes. In addition to this broad diversification, investors in these products may benefit from professional management. This management includes conducting due diligence on the underlying funds to which the manager has allocated as well as periodically rebalancing the target risk fund. Finally, these products are appropriate for people that have neither the time nor the expertise necessary to construct an asset allocation, conduct due diligence on fund managers, allocate to those funds, and periodically rebalance their portfolio.

The disadvantages of investing in target risk funds in lieu of purchasing individual mutual funds are similar to disadvantages of investing in mutual funds in lieu of purchasing individual securities: investors generally pay higher fees and have more taxable events. While managers of target risk products typically invest in the lowest-cost share class of the underlying funds, this fee break is typically offset by the added management cost of the target risk fund.[lxii] Additionally, the periodic rebalancing of the target risk product may create a taxable event for investors who own this fund within taxable accounts. While rebalancing a portfolio is a prudent aspect of managing a personal portfolio, when purchasing a target risk fund this responsibility is explicitly transferred by the investor to the fund manager, who often executes this responsibility without consideration of the tax consequences to the underlying investor. Despite these disadvantages, target risk funds grew in popularity particularly in the 1990s and 2000s when the total number of funds grew from 68 in 1997 to 249 in 2007—while assets grew from $13.2 billion in 1997 to $238.0 billion in 2007.[lxiii] Assets in target risk products in the U.S. have largely plateaued, having peaked in 2014 at $394.7 billion. In fact, net flows into these products were negative for six of the seven years between 2011 and 2017.[lxiv] But, this isn't to suggest that there is an inherent problem with these funds; rather, target date funds have become the preferred one-stop and default investment for investors.

TARGET DATE FUNDS

In November 1993,[lxv] Wells Fargo launched five asset allocation funds with a unique twist. Unlike typical target volatility funds with a relatively static allocation to equities, fixed income, and other asset classes, the asset allocation for these funds would evolve over time. Specifically, these funds had *target dates* at 10-year intervals from 2000 to 2040, which roughly corresponded to the date when the investor anticipated retiring. The further from that target date, the more aggressive the investments would be. In practice, this means that the allocation was highest to equities when the time to the target date is longest, whereas the allocation to equities is lowest at the target date. Wells Fargo named the suite its LifePath Funds and they were to be managed by Wells Fargo Nikko Investment Advisers, which at the time was managed jointly by Wells Fargo and Nikko Securities of Japan.[lxvi]

The LifePath Funds were unique in their approach to asset allocation and offered a clever differentiator in what was an increasingly crowded space for asset allocation products. These funds incorporated a *glidepath*, which is to say that the funds automatically de-risk as the products seasoned. For example, in 1993, an investor in the 2040 LifePath Fund was essentially investing in an aggressive target volatility fund. Fast forward to 2013—that same investor in the 2040 LifePath Fund would be invested in the Wells Fargo equivalent of a moderate target volatility fund. Finally, fast forward again to 2033, and that same investor in the 2040 LifePath Fund would be invested in the Wells Fargo equivalent of a conservative target volatility fund. In addition to the appeal of gradual de-risking as the fund investor neared retirement, these LifePath Funds allocated to 14 different asset classes, meaning they offered meaningful asset-class diversification. Wells Fargo sold these products primarily through 401(k) plans. At the time, Wells Fargo and Nikko managed $17 billion of 401(k) assets.[lxvii] Less than two years after the launch of the LifePath Funds, Barclays Bank purchased Wells Fargo Nikko Investment Advisers for about $440 million[lxviii] and rebranded the group as Barclays Global Investors (BGI). BGI was sold to BlackRock in 2009 for $13.5 billion, 14 years after being acquired from Wells Fargo.[lxix]

Popularity in target date funds grew steadily and in 2005, 12 years after their introduction, there were 124 target date funds offered in the United States—managing $70.5 billion in assets. By comparison, in 2005 there were 201 target risk funds managing $131.6 billion in assets.[lxx] Then, the U.S. Congress passed the Pension Protection Act (PPA) of 2006, which permanently changed the outlook for both 401(k) plans and the popularity of target date funds. Prior to the passage of this act, less than 10% of employers automatically enrolled employees in 401(k) plans, owing in part to the fact that 26 states prohibited wage deductions without the written permission of the employee.[lxxi] The PPA of 2006 included several provisions designed at increasing employee savings rates and the appropriateness of those investments. Two of those provisions included the authority of employers to automatically enroll employees in 401(k) plans without their consent, which supersedes state laws otherwise prohibiting this. Second, the law established safe harbor investments, or Qualified Default Investment Alternatives (QDIA), which would protect employers from liability should employees who were automatically enrolled experience investment losses.[lxxii] The Department of Labor then specified what falls into the QDIA category. Those options are a life-cycle or targeted-retirement-date fund, a balanced fund, or a professionally managed account.[lxxiii] Not included in this list of QDIAs were principal preservation investments, such as money market funds. This is significant because principal preservation investments were the most common investment default option at the time.[lxxiv] Owing to the PPA, by 2017 the number of plan sponsors with auto enrollment increased from 23% in 2004[lxxv] to 71% in 2017[lxxvi] while 85% of new participants defaulted into target date funds.[lxxvii] Owing to these tailwinds, assets in target date products grew dramatically. As of December 31, 2017, Vanguard, Fidelity, and T. Rowe Price managed the lion's share of target date assets at $623 billion, $244 billion, and $232 billion, respectively.[lxxviii]

The benefits of target date products are numerous, which explains their recent explosion in popularity. For plan sponsors, which are the companies that offer 401(k) plans, defaulting employees into target date funds shields the plan sponsors from future lawsuits should the plan participants lose money. Additionally, there is a growing body of academic literature suggesting a target date fund is the most appropriate default investment for a typical employee, which benefits both the plan sponsor and the plan participant. From the perspective of the plan participant, these target date funds offer diversification, professional management, and a glidepath that allows an investor to "set it and forget it." The disadvantages in target date funds are similar to the disadvantages of target risk funds: the investor pays fees to both the manager of the fund's asset allocation as well as fees to the underlying manager of fund assets. Additionally, the most popular target date suites are closed architecture, and the fund managers only use their own affiliated funds to build diversified portfolios. This suggests that investors may not invest in best-in-class underlying funds. One last thing, owing to the management of both the underlying funds as well as the management of the allocation to the underlying funds themselves, there are frequent and material taxable events in which the holder will regularly incur capital gains and ordinary income. For this reason, target date funds are most appropriate for qualified accounts such as a 401(k) or an IRA. Not surprisingly, as of 2017, 87% of all target date investments were held in defined contribution plans (including 401(k), 403(b), 457 plans, etc.) and IRAs.[lxxix]

ANNUITIES

The final pooled investment vehicle we will cover is possibly the oldest vehicle still in use today—the annuity. In 225 AD, Gnaeus Domitius Annius Ulpianis, a Roman speculator and possible creator of the first actuarial table, created an *annua* contract, or in other words, an annual payment to Roman soldiers as compensation for military service.[lxxx] Presumably, the annua, which we now refer to as an annuity, continued until the death of the solider. This contract existed in a variety of forms throughout the ages and first appeared in America in 1759. That year, the first life insurance company was established in Philadelphia and offered annuities to Presbyterian ministers and their families.[lxxxi]

Since then, the number of annuity offerings has grown dramatically but one constant remains—only life insurance companies offer these products. A purchaser of an annuity contract is exchanging cash for a stream of payments, and thus the purchaser is assuming the risk that the insurance company becomes insolvent prior to the maturity of the annuity. For this reason, insurance companies in general and annuities in particular are heavily regulated. Owing in part to both these regulations and the creditworthiness of insurance companies, annuities are popular among retirees. In a survey conducted in 2013 by The Gallup Organization and Mathew Greenwald & Associates, the data showed that 47% of annuity holders purchased their first annuity between the ages of 50 and 64, the average age of annuity holders was 70, and 65% of annuity holders are retired.[lxxxii] In 2017 in the U.S., there were approximately $2.2 trillion in annuity reserves of which $1.8 trillion were variable annuities.[lxxxiii] TIAA-CREF, Jackson National, and Prudential Financial are the three largest variable annuity issuers with over $800 billion in reserves between the three organizations as of Q3 2017.[lxxxiv]

The breadth of annuities currently available to investors has grown in lock-step with asset growth over the past 20 years. There are dozens of bespoke annuities from which an investor can choose, but these products generally fall into four categories:

- *Fixed annuity or single premium immediate annuity (SPIA)*: a purchaser of this type of annuity exchanges an up-front payment for a contractually agreed-upon stream of payments. Depending on the policy, these payments will be fixed and for a predetermined period (say, 10 years), until the death of the policyholder, or until the death of the policyholder and his or her spouse.
- *Deferred annuity*: this is like an SPIA except that the purchaser has the option of waiting for a prespecified period prior to the start of receipt of a stream of payments. During the deferred period, the principal value of the annuity will grow for a predetermined period. Following that period, investors may have the option of beginning payments, cashing out, or selecting another option altogether.
- *Index annuity*: this is also like an SPIA except the interest paid on the annuity, also referred to as the credited interest, is linked to an index like the S&P 500. The contract is usually structured so that the credited interest is higher if the reference index appreciates over a stated period while the credited interest is lower if the reference index falls over a stated period. The credited interest is not lower than 0%—meaning that if the equity index falls, the annuity holder will not experience a principal loss but will also not receive an interest payment. The credited interest is also capped—meaning that the annuity holder doesn't receive the full benefit should the reference index significantly appreciate.
- *Variable annuity*: unlike a fixed annuity where the principal and crediting rate for the policyholder are fixed and known at initiation, the principal and credit rate can vary. With this option, which is the most popular among annuity purchasers, the annuity holder may select a mutual fund or fund of funds offered by the insurance company in which the policyholder's assets will be invested. This underlying fund may appreciate or depreciate, which will directly impact the value of the payment received by the annuity holder.

Like any investment vehicle, there are clear advantages and disadvantages to annuities. The first advantage an annuity offers is that it may be considered a *safe* purchase since the policy is being written with a highly rated and heavily regulated insurance company. Second, annuities offer a tax deferral status like that of a 401(k) or IRA. However, unlike a 401(k), there is no limit to the amount of money placed in them, making them highly attractive for high-net-worth individuals. An additional benefit offered by annuities is a guaranteed payout that will continue either for a fixed period or until the death of the annuity holder. In the previously mentioned 2013 survey of owners of annuities, 90% of respondents purchased annuities because they are safe, 86% purchased annuities for reasons relating to their tax treatment, and 81% purchased annuities relative to their lifetime guarantee payment.[lxxxv]

The primary disadvantage of annuities is their high fee. These fees include commissions for brokers who sell the annuities, surrender charges should the holder of the annuity withdraw prior to a prespecified period, and high annual management fees. Taken together, variable annuities are one of the most expensive vehicles available to investors. So, it should be no surprise that annuity sales fell in 2017 after the U.S. Department of Labor (DOL) expanded the *investment advice fiduciary* definition to include insurance agents.[lxxxvi] Insurance agents looked at their commissions and the fees associated with annuities and were concerned they may be in breach of their fiduciary responsibility should they sell additional policies. In June 2018, the U.S. Appeals Court for the 5th Circuit vacated the Labor Department's fiduciary rule after lawsuits were brought by the U.S. Chamber of Commerce, the American Council of Life Insurers, and the Indexed Annuity Leadership Council.[lxxxvii] As a result, annuity sales have begun to rebound. A final disadvantage of annuities is that they are not insured by the U.S. federal government or the FDIC. Rather, annuities are insured by each State's Guarantee Fund, and this guarantee varies by state.[lxxxviii]

PRIVATE INVESTMENT COMPANIES

All mutual funds are offered to all retail investors and may be marketed publicly. However, there is another class of commingled vehicles that are neither offered to retail investors nor marketed publicly—private investment companies. Like their public counterparts, private investment companies generally commingle investor capital, structure their funds as a separate legal entity such as an LLC, have a prospectus with a clearly defined investment objective and investment universe, and utilize an administrator, custodian, and transfer agent. However, there are several material differences between these products that preclude them from being offered to the public. These differences include, but are not limited to:[lxxxix]

- Legal exemption from periodic reporting requirements, which allows fund managers to not disclose their holdings or to do so on a delay.
- Legal exemption from limits on leverage, which allows fund managers to borrow capital and leverage their funds. Leverage is limited only by the guidelines that have been written by the manager and found in the prospectus. There may be no limit to fund leverage.
- Legal exemption from the requirement that investors have access to daily liquidity to redeem their investments. This means investor capital may be "locked up" for a period defined in the prospectus. Opportunities for an investor to redeem may also be limited to specific times and subject to gates, which may also be at the manager's discretion. Private funds do not trade on an exchange.

For an investment company to qualify for these exemptions, it must meet criteria established in 3(c)(1) or 3(c)(7) of the Investment Company Act of 1940. The 3(c)(1) exemption applies if there are fewer than 100 beneficial owners (investors) and the issuer is not making or proposing to make a public offering of its securities. The 3(c)(7) exemption also requires the issuer to not make a public offering of its securities, and while it does not limit the number of beneficial owners, it does require that all investors are qualified purchasers. The SEC defines *qualified purchasers* as natural persons or family-owned companies who own not less than $5 million in investments; certain trusts; and persons, acting for their own accounts or the accounts of other qualified purchasers, who in the aggregate own and invest on a discretionary basis, not less than $25 million in investments (e.g., institutional investors).[xc] The U.S. Congress defined a qualified purchaser in these terms in 1996 following the passage of the National Securities Markets Improvement Act of 1996. Congress's rationale is that private funds are only appropriate for sophisticated investors who are more likely able to sustain a large loss than a less sophisticated investor.[xci]

Despite being unable to publicly market their products because of their status as private funds, hedge funds are almost exclusively organized as private funds for several reasons. First, limited reporting requirements allow hedge funds to purchase and sell securities without their holdings becoming public knowledge. This can allow some hedge funds to rapidly trade in and out of securities anonymously or amass large positions in target companies without this becoming public knowledge. Second, the ability to engage in leverage allows managers to identify and exploit pricing anomalies that might otherwise be too small to warrant a dedicated strategy. For example, convertible arbitrage-strategies hedge funds typically employ significant leverage.[xcii] When implementing their strategy, these managers purchase convertible bonds and then sell the equity exposure by shorting stock in the same company. Convertible bond managers can post their convertible bond holdings as collateral and continue to leverage until a desired amount of portfolio volatility is achieved. Finally, hedge funds often invest in less-liquid or illiquid assets. Because hedge funds do not need to provide daily liquidity, these funds can take advantage of a *liquidity premium* by purchasing assets that would otherwise be inappropriate for a traditional mutual fund. Conversely, a mutual fund cannot invest more than 15% of its assets in securities that are deemed illiquid.[xciii] Additionally, hedge funds often include initial capital lock-ups, long lead times to make withdrawals (like 60 days' notice ahead of a redemption date), limit redemptions during the year (e.g., once a quarter), and often have gates whereby managers may limit some or all of a client's redemption if aggregate redemption requests exceed a threshold. These bespoke liquidity and redemption features are one of the reasons private equity funds are typically organized as private investment funds.[9]

SEPARATELY MANAGED ACCOUNTS

The final investment vehicle we will cover are separately managed accounts (SMAs), which are also known as managed accounts. An SMA is a segregated account that is owned and controlled by the investor, while the day-to-day management of the account's assets are delegated to an investment adviser. An SMA is structured as a separate legal entity, and unlike a registered fund whereby an independent board monitors all decisions on behalf of the shareholders, with a managed account, the investor takes the role of the trustee. As a result, the investor maintains control over all aspects of the account's management, including the hiring of an administrator, custodian, and an investment adviser. A managed account has an investment management agreement (IMA), which states the investment terms (the portfolio strategy, objective, benchmark, investment universe, and guidelines) as well as the commercial terms (fees paid to the investment adviser). Should the investor want to replace the investment manager, the investor would only have to revise the IMA—and it can do so at its sole discretion. Because the investor retains complete control over the investments and is the sole investor in the account, the investor may direct the investment adviser to sell or purchase securities, raise cash, or engage in other activities that would normally not be appropriate in a commingled vehicle. Furthermore, the investor maintains full transparency with respect to the portfolio positions.[xciv] The primary drawback of SMAs is cost; there are many fixed costs to managing an investment vehicle. As a result, SMAs need to be large—often $50 million or

---

[9] Note: while private investment companies aren't subject to regulation under the 1940 Act, their investment advisers are likely required to be registered under the Advisers Act and are thereby subject to regulation.

more—to be economically feasible. As a result, typically only the largest institutional investors heavily utilize SMAs.

SUMMARY AND INVESTMENT IMPLICATIONS

Summary

The investment vehicles that are available to individual investors have dramatically expanded over the past three generations, and current investors are the beneficiaries of the financial industry's maturation. My grandfather, a fine saver, investor, and pharmacist, did well by his family as he built a nest egg by purchasing stocks in his local brokerage account because mutual funds at that time were not widely utilized by savers. Since that time, the mutual fund industry has grown and matured, and investing in commingled vehicles is now the primary vehicle through which individuals build portfolios of stocks and bonds. These professionally managed portfolios offer diversification and liquidity—albeit for a fee and with the potential of reoccurring taxable events. With this in mind, the following section lists a few parting thoughts with respect to how individuals and institutions can best navigate today's financial landscape and the plethora of investment vehicles available to them.

Investment Implications

- Individuals typically underperform professional investment managers. Therefore, retail investors should consider utilizing mutual funds, whether they are open-end, closed-end, ETFs, target date, target risk, or annuities.
- Target risk (lifestyle) funds are useful for investors who have a strong desire to hold a single investment and allow a manager to ensure that the portfolio remains diversified.
- Target date funds have surpassed target risk funds in terms of assets under management and availability in 401(k) plans. Target risk funds are favored by plan sponsors, who must select a default investment for employees who participate in their corporate-sponsored retirement plan.
- Annuities can be appropriate for retirees but are not investments per se and they may involve high management fees.
- Investors should maintain tax awareness. Open-end mutual funds, target date, and target risk funds regularly have taxable events since the managers make distributions to investors. Therefore, investors should consider holding these fund types in tax-sheltered or qualified accounts like a 401(k) or IRA. Conversely, ETFs and closed-end funds have few

distributions, leading to far fewer taxable events. Additionally, annuities typically grow tax-free until the investor takes distributions. Therefore, these products are appropriate for a nonqualified (non-tax-deferred) account like a brokerage account.

- Investors should maintain fee awareness. All things being equal, lower-fee products will outperform higher-fee products. Therefore, prior to purchasing a fund, review its fees on Morningstar.com or FINRA.org and select the lowest-fee share class given your investment horizon.
- High net worth and institutional investors have access to private funds. These products invest in generally less-liquid instruments and are the preferred investment vehicle for hedge funds and private equity funds. They involve additional risks and are considered appropriate only for sophisticated investors.
- Large institutional investors often prefer the use of separately managed accounts, as they maintain a high degree of control over their investments.

CITATIONS

i. *2018 Investment Company Fact Book*. Investment Company Institute. Table 1, p. 208.
ii. Board of Governors of the Federal Reserve System (U.S.). "Households and nonprofit organizations; total financial assets." Level (DISCONTINUED) [HNOTFAQ027S], retrieved from FRED, Federal Reserve Bank of St. Louis; https://fred.stlouisfed.org/series/HNOT FAQ027S. April 25, 2018.
iii. "Mutual Funds and ETFs: A Guide for Investors." U.S. Securities and Exchange Commission Office of Investor Education and Advocacy.
iv. Moehrke, Scott and Andrew Wright. Kirkland & Ellis LLP. "Investment Funds 2009." United States. http://www.practicallaw.com/9-384-6412.
v. Vanguard 500 Index Fund Prospectus. (April 25, 2018). https://personal.vanguard.com/pub/Pdf/p040.pdf.
vi. "Mutual Fund Manager Putnam Pays $40 Million Fine to Settle SEC Enforcement Action." (March 23, 2005). SEC Press Release. 2005–40. https://www.sec.gov/news/press/2005-40.htm.
vii. SEC. Administrative Proceeding. File No. 3-11317. (May 3, 2013). https://www.sec.gov/litigation/admin/2013/ia-3600.pdf.
viii. Warburton, A. Joseph. (July 3, 2008). "Should Mutual Funds Be Corporations? A Legal & Econometric Analysis." *Journal of Corporation*

Law. Vol. 33, No. 3. Available at SSRN: https://ssrn.com/abstract= 1155243.

ix. https://www.sec.gov/fast-answers/answersmfinvcohtm.html.

x. "Mutual Funds and ETFs: A Guide for Investors." (August 2012). U.S. Securities and Exchange Commission Office of Investor Education and Advocacy.

xi. "Mutual Funds and ETFs: A Guide for Investors." U.S. Securities and Exchange Commission Office of Investor Education and Advocacy.

xii. "Massachusetts Investors Trust Prospectus." (August 28, 2018). p. 6.

xiii. *A Guide to Closed-End Funds.* (2011). Investment Company Institute.

xiv. AllianceBernstein Income Fund, Inc. (March 1, 2016). "Shareholders Approve the Acquisition of Assets of AllianceBernstein Income Fund, Inc. by AB Income Fund, A Series of AB Bond Fund, Inc." PR Newswire. https://www.prnewswire.com/news-releases/shareholders -approve-the-acquisition-of-assets-of-alliancebernstein-income -fund-inc-by-ab-income-fund-a-series-of-ab-bond-fund-inc -300229120.html.

xv. Fertig, Maury. (October 5, 2015). "Activism Rising in Closed-End Funds." *Forbes.* https://www.forbes.com/sites/mauryfertig/2015/10/05/ activism-rising-in-closed-end-funds/#3ff4c75d3ccc.

xvi. NASD Notice to Members 00-53.

xvii. "Interval funds: An unexpected revival for an old vehicle structure." (July 2018). Ernst & Young LLP.

xviii. https://www.intervalfundtracker.com/2018/10/01/interval-fund -market-2018q3-update/.

xix. "A Guide to Unit Investment Trusts." (2007). Investment Company Institute.

xx. Investor Bulletin: Exchange-Traded Funds (ETFs). Securities and Exchange Office of Investor Education and Advocacy.

xxi. *2018 Investment Company Fact Book.* Investment Company Institute. pp. 84–95.

xxii. Norton, Leslie P. (January 7, 2017). "These Ancient Closed-End Funds Still Deliver." *Barron's.*

xxiii. Allen, David Grayson. (2015). *Investment Management in Boston: A History.* Amherst and Boston, MA: University of Massachusetts Press.

xxiv. Levitt, Aaron. (September 2, 2014). "A Brief History of Mutual Funds" MutualFunds.com.

xxv. DeLong, J. Bradford and Andrei Shleifer. (1991). "The Bubble of 1929: Evidence from Closed-End Funds." Journal of Economic History, 51(3): 675–700. Appendix: Pre-1930 Observations of Closed-End Fund Premia and Discounts.

xxvi. Lee, Charles, Andrei Shleifer, and Richard Thaler. 1990. "Investor Sentiment and the Closed-End Fund Puzzle," NBER Working Papers 3465, National Bureau of Economic Research, Inc. Figure 3.

xxvii. www.sec.org. "What We Do."

xxviii. Division of Investment Management United States Securities and Exchange Commission. (May 1992). "Protecting Investors: A Half Century of Investment Company Regulation." pp. iv, xix.

xxix. Division of Investment Management United States Securities and Exchange Commission. (May 1992). "Protecting Investors: A Half Century of Investment Company Regulation." p. 432.

xxx. *2018 Investment Company Fact Book*. Investment Company Institute. Table 1. p. 208.

xxxi. ———. Investment Company Institute. Table 1. p. 208.

xxxii. U.S. Bureau of Economic Analysis, Personal Saving Rate [PSAVERT], retrieved from FRED, Federal Reserve Bank of St. Louis; https://fred .stlouisfed.org/series/PSAVERT. (December 25, 2018).

xxxiii. Investment Company Institute. "How many American households own mutual funds?" https://www.ici.org/faqs/faq/mfs/faqs_mf _shareholders.

xxxiv. *2018 Investment Company Fact Book*. Investment Company Institute. Table 1. p. 208.

xxxv. Fix, Janet L. (January 14, 1990). "'80s Saw Mutual Admiration But Economic Uncertainty Could Make '90s Difficult." *Chicago Tribune*.

xxxvi. *2018 Investment Company Fact Book*. Investment Company Institute. Table 1. p. 208.

xxxvii. SPDR® S&P 500® ETF Trust. Prospectus (January 18, 2018). p. 1.

xxxviii. Fact Sheet. (March 3, 2018). State Street Global Advisers. S&P 500 ETF.

xxxix. *2018 Investment Company Fact Book*. Investment Company Institute. Figure 2.1. p. 34.

xl. ———. Investment Company Institute. p. ii.

xli. ———. Investment Company Institute. Table 1. p. 208.

xlii. ———. Investment Company Institute. Table 9. p. 216.

xliii. ———. Investment Company Institute. Table 11. p. 218.

xliv. ———. Investment Company Institute. Table 14. p. 221.

xlv. ———. Investment Company Institute. Table 11. p. 218.

xlvi. ———. Investment Company Institute. Table 1. p. 208, Table 9. p. 216, Table 12. p. 219.

xlvii. Thomas, Jason M. "Where Have All the Public Companies Gone?" (November 16, 2017). *Wall Street Journal*.

xlviii. Barber, Brad M. and Terrance Odean. (April 2000). "Trading Is Hazardous to Your Wealth: The Common Stock Investment Performance of Individual Investors." *The Journal of Finance.* Vol. LV, No. 2.

xlix. Gastineau, Gary L. *The Exchanged-Traded Funds Manual.* p. 6.

l. ICI Research Perspective. (April 2018). "Trends in the Expenses and Fees of Funds, 2017." Vol. 24, No. 3. p. 1.

li. Mutual Fund Fees and Expenses. Investor Bulletin. SEC Office of Investor Education and Advocacy. SEC Pub. No. 162 (5/14).

lii. U.S. Securities and Exchange Commission. Fast Answers: Mutual Fund Classes. www.sec.org.

liii. https://www.finra.org/content/finra-fund-analyzer.

liv. *2018 Investment Company Fact Book.* Investment Company Institute. Figure 6.1. p. 119.

lv. Benz, Christine. (September 23, 2015). "Solid Funds, But Far From Tax-Friendly." www.morningstar.com.

lvi. Friedrich, Otto. (August 22, 1971). "The Fund of Funds he named it, and the money poured in." *The New York Times.*

lvii. Arenson, Karen W. (November 5, 1981). "Anderson Firm is found Guilty of Fraud." *The New York Times.*

lviii. *2018 Investment Company Fact Book.* Investment Company Institute. Figure 8.26.

lix. https://investor.vanguard.com/mutual-funds/lifestrategy/#/mini/holdings/0122.

lx. Elton, E.J., M.J. Gruber, and A. de Souza. (2016). "Target Risk Funds." *European Financial Management,* 22(4), 519–539. p. 19.

lxi. *2018 Investment Company Fact Book.* Investment Company Institute. p. 196.

lxii. Elton, E. J.; Gruber, M. J.; and Souza, A. de. (2016). "Target Risk Funds." European Financial Management. 22(4), 519–539. Table 3. p. 30.

lxiii. *2018 Investment Company Fact Book.* Investment Company Institute. Table 56. p. 263.

lxiv. ———. Investment Company Institute. Table 56. p. 263.

lxv. "Industry's First Target-Date Fund Celebrates 15 Years Since Groundbreaking Launch." (November 7, 2008). (Press release). Barclays Global Investors. via Marketwired.

lxvi. Hansell, Saul. "Wells Fargo to Offer Funds Designed for Baby Boomers." (March 3, 1994). *The New York Times.*

lxvii. ———. "Wells Fargo to Offer Funds Designed for Baby Boomers." (March 3, 1994). *The New York Times.*

lxviii. Truell, Peter. "Barclays to Acquire a Unit of Wells Fargo and Nikko." (June 22, 1995). *The New York Times.*

lxix. "U.S. giant BlackRock buys arm of Barclays bank." (June 12, 2009). *The Guardian.* UK. Press Association.

lxx. *2018 Investment Company Fact Book.* Investment Company Institute. Table 56. p. 263.

lxxi. Engelhardt, Gary V. (2011). "State wage-payment laws, the Pension Protection Act of 2006, and 401(k) saving behavior." Economics Letters 113.

lxxii. Pension Protection Act of 2006. 109th Congress Public Law 280. From the U.S. Government Printing Office. DOCID: f:publ280.109.

lxxiii. Fact Sheet: Default Investment Alternatives Under Participant-Directed Individual Account Plans. (September 2006). U.S. Department of Labor Employee Benefits Security Administration.

lxxiv. Deloitte Consulting LLP's Annual 401(k) Benchmarking Survey 2005/2006 Edition, Exhibit 17.

lxxv. Deloitte Consulting LLP's Annual 401(k) Benchmarking Survey 2005/2006 Edition, Exhibit 15.

lxxvi. 2018 Defined Contribution Trends Survey. Callan Institute. p. 2.

lxxvii. ———. p. 24.

lxxviii. "Largest providers of target-date funds." (March 19, 2018). *Pensions & Investments.*

lxxix. *2018 Investment Company Fact Book.* Investment Company Institute. Figure 8.26.

lxxx. Wilson, T. (2015). *Value and Capital Management: A Handbook for the Finance and Risk Functions of Financial Institutions.* Wiley: Chichester. p. 153.

lxxxi. "American Council of Life Insurers." *2017 Life Insurers Fact Book.* p. 151.

lxxxii. "2013 Survey of Owners of Individual Annuity Contracts." (2013). The Gallup Organization and Mathew Greenwald & Associates for The Committee of Annuity Insurers. p. 8.

lxxxiii. *2018 Investment Company Fact Book.* Investment Company Institute. Figure 8.6 and Table 58.

lxxxiv. Iacurci, Greg. (February 17, 2018). "2017 largest variable annuity providers." InvestmentNews.com.

lxxxv. 2013 Survey of Owners of Individual Annuity Contracts. (2013). The Gallup Organization and Mathew Greenwald & Associates for The Committee of Annuity Insurers. Table 4, p. 30.

lxxxvi. Iacurci, Greg. (February 21, 2018). "DOL fiduciary rule continues to take toll on annuity sales" InvestmentNews.com.

lxxxvii. Case: 17-10238 Document: 00514522719. 06/21/2018. United States Court of Appeals. Fifth Circuit. Office of the Clerk.

lxxxviii. https://www.annuityadvantage.com/resources/state-guaranty -associations/.

lxxxix. SEC Office of Investor Education. Investor Bulletin. Hedge Funds. SEC Pub. No. 139 (2/13).

xc. National Securities Markets Improvement Act of 1996 § 209(a); Investment Company Act § 2(a)(51)(A).

xci. "Report on the Review of the Definition of 'Accredited Investor.'" (December 18, 2015). U.S. Securities and Exchange Commission. p. 25.

xcii. Agarwal, Vikas et al. (2011). "Risk and return in convertible arbitrage: Evidence from the convertible bond market." *Journal of Empirical Finance*, 18. pp. 175–194.

xciii. Revisions of Guidelines to Form N-1A, SEC Release No. IC-18612, 57 Fed. Reg. 9828 (March 20, 1992).

xciv. "Accessing hedge funds through managed accounts: The future is now." (November 2015). KPMG International.

3

INSTITUTIONAL INVESTORS

Matthew H. Brenner, CFA
Managing Vice President
ICMA-RC

David E. Linton, CFA
Director, Portfolio Construction and Manager Research
Pacific Life Fund Advisors LLC

It was July 1990. Iraq had moved from accusing Kuwait of stealing oil from the Rumaila oil field to amassing its formidable army on the Kuwaiti border. I was very concerned that war would lead to higher oil prices, higher inflation, and a general flight to safety. I was also about to turn eight years old. So, I convinced my parents to open a Uniform Transfer to Minors Act (UTMA) account in my name with Vanguard. Given my geopolitical and market concerns, I purchased $500 of the Vanguard Gold and Precious Metals (VGPMX) mutual fund as soon as the account was opened. The thesis seemed to play out well and by mid-August, both gold and my mutual fund were up +15% from where I purchased it. But, by the end of January 1991, VGPMX had fallen almost 15% from when I purchased the fund while gold was roughly unchanged from the prior July. That seemed like pretty awful underperformance, so naturally I did what any concerned eight-year-old would do in this situation. I looked up the name of the portfolio manager in the fund prospectus and called the main customer support number (I don't recommend this to my readers).

"How can I help you?" the friendly operator began.
"I'd like to talk to (whatever his name was)."
"What is the nature of your inquiry?"
"His fund stinks and I want to know why."
"Um, are you an investor?"

> "Yes! My whole life savings!"
>
> "Okay, one moment please."
>
> A few minutes later, the portfolio manager was on the phone. "What questions do you have?"
>
> "Why is your portfolio down over the past six months when gold isn't?"
>
> "Well, this portfolio doesn't invest in just gold, it invests primarily in miners. While their profitability is linked to the price of gold, this fund will not move in tandem with gold prices. Thank you for your investment." Click.

I sat at my desk for a moment, and I began to ponder the difference between the person with whom I had just spoken and me. We're both investors, right? But, he's there and I'm here. I have $425 in my account, while he is probably managing, well, a whole lot more than $425. I call him, he doesn't call me. He's the steward of my money, not the other way around. With time I began to realize that not all investors are the same—Vanguard and other large fund managers are institutions, while as an individual, I am a retail investor. For this reason, I will not have the same access to companies, execution, information, or other managers. But, I did get to talk to a portfolio manager, which I believe is a testament to Vanguard's commitment to customer support. In this chapter, we will define *institutional investors* and classify them into seven categories: corporations, endowments, pension plans, commercial banks, insurance companies, mutual and hedge funds, and family offices. Additionally, we explain each investor's objectives and reaction function. Finally, we will close with investment implications both for these institutional investors and others looking to better position their portfolios.

INSTITUTIONAL INVESTORS

An institutional investor, as the name suggests, is a non-person investing entity that deploys capital (invests) on behalf of its stakeholders. As just mentioned, the subcategories of institutional investors vary, but the six most common include: corporations, endowments, pension plans, commercial banks, insurance companies, and mutual and hedge funds. Family offices, and the ultra-high net worth individuals whom they service, are often classified as qualified purchasers by the Securities and Exchange Commission (SEC[i]) and their portfolios are generally classified as *institutional accounts* by the Financial Industry Regulatory Authority (FINRA[ii]). Owing to their size and sophistication, we will include family offices in my definition of an institutional investor, bringing the number of types of institutional investor to seven. Understanding institutional investors' mandates and anticipating their reactionary functions are highly relevant skillsets to an investor of any size considering the institutional investors' collective size. In fact, Goldman Sachs Global Investment Research estimates that the share of institutional ownership of U.S. equities has risen from under 10% in 1945 to 63% by Q3 2017.[1,iii] Thus, like an elephant in a bathtub, institutional investors regularly make a splash when they move—and they often move in herds.

Being an institutional investor comes with some distinctive advantages over an individual investor. First, the size of the institutions allows them to achieve significant economies of scale—they can hire teams of well-educated and seasoned professionals to manage their assets, either employing them directly or by accessing top-tier asset managers. Additionally, institutional investors have access to significant research and tools, offering them insight into stocks, bonds, and other investments that are not available to individuals. Next, institutional investors can trade directly with broker dealers, eliminating some of the middlemen, and their size may allow them to get superior execution as large orders are handled with white gloves. When companies issue stock or bonds in the primary market, banks acting on behalf of the issuing company regularly solicit orders exclusively from institutional investors and then issue these securities at a modest discount to where they are expected to trade shortly after issuance. Finally, institutional investors are eligible to purchase private placement securities (securities not registered with the SEC) under Rule 506 of Regulation D,[iv] whereas individuals generally may not purchase private placements.

There is a major disadvantage to being an institutional investor however—they might not be nimble. Rather, they are generally large and lumbering, and they may unintentionally make waves when they move. They also could be subject to cumbersome procedures or bureaucracy (such as board or committee approvals or amendments to investment policy statements) that may prevent timely actions. Because of these limitations, it may take weeks or months for an institutional investor to take a meaningful stake in a stock or bond without causing the security to materially appreciate while the investor builds a position. Conversely, if the outlook for an investment deteriorates, the institutional investor may have difficulty exiting the position before other investors catch on and the investment declines in value. Recognizing this reality, institutional investors generally have relatively long time horizons as the costs to quickly enter or exit a position may be prohibitively expensive. Finally, owing to their

---

[1] The Goldman Sachs report decomposes ownership of U.S. equities in seven categories: households (37%), mutual funds (24%), ETFs (6%), pension and government retirement funds (13%), international investors (15%), hedge funds (3%), and other (3%). We consider *institutional* investors to be all categories except households. *Source*: David J. Kostin. (January 2018). Where to Invest Now, Year 2. Global Investment Research. The Goldman Sachs Group. p 82.

size, institutional investors may be the targets of front-running. Front-running is considered by some to be a *parasitic* trading strategy whereby traders extract profits from investors or other traders but without rendering a service—like matching a buyer and seller. Front-running occurs when another trader or organization identifies the placement of a large institutional order and attempts to purchase or sell shares of a stock at a preferential price. If done effectively, the front-run institutional investor pays a higher price when purchasing a security and a lower price when selling the security than would have been the case had it not been front-run. As this type of trading is zero-sum, the institutional investor's loss is someone else's gain. It would be naïve to assume that this hasn't always been an issue with financial markets; what makes this issue particularly concerning has been the proliferation of high-frequency traders.[v]

Whether you are an individual investor or a high-profile institutional portfolio manager, it is useful to understand who the major institutional investors are, what they are doing, and why. As mentioned, because of their size, institutional investors have the potential to create or eliminate investment opportunities as they implement their own investment strategies. Additionally, some institutional investors may have motives other than profit maximization, such as meeting regulatory requirements, maximizing book yield, or implementing broad government policy. Because of these market participants not prioritizing the maximization of their risk-adjusted returns, as they implement their policy they may create opportunities for scrupulous investors to exploit. As such, we'll cover each major institutional investor category separately and detail how knowledge of their respective objectives, strategies, and investment approaches may enhance your ability to meet your own investment objectives.

Corporations

Broadly speaking, corporations are companies or businesses that are established to have a continuous existence separate and apart from the individuals or members who create it. There has been a proliferation of corporate entities, both in the United States and overseas, providing multiple options based on the number of owners, the type of ownership, tax regimes, exposure to liabilities for corporate actions, and other factors. In the context of institutional investing, most of this is not directly relevant. After all, the business of business is supposed to be—business. Sure, corporations have been the major drivers of pension plans, a discussion of which follows later. But increasingly in an era of mega corporations, many corporations utilize their corporate treasury assets, or balance sheet, for institutional investing that is separate and apart from their primary focus as businesses.

Consider a hypothetical company named *HypoCo* that manufactures iWidgets. iWidgets become a must-have holiday item, and HypoCo's business takes off, with increasing revenues and profitability. Normally, HypoCo might engage in capital expenditures to either expand their iWidget business or launch a new business line. Or, it might increase dividends or share buybacks to return capital to investors or boost its stock price. But for a variety of reasons, HypoCo is cautious about increasing its capital expenditures and still has plenty of money left over after increasing dividends and buying up some shares. HypoCo doesn't want to sit on cash without any returns, so it might start investing in some short-term bonds—first governmental bonds and later corporate and mortgage securities. HypoCo sees that this might provide some diversification benefit relative to its iWidget business, so with a portion of its extra cash, it gets more aggressive—first with fixed income and later with equities and real assets. Eventually, HypoCo commits to an ongoing strategic allocation to the capital and private markets, even though this doesn't really relate to its primary business strategy manufacturing iWidgets.

Is the HypoCo example truly hypothetical or does this reflect actual corporate behavior? In 2017, S&P estimated that total corporate cash held by 2,000 U.S. companies surveyed exceeded $1.9 trillion.[vi] Of that amount, over half of it was held by just the top 25 companies. Moreover, many companies also had significant debt obligations on their balance sheets, indicating that some companies might be hoarding cash in anticipation of debt payments, or perhaps attempting to arbitrage the market by generating higher returns with their cash balances than their debt payments. The majority of companies, it seems, may not be willing or able to invest their balance sheet assets as aggressively as HypoCo.

Still, if even 25 companies have approximately $1 trillion to deploy, that alone constitutes a significant amount of institutional assets. Indeed, one company alone, Apple, continued to set records and make headlines with its balance sheet—with its balance of cash, cash equivalents, and marketable securities exceeding $245 billion (down from $285 billion) as of year-end 2018.[vii] It is very difficult to discern Apple's investment strategy for its cash balance, but the mere fact of its continued existence demonstrates that Apple has insufficient capital expenditures relative to its cash and therefore prefers to invest in financial assets. Apple is not alone in this trend. The Association for Financial Professionals surveys corporations on a quarterly basis about their cash holdings, and through the end of 2018, corporations continued to increase their cash and short-term investments.[viii]

For public companies that have daily-traded stock, large cash balances could lead to demands by shareholders for higher dividends, increased share buybacks, or more capital expenditures to reduce those cash balances. However, the robust performance of the stock market in recent years has done little to prevent the aggregate corporate cash balances from its upward climb. Changes to the U.S. tax code in 2017 were designed to promote capital expenditures, but in the early stages of its implementation, the shift away from cash balances did not occur. For the foreseeable future, it seems corporate cash balances will continue to constitute a sizeable pool of institutional assets.

Relative to other institutional investors, corporations do maintain greater flexibility with how they deploy their balance sheet assets. Specifically, corporations are designed to deploy capital to its best usage, and therefore are less likely to be limited by lengthy board approval cycles or changes to investment policy statements. This is significant because corporations could be more nimble in responding to various market or macroeconomic environments. For example, changes in interest rates may lead corporations to different investment strategies, including managing the size of their balance sheets. Falling interest rates could lead corporations to refinance existing debt or issue new debt, increasing the amount of cash on hand in order to invest assets and attempt to arbitrage their own financing rate. Rising interest rates also could result in multiple outcomes, from debt reduction on variable interest rate loans, to the hoarding of cash through short-term investments as a cushion against the potential impact of contractionary business conditions. Even though corporations may possess a quicker reaction function to market events, that does not necessarily mean that they will deploy capital effectively. Indeed, share buybacks seem to accelerate as equity markets rise, yet may fall as the equity markets decline, meaning that corporations could inadvertently be employing a *buy-high* strategy. Ultimately, for all their ability to be nimble, corporations may simply be inclined toward a posture that maximizes their optionality on deploying their balance sheet assets. A company may want to jump on the opportunity to acquire a competitor, ramp up hiring, or increase their widget manufacturing. These short-term considerations tip the scales such that corporations will likely continue to favor shorter term investments with their balance sheet assets.

Endowments

Endowments, or more specifically endowment funds, are pools of assets established by foundations. Typically, these foundations are nonprofit institutions such as universities, hospitals, religious congregations, or other charities. The endowments are typically funded by donors, and these assets are intended to assist the foundation in achieving its objective. By far, the largest endowments are university endowments. In 2017, the National Association of College and University Business Officers (NACUBO) collected data from 809 colleges and universities and reported that aggregate university endowment assets were

$566.8 billion, while the median endowment was $127.8 million.[ix] The size of endowments is heavily skewed and the 10 largest endowments (including Harvard, Yale, University of Texas, Stanford, and Princeton) collectively control approximately $200 billion in assets. In addition to universities, there are several endowments dedicated to human rights, health, and medical research and development. The largest of these in the United States are the Bill & Melinda Gates Foundation ($40.3 billion)[x] and the Howard Hughes Medical Institute ($21.1 billion).[xi]

Endowments enjoy a tax advantage: if the recipient of the endowment's investment income is also a nonprofit, the recipient does not pay tax on the endowment's investment income. Separately, donors typically also receive tax deductions for donations. In November 2017, Republicans proposed limiting the tax-exempt status for university endowments that held greater than $100,000 in assets per student. The initial proposal included a modest 1.4% tax on net investment income, which would raise an estimated $3 billion in tax revenue between 2018 and 2027.[xii] Universities balked, lobbied congress, and the final version of the bill levied a 1.4% tax on investment income for endowments that exceeded $500,000 per student. While the final details of the tax were left to the Internal Revenue Service, the new university endowment tax is expected to impact about 30 of the largest university endowments and raise $1.8 billion in tax revenue over the next 10 years.[xiii]

To assist the university or nonprofit to which the endowment is attached, a portion of the endowment assets are donated to the university or nonprofit—for example, 5% per year. Since the objective and time horizon of the endowments are typically perpetual, managers of endowments target a growth rate that is equal to or greater than its donation rate. This suggests that some, but not all, of an endowment's interest and capital gains will be paid to its corresponding university or nonprofit. As such, endowments typically create investment policies establishing return and volatility targets as well as limiting different investment types. David Swenson, chief investment officer of the Yale University endowment, and Dean Takahashi, senior director of investments, have been credited with the creation of the *Yale model*, which is also known as the endowment model. This approach to asset allocation begins by recognizing that endowments have a perpetual time horizon and only a modest need for immediate liquidity—such as 5% per year. Additionally, dividend income, rental payments, interest income, and donations all constitute steady sources of liquid inflows. Therefore, it may be appropriate for an endowment to invest in illiquid assets and only modest amounts in more traditional assets including cash, fixed income, and equities.[xiv] As shown in Figure 3.1, in 2017 the Yale endowment held only 1% of its assets in cash and 9% between domestic equities and fixed income. Rather, a bulk of its assets were invested in illiquid asset classes including

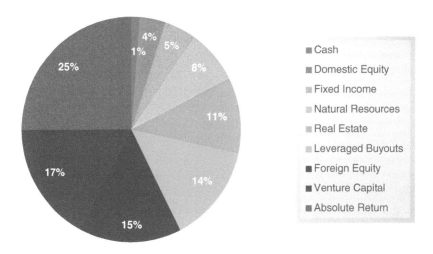

Figure 3.1   2017 Yale endowment asset allocation. *Source*: Yale Investments Office

real estate (11%), leveraged buyouts (14%), venture capital (17%), and *absolute return* which we may interpret as some form of hedge fund (25%).

So, how has the endowment model performed? The results are mixed. Yale is an outlier and has generated a +12.1% annualized return for the 20-year period that ended 6/30/2017, while domestic equities (S&P 500) returned +7.9% annually and domestic bonds (Barclays U.S. Aggregate) returned +5.2% annually over the same period.[xv] That's truly a remarkable track record, making it understandable that so many endowments have adopted Mr. Swenson's investment philosophy. Meanwhile, over the past 10 years, the average annual net university endowment return has varied from −18.7% in 2009 to +19.2% in 2011.[xvi] For the 10-year period that ended 6/30/2017, despite the strong performance since 2009, the average university endowment has returned a modest +4.6%[xvii]—underperforming domestic equities (S&P 500), which returned +8.6% and modestly outperforming domestic bonds (Barclays U.S. Aggregate), which returned +4.4% annually. Meanwhile, investors and alumni alike were shocked to learn that in the 2009 fiscal year, the Yale endowment shed 28.6% ($6.6 billion) of its value while the Harvard endowment shed 29.8% ($11.0 billion)![xviii] In fact, having been slightly leveraged prior to the 2008–2009 financial crisis, Harvard had insufficient liquidity and was forced to issue approximately $2.5 billion in bonds in late 2008 and early 2009 at interest rates ranging from 3.2% to 6.5%.[xix] Both Stanford and Princeton also issued $1 billion each in debt during the same period, perhaps indicating a greater need for liquidity than is generally appreciated.

Still, given their size, sophistication, generally low need for liquidity, and stable long-term return objective, there is some degree of predictability to endowment investment preferences and reaction functions. Specifically, as interest rates rise, endowments may be more inclined to invest in long-duration instruments. However, given their desire to generate an illiquidity premium, their investments in U.S. Treasuries, investment grade corporate bonds, and other similar fixed income instruments, will remain muted. Rather, endowments will likely maintain relatively high allocations to *alternative* asset classes including commodities, real assets (like timber), hedge funds, and private equity. As a result, in significant market downturns, these institutions will likely be unable to provide liquidity by buying cheap assets, as they have little spare liquidity. Instead, endowments will be more likely to be shopping illiquid holdings, like seasoned investments in real assets or private equity funds, at significant discounts. Knowing this, the scrupulous investor that maintains sufficient liquidity to deploy during severe market downturns may find assets at fire-sale prices as the Harvards and Yales look to unload assets.

Pension Plans

A pension plan, broadly defined, is a pool of assets that provides participants with income while in retirement. There are two types of plans: defined benefit (DB) and defined contribution (DC). DC plans are far more common among private-sector workers, involve a *plan sponsor* (a company offering the retirement plan), and involve both an employer and employee contributing into a retirement account in the employee's name. There is no guarantee of future income or asset value at retirement. Conversely, DB plans are more common among public-sector workers. Unlike DC plans, DB plans offer a guaranteed monthly benefit at retirement based on a predetermined formula. The formulas vary and may be a dollar value times the number of years worked, or a value equal to a percentage of the salary earned by the employee in his or her final year or several years of employment.[xx] While DC plans are a type of pension plan, in general, when practitioners speak of pension plans they are usually referring to the large public and private DB plans. For this reason, in this chapter we'll focus on this type of pension plan and we will use the terms *pension plan* and *DB plan* interchangeably.

In 1875, 25 years after its founding, The American Express Company became the first company in the United States to offer a pension to its employees. The initial plan was intended to ease out of the workforce employees who had been injured on the job. In 1893, the plan was expanded to include fixed retirement benefits for employees who had worked for at least 20 years and were at least 40 years old.[xxi] In 1913, the California State Teachers' Retirement System

(CalSTRS) was created to provide California teachers with retirement benefits without requiring employee contributions.[xxii] In 1920, the U.S. Congress passed the Civil Service Retirement Act, creating the first DB retirement system for federal employees.[xxiii] Congress continued to encourage the growth of private pensions by passing the Revenue Acts of 1921 and 1926, which allowed employers to deduct pension contributions from corporate income, as well as allowing the income of the pension fund's portfolio to accumulate tax free.[xxiv] Finally, in 1935, in the depth of the Great Depression, the U.S. Congress passed the Social Security Act, providing retirement benefits to all Americans age 65 and older; at the time, life expectancy was 60 years.[xxv]

Since the 1930s, growth in both pension assets and liabilities has been dramatic. In 2017, total state and local government pension assets rose to approximately $4.33 trillion.[xxvi] However, continuing with the precedent set in 1913 with CalSTRS, on average, governments for generations have failed to save for future pensioners. In 2016, the American Enterprise Institute estimated that state and local government pensions may have unfunded liabilities of over $5.0 trillion![xxvii] This shortfall will eventually be made up from higher taxes, lower future benefits, or a combination of the two. Meanwhile, at the end of 2016, the U.S. Social Security Administration paid benefits to 61 million people, collected taxes on 171 million people, and held $2.8 trillion in reserves, which are exclusively U.S. Treasuries.[xxviii] However, assuming that the life expectancy of U.S. workers continues to lengthen and the ratio of workers to retirees grows, the unfunded social security benefits liability as of 2017 (through 2091) is estimated by the U.S. Social Security Administration to be $12.5 trillion![xxix] Meanwhile, U.S. corporate pensions have amassed $3.7 trillion in assets through 2017.[xxx] Willis Towers Watson estimated that the largest DB plans are roughly 83% funded[xxxi]—if we apply that funding ratio to all plans, that suggests total U.S. corporate pensions liability is around $4.5 trillion. Still, a funding status of 83% is better than the roughly 72% funded ratio for state and local pensions, according to the Center for Retirement Research (CRR) at Boston College and the Center for State and Local Government Excellence (SLGE).[xxxii] The comparatively strong funding status of U.S. corporate pensions can largely be attributed to the Employee Retirement Income Security Act (ERISA) of 1974, which established minimum funding requirements for U.S. private pension plans.

Over the past thirty years, the usage of DB plans has waned, as shown in Figure 3.2. In 1989, according to the CRR at Boston College, 32% of workers in the United States participated in a DB plan either exclusively or in addition to a DC plan. That figure has declined to 13% in 2016. Meanwhile, the usage of DC plans has dramatically increased, as workers that participate in only a DC plan has risen from 15% to 34% over the same period.[xxxiii] In 2008, The Pensions Institute (a UK academic research center) published "Large Declines in Defined

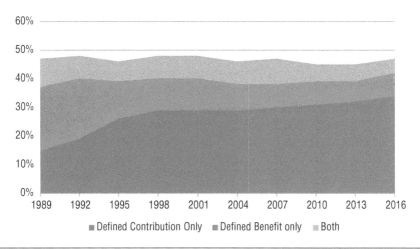

Figure 3.2   Pension participation of all workers, by type of plan, 1989–2016.
Source: CRR at Boston College

Benefit Plans Are Not Inevitable," in which they identified several reasons why companies favor offering DC plans to DB plans. These reasons include: lower compliance costs, lower regulatory burden, tax laws that may disincentivize overfunding of DB plans, volatility of funding status and required contributions, and preferential accounting treatment given to DC plans.[xxxiv] While companies may prefer DC plans for these reasons, workers are less enthused with this transition, given that their funding liability for retirement has shifted to them and they can neither rely on a predictable pension nor can they access similarly robust investment strategies and resources. As the name of the study suggests, the decline in DB plans is not inevitable, but there is little reason to think that these plans won't continue to shrink for the aforementioned reasons. Public pensions, however, are unlikely to be replaced by DC plans in the near future because DB plans are popular among unions, workers who are near retirement, and people who are currently retired. This can be evidenced by the failure of George W. Bush to reform and partially privatize Social Security in 2005 following significant pushback from Americans United to Protect Social Security (a nonprofit *advocacy group* founded in 2005) and the AARP.[xxxv]

Excluding the U.S. Social Security reserves, which by law are exclusively U.S. Treasuries, public and private DB pensions in the United States have amassed over $8.0 trillion in assets as of 2017. Because these institutional investors generally have similar mandates as well as market reaction functions, investors may be able to anticipate their future allocation of capital and position themselves accordingly. A commonality among all DB pensions is that each of these investors are tasked with accumulating assets and responsibly investing those assets to pay future retirement benefits. The present value of those retirement benefits varies by the pension since that figure is driven by the number of employees, the formula used to determine future benefits, the average age of current and retired employees, and so on. However, one component of the liability calculation that is identical to all pension plans is that future liabilities are discounted at an interest rate to determine the present value of those liabilities. Holding all other things equal, as interest rates rise, the present value of future liabilities declines, meaning the funding statuses of all pension plans improve; conversely, as interest rates fall, pension plan funding status worsens. A second commonality is that a majority of pensions have a mix of both equities and bonds. Therefore, as equities appreciate, pension plan funding status improves; as equities depreciate, pension plan funding status deteriorates.

Taken together, we know that an ideal situation for pension plans is an environment in which equities appreciate and interest rates rise, while a nightmare scenario is when equities depreciate and interest rates fall. In the second scenario (equities fall and interest rates fall), the managers of corporate pensions, because of both ERISA requirements and their fiduciary duties to pensioners and employees, have a menu of options ranging from bad to terrible. These options include: reduce future pension benefits either by reducing the monthly payout or increasing the retirement age, increase annual payments into the DB plan (via a reduction in worker wages, dividends, share buybacks, or capital investments), issue equity or debt to fund the shortfall, or increase the return target for the remaining pool of pension assets. Early in 2003, many pensions faced this dilemma: the S&P 500 had fallen 37.6% in the 3-year period that ended 12/31/2002, while 10-year U.S. Treasury yield had fallen 2.63% to 3.82% over the same period. At that time, General Motors (GM) was in a particularly dire situation: GM had a $19 billion shortfall with a 76% funding ratio. Additionally, its plan was *mature* with only 2.5 workers per retiree. How did GM respond? In 2003, it issued $17.6 billion in debt, of which $13.2 billion was immediately contributed to its pension plan. Additionally, GM increased its return target to 9% and invested a large portion of its proceeds in high-yield bonds, emerging markets, real estate, and hedge funds.[xxxvi] While the case can be made that GM was essentially rolling the dice with the future of its pensioners at stake, it is nevertheless a prime example of how declining equities and interest rates incentivizes pension plan managers to engage in risk-seeking behavior. Furthermore, this risk-seeking behavior is implemented by issuing and selling debt and purchasing equities and other higher-risk, higher-return assets. Thus, as an unintended consequence of the accounting surrounding pension liabilities, large institutional investors become material buyers of risky assets in depreciating equity and falling interest rate environments.

The same can also be said in the reverse situation: large pension managers become marginal sellers of risky assets and buyers of fixed income when both equities appreciate and interest rates rise. In the 18-month period that ended 12/31/2017, the S&P 500 appreciated +31.4% while the 10-year U.S. Treasury rate rose +0.94% to 2.41%. At the same time, according to the 2018 edition of the Milliman Corporate Pension Funding Study of the 100 largest corporate DB pension plans, the average funding ratio improved from 81.1% to 86.0% in 2017, resulting in a $72 billion reduction in the funding deficit.[xxxvii] In response, in January 2018 alone, U.S. pension funds purchased $24 billion in bonds and sold $12 billion in equities.[xxxviii] This is essentially the opposite *trade* GM made in 2003 when its funding status was deteriorating. Of interest to bond managers is that when pension funds purchase debt, they typically purchase long-duration bonds (or bonds that mature in greater than 20 years). This is because pension liabilities are also long-duration, meaning that retirement benefits won't be paid to current employees for decades. Therefore, to sterilize[2] these liabilities, long-duration bonds are highly appropriate for pension plans. So, when the yield curve *steepens*, or when the difference between the interest rate of a short-duration and a long-duration bond increases, pension funds become a significant marginal buyer of long-duration bonds, or just *buyers of duration* as is typically referenced by bond managers.

Commercial Banks

Commercial banks are financial institutions that provide a variety of services to their customers, including accepting deposits, issuing CDs, and extending loans to both individuals and businesses. The size and breadth of commercial banks vary dramatically—from small regional banks with a limited physical and online presence to major multi-national banks with thousands of physical locations and a significant online presence. Additionally, depending on the type of bank, the primary federal regulator may be the Federal Deposit Insurance Corporation (FDIC), the Office of the Comptroller of the Currency (OCC), or the Federal Reserve.[xxxix] Some banks offer services to large institutions including underwriting corporate transactions as well as facilitating the issuance and trading of equity, debt, and derivatives; in the past these services were performed by *investment banks*. In 1933, the U.S. Congress passed the Banking Act of

---

[2] *Sterilize* is a term that is regularly utilized by managers who are engaged in *liability-driven investing*, (LDI). A liability that is fully *sterilized* will be matched with an offsetting asset to have a zero *shortfall*, meaning the value of the asset is equal to the value of the liability. Because pension plans have long-duration liabilities, the present value of these liabilities is sensitive to changes in interest rates. Therefore, LDI investors purchase assets with similarly long durations to match the assets and liabilities' interest rate sensitivity, thereby eliminating volatility in their funding ratio.

1933, often referred to as the Glass-Steagall Act after Senator Glass of Virginia and Congressman Steagall of Alabama. Among other things, this act limited activities of banks and separated them into *commercial banks*, which primarily interacted with individuals and small businesses and *investment banks*, which primarily worked with large institutions.[xl] At the time, it was believed that separating these two activities would improve the stability of the U.S. financial system. However, decades later the U.S. Congress passed the Gramm–Leach–Bliley Act, also known as the Financial Services Modernization Act of 1999, which repealed the prohibitions ensuring the separation of investment banks, commercial banks, and insurance companies.[xli] As a result, today in the United States, commercial banks with deposits from individuals, such as J.P. Morgan or Bank of America, now offer services previously limited to investment banks.

But, despite their differences in size and scope of services, there are many commonalities among banks that allow a discerning investor to anticipate how these institutions will react in a variety of market conditions. First, all banks irrespective of their size, level of sophistication, or customers, attempt to maximize the spread on the bank's liabilities (such as bank deposits or debt issue by the bank) and the interest rate on the bank's assets (such as loans extended by the bank); this is known as the net interest margin. Second, banks *borrow short* and *lend long*. This means that the average duration of a bank's liabilities is generally shorter than the average duration of its assets. For example, a bank's liabilities, such as customer deposits in savings and checking accounts, may be withdrawn in a single day. Alternatively, bank assets—like loans to individuals for cars or homes or loans to businesses for multi-year lines of credit—typically have agreements that are up to 30 years. Third, banks are sensitive to both the level and shape of the yield curve. Specifically, owing to their propensity to borrow short and lend long, bank profitability declines when the yield curve flattens (2-year interest rates rise relative to 10- and 30-year rates), while bank profitability increases when the yield curve steepens (2-year interest rates fall relative to 10- and 30-year rates). Additionally, bank net interest margins shrink as interest rates fall while net interest margins increase when interest rates rise.[xlii] Fourth, banks attempt to maximize their return on equity (ROE). ROE can be roughly calculated as: (net interest margin × total bank assets) × (total bank assets / shareholder's equity). The first part of the equation corresponds to net income, while the second part of the equation is a rough measure of leverage. Thus, if a bank's only objective were to increase ROE, a bank would maximize its leverage. It is the responsibility of regulators to ensure that this doesn't occur. Finally, all banks attempt to minimize the implicit costs associated with regulatory requirements and will adjust their mix of assets and liabilities as regulations change.

Total assets of U.S. commercial banks as of September 2018 were $16.7 trillion. Total assets for U.S. commercial banks previously peaked in December 2008 at $12.3 trillion and troughed at $11.7 trillion in January 2010 before continuing a shallower growth trajectory than in the years prior to the 2008–2009 recession. Most bank assets are currently loans and leases ($9.4 trillion), which includes commercial and industrial loans ($2.2 trillion), consumer loans ($1.5 trillion), and real estate (home) loans ($4.4 trillion). U.S. commercial banks collectively hold $2.2 trillion in cash, a majority of which are excess reserves earning an interest rate at the Federal Reserve (more on this in Chapter 4). Finally, banks hold $3.4 trillion in securities, including U.S. Treasuries, mortgage-backed securities, and other debt instruments.[xliii,xliv] While this is a snapshot of the asset-side of U.S. commercial bank balance sheets in 2018, the composition of balance sheets vary from year to year and are impacted by regulations, interest rates, implied risk premiums, and other market forces. In 2015, the Brookings Institution released a paper analyzing the changing composition of the four largest U.S. banks known as the *Big Four*, which includes J.P. Morgan Chase, Bank of America, Citigroup, and Wells Fargo. The study showed that from 2003 through 2008 the Big Four's bank asset growth was driven primarily by increases in loans and leases, while from 2009 to 2014, commercial bank asset growth had been primarily driven by increases in interest-bearing assets, such as deposits at the Federal Reserve.[xlv] This can be seen in Figure 3.3. Following 2008, cash assets grew significantly as a percentage of bank assets, whereas loans and leases fell as a percentage of bank assets.

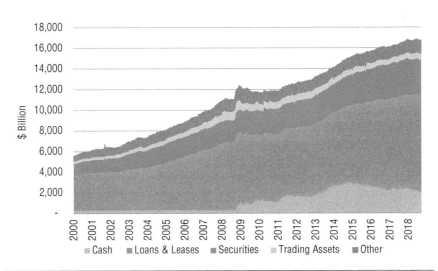

Figure 3.3   All U.S. commercial banks total assets. *Source*: Federal Reserve Bank of St. Louis

The authors of the aforementioned Brookings Institution paper highlight two factors that have directly impacted the composition of commercial bank assets since the financial crisis. First, five years of monetary expansion known as *quantitative easing* was executed by the U.S. Federal Reserve by purchasing U.S. Treasuries and mortgage-backed securities. This led to banks shedding these assets in favor of interest-bearing deposits at the Federal Reserve. Said another way, as the Federal Reserve was expanding its balance sheet by purchasing assets in the secondary market, U.S. commercial banks regularly sold these securities to the Federal Reserve and then immediately placed the cash from the sale of those securities back at the Federal Reserve in the form of interest-bearing deposits. The second factor impacting bank balance sheet composition are the new rules and regulations authorized under Dodd-Frank. Specifically, new liquidity requirements incentivize banks to hold high-quality, liquid securities in lieu of riskier, less liquid assets. This led the Big Four to reduce their emphasis on trading and market-making operations.[xlvi]

The change in U.S. commercial balance sheet composition has several investment implications. First is that the reaction by banks to the Federal Reserve purchasing its securities in the secondary market—which was to deposit the cash back at the Federal Reserve—limited the impact of the Federal Reserve's policy since the banks were not using this cash to increase loans. This may explain in part why loan growth, and thus economic growth, remained on a shallower trajectory than prior to the 2008–2009 recession. Second, U.S. banks' de-emphasis in trading operations, which has led to a reduction in securities earmarked for trading and market making, has led to a decline in the liquidity of many fixed-income assets, according to a separate Brookings Institute paper from 2015. While in 2015, the bid/offer spreads, a common metric to gauge liquidity, were similar to 2006, the reduction in trading operations may have contributed to several instances of what the authors define as *extreme volatility*. These instances include the May 2013 *taper tantrum* when the value of the 10-year U.S. Treasury fell 3% in two days and the dramatic intra-day move in U.S. Treasuries on October 15, 2014.[xlvii] While a reduction in liquidity and heightened instances of significant interest rate moves is generally a bad development for investors, it does create additional opportunity for active bond managers to add value for their investors. Specifically, active bond managers will likely have more opportunities to purchase securities that have cheapened for technical reasons, thereby acting as the marginal bidder and a liquidity provider.

Insurance Companies

As mentioned in Chapter 2, life insurance companies are the institutions that underwrite and sell annuity contracts, life insurance, and other financial products that are directly related to life and death. By contrast, property and casualty

(P&C) insurance companies underwrite and sell policies directly related to property. For example, property insurance will reimburse the owner of property (such as homes, cars, or equipment) if the property is damaged or stolen without fault of the policyholder. Casualty insurance will reimburse the policyholder, thereby indemnifying that person subject to a limit, for costs incurred if the insured person becomes legally liable for injury to another or damage to another's property. For example, auto insurance typically insures the driver's vehicle and losses the policyholder incurs following an accident, such as damaging another driver's car, assuming the policyholder wasn't negligent at the time.

Whether it is a life insurance or a P&C insurance policy, in both instances the policy begins with a contract that is purchased by the policyholder. At that time, the insurance company receives an asset in the form of a premium and incurs a liability in the form of a potential future payment to the policyholder or someone with a claim against the policyholder. With respect to a life insurance policy, the insurance company will make a future payment with a high degree of certainty; the uncertainty lies with respect to the duration of those payments, which is to say how long the policyholder lives to receive the payments. By contrast, the insurance company has no degree of certainty on whether it will ever make a P&C payment, and if it does, for what amount. Plus, a typical P&C policy is a year, further reducing the likelihood that a claim will occur during any given contract (as opposed to over a multi-year period). However, should the P&C company make a payment to a policyholder owing to a claim, that payment will likely significantly exceed the premium originally paid to the P&C company. So, irrespective of whether it is a life insurance or P&C insurance company, both institutions need to save and invest the unpaid premiums, called a *float*, with the expectation that this capital grows and is sufficient to meet future claims. As of Q2 2018, U.S. P&C insurance companies held $2.4 trillion in financial assets of which at least $1.1 trillion are debt securities,[xlviii] while life insurance companies held $7.7 trillion in financial assets of which at least $3.5 trillion are debt securities.[xlix]

Because both life and P&C insurers invest significant portions of their floats in fixed income assets, both types of insurers are sensitive to changes in interest rates. In 2015, a working group of members in the Casualty Actuarial Society published their findings on the P&C industry's sensitivity to interest rates. In it, they highlight that a low interest rate environment has reduced the industry's overall profitability because it has reduced the interest income from their collective float. In response to lower yields on their portfolios, P&C insurers have increased overall premiums on their products. Additionally, P&C insurers are concerned about a sudden rise in interest rates since this could cause the market value of their positions to decline. As a result, P&C insurers have generally reduced the duration of their assets—both to match the generally low-duration nature of their policies as well as reduce their float's interest rate sensitivity.[l]

Life insurers are even more exposed to interest rate sensitivity than P&C insurers. Unlike P&C policies, which often cover only a single year in duration, life insurance products are long term in nature. Because policyholders receive a stream of cash flows for years, often starting years after the policy is first written, life insurers must invest assets in a way that is appropriate given the long-duration nature of its liabilities. Additionally, many life insurance policies involve *riders* or guaranteed minimum returns, whose present values are also sensitive to changes in interest rates. In 2010, 95% of all life insurance policies contained a guarantee of 3% or higher.[li] As interest rates such as the 10-year U.S. Treasury bond fall below 3%, plans with a 3% or higher guarantee are now *in the money*. In this environment, life insurance assets may not generate sufficient returns to cover the guarantee and any interest rate shortfall directly reduces firm profitability. Additionally, new policies with low annual return guarantees that are offered in low interest rate environments are generally unattractive to life insurance purchasers, leading to lower life insurance product sales.

Interestingly, while the mission statements of life and P&C insurance companies share little in common with those of DB plans, these institutions' investing objectives share several commonalities. First, both pensions and insurance companies view their operations as *going concerns* with perpetual horizons. Insurance Company of America (now a part of Cigna)—the oldest insurance company in the United States—celebrated its 226-year anniversary in 2018;[lii] meanwhile, the American Express Company pension celebrated its 143-year anniversary the same year.

Second, both pensions and insurance companies anticipate making regular payments to their beneficiaries. Being *going concerns*, neither institution wants its annual payments to significantly exceed the returns earned by their portfolios. Otherwise, their ability to operate into the future indefinitely will be compromised; insurance companies' shareholder equity and pension plans' principal will fall if payments consistently exceed investment income plus other forms of income.

Third, both institutions have relatively low current liquidity needs. Pensions are constantly receiving contributions from current workers and generating interest income, while insurance companies are regularly selling new policies and are also generating interest income. Given their relatively predictable outflows and steady streams of income, both institutions may invest some portion of their portfolios in illiquid assets. Finally, both institutions have difficulty meeting their targeted return objectives in low interest rate environments. A low interest rate environment, as previously mentioned, reduces the annual interest income for these institutions, while their current liabilities are generally un-changed and the present value of future liabilities is higher.

Given their similarities, it should be no surprise that both pensions and in-surance companies have somewhat similar reaction functions to low interest rate environments. Specifically, both institutions *reach for yield* and begin in-creasing the riskiness of their portfolios when yields on fixed income assets decline. However, unlike private pension plans that have comparatively loose guidelines with respect to the investments in their pension plans, insurance companies are heavily regulated. There is no federal regulator for insurance companies; instead, each state is responsible for regulating insurance compa-nies that operate within their territories. To standardize interstate regulations, in 1871 state insurance regulators formed the National Insurance Convention, which eventually became the National Association of Insurance Commissioners (NAIC). This body is tasked with establishing accounting standards and best practices, conducting peer review, and coordinating regulatory oversight.[liii] This regulatory oversight includes recommendations for minimum capital, measure-ments of capital riskiness (risk-based capital), and the classification of capital's riskiness. State regulators regularly adopt these measures, although there isn't complete uniformity across states, to ensure that insurance companies are highly capitalized and unlikely to become insolvent.

As such, while some pension plans, such as GM, issued debt and invested those proceeds in risky assets when unfunded liabilities grew as interest rates fell, insurance companies' collective response has been more muted, but still measurable. Collectively, insurance companies' holdings of securities rated NAIC-1 (the highest quality bonds) fell from 75.5% in 2007 to 66.6% in 2016, while holdings of NAIC-2 (slightly lower-quality than NAIC-1 bonds) rose from 19.7% in 2007 to 27.5% in 2016. This aggregates to a net $500 billion increase in corporate bonds that do not hold the highest credit rating.[liv] Yet, given their limited ability to engage in risk-seeking behavior, combined with a reduction in profitability and marketability of its products, it is no surprise that the equity returns for insurance companies have materially lagged the broader market. For the 10-year period that ended 6/15/2018, insurance companies have appreciated +28.3% while the S&P 500 has appreciated +98.5% over the same period.[lv]

Mutual Funds and Hedge Funds

The next institutional investors we'll review are mutual funds and hedge funds, or more accurately, the investment management firms that manage these products. As described in Chapter 2, mutual funds are commingled vehicles, meaning investor capital is aggregated and each investor owns a fraction of the fund. In the U.S., these funds are regulated by the SEC following the Investment

Company Act of 1940. Mutual funds must publicly disclose holdings, have strict limits on leverage, and have minimum liquidity requirements.[lvi] Hedge funds are like mutual funds in that they are commingled investment vehicles; however, unlike mutual funds, only accredited investors may invest in hedge funds. Accredited investors are defined as banks, private businesses, trusts with assets exceeding $5 million, individuals that make $200,000 (or couples that make $300,000) per year and expect to continue to do so, and individuals with greater than $1 million in net worth.[lvii] Unlike their mutual fund counterparts, hedge funds can utilize leverage and may not be required to file public reports with the SEC. While hedge funds are subject to the same prohibitions against fraud, hedge fund investors do not receive all of the state and federal law protections that are extended to mutual fund investors.[lviii]

Both hedge funds and mutual funds are managed according to prespecified objectives and limited by guidelines that are detailed in their respective prospectuses. Given the less-regulated nature of hedge funds, these funds often invest in less-liquid markets, utilize leverage, and may experience greater volatility than traditional mutual funds. The mutual fund and hedge fund industries are enormous. In the United States alone at the end of 2017, open-end mutual funds collectively controlled $19.2 trillion in financial assets. Globally, assets in open-end mutual funds reached $49.3 trillion in 2017.[lix] The largest global mutual fund managers in 2017—aggregating only mutual funds and not exchange-traded funds (ETFs), separately managed accounts, or other private vehicles—are The Vanguard Group ($3.8 trillion), Fidelity Investments ($2.1 trillion), and Capital Research & Management, a.k.a. Capital Group ($1.7 trillion).[lx] Meanwhile, globally, hedge funds collectively managed approximately $3.2 trillion in financial assets at the end of 2017.[lxi] The largest global hedge fund managers in 2017 are Bridgewater Associates ($132.8 billion), AQR Capital Management ($83.7 billion), and Man Group ($59.1 billion).[lxii]

As both mutual funds and hedge funds generally have clearly defined objectives and external benchmarks, the ability of fund managers to respond to changing economic environments is generally limited: managers benchmarked against the S&P 500 will continue to invest almost exclusively in equities, while managers benchmarked against the Bloomberg Barclays U.S. Aggregate will continue to invest almost exclusively in bonds, irrespective of the recent changes in equity and bond prices. The exceptions to this rule are asset allocation and target risk products; however, these products constitute a small portion of the entire hedge and mutual fund environment. Thus, unlike pensions, endowments, banks, or other institutions, fund managers do not have highly pronounced reaction functions with respect to allocating between asset classes. However, this does not mean that they are immune to changing environments and the assets in which they invest. Rather, fund managers are beholden to the flows in and out of their products, and those flows are highly correlated to recent performance.

In fact, there is a rather large body of academic research that has established the link between past performance and both hedge and mutual fund flows. Said another way, if bank loans performed well last year, bank loan mutual funds will receive outsized inflows this year; if technology stocks performed poorly this year, technology stock mutual funds will experience outsized outflows next year, ceteris paribus.[lxiii,lxiv] Finally, the top managers in any given sector, such as small-cap U.S. equities, will receive the lion's share of flows into that sector, often at the expense of the poorest performing managers in the same sector. So, do these flows impact future performance, and is there a trading strategy that can incorporate this flow information? In 2015, Martin Rohleder addressed this question in a study published in the International Journal of Financial Studies. He found that a simple investment strategy of rotating out of funds with low or negative flows, and purchasing funds with high recent flows, resulted in statistically higher performance than a simple buy-and-hold strategy with no notable increase in investment volatility. This is true for both equity and bond mutual funds. However, when incorporating transaction costs, such as loads and taxes, the simple buy-and-hold strategy outperformed the flow-driven investment strategy. Mr. Rohleder concluded, "It is, therefore, not possible to exploit the information content in lagged flows via these simple investment strategies."[lxv] Guillermo Baquero and Marno Verbeek found the same to be true in 2015 when analyzing hedge fund flows and subsequent performance. They concluded that hedge fund investors "overweigh the importance of performance streaks . . . and underperform, ex post, simple model allocation rules."[lxvi]

Family Offices and Ultra-High Net Worth Individuals

A family office is a private wealth management firm that meets the needs of ultra-high net worth individuals and their families. While these needs vary by family or individual, family office services generally include asset management, cash management, estate and succession planning, philanthropic activities, management of physical assets such as homes and yachts, and other *concierge* services. The most common types of family offices are the single-family office (SFO) and the multi-family office (MFO), which as the name implies, manages the wealth and finances for one or multiple families. It is uncertain how many family offices operate worldwide, but Ernst and Young estimates that as of 2016, there were at least 10,000 family offices globally and at least half of these offices were established in the last fifteen years.[lxvii] We can assume that the rapid growth in family offices has mirrored the growth in billionaires. In 2002, Forbes counted 497 billionaires globally[lxviii] and in 2018 Forbes counted 2,208 billionaires including 585 in the USA and 373 in China.[lxix] Owing to the fact that family offices manage the combined wealth of families, and since there are more families than individuals in the *three comma club*, we should expect the number of family offices to remain well above the number of individual billionaires tracked by Forbes.

The motivations for establishing a family office vary but may include family privacy and confidentiality, elaborate governance and efficient management of family assets, alignment of interests between family members, and the potential for superior portfolio risk-adjusted returns. Additionally, given the variety between families, the source of their wealth, their tax regimes, their domiciles, and their medium- and long-term objectives, family offices are sufficiently nimble to develop and implement custom solutions. While family offices vary in size and scope to fit the needs of the family they service, they often have several items in common, including:

- *Expenses*: the average family office spends $11.4 million in services per year. The single largest line-item expenses are asset allocation, risk management, and manager selection services.[lxx]
- *Size*: because of the nontrivial expenses, family offices must be large to operate profitably. As such, most family offices have at least $250 million in total assets under management, while the average family office in 2018 managed $697 million, and the average multi-family office managed $1.4 billion.[lxxi]
- *Small teams*: the average family office employs eleven full-time and four part-time members.[lxxii]
- *Breadth of teams*: the teams generally have experts in specific areas of accounting, tax law, estate planning, asset management, and risk management.

Of all the previously mentioned institutional investors, family offices are most like endowments in terms of their size, investment horizon, ability to assume risk, sophistication, low current cash needs, and affinity for illiquid and alternative investments. So, it should be no surprise that family offices have gravitated toward the endowment (or Yale) model with respect to their asset allocation. For the 2018 UBS/Campden Wealth Global Family Office Report, 311 family offices completed a survey that includes their asset allocation. As shown in Figure 3.4, for the average family office, only 7% of investments were cash or cash equivalents and 44% of investments were traditional equities or fixed income, with most of those investments in developed markets. The balance of 49% of family office portfolios were in *alternative* assets, including real estate, private equity, hedge funds, and hard assets such as agriculture, gold, or commodities. The survey, interestingly, showed that there was only a modest differentiation in

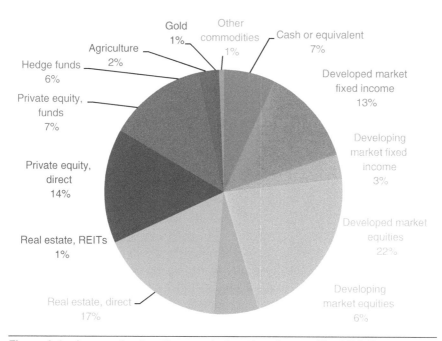

Figure 3.4 Average family office asset allocation. *Source*: The UBS/Campden Wealth Global Family Office Report 2018

terms of asset allocations between family office sizes, strategy, and region. For example, fixed income investments generally ranged from 13% to 23%, equities ranged from 25% to 31%, alternatives ranged from 37% to 54%, and cash and cash equivalents ranged from 5% to 12%.[lxxiii]

Like endowments, family offices have perpetual horizons and annual liquidity requirements, which involve disbursements to fund the lifestyles of their family members. To state the obvious, these portfolios are subject to market fluctuations and changes in liquidity conditions like any other portfolio. According to a 2009 study by the Wharton Global Family Alliance (GFA) and IESE Business School, 45% of surveyed family offices reported returns below negative 6% for the most recent one-year period (likely the one year ended March 31 or June 30, 2009).[lxxiv] While family office portfolios are constructed similarly to those managed by endowments, the family office reaction functions differ in one meaningful way to endowments: the families and individuals for whom the offices work may more easily elect to reduce current consumption following a year of poor performance. Meanwhile, endowments support universities and other nonprofit organizations that have included expected endowment disbursements years in advance. As a result, endowments are more likely to find themselves in a situation of being insufficiently liquid to meet current cash needs, as was the case with Harvard in 2009. There is no public information available to emphasize this point, but we suspect that family offices will vary in their willingness and ability to either supply or demand liquidity in highly volatile markets.

SUMMARY AND INVESTMENT IMPLICATIONS

Summary

As a young retail investor, while my $500 investment in a gold and precious metals mutual fund was material to me, it was largely irrelevant with respect to the market. Unless millions of people just like me moved in lockstep, my investment and reaction function had no bearing on the next investor. I wasn't a *real money* investor. However, there are many *real money* institutional investors that do move markets and they're worth understanding. Because of their size, institutional investors have the potential to create or eliminate investment opportunities since these institutions implement their own investment strategies. Institutional investors generally move slowly, often in the same direction, in large size, and they react similarly to various investment environments. As such, institutional investors may provide price support or price pressure to various asset classes as they implement their strategies. Knowing the likely direction of institutional investor flows may offer a discerning investor an opportunity to either ride the wave of significant institutional inflows, or reduce exposure to an asset class that might soon experience pricing pressure because of institutional investor outflows.

Investment Implications

Below is a summary of how institutions have empirically responded to various market environments and what we should anticipate in the future:

- *Corporations:* these institutions engage in business activities that result in their retained earnings sitting on their balance sheets. The very largest corporations have amassed huge cash balances, leading many to employ a somewhat diversified approach to investing their cash in diversified fixed income and even equities and alternatives. The bulk of corporate balance sheet assets, however, tend to be invested in shorter-duration fixed income or cash equivalents, enabling corporations to maintain optionality and flexibility to deploy capital toward their core businesses or toward dividends or share buybacks.
- *Endowments*: these institutions are large investors in illiquid and alternative assets because of their low current liquidity needs, the long-duration

nature of their objectives, minimal regulation, and belief in their own investment sophistication. However, in times of significant market downturns, these institutional investors may find themselves unable to meet current commitments and have become sellers of risky and illiquid assets at exactly the worst possible time.

- *Pension plans*: these institutions also have long time horizons and generally have the liability that is associated with increases in payments to pensioners every year. Thus, pensions must save aggressively for the future. As interest rates fall, the present value of future liabilities increases and funding ratios decline, thereby incentivizing pension plans to increase their exposure to risky assets and shed fixed income assets. The same is true in reverse; as interest rates rise, the present value of future liabilities fall and funding ratios increase, thereby incentivizing plans to increase their exposure to long-duration fixed income assets and shed equity exposure. This leads to a strong bid for bonds as long-duration interest rates rise, offering long-duration investors with a positively convex return.

- *Commercial banks*: these are profit-maximizing entities that incur short-term liabilities and own long-term assets; these assets may be loans that banks originate or purchase in the secondary market, whereas liabilities are predominately deposits, such as savings or checking accounts. The profitability of banks depends on the current and future regulatory environment, as well as macroeconomic variables such as the steepness of the yield curve. An inverted yield curve is a headwind to bank profitability, which may also lead to a reduction in loan origination. Separately, the requirement by regulators of higher capital for secondary market trading operations may lead to fewer banks acting as *circuit breakers* in times of large market movements—and this may lead to more instances of extreme short-term volatility.

- *Insurance companies*: insurance companies receive premiums at the time they sell policies while incurring a liability in the form of future payments to policyholders. To have sufficient capital to make these future payments, insurance companies must invest these premiums, called a float. Insurance companies, such as pension plans, tend to *reach for yield* in low interest rate environments since low interest rates are an impediment to the profitability of insurance companies. However, their ability to significantly increase the riskiness of their portfolios is limited by state regulations that ensure that insurance companies remain well-capitalized and highly creditworthy entities.

- *Mutual and hedge funds*: mutual and hedge funds are the primary vehicles through which commingled investor capital is invested. Except for multi-asset products, most funds generally focus on specific asset classes and have prespecified third-party benchmarks, such as the S&P 500 or the Bloomberg Barclays U.S. Aggregate Index, against which managers are evaluated. While these managers have a limited ability to respond to changing market environments because fund objectives and guidelines are rarely revised, the investors who utilize these vehicles can respond to market environments. Specifically, there is a growing body of evidence demonstrating that investors tend to over-allocate to assets classes and managers in those asset classes who have experienced recent strong performance. These flows may provide near-term price support for the underlying securities in which these funds invest; however, rotating into recent *winners* is not a viable trading strategy, owing to transaction costs.

- *Family offices and ultra-high net worth individuals*: these are the private wealth management firms that address the financial, legal, tax, accounting, philanthropic, and other needs of ultra-high net worth individuals and their families. These organizations are generally small in terms of their employees (usually 10–15 investment professionals), and they manage an average of around $1 billion apiece—although some can be much larger. There are over 10,000 such offices, and their popularity continues to grow as the number of global billionaires increases each year. The portfolios that these offices manage are most like endowments in that they hold significant portions of their assets in illiquid alternatives including real estate, private equity, hedge funds, and other hard assets. Additionally, the families for whom these offices service have long horizons and low current liquidity needs. Owing to their flexible mandates and long investment horizon, family offices are likely to be purchasers of risk assets that have recently cheapened. However, their ability to provide liquidity during periods of significant market volatility will vary by office.

CITATIONS

i. "Report on the Review of the Definition of 'Accredited Investor.'" (December 18, 2015). U.S. Securities and Exchange Commission. p. 25.
ii. FINRA Rule 4512(c).
iii. Kostin, David J. (January 2018). "Where to Invest Now, Year 2." Global Investment Research. The Goldman Sachs Group. p. 82.
iv. "Report on the Review of the Definition of 'Accredited Investor.'" (December 18, 2015). U.S. Securities and Exchange Commission. p. 25

v. Adrian, Jacob. (2016). "Informational Inequality: How High Frequency Traders Use Premier Access to Information to Prey on Institutional Investors." *14 Duke Law & Technology Review*. pp. 256–279.

vi. Manzi, James et al. (May 25, 2017). "U.S. Corporate Cash Reaches $1.9 Trillion But Rising Debt and Tax Reform Pose Risk." S&P Global.

vii. Apple Inc., Q1 2019 Form 10-Q. p. 3.

viii. AFP Corporate Cash Indicators®. (January 2019). "Association for Financial Professionals." p 1.

ix. Luke, Keith et al. (January 25, 2018). "Educational Endowments Report Decline in 10-Year Return Despite 12.2% Return for FY2017, Up Significantly from −1.9% Reported for FY2016." Press Release. Nacubo.org.

x. Bill & Melinda Gates Foundation Consolidated Financial Statements (PDF). (December 31, 2016). Bill & Melinda Gates Foundation.

xi. Consolidated Financial Statements 2016 (PDF). (August 31, 2016). Howard Hughes Medical Institute.

xii. Lorin, Janet. (November 2, 2017). "Colleges Blast Endowment Target in Republican Tax Bill." *Bloomberg*.

xiii. Stratford, Michael and Benjamin Wermund. (December 22, 2017). "The new tax on Harvard." Politico.com.

xiv. Swensen, David F. (2009). *Pioneering Portfolio Management: An Unconventional Approach to Institutional Investment*. Fully Revised and Updated. Simon and Schuster. p. 161.

xv. Comtois, James. (October 11, 2017). "Yale endowment posts 11.3% return." *Pensions & Investments*.

xvi. Williamson, Christine. (February 6, 2017). "Large endowments struggled with returns in fiscal 2016" *Pensions & Investments*.

xvii. 2017 NACUBO-Commonfund Study of Endowments® (NCSE).

xviii. "The 10 Worst-Performing College Endowments." (January 28, 2010). *Forbes*.

xix. Condon, Bernard and Nathan Vardi. (February 26, 2009) "Harvard: The Inside Story of Its Finance Meltdown." *Forbes*.

xx. Topoleski, John J. (March 29, 2018). "Multiemployer Defined Benefit (DB) Pension Plans: A Primer and Analysis of Policy Options." Congressional Research Service.

xxi. Tackett, Michael. (December 3, 1989). "Pensions Began As Reward, Remain Employers Option." *Chicago Tribune*.

xxii. Overview of the California State Teachers' Retirement System and Related Issues. (January 1, 2012).

xxiii. www.benefits.gov/.

xxiv. Georgetown University Law Center. "A Timeline of the Evolution of Retirement in the United States." Workplace Flexibility 2010. Georgetown University Law Center. p. 1.

xxv. Georgetown University Law Center. "A Timeline of the Evolution of Retirement in the United States." Workplace Flexibility 2010. Georgetown University Law Center. p. 2.

xxvi. National Association of State Retirement Administrators. QUARTERLY UPDATE (Q4 2017). Public Pension Assets.

xxvii. Biggs, Andrew G. (July 5, 2016). "Are State and Local Government Pensions Underfunded by $5 Trillion?" http://www.aei.org.

xxviii. The 2017 Annual Report of the Board of Trustees of the Federal Old-Age and Survivors Insurance and Federal Disability Insurance Trust Funds. Social Security Administration. p. 2.

xxix. 2017 OASDI Trustees Report. Table VI.F1.—Unfunded OASDI Obligations Through the Infinite Horizon, Based on Intermediate Assumptions.

xxx. Kozlowski, Rob. (February 5, 2018). "Largest U.S. retirement funds set record at $10.3 trillion in assets." *Pensions & Investments.*

xxxi. Kilroy, Meaghan. (January 2, 2018). "Willis Towers Watson: U.S. corporate pension funding increases in 2017." *Pensions & Investments.*

xxxii. Center for Retirement Research at Boston College (CRR) and the Center for State and Local Government Excellence (SLGE). http://publicplansdata.org/quick-facts/national/. Actuarial Funding Table.

xxxiii. Center for Retirement Research at Boston College. Pension Participation of All Workers, by Type of Plan, 1989–2016. http://crr.bc.edu/wp-content/uploads/2015/10/Pension-coverage.pdf. Table 1.

xxxiv. Turner, John and Gerard Hughes. (2008). Large Declines in Defined Benefit Plans Are Not Inevitable: The Experience of Canada, Ireland, the United Kingdom, and the United States.

xxxv. Pear, Robert. (November 12, 2004). "AARP Opposes Bush Plan to Replace Social Security with Private Accounts." *The New York Times.*

xxxvi. Viceira, Luis M. and Helen H. Tung. (July 5, 2005). General Motors U.S. Pension Funds. HBS Publishing Case No.: 9-206-001; Teaching Note No.: 5-206-098.

xxxvii. Perry, Alan H., Charles J. Clark, and Zorast Wadia. (2018). "Milliman Corporate Pension Funding Study (PFS)."

xxxviii. Chappatta, Brian and Edward Bolingbroke. (January 24, 2018). "Wall Street Warns of Seismic Pension Shift Into Bonds This Month."

xxxix. Stackhouse, Julie. (April 25, 2017). "Why Are There So Many Bank Regulators?" St. Louis Federal Reserve.

xl. Public Law 73-66, 73d Congress, H.R. 5661. Banking Act of 1933 (Glass-Steagall Act). (June 16, 1933).

xli. Public Law 106-102, 106th Congress, H.R. 10. GRAMM–LEACH–BLILEY ACT. (November 12, 1999).

xlii. Alessandri, Piergiorgio and Benjamin Nelson. (2014). "Simple Banking: Profitability and the Yield Curve." No. 945, Temi di discussione (Economic working papers). Bank of Italy. Economic Research and International Relations Area.

xliii. https://www.federalreserve.gov/releases/h8/current/.

xliv. Board of Governors of the Federal Reserve System (U.S.). (June 8, 2018). Bank Credit at All Commercial Banks [LOANINV], retrieved from FRED, Federal Reserve Bank of St. Louis. https://fred.stlouisfed.org/series/LOANINV.

xlv. Baily, Martin Neil, William Bekker, and Sarah E. Holmes. (May 2015). "The big four banks: The evolution of the financial sector, Part I." Economic Studies at Brookings.

xlvi. Ibid.

xlvii. Elliott, Douglas J. (June 2015). "Market Liquidity: A Primer." Economic Studies at Brookings.

xlviii. Board of Governors of the Federal Reserve System (U.S.). Financial Accounts of the United States—Z.1, L.115 Property-Casualty Insurance Companies.

xlix. Board of Governors of the Federal Reserve System (U.S.). Financial Accounts of the United States—Z.1, L.116 Life Insurance Companies.

l. "Low Interest Rate Environment Issues Faced by Property-Casualty Insurance Companies." (2015). Casualty Actuarial Society (CAS).

li. Berends, Kyal et al. (2013). "The sensitivity of life insurance firms to interest rate changes." Federal Reserve Bank of Chicago.

lii. Best's Insurance Reports. Fire and Miscellaneous, 9th ed. (New York: A.M. Best Company, Inc., 1908–1909). p. 140.

liii. http://www.naic.org/index_about.htm.

liv. Wong, Michael. (March 13, 2018). National Association of Insurance Commissioners & The Center for Insurance Policy and Research. Capital Markets Special Report "U.S. Insurance Industry's Exposure to Bonds with NAIC 2 Designations."

lv. https://eresearch.fidelity.com.

lvi. Division of Investment Management United States Securities and Exchange Commission. (May 1992). "Protecting Investors: A Half Century of Investment Company Regulation."

lvii. Title 17: Commodity and Securities Exchanges. PART 230—GENERAL RULES AND REGULATIONS, SECURITIES ACT OF 1933. §230.501 Definitions and terms used in Regulation D.

lviii. U.S. Securities and Exchange Commission. "Fast Answers: Hedge Funds". www.sec.gov.

lix. 2018 Investment Company Fact Book. Investment Company Institute. Figure 1.1.

lx. Benjamin, Jeff. (August 8, 2018). "10 largest mutual fund companies by assets." www.InvestmentNews.com.

lxi. HFR Global Hedge Fund Industry Report—Q4 2017. Hedge Fund Research (HFR). www.hedgefundresearch.com.

lxii. "The largest managers of hedge funds." (September 17, 2018). *Pensions & Investments*.

lxiii. Huang, Jennifer, Kelsey D. Wei, , and Hong Yan. (2007). "Participation costs and the sensitivity of fund flows to past performance." *Journal of Finance 62*. pp. 1273–1311.

lxiv. What Factors Drive Investment Flows? (May 22, 2018). Quantitative Analytics Quarterly. Morningstar.

lxv. Rohleder, Martin. (February 4, 2015). "The Relation between Past Flows and Future Performance: Simple Investment Strategies in the Mutual Fund Sector." International Journal of Financial Studies. 3, 3–10.

lxvi. Baquero, Guillermo and Marno Verbeek. (2015). "Hedge fund flows and performance streaks: How investors weigh information." ESMT Research Working Papers ESMT-15-01, ESMT European School of Management and Technology.

lxvii. Van Rij, Marnix et al. (2016). EY Family Office Guide: Pathway to successful family and wealth management. Ernst & Young GmbH. p. 5.

lxviii. Luisa Kroll with Lea Goldman. (February 28, 2002). The World's Billionaires. *Forbes*. https://www.forbes.com/2002/02/28/billionaires .html#6381bc79797b.

lxix. Kroll, Luisa and Kerry Dolan. (March 6, 2018). Meet the Members of the Three-Comma Club. *Forbes*. https://www.forbes.com/ billionaires/#5b46214a251c.

lxx. The UBS/Campden Wealth Global Family Office Report 2018. p. 11.

lxxi. The UBS/Campden Wealth Global Family Office Report 2018. p. 16.

lxxii. The UBS/Campden Wealth Global Family Office Report 2018. p. 17.

lxxiii. The UBS/Campden Wealth Global Family Office Report 2018. Figures 1.5 and 1.6.

lxxiv. Amit, Raphael and Heinrich Liechtenstein. (November 2009). "Benchmarking the Single Family Office: Identifying the Performance Drivers." Wharton Global Family Alliance. Figure 7.

4

GLOBAL CENTRAL BANKS
AND THE FEDERAL RESERVE

In his September 2016 Investment Outlook, Bill Gross made headlines when he wrote:

> *Speaking of practice, and mastering a game, Fed Chairwoman Janet Yellen has been at it a long time, as have her predecessors and contemporaries in other central banks. All have mastered the art of market manipulation—and no, that's not an unkind accusation—it's one, in fact, that Ms. Yellen and other central bankers would plead guilty to over a cocktail at Jackson Hole. . . .*[i]

Gross has a long history of making headlines when delivering direct, memorable, accurate, and at times, punitive market commentary. For example, in March 2002, he took aim at GE Capital and wrote that GE "is using near-hedge fund leverage"—attributing earnings growth to GE's reliance on cheap financing from its $127 billion in short-term debt. He went on to state that his fund would not own GE debt.[ii] By mid-April, GE stock had fallen 17.9% versus the S&P 500 falling 4.2%. In the following years, GE's *AAA* credit-rating was downgraded, and in June 2018, GE was removed from the Dow 30 after 110 years of continuous membership. In June 2007 in another famous Investment Outlook, when referring to AAA-rated securities, Gross wrote that "Mr. Moody's and Mr. Poor's" had been "wooed by the makeup, those six-inch hooker heels, and a tramp stamp" and "many of these good-looking girls are not high-class assets worth 100 cents on the dollar."[iii] By 2010, hundreds of billions of dollars' worth of AAA-rated securities had been downgraded to *junk* status.[iv] Lawsuits over S&P and Moody's rating methodologies ensued, and in 2013 S&P and Moody's settled with private institutions for an undisclosed amount,[v] and in 2015 S&P agreed to pay $1.5 billion to the U.S. Department of Justice along with 19 states and the District of Columbia.[vi]

With a track record like that, when Gross takes aim at an institution, market participants take note. But, unlike GE or S&P, the central banks to which Gross is referring are not profit-maximizing private institutions that are held accountable by stakeholders and regulators. Rather, central banks are public institutions with their own objectives and tools—they are the regulators, and per Gross's observation, have become masters at market manipulation. This observation begs many follow-up questions:

- What are central banks and what are their objectives?
- What are their motivations and reaction functions?
- How do they engage in this manipulation?
- And most important: given these motivations, tools, and reaction functions, how can we as investors benefit from this knowledge?

These are critical questions, and one's I'll tackle in this chapter.

BRIEF HISTORY OF THE BANK OF ENGLAND AND THE FEDERAL RESERVE

In the late-17th century in England, the Kingdom of England's public finances were in a precarious state caused by a costly war with France. The short-term solution came in 1694 in the form of establishing the Bank of England; this private institution would issue bank notes, or paper currency as we use today, with public debt as collateral.[vii] At the time, the bank's mandate was limited to supporting the raising of public debt, which ensured that public services could continue. The Bank of England's importance and mandate grew in the subsequent decades, and in 1844 the Bank of England was given the exclusive power to issue bank notes following the passage of the Bank Charter Act.[viii] Despite this public mandate, the Bank of England still largely operated as a private institution; during a series of banking panics from 1825 to 1866, the bank elevated the interests of its shareholders above that of the public financial system. This changed in 1873 when the Bank of England assumed the role as lender of last resort when it adopted the Thornton-Bagehot *Responsibility Doctrine*.[ix] This doctrine, named for framers Henry Thornton and Walter Bagehot, includes six principles:

1. Protecting the money stock and not institutions
2. Allowing insolvent institutions to fail
3. Only accommodating sound (solvent) institutions
4. Charging penalizing rates

5. Requiring sound collateral for loans
6. Announcing the terms of support (collateral, rates, etc.) ahead of a banking crisis

This doctrine, and the responsibility that the Bank of England assumed following its adoption, made the Bank of England the lender of last resort *par excellence* through the late-20th century.[x]

Across the pond, the United States had experienced a banking crisis in 1873 and in 1893, yet support for the chartering of a central bank was limited; but this changed in the early 1900s. On October 22, 1907, Knickerbocker Trust experienced a bank run and was forced to suspend operations.[xi] The most famous banker at the time, J.P. Morgan, examined Knickerbocker Trust's assets and had concluded that the trust was not solvent; so, he opted to not lend to the institution and sealed its fate. Panic spread, and other trust companies experienced significant withdrawals, including Trust Company of America. After an audit of Trust Company of America's books by J.P Morgan's lieutenants revealed the institution to be solvent, J.P. Morgan asserted, "This is the place to stop the trouble, then." He quickly organized a consortium including other trust companies, the U.S. Treasury, and John D. Rockefeller in order to extend loans to the trust to ensure it could continue to operate. A rapid withdrawal of deposits continued among several other trusts and a week later J.P. Morgan assembled the city's most senior bank and trust officials in his personal library at his residence to discuss the extension of $25 million in loans from the stronger trusts to the weaker trusts. The bankers initially balked but soon learned they had been locked into J.P. Morgan's library and would not be able to leave until they had agreed to the plan of raising the necessary funds to ensure that all trusts remained liquid. At 4:45 a.m., the bankers signed an agreement to pool their reserves and were allowed to return home.[xii] With this action, the banking crisis subsided.

Because the United States did not have a lender of last resort akin to the Bank of England, J.P. Morgan assumed this role to the benefit of the nation. Additionally, while not required by law, his actions followed the Bank of England's *Responsibility Doctrine* and were viewed by many U.S. citizens and Europeans as heroic. However, others in the U.S. viewed his actions with skepticism and feared the power that an unelected individual had over the country's banking system. As a result, in the aftermath of the Panic of 1907, the need for a more appropriate backstop became self-evident. In 1911 the National Monetary Commission published a paper recommending the creation of a central bank in the U.S., and in 1913 the U.S. Congress passed the Federal Reserve Act, forming the U.S. Federal Reserve System.[xiii]

THE FEDERAL RESERVE AND OTHER GLOBAL CENTRAL BANKS

Central Bank Objectives

While the genesis of each of today's global central banks varies, their mandates and tools are nearly identical. The world's most influential central banks include the U.S. Federal Reserve (Fed), the European Central Bank (ECB), the Bank of Japan (BOJ), the Bank of England (BOE), and the People's Bank of China (PBC). These institutions are responsible for conducting their nations' monetary policy in accordance to their mandated objectives. These objectives generally include price stability (i.e., low inflation), financial stability, stable economic growth, or in the case of the U.S., *maximum employment*. These institutions also promote the soundness of financial institutions within their jurisdictions, ensure their currencies remain stable and available for settlement and exchange of goods and other currencies, and they may promote consumer protection. That said, should central bank objectives ever conflict, the highest priority objective for central banks (including the ECB, BOJ, and BOE) is price stability (low inflation). For the remainder of this chapter, I will focus exclusively on the U.S. Federal Reserve because it is the world's most powerful central bank and because it shares enough in common with other central banks in terms of its objectives, policies, and tools that a review of each central bank would be largely redundant.

Meetings, Policies, and Statements

The Federal Reserve was granted sole authority to create bank notes, or official U.S. currency following the passage of the Federal Reserve Act in 1913.[xiv] Additionally, this act established a Federal Reserve Board of Governors to serve as the chief governing body of the Federal Reserve system; it was made up of seven members who would be nominated by the President and confirmed by the Senate. The Banking Act of 1935 further defined the structure of the Federal Reserve; specifically, this act established the members of the Board of Governors, along with five rotating members of the twelve Federal Reserve Banks, would constitute the 12-member Federal Open Market Committee (FOMC), as shown in Figure 4.1. The FOMC is responsible for setting monetary policy in accordance with the Federal Reserve's mandate.[xv]

The Federal Reserve's mandate, as it relates to employment and inflation, wasn't added until 1977. In 1974, Congress adopted Resolution 133, which instructed the Federal Reserve to "maintain long-run growth of the monetary and credit aggregates commensurate with the economy's long-run potential to

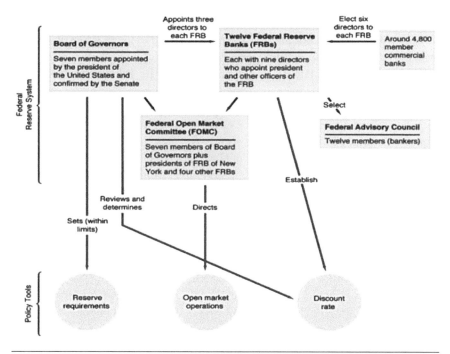

Figure 4.1   Structure of the Federal Reserve. *Source*: Mishkin, Frederic S. *The Economics of Money, Banking, and Financial Markets*[xvi]

increase production, so as to promote effectively the goals of maximum employment, stable prices, and moderate long-term interest rates."[xvii] In 1977, Congress amended the Federal Reserve Act to incorporate the maximum employment, stable prices, and moderate long-term interest rate objectives. In practice, many central bank officials contend "moderate long-term interest rates" are a result of price stability and an economy at full employment; therefore, targeting long-term rates is not a focal point of policy discussions. Thus, the Federal Reserve is left with what is today referred to as a *dual mandate* of low inflation and low unemployment.

Eight times a year, the Board of Governors and the presidents of the twelve Federal Reserve Banks gather in Washington D.C. Approximately two weeks before the meeting, the Federal Reserve releases to the public its *Beige Book*. This book is a compilation of anecdotal information on economic conditions collected by each of the twelve Federal Reserve Banks from interviews with business contacts, economists, and other sources. FOMC members review this as well as the *Tealbook* (discussed later) in preparation for the biquarterly meeting. During the two-day meeting, which occurs roughly every six weeks, the FOMC considers three questions: (1) How is the U.S. economy likely to evolve in the near and medium term, (2) what is the appropriate monetary policy setting to help move the economy over the medium term to the FOMC's goal of 2% inflation and maximum employment, and (3) how can the FOMC effectively communicate its expectations for the economy and its policy decisions to the public?[xviii]

The agenda for these meetings is relatively standard and typically begins with housekeeping items such as the election of committee officers or the review of special topics by committee members. Next, the committee hears a report from the Federal Reserve Bank of New York staff covering recent financial developments and the status of open market operations. Committee members then hear from staff members who review *Tealbook A*, subtitled *Economic and Financial Conditions: Current Situation and Outlook*. Following this review, committee members then discuss the staff report and develop their own outlook. After this discussion, committee members then hear from staff members who review *Tealbook B*, subtitled *Monetary Policy: Strategies and Alternatives*. After this, committee members discuss their views on appropriate monetary policy and attempt to come to a consensus. Once an action (including the decision to not act) is agreed upon, the meeting concludes with members discussing how they will communicate their policy decision. Following the conclusion of the meeting on the second day, the FOMC releases a statement irrespective of whether or not there was a change in policy. The chairman then holds a press conference that includes a prepared statement and Q&A. Every other meeting, the Fed also releases an updated summary of economic projections (SEP), which includes the Fed's forecasts for gross domestic product (GDP) growth, inflation, and the policy rate. The minutes for the meeting are released about three weeks after the meeting.[xix]

Answering the Three Most Important Questions

As mentioned previously, the first question the members of the FOMC must answer is: how is the U.S. economy likely to evolve in the near and medium term? *Tealbook A* is intended to assist members with answering this question by keeping FOMC members highly informed and facilitating discussion during the two-day meeting. The data included in this book includes (but is not limited to) employment figures (unemployment, job creation, labor force participation), manufacturing production, commodity prices, residential construction, consumer and business sentiment, fiscal outlook, market conditions for including equity prices, interest rates, credit spreads, etc. Given this information, the staff generates its outlook for GDP growth, inflation, and employment over the next one to two years.[xx] To create these forecasts, staff members use a variety of mathematical and empirical models (there is no shortage of highly intelligent

PhD's on staff at the Federal Reserve) and much of the methodology for their models can be traced to economic literature. Once the FOMC has opined and the forecasts for GDP, employment, and inflation are finalized, the focus of the economic discussion can shift from point estimates (what will unemployment or inflation be in two years) to answering the question: how will the economy *evolve*? The evolution of the economy is more relevant to the subsequent discussion concerning appropriate monetary policy since achieving the Federal Reserve's mandates requires it to be proactive and not reactive. For example, imagine unemployment is forecast to be 6% in the following year; what should the Federal Reserve do, given this point estimate? If unemployment is currently 5%, a 6% unemployment forecast indicates that the economy will weaken, whereas if unemployment is currently 7%, then a 6% forecast indicates that the economy will strengthen. Similarly, the FOMC will forecast inflation and GDP growth, and, conditional on the starting circumstances, the committee is able to forecast whether economic growth is increasing or decreasing, whether inflation is accelerating or decelerating, and whether employment is improving or deteriorating. Given this collective outlook, the FOMC can address what it views as the *balance of risks*, meaning, what is of greatest concern to the Federal Reserve (inflation, economic output, or unemployment).[xxi]

Once the FOMC has reached a consensus on the near- and medium-term economic outlook and balance of risks, the FOMC is now able to answer the second question: what is the appropriate monetary policy setting to help move the economy over the medium term to the FOMC's goal of 2% inflation and maximum employment? In general, if the FOMC views inflation as being of greater concern, this concern warrants a *tightening* in financial conditions, such that credit, money, and an economic expansion will slow. In theory, this should lead to a deceleration in price inflation. Conversely, if the FOMC views unemployment or a recession as the greater concern, this would warrant a *loosening* in financial conditions, leading to an expansion in credit and the money supply, thus stimulating economic growth and improving the demand for labor. If the FOMC views the risks to the economy and inflation to be balanced, this might warrant no change in financial conditions or monetary policy. But, how should the FOMC measure current financial conditions, as they relate to their current policy?

To help answer this question, FOMC members review and reference the staff-prepared *Tealbook B*. The data in this book includes the Federal Reserve staff outlook on the what it believes is the equilibrium (or *natural* or *neutral*) real interest rate, r*, as well as optimal policy rate given r*, and the staff's forecasts for economic growth, inflation, and employment. The FOMC defines r* as: *the level of the real short-term interest rate that, if obtained currently, would result in the economy operating at full employment or, in some simple models of* *the economy, at full employment [while achieving] price stability.*[xxii] So, how does the staff forecast the optimal policy rate given all of these inputs? The Federal Reserve staff uses several economic models, but the original and most easily understood (and still used today) is the *Taylor Rule*. This *rule* was first proposed by economist John B. Taylor in 1993[xxiii] in his paper titled "Discretion versus policy rules in practice." In it, he includes an equation that suggests an appropriate monetary policy rule is:

$$r = p + .5y + .5(p - 2) + 2$$

where:

   r is the federal funds rate
   p is the rate of inflation over the previous four quarters
   y is the percent deviation of real GDP from a target

This rule has been popular among both economists and FOMC officials because it offers a simple policy prescription given the measurable and relevant inputs including the current policy rate, inflation, and economic output. This *rule* is also highly relevant for investors to monitor because it provides insight into the Federal Reserve's reaction function—the likely future path of the policy rate. Specifically, not only do we know that the Federal Reserve will raise its policy rate if economic growth or inflation increase, but by using this model, we can estimate the magnitude of that move. Conversely, if GDP growth or inflation falls, the Federal Reserve will lower its policy rate, and using this model we can estimate the magnitude of that change as well.

Once the FOMC has established a near-term economic outlook and settles on whether or not this outlook warrants tightening, loosening, or no change to monetary policy, the FOMC is in a position to answer its final question: how can the FOMC effectively communicate its expectations for the economy and its policy decisions to the public? This communication initially comes in the form of a statement that is released at the end of each two-day meeting. Also included in *Tealbook B* are the last FOMC statement as well as three potential revisions to the statement, written by Federal Reserve staff members; this "menu" of policy statements includes a rationale for each statement. FOMC officials then discuss each statement and either select one of the three statements, or revise one of the statements to best reflect the FOMC's views on the balance of risks. Typically, at 2:00 p.m. EST on the second day of the meeting, the new FOMC statement is released to the media and uploaded to the Federal Reserve website. Within seconds, interest rates move higher or lower as market participants dissect each word of the statement in order to glean information regarding the likely path of interest rates. Particular focus is given to revisions to the prior statement that relate to the economy, inflation, and employment. Modest changes that include qualifiers like *strengthened*, or *moderated*, may indicate the Fed is becoming increasingly hawkish (worried about inflation) or dovish (worried about employment). Additionally, the FOMC statement usually mentions the word "risk" in a single sentence. In that sentence the FOMC highlights what it perceives to be the greater risk to achieving its dual mandate. For example:

- June 13, 2018: *Risks to the economic outlook appear roughly balanced.*
- January 25, 2012: *Strains in global financial markets continue to pose significant downside risks to the economic outlook.*
- December 11, 2007: *The committee judges that some inflation risks remain, and it will continue to monitor inflation developments carefully.* (They got that wrong.)

Fed Day—What to Look For

As mentioned, the FOMC meets eight times a year, after which a statement is released, the chair then reads a prepared statement, and he or she then holds a public Q&A. Additionally, after every other meeting the FOMC releases an updated SEP that shows the FOMC's forecasts for GDP growth, inflation, and the policy rate. So, what do market participants care about on Fed day? And, if you work in a capacity that is impacted by the FOMC policy rate, what should *you* care about? In short, participants focus primarily on changes in FOMC views. Changes in views, including the Federal Reserve's assessment of the economy, labor market, and inflation, portend changes in FOMC policy. Therefore, upgrades to the economic outlook or labor conditions are considered *hawkish*, which is another way of saying that the FOMC is inclined to reduce liquidity and increase the policy rate. Meanwhile, downgrades to the economic or labor outlook are considered *dovish*, which is to say that the FOMC is inclined to support the financial sector by increasing liquidity and reducing the policy rate. Meanwhile, an increase in the inflation forecast is considered *hawkish* while a decrease in the inflation forecast is considered *dovish*. A change in the economic, labor, or inflation outlook may come in the form of a revision to the statement, a change in the SEP, part of the chairman's speech, or even an off-the-cuff remark. With respect to the FOMC statement, the single most important sentence is what the FOMC describes as its *balance of risks*. If the balance of risk shifts from *balanced* to concern with the economy or labor market, the FOMC is telegraphing future policy will be dovish. Meanwhile, if the balance of risks shifts from *balanced* to concern with higher inflation, the FOMC is telegraphing future policy will be hawkish.

IMPLEMENTING FEDERAL RESERVE POLICY

Once the FOMC has settled on its monetary policy, what tools can the Federal Reserve use to implement this policy? Quite a few. The Federal Reserve's tools can be divided into two categories, as shown in Figure 4.2: *traditional* and *nontraditional*. Traditional tools include open market operations, excess reserve borrowing, discount window lending, and reserve requirement management. Nontraditional monetary policy includes forward guidance and asset purchases. I'll cover each tool, one by one.

Open Market Operations

Open market operations include the purchase and sale of typically U.S. Treasuries to primary dealers—such as Bank of America, J.P Morgan, and Citigroup—and this is done on behalf of the System Open Market Account (SOMA). SOMA is the account into which all assets that are purchased by the Federal Reserve are housed.[xxv] Since 1936, the New York Fed has been selected among the 12 reserve banks to engage in open market operations on behalf of all of the Federal Reserve Banks. To engage in these operations, the New York Fed utilizes its own trading desk.[xxvi] The objective of open market operations is to set short-term (generally overnight) interest rates. The FOMC, in each announcement following its two-day meeting, specifies the federal funds rate, which is also its *policy rate*. The federal funds rate is the interest rate at which depository institutions trade federal funds, which are balances held at Federal Reserve Banks,

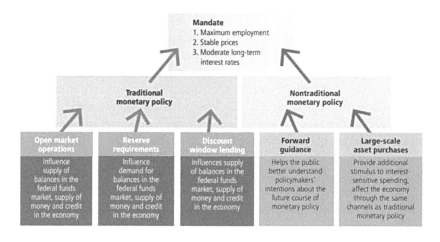

Figure 4.2   The Federal Reserve's mandate and tools. *Source*: The Federal Reserve[xxiv]

with each other for an overnight term.[xxvii] This federal funds target includes a 0.25% range (e.g., 1.75% to 2.0%); prior to December 2008 the target was a specific point (e.g., 1.0%).[xxviii] The balances held at Federal Reserve Banks are the required reserves that banks must place with the Federal Reserve plus any balances that banks voluntarily choose to deposit with the Federal Reserve. For example, if required reserves are set at 10% of bank deposits, for each $100 a customer deposits at a commercial bank, that bank must then deposit $10 in their local Federal Reserve Bank. This reserve requirement limits the ability of the bank to generate new loans, which in turn caps the aggregate money supply.

If a bank ever falls short of its required reserves, that bank can borrow reserves from another bank at the Federal Fund rate. For example, let's say there are two banks, each with $100 million in deposits and each is required to post $10 million to their local Federal Reserve Bank. If Bank A only has $8 million deposited at the Federal Reserve, while Bank B has $12 million deposited at the Federal Reserve, Bank B may lend $2 million to Bank A, and the rate that Bank A pays to Bank B for an overnight loan is the federal funds rate. The FOMC sets the rate at which the two banks transact by engaging in open market operations. Imagine that the interest rate that the two banks negotiate is 1.875% (the mid-point of the targeted federal funds rate), and the following day the FOMC raises the targeted Federal Fund rate by +0.25% to 2.0% to 2.25%. Following this update in FOMC policy, the Federal Reserve Bank of New York will respond by making liquidity more expensive. To do this, the New York Fed will sell Treasuries to other banks (in the open market). Imagine now that the Federal Reserve sells Bank B $2 million of a short-term Treasury with an interest rate at 2.125%; in this case, Bank B will no longer have $2 million in excess reserves available to lend to Bank A. Bank A, in turn, will have to find another bank with excess reserves, and Bank A will likely pay an interest rate in excess of 2.125%. Thus, through this simple exchange of a short-term Treasury for cash, the Federal Reserve would have accomplished its objective of raising the overnight borrowing costs for banks.

For decades this approach was successful as banks, which are profit maximizing entities, attempted to minimize the quantity of reserves it held at the Federal Reserve. On any given day in the early 2000s, about $200 billion in federal funds traded as banks with reserve shortages used this market to ensure that they posted sufficient reserves at the Federal Reserve. Additionally, by injecting or removing relatively small amounts of cash in the banking system, the FOMC could directly impact the interest rate at which these banks transacted. However, this changed in 2008 following the global financial crisis for two reasons. First, the Federal Reserve reduced interest rates to roughly 0.0%, and it did this by purchasing Treasury securities from banks, which in turn raised bank cash balances. Second, the Federal Reserve began paying interest on excess reserves at a rate higher than the federal funds rate. As a result, almost overnight banks became incentivized to place growing excess reserves at the Federal Reserve and not lend excess reserves in the federal funds market. Owing to these two developments, the daily volume of federal funds fell from around $200 billion to $400 billion in 2008 to around $50 to $100 billion by 2012.[xxix]

The reduction in the size of the federal funds market would not be a material concern to the FOMC if it intended to maintain the policy rate at ~0.0%. However, Federal Reserve officials knew that when the FOMC began raising the policy rate, the Federal Reserve would need to remove excess cash from the banking system. One option would be to sell many of the securities that the FOMC had purchased in the preceding years; however, fearing the impact on the shape of the yield curve should the FOMC begin a rapid sale of securities, FOMC officials developed a new tool to help increase the cost of overnight financing: a reverse repurchase facility. In March 2010, the Federal Reserve Bank of New York announced that it was initiating a program whereby it would conduct "temporary open market operations" directly with eligible money market mutual funds.[xxx] Specifically, the Federal Reserve Bank of New York would engage in transactions whereby money market funds would transfer cash to the SOMA portfolio and receive treasury collateral in return. These loans would generally be overnight, and at the expiry of the loan, cash plus interest would be transferred to the money market funds and collateral would be transferred back to the SOMA portfolio. The interest rate for these overnight loans would be equal to the lower-bound of the federal funds target rate, which in theory would provide a *floor* to the targeted federal funds rate. At the time of the announcement, there was $2.6 trillion in money market fund assets,[xxxi] and while only a small fraction of the managers responsible for those assets would become eligible counterparties, the FOMC believed trading with an additional body of institutions would be a useful complement following the shrinking federal funds market. As of December 2018, there are 30 fund managers and 98 money market funds that are approved to trade directly with the Federal Reserve Bank of New York.[xxxii] As of Q2 2018, daily usage of this facility is relatively light ($0 to $10 billion); however, usage of the facility regularly spikes around year-end and was $319 billion on December 29, 2017.[xxxiii]

While transacting with commercial banks and select money market funds constitutes the primary open market operations that are currently in use, it is worthwhile to briefly mention several of the facilities that were created in 2008 and 2009, and subsequently retired in 2009 and 2010. These facilities include:[xxxiv]

- Commercial Paper Funding Facility: which purchased and rolled commercial paper from eligible issuers. This alleviated short-term financing needs of highly rated commercial paper issuers.

- Money Market Investor Funding Facility: which provided short-term financing to money market funds in exchange for highly rated collateral. This facility gave money market funds the ability to meet client withdrawals without selling short-term holdings.
- Primary Dealer Credit Facility: which extended short-term financing to primary dealers, like Morgan Stanley or Bank of America, in exchange for eligible collateral. This was created following the failure of Bear Stearns and was intended to alleviate short-term funding needs of other primary dealers.
- Term Securities Lending Facility: which extended loans with a tenor of at least one month to eligible primary dealers. This facility allowed dealers to better manage intermediate-financing needs.
- Term Asset-Backed Securities Loan Facility: which extended financing to institutions that purchased eligible collateral, including auto loans, student loans, credit card loans, equipment loans, insurance premium finance loans, and loans guaranteed by the Small Business Administration. This facility helped with the demand for assets that were trading at fire-sale prices.
- Fed swap lines, which lent U.S. dollars to other global central banks in exchange for their foreign currency. In mid-2007, European banks began experiencing a dollar shortage, which caused dollar financing levels to rise and intraday volatility in the U.S. federal funds market. The shortage of dollars dramatically increased following the failure of Lehman Brothers in September 2008, and this shortage led to significant stress among both advanced and emerging economies. In response, the Fed opened swap lines with the ECB and the Swiss National Bank (SNB) in December 2007. In September and October 2008, the Fed expanded the swap program to eight additional advanced and four emerging economies, and the Fed removed caps on several of the swap lines. This effectively allowed the U.S. Federal Reserve to function as the world's reserve currency lender of last resort. Use of these lines peaked at $580 billion in late 2008 and were closed in February 2010.[xxxv]

Each of these facilities was approved by the Federal Reserve System Board of Governors under Section 13(3) of the Federal Reserve Act, which specifies the powers of the Federal Reserve Banks. The creation of facilities marked a dramatic, albeit temporary, increase in the Federal Reserve's influence in the day-to-day functioning of the financial markets. In short, these facilities accomplished their objectives and were successfully wound down without incurring losses to the Federal Reserve or the taxpayer. While these facilities are no longer in existence, the legacy of the Federal Reserve's actions in 2008 and 2009 still impacts today's financial markets. I'll explore that impact later in this chapter.

Discount Window Lending

When the Federal Reserve System was established in 1913, the discount window was expected to be the primary mechanism by which the Federal Reserve implemented monetary policy, established a policy rate, and enhanced the stability of the financial system during a crisis. And until 1923,[xxxvi] when open market became the Federal Reserve's primary mechanism for establishing a policy rate, the discount window served this purpose. But what is the discount window? The *discount window* is the permanent lending facility, offered by each regional Federal Reserve Bank, and is accessible to commercial banks and other depository institutions. The *discount* portion of the name indicates that when collateral is posted to a Federal Reserve Bank, the size of that loan was given a discount (typically referred to as a *haircut* today) to the value of the collateral. The *window* is a historical reference to when a customer would go to a bank teller and would typically interact with the teller through a window. The discount window currently offers:[xxxvii]

- *Primary credit*: generally overnight loans at a rate above the federal funds rate
- *Secondary credit*: generally overnight loans at a rate +0.50% above the *primary credit*
- *Seasonal credit*: loans intended to help small depository institutions manage seasonal swings in deposits
- *Emergency credit*: loans approved by the Secretary of the Treasury

So, what is the facility's utility, and why did the architects of the Federal Reserve believe this would be the mechanism for increasing financial stability? Remember from earlier in this chapter that in 1873 the BOE adopted the Thornton-Begehot *Responsibility Doctrine*. This doctrine established the BOE as the lender of last resort, which would provide temporary financing to solvent institutions in exchange for collateral, while charging a penalizing rate to discourage banks from using this facility in normal circumstances. Additionally, the availability of this window and the terms of its usage would be announced in advance of a crisis. Also, remember that during the U.S. Panic of 1907, there was no central bank in the United States that was able to act as the lender of last resort, and so J.P. Morgan was forced to assume this responsibility. So, when the Federal Reserve was established in 1913, its architects believed the discount window would allow the Federal Reserve to function as America's lender of last resort. It was further believed that had the discount window been available to banks in 1907, the *panic* would have been much more subdued and J.P. Morgan would not have needed to have gone to the great lengths he did to avert a financial crisis.

Currently, the primary credit discount rate is 0.50% above the upper band of the federal funds target. When the FOMC announces a change in the federal funds rate, the discount rate regularly moves in the same direction and by the same magnitude. As a result, the discount rate serves as a theoretical *upper bound* of the targeted short-term interest rate corridor. To understand this principle, imagine that the federal funds target rate is 1.75% to 2.0% and the discount rate is 2.50%. In an instance when banks experience a large, sudden, and unexpected withdrawal of deposits (like in 1907 or 2008), bank reserves will fall. A bank that is needing reserves will borrow excess reserves from other banks at any rate below 2.50%, but not higher. Why? If a bank has the option of borrowing from another bank at 2.51% or from the Federal Reserve at 2.50%, they will borrow from the Federal Reserve at 2.50%. In practice, the actual rate at which banks borrow reserves may exceed the discount rate because utilizing the discount window has a stigma associated with it.[xxxviii] In 2007, general usage of the facility remained less than $1 billion, but it spiked to over $400 billion in October 2008, despite both the stigma and other lending facilities being available to banks. By 2013, usage of the facility was once again generally less than $1 billion.[xxxix]

Excess Reserve Targeting

Excess reserves are the reserves commercial banks deposit with the Federal Reserve in excess of the required reserves, as the name suggests. Many global central banks pay an interest rate on these reserves because it further enables the central bank to ensure its policy rate remains within a narrow band. How's that? Imagine the targeted federal funds rate is 2.0% to 2.25%, and the interest rate the Federal Reserve will pay on excess reserves is set at 2.0%, and the discount rate is 2.50%, as shown in Figure 4.3. Remember, the federal funds rate is the rate banks charge each other for overnight loans for reserves. If the Federal Reserve paid an interest rate of 2.0% on excess reserves, the federal funds rate would never trade below 2.0%. This is because no bank would agree to lend reserves at a rate lower than the rate it would earn if it deposited excess reserves at the Federal Reserve. Conversely, in this example the Federal Reserve could set a ceiling of the federal funds rate equal to the discount rate, as mentioned previously. Thus, the Federal Reserve has created a corridor which will ensure its policy rate remains in a tight range every day.

Despite the utility of paying interest on reserves, not all central banks offered interest on excess reserves (IOER). In 1999, the ECB was established and its officials received the authority to pay IOER.[xl] Seven years later, the Federal Reserve also gained this authority when the U.S. Congress passed the Financial

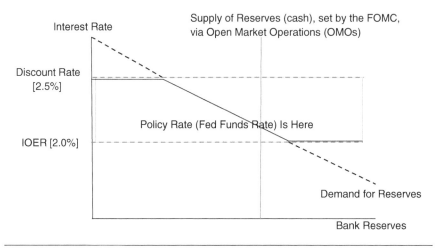

Figure 4.3   Envisioned policy rate corridor before 2008

Services Regulatory Relief Act of 2006,[1] which would allow the Federal Reserve to start paying IOER in 2011.[xli] At the time this law was passed, excess reserves were around $1.9 billion,[xlii] while around $200 billion in reserves traded daily in the federal funds market. So, in 2006, lawmakers and Federal Reserve officials anticipated the actual interest paid on these reserves would be relatively small, and this complementary tool would merely serve to assist the Federal Reserve Bank of New York to more tightly manage the federal funds rate. That's not what happened.

Following the failure of Lehman Brothers, the U.S. Congress passed the Emergency Economic Stabilization Act of 2008, which authorized the U.S. Treasury to purchase up to $700 billion in distressed assets. Included in this bill was the authorization of the Federal Reserve to immediately begin paying interest on excess reserves. At the same time that the Federal Reserve was establishing the aforementioned liquidity facilities, banks began depositing reserves with the Federal Reserve en masse. By November 2008, excess reserves had jumped to $558 billion. Then on November 25, 2008, the Federal Reserve announced it would initiate a program to purchase $600 billion in assets, of which $500

---

[1] In 1969, Nobel Laureate Milton Friedman presented a theoretical rationale for the payment of IOER; the argument was that the optimal opportunity cost of holding money (and by extension, the opportunity cost of a commercial bank's deposits at the Federal Reserve) should be zero. In order to achieve a zero-marginal cost of holding currency or excess reserves, the central bank must pay interest on those reserves. In practice, central bankers desired this tool—not because this interest rate properly balanced a theoretical monetary formula, although it was nice that Dr. Friedman agreed, but because interest on excess reserves could act as a floor to a central bank policy rate.

billion would be mortgage-backed securities.[xliii] The Federal Reserve would later announce two more similar programs. The net impact of these purchases and liquidity facilities was a fantastic increase in excess reserves. How did this happen? The Federal Reserve would purchase securities from a commercial bank (say, $1 billion of U.S. Treasuries). The commercial bank would in turn deposit that $1 billion back at the Federal Reserve in the form of excess reserves. So, why did the commercial bank deposit the cash with the Federal Reserve? It did this because the bank had no creditworthy borrowers in need of cash, its treasury was just purchased by the Federal Reserve, the bank is required to keep high-quality collateral by regulators, and the Federal Reserve was now paying IOER. Excess reserves would eventually peak in August 2014 at $2.7 trillion, as shown in Figure 4.4. In May 2018, excess reserves had fallen to $1.65 trillion.[xliv]

While Federal Reserve officials initially anticipated IOER would function as a floor for its policy rate, in 2009 IOER became the ceiling of its policy rate corridor. Remember that the federal funds market is the market in which a bank that requires reserves can borrow those reserves from another bank with excess reserves. But, what happens if there are no banks that need to borrow reserves because all banks have excess reserves? Then, the federal funds market largely ceases trading and all banks simply place their reserves at the Federal Reserve and earn IOER. In practice, there are a few institutions that can lend cash in the federal funds market but do not have access to IOER—but these are the exceptions and not the rule. These institutions with excess cash will then lend their cash to banks that have access to IOER, but at a discount to IOER. Thus, the clearing level for the federal funds market is below that of IOER, as shown

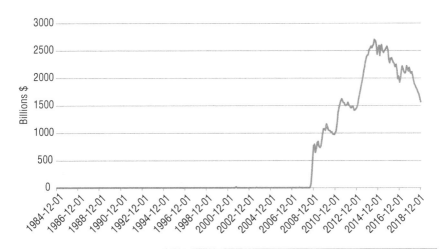

Figure 4.4 Excess reserves of U.S. depository institutions. *Source*: Federal Reserve[xlv]

in Figure 4.5. As of May 2018, the daily volume of federal funds is around $65 billion[xlvi]—or 4% the size of the excess reserves deposited at the Federal Reserve. While never formally admitted by FOMC officials, owing to the policies that the Federal Reserve put in place beginning in 2008 that led to the growth of the stock of excess reserves, *the de facto policy rate is no longer the federal funds rate, but the IOER rate.* Today, IOER is within a few basis points of the high end of the Federal Fund range specified by FOMC officials. In my opinion, IOER will remain the de facto policy rate until excess reserves decline to roughly zero and the federal funds market is once again the primary market utilized by banks to manage their reserve balances.

Additionally, the new floor for the federal funds rate has unintentionally become the Federal Reserve repurchase (repo) rate. Mentioned earlier in the chapter, the creation of this facility was announced in 2010 and it is the facility utilized by a limited number of money market funds in order to lend cash to the Federal Reserve. So, how is this the de facto floor for the Federal Reserve policy rate? Remember, the federal funds rate is the rate a bank will borrow cash to deposit with the Federal Reserve. Imagine, the reverse repo rate is 1.75% and interest on excess reserves is 2.0%. In this case, a money market fund will not lend cash to a bank at a rate lower than the reverse repo rate (1.75%) because a money market fund with excess cash will always attempt to maximize the interest earned on that cash. Said another way, a money market fund will not lend cash to a bank at 1.74% or lower when it can place cash at the Federal Reserve at 1.75%. Therefore, a bank looking to raise cash will borrow it from a money market fund at a rate no lower than 1.75%, which is the overnight rate of the reverse repo facility, the effective floor for the federal funds rate.

Between 2015 and 2018, the FOMC raised interest rates nine times. As shown in Figure 4.6, in each instance the FOMC simultaneously raised the discount

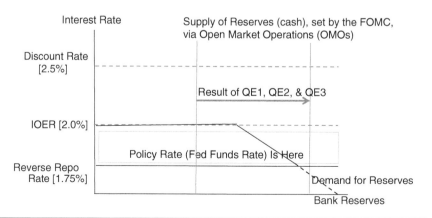

Figure 4.5   Current policy rate corridor

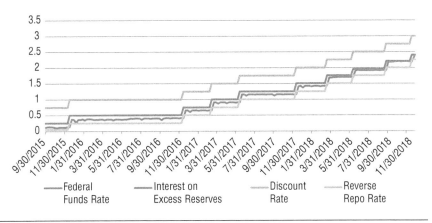

3.5
3
2.5
2
1.5
1
0.5
0

9/30/2015 11/30/2015 1/31/2016 3/31/2016 5/31/2016 7/31/2016 9/30/2016 11/30/2016 1/31/2017 3/31/2017 5/31/2017 7/31/2017 9/30/2017 11/30/2017 1/31/2018 3/31/2018 5/31/2018 7/31/2018 9/30/2018 11/30/2018

──── Federal Funds Rate   ──── Interest on Excess Reserves   ──── Discount Rate   ──── Reverse Repo Rate

Figure 4.6   Policy rate corridor: 2015–2018. *Source:* Bloomberg

rate, interest on excess reserves, the federal funds rate, and the reverse repo rate. Additionally, the spread between each rate remained constant. In the future, when excess reserves decline to roughly zero, the federal funds rate will drift higher than the interest on excess reserves rate but will always remain below the discount rate. Until then, the federal funds rate will remain below the excess reserves rate and above the reverse repo rate.

Reserve Requirements

As mentioned earlier in this chapter, the reserve requirement is the amount of funds that a depository institution must hold against specific liabilities. These reserves must be held in the form of vault cash or, more typically, deposits at a Federal Reserve Bank. The current reserve requirement as of 2018 for deposits at a bank in excess of $124.2 million is 10%.[xlvii] So, this means for every $100 you deposit at a mid-sized or large bank, $10 is transferred to a Federal Reserve Bank where it earns interest at a rate set by the FOMC. But what is the utility of reserve requirements? To answer this, we must briefly discuss a fractional reserve banking system and how this leads to the creation of money.

Imagine a small closed economy in which there are one million gold coins minted and used as currency. In this instance, the money supply is stable, and assuming economic output remains unchanged year over year, the price for those goods will also remain unchanged. Over time, people decided that using gold coins is inconvenient because of the risk that they are easily lost or stolen, or simply because they are heavy to carry. So, people deposit these gold coins at a bank, which then issues paper certificates that may be redeemed at any time for the gold coins (the coins are kept in a bank vault). These paper certificates eventually become a de facto currency as people exchange the gold coins for bank certificates. Now, if that bank issues only one paper certificate for each gold coin, then the bank essentially has a reserve of 100% because each liability of a deposit is fully covered by gold coins in a bank vault. But what happens if a person comes to the bank and requests a loan, and the bank accommodates by issuing additional paper certificates that are redeemable for gold coins? The bank has just created money! If this process is repeated and the bank extends a total of one million in loans against its one million in deposits, the total amount of paper currency now in circulation has become two million and the bank holds 50% in reserves. Assuming the output of our small closed economy remains unchanged, there will be significant price inflation as the quantity of money has doubled.

In this simple example, we see that bank lending practices directly impact the money supply. Our banking system today is a *fractional reserve* system whereby banks are required to hold reserves that are a fraction of their deposits, and this system gives banks the power to create and retire what we generally consider to be *money*. As such, while the Federal Reserve determines the monetary base—which is the quantity of paper currency in circulation plus bank deposits with Federal Reserve banks—the Federal Reserve does not directly control the money supply (which includes anything that can be quickly converted into cash). The relationship between the monetary base and the money supply can be approximated as:

- Money supply = monetary base × money multiplier
- Money multiplier = (1 / reserve requirement percentage)

Thus, if the reserve requirement is 10%, the money supply will be roughly 10× the monetary base. In practice, the actual money supply will be smaller than this due to banks choosing to hold excess reserves and people choosing to hold paper currency. Globally, as of 2010, around 93% of surveyed central banks have mandated reserve requirements and most banks' reserve requirements are between 6% and 15%.[xlviii]

Pivoting now to the Federal Reserve's reaction function when implementing policy, should inflation begin to increase, mathematically speaking, reducing the economy's money supply should reduce inflation. In short, fewer dollars chasing the same amount of goods will increase the relative value of the currency and reduce or reverse price inflation. This suggests the Federal Reserve should respond to increases in inflation by increasing bank reserve requirements. Conversely, if economic growth slows, the Federal Reserve should respond by reducing reserve requirements; doing so should stimulate loan growth and increase the money supply. This is what several global central banks chose to do in 2008 and 2009,[xlix] and it is not uncommon for some central banks around the world to regularly revise their reserve requirement percentage. For example, the PBC revised the required reserve ratio more than forty times from mid-2006 through February 2015.[l] However, the Federal Reserve takes a different approach; while each year it changes the threshold after which the required reserve ratio is 10%, the last time it changed the maximum requirement was in 1992 when it was reduced from 12% to 10%.[li] Why is the Fed averse to changing the required reserve ratio as a tool to implement monetary policy? In 1965 Milton Friedman argued that small changes in reserve requirements have outsized impacts that necessitate offsetting open market operations. The net effect is of dubious benefit but potentially a material cost as the FOMC may unintentionally tighten or loosen the requirement by more than intended. Dr. Friedman went on to write, "Anything that can be done with reserve requirement changes can be done with open market operations. Hence, the power to vary reserve requirements ought to be abolished."[lii] Heeding Dr. Friedman's advice, by the early 1980s the Federal Reserve had largely shifted away from targeting the monetary base (cash + reserves) as a means by controlling inflation, and instead it focused on the price and availability of loans to individuals and institutions. It is reasonable to expect the Federal Reserve required reserve ratio to remain largely unchanged into the future.

Forward Guidance

Forward guidance is the first of two nontraditional tools used by the Federal Reserve, and this term is a euphemism for letting market participants know the likely future path of the FOMC policy rate. This guidance is particularly useful when the Federal Reserve is attempting to influence the shape of the yield curve. The yield curve is the curve that can be graphed when plotting the market interest rate at different tenors. The Federal Reserve can influence the curve by indicating what the short-term interest rate will be at some point in the future. For example, imagine the overnight policy rate is 1.0% annualized and the 5-year U.S. Treasury is 3%. If the FOMC were to state, following their next policy meeting, that the FOMC will keep the overnight policy rate at 1.0% for exactly five more years, the 5-year U.S. Treasury yield would likely fall to just over 1.0%. This is because an institutional investor should be roughly indifferent with respect to keeping cash at a Federal Reserve Bank earning 1.0% for five years or holding a 5-year U.S. Treasury earning slightly over 1.0%.

The FOMC used forward guidance in March 2009 when it stated in its FOMC statement that it intended to keep the federal funds rate "exceptionally low" for "an extended period." At the time, the FOMC's objective was to reduce long-term interest rates in support of the economic recovery.[liii] It was effective. The 10-year U.S. Treasury fell from 3.40% in March 2008 to 2.28% in December 2009. Occasionally, forward guidance has the opposite effect as was intended by

Federal Reserve officials. On May 22, 2013 when presenting to the U.S. Congressional Joint Economic Committee, then Chairman Ben Bernanke was asked about the future of asset purchases. During the meeting, he stated, "A step to reduce the flow of purchases would not be an automatic, mechanistic process to end the program," and the FOMC would make an announcement for when this process would begin "in the next few meetings."[liv] This marked the beginning of what would later be known as the *Taper Tantrum*—when the 10-year U.S. Treasury would rise from 2.04% to 2.99% within four months. The consensus among financial professionals is that Dr. Bernanke did not intend for the 10-year U.S. interest rate to rise by roughly 1.0% after he indicated the Federal Reserve purchase program would begin to wind down later that year.

Asset Purchases

From 1951[2] until 2008, the FOMC rarely utilized long-term asset purchases to implement monetary policy. In 2002, in a speech given by then Federal Reserve Governor Ben Bernanke to the National Economists Club entitled "Deflation: Making Sure 'It' Doesn't Happen Here," Dr. Bernanke laid out what the Federal Reserve could do to support banks and avoid deflation should the U.S. financial system experience a banking crisis on the same order of magnitude as was experienced during the Great Depression. In this speech, he explained that the Federal Reserve could inject money into the economy by both expanding the "scale of asset purchases" and "expand[ing] the menu of assets."[lv] Fast forward six years—several of the largest banks had just failed, the economy was rapidly contracting, and financial markets had begun pricing in the likelihood of sustained deflation. In response, as Dr. Bernanke had described in that prescient speech on November 25, 2008, the FOMC announced it would begin the purchasing of $600 billion in assets including $100 billion government sponsored entity (GSE) direct obligations (like Fannie Mae or Freddie Mac debt) as well as $500 billion in mortgage-backed securities (MBS).[lvi]

This was the first announcement of a large-scale asset purchase (LSAP), a policy that would later be termed as *quantitative easing* (QE). LSAP programs are the second nontraditional tool used by the Federal Reserve. In March 2009, the FOMC expanded its original program from $600 billion to $1.25 trillion in asset purchases. In November 2010, the FOMC announced it would purchase an additional $600 billion in U.S. Treasuries (later known as QE2). Next, in

---

[2] During and after WWII, asset purchases were effectively utilized to influence long-term interest rates; in fact, long-term bond interest rates were capped at 2.5% until 1951.

September 2011, the FOMC announced a *maturity extension program* whereby the FOMC would sell $400 billion worth of bonds with maturities less than three years and purchase $400 billion worth of bonds with maturities between 6 and 30 years (later known as *Operation Twist*). Finally, in September 2012, the FOMC announced an open-ended commitment (i.e., it didn't set a final dollar value it would purchase) to buy $40 billion per month of MBS—and in December, the FOMC announced it would also purchase $45 billion per month of Treasuries (later known as QE3). When QE3 ended in October 2014, the FOMC had purchased an additional $1.7 trillion worth of assets. In total, the FOMC purchased over $4.0 trillion worth of assets between September 2008 and October 2014, expanding its balance sheet from $900 billion to $4.5 trillion during that period, and extended the duration of securities held by the Federal Reserve from 5.2 years to 5.9 years.[lvii]

At their initiation, FOMC officials knew that LSAPs were an unconventional tool that would have long-lasting influences on financial conditions and the economy. Additionally, such purchases had no historical precedence. So, why do it? In short, the Federal Reserve officials believed that weak economic conditions warranted an exceptionally *loose* monetary policy. Returning to the *Taylor Rule*, at the time the FOMC was engaging in LSAPs, the targeted federal funds rate should have been negative due to weak economic growth and inflation below its 2% target. But, after the FOMC reduced the federal funds rate to zero, how could the FOMC further ease monetary conditions? The answer, as explained by Dr. Bernanke in 2002, was to engage in LSAPs to further reduce intermediate and long-term interest rates. Were these programs effective? In short, yes. In 2017, Federal Reserve economists released a short paper indicating that the midpoint for the estimated downward impact on the 10-year U.S. Treasury was 1.05% between all three LSAPs and the maturity extension program. Furthermore, at the end of 2017, the 10-year U.S. Treasury yield was estimated to be 0.85% lower because of the lingering effects of these programs—and the LSAPs would continue to exert waning downward pressure on the 10-year U.S. Treasury yield until the Federal Reserve's balance sheet had fully normalized.[lviii] It should be noted that this is merely an estimate and since the FOMC officials can't go back in time to see what the 10-year rate would have been had they not engaged in asset purchases, the economists must rely on mathematical models to estimate how purchases impacted the market term premium. So, can we expect further LSAPs as part of the FOMCs toolkit? Unlikely. Unless there is another Great Recession that might warrant negative long-term real interest rates to stimulate the economy, this unconventional tool will likely be used only in exceptional circumstances.

Putting It All Together: The Federal Reserve's Balance Sheet

Like any entity following generally accepted accounting principles, the Federal Reserve has both assets and liabilities. Until 2008, its assets were primarily U.S. Treasury securities. But what about its liabilities? The Federal Reserve is unique in that it can issue fiat currency without the backing of something else into which it can be exchanged (like a precious metal or other commodity). Beginning in 1971, President Nixon suspended the convertibility of U.S. dollars for gold, meaning the Federal Reserve's liabilities were no more. However, for accounting purposes, when the Federal Reserve creates dollars—whether they be coins, paper, or even electronic—it records these dollars as liabilities. So, what does the Federal Reserve do with dollars after they're created? Prior to the Great Recession, the Federal Reserve primarily purchased U.S. Treasuries and recorded these Treasuries as assets, as shown in Figure 4.7. The purchase of Treasuries served two functions: first, purchasing Treasuries injects dollars into the economy, and second, holding only U.S. Treasuries ensures that the Federal Reserve's balance sheet maintains the highest credit quality. But why create currency and buy Treasuries at all? Remember—price stability is one of the Federal Reserve's mandates. Ignoring for the moment the money multiplier or the velocity of money (how regularly currency changes hands during a year), when the economy grows, its money supply must also grow to maintain constant prices. Imagine for a moment that the economy doubles in size but its money supply remains unchanged. In that case, all prices would fall by ~50% since this hypothetical economy has the same money supply chasing twice as many goods. So, in general, the Federal Reserve will print money (expend its monetary base) and purchase U.S. Treasuries with that money as the economy grows; doing so ensures that prices remain mostly unchanged, thus avoiding deflation.

Beginning in late 2008, the Federal Reserve began rapidly expanding its balance sheet for all of the aforementioned reasons. To implement its loose monetary policy, the Federal Reserve began by creating electronic currency and using this currency to purchase assets from banks—including Treasuries, agency debt, mortgage debt, and a host of other securities. However, unlike in the pre-recession period, the rate of the monetary base expansion far exceeded the growth rate of the U.S. economy. As a result, banks that sold the securities to the Federal Reserve didn't need the cash in order to originate new loans. So, banks placed these dollars back with the Federal Reserve in the form of excess reserves, which was added to the Federal Reserve's list of liabilities. For this reason, we can see that roughly for each additional dollar the Federal Reserve created during the QE programs, the Federal Reserve's liabilities in the form of excess reserves grew and their assets in the form of securities also grew at an approximate 1:1 ratio.

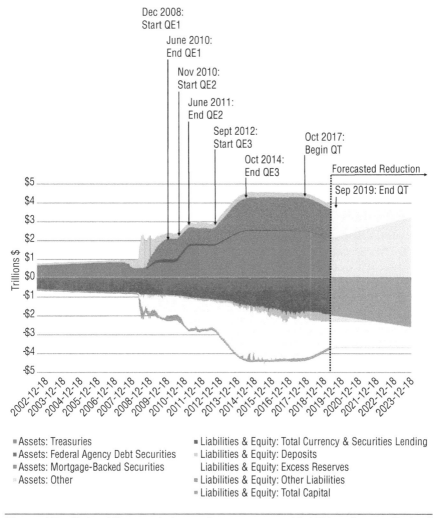

Figure 4.7   Federal Reserve balance sheet: assets and liabilities. *Source*: Federal Reserve

So what happens when a Treasury (or other security) matures? Prior to October 2017, when a Treasury matured, the Federal Reserve would place a non-competitive bid with the treasury, and this bid would be treated as an *add-on* to the previously announced auction size. For example, if $5 billion worth of 10-year Treasuries that were held by the Federal Reserve were maturing, the Federal Reserve would inform the treasury that it would like to roll that $5 billion of 10-year Treasuries. In this example, if the treasury had already announced that it is selling $25 billion 10-year Treasuries on a certain date, the treasury would still sell $25 billion 10-year Treasuries to the public and then issue an *additional* $5 billion worth of 10-year Treasuries. The $5 billion *add-on* is then transferred to the Federal Reserve in exchange for the maturing 10-year treasuries.[lix]

Beginning in October 2017, as the final stage in unwinding the extraordinary monetary accommodation, the Federal Reserve began allowing its balance sheet to gradually shrink. To do this, the Federal Reserve is allowing Treasuries and MBS to gradually mature according to a previously announced schedule.[lx] Specifically, beginning in October 2017, the Federal Reserve began allowing $6 billion in U.S. Treasuries and $4 billion in agency MBS debt to mature per month in a process colloquially known as quantitative tightening (QT). The size of the monthly maturities increased quarterly so that by Q4 2018 up to $30 billion U.S. Treasury securities and $20 billion agency MBS securities will mature. As securities mature and the Federal Reserve collects principal payments, it will *retire* cash, causing its liabilities to fall by an amount equal to the decline in its assets. This process will also cause bank excess reserves to fall by an amount roughly equal to the value of the maturing securities. If the Federal Reserve had allowed this process to continue, excess reserves would likely have fallen to pre-crisis levels by late 2022, according to Federal Reserve estimates.[lxi] However, in March 2019, the FOMC announced it would slow the balance sheet reduction beginning in May and cease it in September 2019. As a result, we can expect the asset side of the Federal Reserve balance sheet to remain around $3.5 trillion from 2020 through 2024 (or longer). The composition of its assets will evolve so that as MBS mature, they will be replaced with treasury holdings (subject to a cap of $20 billion per month).[lxii] Meanwhile, the Federal Reserve's liabilities will also remain around $3.5 trillion; however, its composition will also evolve. Specifically, there will be a gradual (multi-year) reduction in excess reserves as banks withdraw these reserves and find uses for them (such as to originate loans or buy securities). As banks withdraw reserves, the Federal Reserve's liability of *total currency* will expand by an equal amount, leaving the total size of the Federal Reserve's liabilities unchanged.

CENTRAL BANK TRANSMISSION MECHANISMS

Following each FOMC meeting, the Federal Reserve banks engage in coordinated actions with the objective of either stimulating or reducing economic output or inflation. So, how do changes in a policy rate, discount rate, reserve ratio, asset purchases, or simply speaking about the economy impact main street? There are at least six channels,[lxiii] as shown in Figure 4.8, and I'll briefly cover each one here:

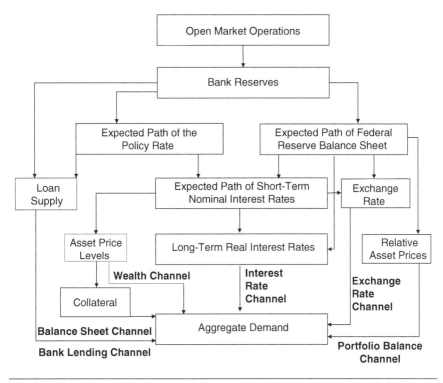

Figure 4.8   Federal Reserve transmission mechanisms. *Source*: McCarthy (2013)[lxiv]

- *Interest rate channel*: this is the primary channel through which FOMC decisions impact the real economy. In this channel, a change in the real interest rate may cause individuals and businesses to cancel, postpone, reduce, increase, or expedite spending. For example, a business that is considering building a factory with an expected return of 5% may elect to make this investment if its opportunity cost is not investing in a U.S. Treasury earning 3%. But, that business may elect to not build a factory if it can buy a U.S. Treasury earning 8%. Home purchase decisions are also directly impacted by this channel. When people buy homes, the binding constraint for how expensive a house the homebuyer can afford is typically the size of the monthly mortgage payment. As interest rates rise, so too does the monthly mortgage payment, which reduces the value of a home that a prospective buyer can afford. In short, a reduction in interest rates stimulates aggregate demand while an increase in interest rates reduces aggregate demand.

- *Bank lending channel*: this is the channel by which households and businesses have access to financing. When the FOMC reduces the reserves that are available to banks (reserves which may otherwise have been used to originate loans), loan origination will slow. This should reduce aggregate spending because spending that is conditional on financing will be reduced.
- *Wealth channel*: this is the channel whereby household spending is influenced by changes in the wealth of that household. For example, in the years prior to 2008, household spending increased due in part to appreciating home values, and in 2008 and 2009 household spending fell as home prices also fell. By reducing interest rates, the FOMC can increase the relative value of existing bonds, stocks, and homes. Thus, a prolonged reduction in rates can cause asset prices to inflate, which in turn will stimulate aggregate demand.
- *Balance sheets channel*: this is related to both the bank lending and wealth channels, but focuses exclusively on how asset prices impact creditors' willingness to extend loans collateralized by assets. Specifically, if asset prices fall, banks are less willing to extend loans against collateral, or they may do so with higher haircuts or charge a higher interest rate. Therefore, a decline in asset prices leads to a reduction in bank lending, which can reduce aggregate demand.
- *Exchange rate channel*: this channel is where a change in a country's interest rates impacts the relative attractiveness of that country's currency, *ceteris paribus* (with other things staying the same). Specifically, an increase in domestic interest rates may lead to currency appreciation, which should reduce that country's net exports and overall economic output.
- Portfolio balance channel: in this channel, it is hypothesized that interest rates change the relative attractiveness of various assets, including cash, bonds, and real assets. So, a change in interest rates can impact the *cost* of holding cash, which will lead to a change in the demand for other assets, which in turn will impact their prices. This phenomenon may have a modest impact on aggregate demand.

NORMALIZING MONETARY POLICY

How Will the Federal Reserve Intend to Unwind Its Exceptional Policy Accommodation?

In June 2008, the Federal Reserve balance sheet held $892 million in assets,[lxv] excess reserves were $2.2 billion,[lxvi] and the effective federal funds rate was 2.00%

(down from 5.25% the prior year).[lxvii] Exactly 10 years later, the Federal Reserve balance sheet held $4.3 trillion in assets,[lxviii] excess reserves were $1.9 trillion,[lxix] and the effective federal funds rate was 1.82% (up from 1.04% the prior year).[lxx] So, now that we know how and why the Federal Reserve lowered its policy rate to 0.0% and dramatically increased the size of the balance sheet, the logical next question is: how will the Federal Reserve *normalize* monetary policy? By normalization, this includes raising the policy rate to a level in the 2%–4% vicinity and reducing the size of its balance sheet such that excess reserves are minimal. To explain to market participants how the Federal Reserve would normalize, in September 2014 the Federal Reserve released a statement entitled: "Policy Normalization Principles and Plans." In it, the FOMC stated that when the FOMC felt appropriate, it would take the following steps (among others):

- *During normalization, the Federal Reserve intends to move the federal funds rate into the target range set by the Committee primarily by adjusting the interest rate it pays on excess reserve balances.* Interpretation: this is a tacit admission that the interest rate on excess reserves will remain the de facto policy rate until excess reserve balances fall to pre-2009 levels.
- *The Committee intends to reduce the Federal Reserve's securities holdings in a gradual and predictable manner primarily by ceasing to reinvest repayments of principal on securities held in the SOMA.* Interpretation: the Federal Reserve will not sell securities to reduce the size of its balance sheet; rather, it will gradually wind down its balance sheet by allowing securities to mature. In short, balance sheet reduction will be gradual.

In March 2015, the Federal Reserve released an addendum in which it stated that the Federal Reserve intends to "set the IOER rate equal to the top of the target range for the federal funds rate and set the offering rate associated with an ON RRP (overnight reverse repo) facility equal to the bottom of the target range for the federal funds rate."[lxxi] In doing so, they confirmed that the targeted overnight interest rate corridor will remain at the level between the reverse repo facility, where money market funds can invest with the Federal Reserve, and the IOER level, which is the interest rate that banks earn when depositing excess reserves.

On December 16, 2015, after seven years with the federal funds rate at 0%–0.25% and believing the economy was sufficiently strong to begin tightening financial conditions, the FOMC announced it was raising the overnight policy target by +0.25% to 0.25%–0.50%;[lxxii] IOER was raised to 0.50% at the same time. The FOMC waited another full year to raise the policy rate, and then hiked it again in March 2017 and June 2017 so that the target federal funds rate was 1.0%–1.25%. At the June 2017 meeting, the FOMC released another addendum to the *Policy Normalization Principles and Plans* in which it stated the Federal

Reserve would soon allow $6 billion worth of Treasury securities and $4 billion of agency debt and MBS to mature per month. Additionally, over the course of a year, the quantity of securities that would not be reinvested would increase to $30 billion of Treasuries and $20 billion of agencies and mortgages each month. Thus, up to $600 billion in securities would be allowed to mature each year. In practice, there are several months each year when less than $30 billion of Treasuries and $20 billion of agencies and mortgages mature; so, the total annual runoff of the SOMA balance sheet is less than $600 billion per year. In September, the FOMC announced it would begin this process in October 2017.[lxxiii] From October 2017 to June 2018, excess reserves fell approximately $550 billion to $1.6 trillion.[lxxiv] As stated previously, had this plan been allowed to continue, reserve balances would likely have fallen to pre-crisis levels by 2022.[lxxv] However, now that this roll off will likely be paused at the end of 2019, it is likely that excess reserves will remain above pre-crisis levels until at least 2024, after which the U.S. economy will eventually *grow into* the size of the currency created by the Federal Reserve.

Issues the Federal Reserve Will Face

As discussed earlier in the chapter, the IOER rate is now the de facto policy rate, and raising the federal funds rate will require an increase in the IOER rate as well. As of July 2018, there were approximately $1.9 trillion in excess reserves.[lxxvi] By setting the policy rate at 2.0%, the Federal Reserve will generate $38 billion in annual payments to banks. Additionally, this transfer payment doesn't include the interest expense incurred by the Federal Reserve as money market funds utilize the reverse repo facility. In 2006, when evaluating the Federal Reserve's request to pay interest on excess reserves (a component of the Financial Services Regulatory Relief Act), the Congressional Budget Office (CBO) estimated that this expense would be between $250 million and $300 million a year.[lxxvii] Knowing this, we might question if the bill would have passed into law had the CBO indicated that the cost of interest on reserves would have been $40 billion or more. Several years ago, I asked Dr. Ben Bernanke if the Fed was concerned about the optics of this transfer payment. "While there's no limit to people's irrationality, the Fed has transferred much more to the Treasury in the form of remittances." So, no, he's not concerned. I asked him later at lunch if he preferred to go by *Dr. Bernanke, Mr. Chairman*, or *Ben*. "Whatever," was his response. Perhaps he didn't seriously consider either of my questions because he suspected that I was a relatively junior investment professional. Whatever.

Speaking of Ben, I think he's a wonderful economist and will be historically judged as being one of the saviors of the U.S. economy in 2008 and 2009, but I question whether he has his pulse on main street's perception of the Federal

Reserve and its officials, and I also question whether he has fully considered the potential political backlash of such a large transfer payment to banks. In January 2018, *Business Insider* described the 2017 Federal Reserve $30 billion in transfer payments to banks attributable to interest on reserves as: "At taxpayer expense: easiest, risk-free, sit-on-your-ass profit ever."[lxxviii] While this story was not front-page news, it might become front-page news as the Federal Reserve continues to raise overnight rates while banks continue to hold large quantities of excess reserves. Additionally, by continuing to suppress the term premium (the additional interest rate pickup for holding 5-, 10-, and 30-year bonds), while simultaneously raising the overnight rates, the Federal Reserve may *invert* the interest rate curve whereby short-term rates are higher than long-term rates. Why is inverting the curve bad? According to research from the Federal Reserve Bank of San Francisco, "Every U.S. recession in the past 60 years was preceded by a negative term spread, that is, an inverted yield curve. Furthermore, a negative term spread was always followed by an economic slowdown and, except for one time, by a recession."[lxxix] So yes, the Federal Reserve would be wise to not invert the yield curve; therefore, the policy option that seems to be the easiest and safest to implement would be for the Federal Reserve to reduce the size of its balance sheet and then raise the policy rate.

CRITICISMS OF THE FEDERAL RESERVE

The Great Depression, The Great Inflation, and The Great Recession

Critiquing Federal Reserve policy decisions, while of great value if done constructively, ought to be performed with the understanding that the vast majority of Federal Reserve employees are thoughtful, intelligent, and well-intentioned. Additionally, policy decisions are often made with imperfect information or may be considered at the time the best of bad options, and sound policies may be implemented utilizing novel and untested tools. However, like an after-action analysis following a military operation, a review of the successes and failures of the Federal Reserve is essential to improving the Federal Reserve's ability to accomplish its objectives in the future. So, when has the Federal Reserve failed to achieve its dual mandate and what can we learn from that? There are several instances when the Federal Reserve may have improved its reaction function or better anticipated financial instability. But, the three instances I'll briefly cover are the Great Depression, the Great Inflation, and the Great Recession.

Frequently cited causes of the Great Depression include the stock market crash of 1929, a reduction in purchasing power (wealth effect) due to this crash, the Smoot-Hawley Tariff of 1930, and even drought conditions nicknamed *The Dust Bowl*. While these factors contributed to a decline in output, none of these factors, even taken together, were material enough to cause unemployment to rise to 25% and cause the GDP to decline approximately 30%. So, what caused the reduction in output in 1929, which started as a modest cyclical correction, to snowball into the most devastating economic contraction in U.S. history? Economists today largely attribute the Great Depression to inappropriate Federal Reserve policy. Between 1929 and 1933, around 7,000 banks failed,[lxxx] which led to a dramatic decline in the money supply; this decline in the stock of money was later termed *The Great Contraction of 1929–1933*. Despite the contraction in the money supply, the increase in unemployment, and the contraction in output, the Federal Reserve responded by *tightening* monetary policy. This further shrunk the money supply and greatly exacerbated the ongoing economic contraction. In their seminal work, *A Monetary History of the United States,* authors Milton Friedman and Anna Schwartz argue that "the contraction is in fact a tragic testimonial to the importance of monetary forces."[lxxxi] Economists today agree. In a speech given to honor Milton Friedman's 90th birthday at the University of Chicago, Governor Ben Bernanke thanked Friedman for his contributions to economists' understanding of the monetary system. Governor Bernanke's concluding remark was, "I would like to say to Milton and Anna: Regarding the Great Depression—you're right, we did it. We're very sorry. But thanks to you, we won't do it again."[lxxxii]

Some 20 years following the conclusion of World War II, U.S. economic growth was strong after a brief recession in 1960, while inflation remained around 1% per year. Inflation began to rise by the late 1960s and reached 12% in 1974 and peaked at nearly 15% per year in 1980.[lxxxiii] This episode of sustained inflation led to prices rising nearly 350% for the 20-year period ending in 1985, a period now known as the *Great Inflation*. Clearly a 3.5× rise in prices is not consistent with the Fed's dual mandate, which includes price stability. So, what went wrong? The error in policy can be largely traced to the acceptance by policymakers of an inverse relationship between inflation and employment called the *Philips Curve*. This curve is a graphical representation of inflation on one axis and unemployment on the other. Following the publishing of Philip's 1958 paper,[lxxxiv] a theory was put forward that policymakers could lower unemployment by increasing inflation, and vice versa. In addition to this errant logic among central bank officials, events outside the Federal Reserve's control also had inflationary influences, including the halting of U.S. dollar convertibility into gold in 1971, deficit spending to finance the Vietnam War, and two energy crises in 1973 and 1979. However, during these episodes, the Federal Reserve maintained loose policy to support employment; unemployment reached 8.8% in 1975, fell over the next five years, and then spiked again to 10.8% in 1982.[lxxxv]

Unfortunately, warnings of the Philips Curve's shortcomings were not heeded until too late. Economists Phelps and Friedman both argued that the Philips Curve was, at best, transitory. According to Friedman, "There is always a temporary trade-off between inflation and unemployment; there is no permanent trade-off."[lxxxvi] With the Philips Curve largely discredited, the legacy from this episode is that policymakers now agree they should not sacrifice longer term prosperity for short-term gains; therefore, running inflation well above target for an extended period is not an appropriate monetary policy, even if unemployment remains elevated.

The final episode I will briefly cover is the *Great Recession* from 2008 to 2009, or more accurately, the eight years preceding the recession. The period between the Great Inflation and the Great Recession had been colloquially termed the Great Moderation among policymakers. During this period, the U.S. economy enjoyed subdued inflation, lower inflation volatility, and lower volatility of economic output. In 2004, then Governor Ben Bernanke attributed this moderation to structural changes in the economy (improved technology and business practices) as well-improved monetary policy.[lxxxvii] In hindsight, we know the latter to be incorrect. During this period, there were dozens of issues that should have warranted significant focus by economists and policymakers. These include (but are not limited to): the use of off-balance sheet structures such as structured investment vehicles by investment banks, the rise of complex securitization models such as collateralized debt obligations (CDOs), the heavy use of short-term financing to financing long-term assets by *shadow bank* complicit rating agencies, aggressive mortgage lending and a dramatic decline in lending standards, and a home construction rate that was well beyond the historic average necessary to accommodate household formation. However, despite these festering issues, the Federal Reserve engaged in a largely loose monetary policy from 2002 through 2005 (due in part to muted inflation) and failed to investigate the growth of leverage from areas that existed outside their traditional purview. The lessons learned by central bankers following the sudden economic collapse in late 2008 are too many to list here; however, I will highlight one: our economy is complex and interconnected. So, to guard against another rapid contraction in credit and output, Federal Reserve officials must look beyond their traditional roles of monitoring the money supply and commercial bank balance sheets. Had they done so in the early 2000s, perhaps some of the previously mentioned concerns would have spurred preemptive action.

FOMC Policy Following The Great Recession

I'll return now to Bill Gross's assertion from his 2016 Investment Outlook that central bankers have "mastered the art of market manipulation." Gross has never been one to mince words. So what does he mean by this? Recall that the

Thornton-Bagehot *Responsibility Doctrine*, which was mentioned at the beginning of this chapter, includes several principles including allowing insolvent institutions to fail, charging penalizing rates, and announcing the terms of support ahead of a banking crisis. Critics point out that central banks moved away from several of these principles from 2008 through 2010. For example, during and immediately after the Great Recession, it is likely that some insolvent institutions were not allowed to fail because they were believed to be *too big to fail*, much of the support provided to market participants was below the market rate (i.e., not penalizing), and many of its responses to the crisis were ad hoc and not stated in advance of the crisis.[lxxxviii]

Additionally, by engaging in exceptionally loose monetary policies for years after the Great Recession, it has become apparent that the Federal reserve will act to suppress financial volatility. As such, large reductions in value of the stock market, declines in the value of bank stocks, and weakness in the labor market will likely generate a strong reaction by the Federal Reserve. This reaction function, while appropriate given the mandate to balance risks of unemployment and inflation, in practice offers investors a *put* whereby they may anticipate that the Federal Reserve will limit the losses to financial assets. Due to the expectation that volatility (downside risk) will continue to be artificially suppressed, investors are encouraged to engage in risk-seeking behavior. In practice, this means investors are inclined to sell their low-risk, low-duration assets and instead purchase riskier assets including high yield bonds, emerging market securities, and equities. As a result, more capital is allocated to riskier ventures than would have been the case. In addition to a broad, market-wide seeking of risk, the Federal Reserve's (and other central banks') aversion to allowing large, systemically important institutions to fail creates a moral hazard. Specifically, executives in these systemically important institutions are also encouraged to engage in risky behavior by increasing leverage and extending credit to high-risk enterprises. Additionally, counterparties of too-big-to-fail banks are inclined to offer these institutions financing, thereby fostering the risk-seeking behavior because the counterparties to the too-big-to-fail institutions can assume that their losses will be limited by central bank intervention. This reduction or elimination of private losses to too-big-to-fail creditors will likely come at the taxpayer's expense.

In addition to the increase in risk-seeking behavior, the Federal Reserve and other central banks may be charged with *manipulation*—due to their ability to inflate financial asset values, and in doing so, generate elevated consumption. In theory, inflating the value of assets (including houses, stocks, and bonds) is appropriate to offset a contraction in aggregate demand. However, if financial assets remain inflated once a cyclical contraction passes, consumption may continue to be *brought forward*. In practice, this means consumers continue to overconsume and under-save for years after loose monetary policy was originally implemented. This lack of savings and emphasis on near-term consumption may lead to lower long-term investments in drivers of production, such as R&D and education. So, is Gross correct in saying that central banks have "mastered the art of manipulation?" I hope so—because if they can, they can ensure that there is never another recession! Otherwise, I think a fairer assertion is that central bank officials have expanded their view, toolkit, and reach, such that their influence in global economies is more ubiquitous and relevant than ever before.

SUMMARY AND INVESTMENT IMPLICATIONS

Summary

The U.S. Federal Reserve was formed in 1913 after the U.S. Congress passed the Federal Reserve Act. The U.S. Federal Reserve's initial mandate was modeled on the Bank of England's Thornton-Bagehot *Responsibility Doctrine*. The six principles of this doctrine include:

1. Protecting the money stock and not the institutions
2. Allowing insolvent institutions to fail
3. Only accommodating solvent institutions
4. Charging penalizing rates
5. Requiring sound collateral for loans
6. Announcing the terms of support ahead of a banking crisis

The Federal Reserve's mandate since then was expanded by the U.S. Congress to also include targeting policies that promote maximum employment and stable prices (low inflation).

The members of the FOMC meet eight times a year to answer the questions:

- How is the U.S. economy likely to evolve in the near and medium term?
- What is the appropriate monetary policy setting to help move the economy over the medium term to the FOMC's goal of 2% inflation and maximum employment?
- How can the FOMC effectively communicate its expectations for the economy and its policy decisions to the public?

Once these questions have been answered, the FOMC employs tools to implement what it believes to be appropriate monetary policy. These tools include targeting market interest rates via open market operations, discount window lending, excess reserve targeting, revising bank reserve requirements, engaging in forward guidance that involves communication to market participants, and engaging in asset purchases.

These policies impact the real economy and occur through six channels: interest rates, bank lending, wealth effect, balance sheet, exchange rates, and portfolio balance. Taken together, the U.S. Federal Reserve attempts to offset economic cyclicality by pulling forward consumption and investment when the economy slows and delaying consumption and investment when inflation accelerates. Whether or not the U.S. Federal Reserve has achieved these objectives is subject to debate, but most participants agree that those who are making the decisions do so with incomplete information and with the best intentions. Thus, their reaction functions, along with the tools they utilize, will continue to evolve and improve.

Investment Implications

While we as investors may be tempted to ask the question, "What *should* the FOMC do?" when discussing the Federal Reserve and investment implications, the correct questions are: "What *will* the FOMC do?" and "Given what the FOMC will do, *how should we position our investments*?" Hopefully this detailed discussion of central bank objectives, tools, and reaction functions will help our readers answer the former question. With respect to the latter question, here are a few takeaways:

- Until the Federal Reserve indicates that the greater risk to the economy is inflation, the FOMC stands ready and willing to engage in loose monetary policy whenever financial assets materially decline in value. This reaction function acts as a volatility suppressor.
  - For a fixed income investor, this suggests that *selling volatility* is an appropriate way to add value to portfolios. Selling volatility, within the context of a fixed income portfolio, means holding securities that typically outperform when interest rate volatility is muted, such as mortgage-backed and other asset-backed securities that are *callable*.
  - For an equity investor or someone who allocates to asset classes more broadly, this suggests maintaining a slight risk overweight. Because the Federal Reserve is willing to support asset prices should they decline, the left tail of the distribution of returns has been cut. Therefore, the expected return of risk assets has risen (vis-à-vis riskless assets), warranting a modest risk overweight.

- Owing to artificially depressed low interest rates, financial assets will appear *rich* to historical pricing metrics. Some of these metrics include yield (for bonds) and price to earnings (or the inverse, which is earnings yield), price to book, or dividend yield (for stocks). As a result, it's important to normalize for an opportunity set whereby investors are allocating to the *cleanest dirty shirt*, which is to say, the best of relatively unattractive investment options as evaluated based on historical metrics.

- The Federal Reserve and other regulators have introduced a moral hazard whereby large financial institutions are too big to fail, and thus prone to taking excessive risk. Knowing this, these institutions will be forced by regulators to maintain historically low levels of leverage. As such, the ability of banks to generate returns for their equity holders will be limited by regulators, not unlike a public utility. This makes financials less attractive to equity holders since earnings power, dividends, or stock buybacks have been capped by regulators. However, high capital requirements make financials more attractive to bondholders since these too-big-to-fail institutions are also highly unlikely to fail. Therefore, a modest overweight to financials in a fixed income portfolio and a modest underweight to financials in an equity portfolio are also appropriate.

- Long-term interest rates have been suppressed due to LSAPs. As the Federal Reserve shrinks its balance sheet, this suppression will gradually unwind, leading to a steepening in the yield curve or an increase in the term premium. A modest term premium makes investing in the intermediate (5–10 year) and long (10 year+) portions of the yield curve relatively unattractive, and this low-term premium has incentivized large corporations to issue long-duration bonds. However, a savvy fixed income investor may find value in investing in long-duration corporate bonds while hedging or selling the long-duration interest rate exposure that is inherent to these bonds. This investor will be left with a credit premium that may offer a reasonable amount of carry or yield pickup.

- Asset allocators should assume lower returns for all asset classes over the next 10 years than has been the case in the previous 10 or 20 years. This can most easily be understood when evaluating the attractiveness of bonds; the annual return of the bond if held until maturity will be approximately equal to its yield to maturity at the time the bond is purchased. Therefore, given historically low bond yields, the future return of fixed income portfolios will be lower than has been historically realized. The same is likely true for investors in other financial assets. For example, equity investors generally earn an equity risk with a premium vis-à-vis bond investment, and while this premium can only be measured ex-post, it is fair to assume that this premium did not increase as bond yields fell. Thus, future equity returns have likely declined as well.

CITATIONS

    i. Gross, Bill. (September 2016). "How I Found My Golf Game but Lost My Wife to a Titleist." Janus Capital Investment Outlook.

    ii. Zuckerman, Gregory and Rachel Emma Silverman. (March 21, 2002). "Fund Manager Gross Lashes Out At GE Over Disclosure, Debt Load." *The Wall Street Journal.*

    iii. *Orange County Register.* (June 27, 2007). "Pimco's Gross says Moody's, S&P fooled by dolled up CDOs."

    iv. McLean, Bethany and Joe Nocera. (2010). *All the Devils Are Here, the Hidden History of the Financial Crisis.* Portfolio, Penguin. p. 111.

    v. Foley, Stephen. (April 27, 2013). "Standard & Poor's and Moody's settle U.S. subprime lawsuits." *Financial Times.*

    vi. Viswanatha, Aruna and Karen Freifeld. (February 3, 2016). "S&P reaches $1.5 billion deal with U.S., states over crisis-era ratings." *Reuters.*

    vii. Bagehot, Walter. (November 5, 2010). Lombard Street: A description of the money market (1873). London, UK: Henry S. King and Co. (e-text by Project Gutenberg).

    viii. Bank Charter Act of 1844. http://www.legislation.gov.uk/ukpga/Vict/7-8/32/enacted.

    ix. Bordo, Michael D. (2014). "Rules for a Lender of Last Resort: An Historical Perspective." Rutgers University, Hoover Institution, Stanford University and NBER.

    x. Humphrey, Thomas M. (1989). "Lender of last resort: The concept in history." Economic Review. Federal Reserve Bank of Richmond, Issue Mar., pp. 8–16.

    xi. Bruner, Robert F., Peter Marcel Debaere, and Sean Carr. The Panic of 1907. Darden Case No. UVA-G-0619. Available at SSRN: https://ssrn.com/abstract=1419820.

    xii. Ibid.

    xiii. Ibid.

    xiv. 12 U.S. Code § 411.

    xv. The Federal Reserve System Purposes & Functions. Board of Governors of the Federal Reserve. 10th Edition.

xvi. Mishkin, Frederic S. (2010). *The Economics of Money, Banking and Financial Markets*. Toronto, Canada: Pearson Addison Wesley. Print. 9th edition. p. 332 [note: there are newer editions to this book].

xvii. Quoted in: Meltzer, Allan H. (2009). A History of the Federal Reserve: Volume 2, Book 2, 1970–1986, Chicago, IL: University of Chicago Press. p. 986.

xviii. The Federal Reserve System Purposes & Functions. Board of Governors of the Federal Reserve. 10th Edition. p 32.

xix. https://www.federalreserve.gov/monetarypolicy/.

xx. https://www.federalreserve.gov/monetarypolicy/fomc_historical.htm.

xxi. Mishkin, Frederic S. (2010). *Mishkin, the Economics of Money, Banking, and Financial Markets*. 9th Edition. Pearson Addison-Wesley. pp. 328–330.

xxii. Minutes of the Federal Open Market Committee. (October 27–28, 2015). p. 2.

xxiii. Taylor, John B. "Discretion versus Policy Rules in Practice." A paper prepared for the November 1992 Carnegie-Rochester Conference on Public Policy.

xxiv. The Federal Reserve System Purposes & Functions. (October 2016). 10th Edition. Federal Reserve System Publication.

xxv. https://www.newyorkfed.org/markets/soma/sysopen_accholdings.html.

xxvi. https://www.newyorkfed.org/markets/domestic-market-operations/monetary-policy-implementation.

xxvii. Board of Governors of the Federal Reserve System (U.S.). (June 26, 2018). Effective Federal Funds Rate [FEDFUNDS]. retrieved from FRED, Federal Reserve Bank of St. Louis; https://fred.stlouisfed.org/series/FEDFUNDS.

xxviii. https://www.federalreserve.gov/monetarypolicy/openmarket.htm.

xxix. Afonso, Gara, Alex Entz, and Eric LeSueur. (December 2, 2013). "Who's Lending in the Fed Funds Market?" Liberty Street Economics and the Federal Reserve Bank of New York.

xxx. Statement Regarding Counterparties for Reverse Repurchase Agreements. (March 8, 2010). Federal Reserve Bank of New York.

xxxi. https://www.ici.org/research/stats/mmf.

xxxii. https://www.newyorkfed.org/markets/rrp_counterparties.html#reverse-repo-counterparties.

xxxiii. Federal Reserve Bank of New York, Overnight Reverse Repurchase Agreements: Treasury Securities Sold by the Federal Reserve in the Temporary Open Market Operations [RRPONTSYD]. (June

27, 2018). retrieved from FRED, Federal Reserve Bank of St. Louis; https://fred.stlouisfed.org/series/RRPONTSYD.

xxxiv. https://www.newyorkfed.org/markets/programs-archive.

xxxv. Nathan Sheets, PhD. (September 2018). "The Fed's Swap Lines During the Crisis: Lender of Last Resort on a Global Scale." PGIM Fixed Income.

xxxvi. Burgess, W. Randolph. (November 1964). "Reflections on the Early Development of Open Market Policy." Federal Reserve Bank of New York. Monthly Review.

xxxvii. https://www.frbdiscountwindow.org/.

xxxviii. Armantier, Olivier et al. (January 2011). "Discount Window Stigma during the 2007–2008 Financial Crisis." Federal Reserve Bank of New York. Staff Reports No. 483.

xxxix. Board of Governors of the Federal Reserve System (U.S.). (July 1, 2018). Discount Window Borrowings of Depository Institutions from the Federal Reserve [DISCBORR]. retrieved from FRED, Federal Reserve Bank of St. Louis; https://fred.stlouisfed.org/series/DISCBORR.

xl. Why did the Federal Reserve start paying interest on reserve balances held on deposit at the Fed? Does the Fed pay interest on required reserves, excess reserves, or both? What interest rate does the Fed pay? (March 2013). Federal Reserve Bank of San Francisco.

xli. Summary of S.2856—109th Congress. (2005–2006). Financial Services Regulatory Relief Act of 2006.

xlii. Federal Reserve Bank of St. Louis, Excess Reserves of Depository Institutions [EXCSRESNS]. (June 29, 2018). retrieved from FRED, Federal Reserve Bank of St. Louis; https://fred.stlouisfed.org/series/EXCSRESNS.

xliii. https://www.federalreserve.gov/newsevents/pressreleases/monetary 20081125b.htm.

xliv. Federal Reserve Bank of St. Louis, Excess Reserves of Depository Institutions [EXCSRESNS]. (December 27, 2018). retrieved from FRED, Federal Reserve Bank of St. Louis; https://fred.stlouisfed.org/series/EXCSRESNS.

xlv. Ibid.

xlvi. Federal Reserve Bank of New York, Effective Federal Funds Volume [EFFRVOL]. (December 27, 2018). retrieved from FRED, Federal Reserve Bank of St. Louis; https://fred.stlouisfed.org/series/EFFRVOL.

xlvii. https://www.federalreserve.gov/monetarypolicy/reservereq.htm.

xlviii. Gray, Simon. (2011). "Central Bank Balances and Reserve Requirements." International Monetary Fund. Figure 3.

xlix. ———. (2011). "Central Bank Balances and Reserve Requirements." International Monetary Fund. Figure 3.

l. Daohua, Dai. (February 2015). "Comparison of China and U.S. Bank Reserves and Their Implications." Economic Review. Bank of China. p. 2.

li. Feinman, Joshua N. (1993). Reserve Requirements: History, Current Practice, and Potential Reform. *Federal Reserve Bulletin*. 79. 569–589. p. 581.

lii. Friedman, Milton. (1965). "A Program for Monetary Stability." In: *Readings in Financial Institutions*. Marshall D. Ketchum and Leon T. Kendall, eds. pp. 189–209. Boston, MA: Houghton Mifflin.

liii. Federal Reserve Education Materials. "Conducting Monetary Policy." https://www.federalreserve.gov/aboutthefed.htm.

liv. Hilsenrath, Jon. (May 22, 2013). "Fed Winddown Strategy Will Test Economy's Reaction and Adjust." *The Wall Street Journal*.

lv. Remarks by Governor Ben S. Bernanke Before the National Economists Club, Washington, D.C. (November 21, 2002). "Deflation: Making Sure 'It' Doesn't Happen Here."

lvi. Federal Reserve 2008 Monetary Policy Releases. (November 25, 2008).

lvii. Ng, Michael and David Wessel. (August 18, 2017). "The Hutchins Center Explains: The Fed's balance sheet." The Brookings Institution.

lviii. Bonis, Brian, Jane Ihrig, and Min Wei. (2017). "The Effect of the Federal Reserve's Securities Holdings on Longer-term Interest Rates." FEDS Notes. Washington: Board of Governors of the Federal Reserve System. April 20, 2017. https://doi.org/10.17016/2380-7172.1977. Figure 3.

lix. https://www.newyorkfed.org/markets/treasury-rollover-faq.html.

lx. Press Release. (June 14, 2017). FOMC issues addendum to the Policy Normalization Principles and Plans. https://www.federalreserve.gov/newsevents/pressreleases/monetary20170614c.htm.

lxi. Ferris, Erin E., Kim Syron, Jeong Soo, and Bernd Schlusch. (January 13, 2017). "Confidence Interval Projections of the Federal Reserve Balance Sheet and Income." FEDS Notes. https://www.federalreserve.gov/econresdata/notes/feds-notes/2017/confidence-interval-projections-of-the-federal-reserve-balance-sheet-and-income-20170113.html.

lxii. Press Release. (March 20, 2019). Balance Sheet Normalization Principles and Plans. https://www.federalreserve.gov/newsevents/press releases/monetary20190320c.htm.

lxiii. Kuttner, Kenneth and Patricia Mosser. (2002). "The monetary transmission mechanism in the United States: Some answers and further questions." BIS Papers chapters, in: Bank for International Settlements (ed.). Market functioning and central bank policy, Volume 12. pp. 433–443. Bank for International Settlements.

lxiv. McCarthy, J. (2013). The Monetary Transmission Mechanism. Speech delivered at The Federal Reserve in the 21st Century: A Symposium for College Professors. Federal Reserve Bank of New York. https://www.youtube.com/watch?v=vCvHVsEZNvE.

lxv. Board of Governors of the Federal Reserve System (U.S.). (July 5, 2018). All Federal Reserve Banks: Total Assets [WALCL]. retrieved from FRED, Federal Reserve Bank of St. Louis; https://fred.stlouisfed.org/series/WALCL.

lxvi. Federal Reserve Bank of St. Louis, Excess Reserves of Depository Institutions [EXCSRESNS]. (July 5, 2018). retrieved from FRED, Federal Reserve Bank of St. Louis; https://fred.stlouisfed.org/series/EXCSRESNS.

lxvii. Board of Governors of the Federal Reserve System (U.S.). (July 5, 2018). Effective Federal Funds Rate [FEDFUNDS]. retrieved from FRED, Federal Reserve Bank of St. Louis; https://fred.stlouisfed.org/series/FEDFUNDS.

lxviii. Board of Governors of the Federal Reserve System (U.S.). (July 5, 2018). All Federal Reserve Banks: Total Assets [WALCL]. retrieved from FRED, Federal Reserve Bank of St. Louis; https://fred.stlouisfed.org/series/WALCL.

lxix. Federal Reserve Bank of St. Louis, Excess Reserves of Depository Institutions [EXCSRESNS]. (July 5, 2018). retrieved from FRED, Federal Reserve Bank of St. Louis; https://fred.stlouisfed.org/series/EXCSRESNS.

lxx. Board of Governors of the Federal Reserve System (U.S.). (July 5, 2018). Effective Federal Funds Rate [FEDFUNDS], retrieved from FRED, Federal Reserve Bank of St. Louis; https://fred.stlouisfed.org/series/FEDFUNDS.

lxxi. Policy Normalization Principles and Plans. Federal Reserve. https://www.federalreserve.gov/monetarypolicy/files/FOMC_Policy Normalization.pdf.

lxxii. Press Release. (December 16, 2015). Federal Reserve issues FOMC statement. https://www.federalreserve.gov/newsevents/pressreleases/monetary20151216a.htm.

lxxiii. Press Release. (September 20, 2017). Federal Reserve issues FOMC statement.

lxxiv. Federal Reserve Bank of St. Louis, Excess Reserves of Depository Institutions [EXCSRESNS]. (July 5, 2018). retrieved from FRED, Federal Reserve Bank of St. Louis; https://fred.stlouisfed.org/series/EXCSRESNS.

lxxv. Bonis, Brian, Jane Ihrig, and Min Wei. (2017). "The Effect of the Federal Reserve's Securities Holdings on Longer-term Interest Rates." FEDS Notes. Washington: Board of Governors of the Federal Reserve System. April 20, 2017. https://doi.org/10.17016/2380-7172.1977.

lxxvi. Federal Reserve Bank of St. Louis, Excess Reserves of Depository Institutions [EXCSRESNS]. (July 5, 2018). retrieved from FRED, Federal Reserve Bank of St. Louis; https://fred.stlouisfed.org/series/EXCSRESNS.

lxxvii. S. 2856. Financial Services Regulatory Relief Act of 2006. Congressional Budget Office Cost Estimate. November 29, 2006. Table 2.

lxxviii. Wolf Richter, Wolf Street. "The Fed paid banks $30 billion on 'excess reserves' for 2017." (January 11, 2018). *Business Insider*. http://www.businessinsider.com/fed-paid-banks-30-billion-on-excess-reserves-for-2017-2018-1.

lxxix. Bauer, Michael D. and Thomas M. Mertens. (March 5, 2018). "Economic Forecasts with the Yield Curve." FRBSF Economic Letter.

lxxx. Wheelock, David C. "The Great Depression: An Overview." The Federal Reserve Bank of St. Louis. www.stlouisfed.org/education.

lxxxi. Friedman, Milton and Anna Jacobson Schwartz. (1963). *A Monetary History of the United States, 1867–1960*. Princeton University Press. p. 300.

lxxxii. Remarks by Governor Ben S. Bernanke. (November 8, 2002). At the Conference to Honor Milton Friedman. University of Chicago, Chicago, IL. https://www.federalreserve.gov/BOARDDOCS/SPEECHES/2002/20021108/default.htm.

lxxxiii. U.S. Bureau of Labor Statistics. Consumer Price Index for All Urban Consumers: All Items [CPIAUCNS]. (March 2, 2019). retrieved from FRED, Federal Reserve Bank of St. Louis; https://fred.stlouisfed.org/series/CPIAUCNS.

lxxxiv. Phillips, A.W. (1958). "The Relationship between Unemployment and the Rate of Change of Money Wages in the United Kingdom 1861–1957." *Economica* 25, No. 100: pp. 283–99. http://www.jstor.org/stable/2550759.

lxxxv. U.S. Bureau of Labor Statistics, Civilian Unemployment Rate [UNRATE]. (March 2, 2019). retrieved from FRED, Federal Reserve Bank of St. Louis; https://fred.stlouisfed.org/series/UNRATE.

lxxxvi. Friedman, Milton. (March 1968). The Role of Monetary Policy. "The American Economic Review." Vol. 58, No. 1. pp. 1–17.

lxxxvii. Remarks by Governor Ben S. Bernanke. (February 20, 2004). At the meetings of the Eastern Economic Association, Washington, DC. https://www.federalreserve.gov/BOARDDOCS/SPEECHES/2004/20040220/default.htm.

lxxxviii. Bordo, M. (2014). "Rules for a Lender of Last Resort: An Historical Perspective." Paper prepared for the Conference—Central Banking in the Next Century: A Policy Conference. Hoover Institution. Stanford, CA.

Part II

Investing and Portfolio Construction

5

INVESTMENT STRATEGIES

Ben Emons
Managing Director
Medley Global Advisors

David E. Linton, CFA
Director, Portfolio Construction and Manager Research
Pacific Life Fund Advisors LLC

It was 1999 and at the age of 16, I had just opened an Ameritrade online brokerage account with $2,000, which was my savings from almost 10 years of birthdays, weekly allowances, and selling candy to kids at my bus stop. I had read several investing books on stock picking and had found an online screening tool that could help me sift through the thousands of equities to find true gems. Ten-baggers, here I come! My first investment was a small-cap U.S. consumer electronics company with big plans for expansion. The firm already had over a thousand different products, including speakers, joysticks, cordless phones, CD players, and many more. It was also cheap, trading around 10× forward earnings, and these earnings would likely grow rapidly as the firm deleveraged following a recent wave of acquisitions. About two weeks after my investment, in March 1999, Recoton Corporation released its earnings; top-line sales were strong and net income (before a one-time charge) rose 41% from the prior year. However, the company disclosed it was adding a $15 million provision for an expected customs settlement, and it announced: "The Company plans to enter guilty pleas to a number of counts involving country of origin mismarking and undervaluation of imports, which will be subject to judicial approval."[i] After the provision, quarterly generally accepted accounting principles (GAAP) earnings would be −$0.53/share versus $0.66/share the prior year. The stock fell 25%. I was devastated. Why couldn't I have been like Ray Dalio, founder of the world's largest hedge fund, whose first stock pick *at age 12* tripled?[ii] I sat in my room, staring at the red in my online brokerage account, and did a bit of soul searching. What could I learn from this, and how can I make back my initial investment? I sold Recoton the next day, even though the investment chat rooms suggested I do otherwise—and it was one of my better investment decisions because the firm filed for bankruptcy protection four years later.[iii]

While my first stock pick was a disaster, I'm happy to say that the story ends well. When I graduated from high school the following year, my brokerage account had experienced the 10× growth that I had naïvely anticipated, and I left for college with around $18,000 in my Ameritrade account. After my Recoton fiasco, I pivoted from fundamental analysis and began day trading and market making with a bias toward shorting stocks that had recently appreciated but their momentum had turned. Truth be told, despite the healthy profits I made while placing limit orders in my broker account from teachers' computers during passing period, some luck was certainly involved. Additionally, I knew relatively little about either investing or speculating and would have had difficulty answering any of these questions:

- What is the difference between investing and speculating?
- What are all the considerations that would lead someone to buy or sell a security?
- What makes investing either *active* or *passive*?
- When should an investor rebalance their portfolio?
- Does buying in insurance constitute a form of investing?

Years later, drawing on some experience and education and after plenty of time for reflection, Ben Emons and I will field these questions in this chapter.

INVESTING AND SPECULATING

In their seminal work, "Security Analysis" (1934), Benjamin Graham and David Dodd distinguish between investing and speculating when they write, "An investment operation is one which, upon thorough analysis, promises safety of principal and a satisfactory return. Operations not meeting these requirements are speculative."[iv] Benjamin Graham further differentiates between investing and speculating in *The Intelligent Investor* (1959) when he states, "An investor calculates what a stock is worth based on the value of its businesses. A speculator gambles that a stock will go up in price because somebody else will pay even more for it."[v] With this insight as a guide, we can further segregate trading activity into investing and speculating based upon three considerations:

- *Pre-transaction due diligence*: investing involves a detailed analysis of cash flows, the riskiness of those cash flows, and the discounting of those cash flows to arrive at a current valuation. Speculating typically involves calculating the potential range of future prices of a security and assessing the likelihood that those prices will be realized in order to arrive at a probability-adjusted future price of a security.
- *Time horizon*: investing usually has a horizon that stretches out over several years. Warren Buffet wrote in his 1988 letter to shareholders of Berkshire Hathaway: "In fact, when we own portions of outstanding businesses with outstanding managements, our favorite holding period is forever."[vi] Conversely, speculators' expected holding period can be as short as days or hours; high-frequency traders (HFTs) may trade in and out of securities in microseconds!
- *Source of profit*: investments derive their profit from an appreciation in the value of an enterprise, which explains Graham and Buffett's relentless focus on identifying well-run businesses. Speculators generate profit from the appreciation of the securities, which may or may not reflect a change in the fundamentals of the enterprise to which they are attached.

So, how does one go about valuing an enterprise, or generating a probability-weighted future price of a security? We will briefly introduce these concepts here.

Fundamental Analysis

Benjamin Graham, and his most famous pupil Warren Buffet, both relied heavily on fundamental analysis prior to purchasing or selling a security or company. The objective of fundamental analysis is to determine the intrinsic value of a business or security, which is the estimate of the current value of future cash flows. However, the future is uncertain, and with the exception of fixed income (bond) investing, future cash flows are highly variable. So, how can we place a dollar value on an investment with an uncertain future? While there are several methods for establishing intrinsic value, two commonly utilized models are the dividend discount model (DDM) and the discounted cash flow (DCF) model.

American economist and professor John Burr Williams is credited with advancing the notion of an investment's intrinsic value in this 1938 text *The Theory of Investment Value*. In 1956, Professors Myron Gordon and Eli Shapiro published *Capital Equipment Analysis: The Required Rate of Profit*. The authors reference Williams but go on to state, "The models he developed were arbitrary and complicated,"[vii] before proposing what would later be known as the *Gordon Growth Model* or *Dividend Discount Model*.

This model is:

$$P = \frac{D_1}{r-g}$$

Where:

P is the price of a stock today,
D_1 is the dividend next year,
r is the discount rate or cost of equity capital, and
g is the growth rate of the dividends.

This model was quickly adopted among professionals for several reasons. First, it is simple and allows an analyst to estimate the degree to which the value of a company, and thus its stock, will respond to changes in assumptions. Specifically, if a company's dividend increases in size, or the company becomes less risky and therefore its cost of equity financing declines, or the expectation for the future dividend growth rate increases, the company's intrinsic value will rise. Second, at the time this model was introduced, most publicly traded companies were dividend-paying industrials, rails, and utilities, almost all of which could be valued with this model. Finally, this model could be utilized to determine which securities were trading below and above their intrinsic value, and which securities were *rich* or *cheap* to their peers.

However, the dividend discount model has several limitations. Some companies pay no dividends (like Berkshire Hathaway) and may not pay dividends in the foreseeable horizon. Additionally, this model assumes that companies that do pay dividends will experience steady growth rates and constant discount rates. Furthermore, this model is highly sensitive to changes in growth rate and discount rate assumptions. Additionally, not all economists agree that dividends are even relevant to the calculation of the value of a company. Franco Modigliani and Merton Miller posited in their famous 1958 article *The Cost of Capital, Corporation Finance and the Theory of Investment*, that a company's value is based on a "stream of profits, not dividends . . . the division of the stream between cash dividends and retained earnings in any period is a mere detail."[viii] Modigliani and Miller further elaborate that whether a company chooses to retain earnings or distribute cash to shareholders, the economic value of the entity remains unchanged. Challenging Modigliani and Miller's assertion of the irrelevance of dividend policy, in 2003, Cliff Asness and Rob Arnott published a paper demonstrating that higher dividend yields correspond to higher future earnings growth in equities.[ix] So, while paying more to investors in the form of a dividend does not make a company more profitable, a high dividend yield may be used as a proxy for the degree to which a company is efficiently run.

To address some of the theoretical and practical shortcomings of the DDM, financial analysts now use a variety of DCF models often in lieu of a DDM. While the process of calculating a present value by discounting expected cash flows had become a common financial practice by the 19th century in England,[x] use of the DCF model has since evolved to value entire enterprises while incorporating standardized accounting data. The DCF model is like the dividend discount model that the objective is to discount future cash flows to arrive at a present value. However, unlike a simple dividend discount model, the various DCF models can be sufficiently bespoke so that any company can be valued even if it pays no dividend, is expected to experience time-varying growth rates, or will experience time-varying leverage and capital expenses. The formula for a DCF model is:

$$DPV = \sum_{t=0}^{N} \frac{FV_t}{(1+r)^t}$$

Whereby:

DPV is the present value of all future cash flows,
FV is the future cash flow at time t,
r is the discount rate at time t,
and N is the time in years.

The cash flow being valued can be either the free cash flow to firm (FCFF), which is the cash generated by a company after all operating expenses and required re-investments in working capital, or the free cash flow to equity (FCFE), which is roughly the FCFF minus debt payments. Assuming there is debt financing and that the leverage of the firm may change through time, the appropriate numerator is FCFF. If using the FCFF in the numerator, the appropriate discount rate is the firm's weighted average cost of capital (WACC). WACC is the discount rate that incorporates at any given period the firm's cost of equity, the percentage of equity capital, the cost of the firm's debt financing, and the percentage of debt financing. Finally, an analyst can incorporate as many time periods as warranted to fully incorporate his or her view of the evolution of the organization's operations and profitability.

While DDM and DCF models will each generate a single point estimate for the value of a company given its inputs, in practice an analyst cannot know, with certainty, each input. So, the next step of fundamental analysis is to generate a range of reasonable valuations. To do this, the analyst begins with the midpoint of their best guess of future growth rates and appropriate discount rates, and then reruns the model with higher or lower growth rates and discount rates.

Doing so allows the analyst to develop a range, or grid, with the output of reasonable valuations, conditional on a variety of assumptions. Once this analysis is complete, the final step is to choose an appropriate *margin of safety*. In *The Intelligent Investor*, Benjamin Graham explains the utility of margin of safety as: ". . . rendering unnecessary an accurate estimate of the future. If the margin is a large one, then it is enough to assume that future earnings will not fall far below those of the past in order for an investor to feel sufficiently protected against the vicissitudes of time."[xi] In practice, this means if an analyst believes an investment is worth between $80 to $120 a share and the stock is currently traded at $99, then there is little or no margin of safety. However, if the stock is currently trading at $79 a share, then there is likely a sufficient margin of safety to warrant an investment.

In November 2009, Berkshire Hathaway announced its intention to purchase the 77.4% stake of railroad Burlington Northern Santa Fe that it did not already own. The price was about $100 in cash and Berkshire Hathaway stock. On the heels of the announcement, Burlington Northern stock jumped from $76.06 to $98.15. In a written statement, Buffett said, "It's an all-in wager on the economic future of the United States," which, at the time, was recovering from the Great Recession.[xii] The relevance to us is that management of Burlington Northern hired Goldman Sachs to assess whether $100 was a *fair* price, and then disclosed this analysis in the SEC Schedule 14A form (which is the form that is filed when management requires a shareholder vote). Depending on the outlook of the U.S. economy and a variety of manager inputs, Goldman assessed the value of BNSF stock to be between $39.44 to $123.01; thus, they concluded that $100 was fair. No doubt Buffett and his team ran their own DCF models and felt more confident with the forward outlook of both the U.S. economy in general and railroads in particular, which was the *all-in* wager to which Buffett alluded.[xiii]

Technical Analysis

In contrast to fundamental analysis, in which the analyst attempts to ascertain the intrinsic value of a security or investment, technical analysis focuses only on the expected future price of a security. Technical analysis does not incorporate earnings, dividends, discount rates, or any other relevant input into a valuation model. Rather, the exclusive focus is analyzing financial markets data to estimate the likely near-term price movement of a security. Charles Henry Dow—an American journalist, cofounder of Dow Jones & Company, and editor of the Wall Street Journal—is credited as advancing the notion that markets have trends that persist over various time periods. In 1912, S. A. Nelson wrote *The ABC of Stock Speculation*, in which he coined the term *Dow Theory* and elaborated on Dow's earlier writings and investment philosophy. Dow believed that price action can be categorized into different trends that last over different time periods. Primary trends last four to six years, secondary trends move counter to the primary trend and last around 30 to 40 days, and minor trends are largely noise that are unrelated to either the primary or secondary trend.[xiv] The implication of this classification system is that if a speculator can identify this trend before it fully plays out, he or she can profit by either purchasing or shorting securities ahead of future price movements.

Technical analysis has been embraced by a minority of traders, many not professional, who exclusively utilize charts and other tools to trade stocks, futures, currencies, and other financial assets. These analysts, or chartists, look for price movement patterns with fun names like *head and shoulders, falling wedge, ascending triangle,* and *cup with handle.* A benefit of this approach is that an analyst with little or no knowledge of a company can develop an investment thesis after identifying a perceived pattern in stock prices; this thesis does not require the hours of painstaking due diligence that a fundamental analyst would employ. Critics of these techniques are many and most academics believe technical analysis to be a pseudoscience. In *A Random Walk Down Wall Street* (1973), Burton Malkiel dismissed technical analysis and wrote: ". . . under scientific scrutiny, chart-reading must share a pedestal with alchemy."[xv] The *Efficient Market Hypothesis,* which states that all past information is incorporated into the current price of a security, and if correct, would indicate that no incremental trading gains can be consistently generated by exclusively analyzing past security price movements. However, in 2000, MIT professors Lo, Mamaysky, and Wang, utilizing academically accepted statistical approaches, analyzed several of the chartist approaches to generating buy and sell decisions. They concluded that "certain technical patterns do provide incremental information," but that "this does not necessarily imply that technical analysis can be used to generate excess trading profits."[xvi]

Separately, in 1997, University of Southern California professor Mark Carhart published *On Persistence in Mutual Fund Performance,* in which he showed that purchasing top-performing funds and selling bottom-performing funds could yield excess returns. Additionally, this excess performance could be largely explained by adding the *one-year momentum anomaly* to a three-factor model.[xvii] In the following years, momentum became a generally accepted *factor.* Technical analysts were quick to point out that momentum is one of the price patterns that chartists are attempting to identify as they look for patterns in stocks. For example, purchasing a security because its price has risen above a simple moving-average line is akin to investing in a stock with a positive exposure to the momentum factor. This argument wasn't lost among financial academics, and at the 2016 Fiduciary Investors Symposium in Chicago, Professor Eugene Fama stated, "Momentum, in my view, is the biggest embarrassment for efficient markets," and that he is ". . . hoping it goes away."[xviii] Therefore, while many academics still scoff at the notion that excess trading returns can be generated by analyzing charts, most admit that the persistence of the *momentum* factor indicates that some valuable information (however small) can be gleaned from analyzing past price movements.

High-Frequency Trading

While high-frequency trading is not technical analysis, there are a few similarities. Technical analysis involves buying and selling securities with short investment horizons and without consideration to the fundamentals of the company. If this approach is taken to the extreme with an investment horizon of a second or less, buy/sell decisions are derived exclusively from trade data, and human intervention or subjective analysis are removed, we arrive at high-frequency trading. High-frequency trading is first and foremost a type of algorithmic trading strategy. An algorithmic trading strategy involves the use of real-time data and computer algorithms to optimize trading execution via order routing, breaking orders into smaller sizes, biding and offering for securities on different exchanges, rapidly canceling and revising those bids and offers, and much more. While people program these algorithms and monitor the trading, people turn over trading authority to computers that can process the data and execute trades within microseconds (one one-millionth of a second). Traditional asset managers may use trading algorithms as a tool to execute orders; for example, if an order is large (say, 1% of the outstanding capitalization of the firm), an asset manager may utilize an algorithm to gradually purchase or sell shares over hours or days with the objective of gaining best execution. HFTs, on the other hand, utilize algorithms not as a tool to implement investment strategies; rather, the computer-generated trading of securities at a profit *is* the investment strategy.[xix]

Investment banks were early adopters of algorithms to complement their human traders. However, in April 2014, the U.S. Department of the Treasury amended Section 619 of the Dodd-Frank Wall Street Reform and Consumer Protection Act (also known as the *Volcker rule*), which generally prohibits insured depository institutions from engaging in proprietary trading.[xx] Proprietary trading involves the use of one's own capital to earn a spread by buying and selling securities with market participants. Because of this regulation, banks in the United States have largely shed their high-frequency trading operations. In Europe, some banks remain active in market making; however, higher capital charges have led them to curtail these operations. This has acted as a windfall to dozens of proprietary trading firms that have filled the hole left by banks and added talent to its ranks and volume to its operations. Some of the largest high-frequency trading firms include: Citadel Securities, Virtu

Financial, Hudson River Trading, Jump Trading, DRW Holdings, and GTS. With respect to their aggregate size, TABB Group, an international capital markets consulting group, estimates high-frequency trading has been responsible for about 50% to 60% of total U.S. equities' daily volume for each calendar year between 2008 and 2017.[xxi]

The most typical strategy employed by high-frequency trading is market making. A market maker is a firm or entity that is ready to purchase or sell a security at any given time, at a price it has posted. A market maker therefore provides a service—standing ready to transact should another investor choose to buy or sell at the advertised price. The primary source of income for a market maker is earning a *spread*, which is the difference in price between the amount paid for a security and the price at which it was sold. This spread is not guaranteed, so the market maker assumes risk while providing other market participants with liquidity (or the ability to transact). Proponents of high-frequency trading are quick to assert that the market-making service they provide is the same service that has been provided for over a hundred years, beginning with a specialist sitting at his post on the floor of an exchange and updating prices on a chalkboard. Additionally, the adoption of algorithms has materially reduced aggregate trading costs since this technology has rendered unnecessary the armies of runners, traders, and their supporting staff. Supporting this claim, Ken French (2006) calculated that the total cost of trading (as a percentage of the total trading volume) U.S. equities fell from 1.46% in 1980 to 0.11% in 2006.[xxii] This reduction in trading costs is a windfall to investors who enjoy significantly tighter bid/offer spreads and lower commissions. Some well-known institutional investors agree. In a 2014 op-ed, AQR Founder Cliff Asness wrote: "How do we feel about high-frequency trading? We think it helps us. It seems to have reduced our costs and may enable us to manage more investment dollars. . . . we devote a lot of effort to understanding our trading costs; and our opinion, derived through quantitative and qualitative analysis, is that on the whole, high-frequency traders have lowered costs."[xxiii]

However, some in the financial industry strongly disagree and believe that high-frequency trading is detrimental to beneficial investors. Taking aim at this industry, in 2014, Michael Lewis published *Flash Boys* in which he described how computers, algorithms, and mathematicians have come to dominate the securities trading landscape. In a *60 Minutes* interview, he summarized his findings when he stated, "The United States stock market—the most iconic market in global capitalism—is rigged," and "high-frequency traders can *identify your desire to buy shares*, buy them, and sell them to you at a higher price."[xxiv] Other critics argue that while high-frequency trading increases volume or number of shares transacting, it does not increase market *depth*, which is the ability to transact large quantities at any one time. This is because HFTs are not market makers as defined by the Securities and Exchange Commission (SEC). The SEC defines a market maker as "an entity that is willing both to buy and sell on a regular or continuous basis at a publicly quoted price."[xxv] Furthermore, some exchanges have a *lead market maker* who agrees with the exchange to make continuous markets.[xxvi] This is highly relevant in instances of severe market volatility, which usually occurs when the value of the stock market falls. Specifically, when the stock market is falling, high-frequency trading algorithms may stop trading whereas true market makers continue to buy and sell securities. So, critics of high-frequency trading argue that these traders provide liquidity when liquidity is plentiful and fail to provide liquidity when it is most needed.

The *Flash Crash* of 2010 provides us with an excellent case study to assess whether algorithmic and high-frequency trading contributes to or is a detriment to market liquidity and financial stability. On May 6, 2010, at 2:32 p.m., a large institution initiated a program to sell a total of 75,000 E-Mini contracts, valued at approximately $4.1 billion, as a hedge to an existing equity position. While the name of the institution was withheld from the official U.S. Commodity Futures Trading Commission and U.S. Securities & Exchange Commission report, it was later leaked that the fund manager was Waddell & Reed Financial Inc., which was acting on behalf of the Ivy Asset Strategy Fund.[xxvii] According to the awkwardly worded official report, "The *sell algorithm* that was chosen by the large trader to only target trading volume, but neither price nor time, executed the sell program extremely rapidly—in just 20 minutes." In the past, algorithms executing similar orders had always limited the rate of selling based on time, market impact, or both. Additionally, the execution of previous similar orders took around five hours and not 20 minutes.[xxviii] By 2:45 p.m., in less than 15 minutes and on the heels of rapid selling without regard to price, the market fell about 7%, which pushed the index to −9% for the day. In that short timespan, nearly $1 trillion worth of equity market value was eliminated. Once selling pressure from the large trade subsided, U.S. equities quickly rebounded and the S&P 500 closed the day at −3.2%. Following the leaks that Waddell & Reed was the unnamed culprit in the U.S. Common Futures Trading Commission (CFTC) and SEC report, Waddell & Reed responded to the report and argued that they were not solely responsible for the *Flash Crash*. In 2015, they were, to a small degree, exonerated. On February 11, 2015, the U.S. District Court of Illinois filed a criminal complaint against Navinder Singh Sarao, a 36-year-old day trader who was living just outside of London. The complaint stated that "he had contributed to the *Flash Crash* by *spoofing* the S&P E-Mini contracts that Waddell & Reed happened to be selling."[xxix] Spoofing involves the placement of large orders to give the appearance of significant interest in the purchasing or selling of a security or index. The individual that places the orders has no intention of executing them, and so these orders are intended to mislead market participants. According to the CFTC, which filed a complaint against Sarao the following April, "These orders represented approximately $170 million to over $200 million worth of persistent downward pressure on the E-mini S&P price and, over the next two hours, represented 20%–29% of the entire sell side of the order book. The orders were replaced or modified more than 19,000 times before being canceled."[xxx] On November 9, 2016, Sarao pleaded guilty to one count of wire fraud and one count of spoofing shortly after being extradited to the United States.[xxxi]

So, are HFTs to blame for the Flash Crash as critics claim? Well, not really. The Flash Crash began when a trader chose an inappropriate algorithm to execute a large block trade, and that trader failed to modify or cancel their order as the market began to rapidly decline. So, while a computer was executing the sell orders, the market-moving poor execution can be largely attributed to human error. Second, a high-speed trader contributed to the rapid decline in the equity market by spoofing, or placing large orders to mislead participants regarding the existence of unexecuted buy or sell orders. However, while an algorithm and high-speed trader were major contributions to the Flash Crash, this rogue trader's actions were illegal and the algorithm was merely the tool used to commit a crime. Finally, what about the claim that during instances of heightened volatility, high-speed traders withdraw liquidity? The 2010 joint report from the U.S. CFTC and SEC is mixed. Specifically, with respect to HFTs, the report states: "We did not find uniformity in response to market conditions on May 6. Although some HFTs exited the market for reasons similar to other market participants, such as the triggering of their internal risk parameters due to rapid price moves and subsequent data-integrity concerns, other HFTs continued to trade actively." However, it concludes that while the HFTs continued to trade, they may have, on average, exacerbated the initial drop in the equity markets. Specifically, the report states: "It appears that the 17 HFT firms traded with the price trend on May 6 and, on both an absolute and net basis, removed significant buy liquidity from the public quoting markets during the downturn."

PASSIVE VERSUS ACTIVE INVESTMENT

Regardless of whether an analyst or firm utilizes fundamental or technical analysis, or some blend of the two, both approaches include the development and execution of an investment thesis prior to purchasing and selling securities. As a result, both approaches are considered *active* investing. In contrast, *passive* investors attempt to merely track market benchmarks, such as the S&P 500, and do not attempt to outperform these benchmarks using fundamental or technical analysis. Passive management is often implemented by holding each of the indices' constituent securities in proportion to their representation in the index. If the quantity of securities is exceptionally numerous or difficult to source, the manager may utilize a rules-based sampling method to develop a portfolio that closely matches the index. A passive investment strategy would require no trading in the absence of changes in index composition or cash flows within the portfolio. Passive investing is not appropriate for all asset classes because it requires an index in which the constituents are publicly traded liquid securities. For this reason, asset classes—for example, private equity, real estate, and other alternatives such as hedge funds—have seen limited adoption of passive strategies. Conversely, equity and fixed income asset classes meet these criteria and have garnered most of the passive flows.

The rationale for the utilization of passive investment strategies was explained by Professor William Sharpe (1991) in his paper *The Arithmetic of Active Management*. In it he states, "If *active* and *passive* management styles are defined in sensible ways, it must be the case that: (1) before costs, the return on the average actively managed dollar will equal the return on the average passively managed dollar, and (2) after costs, the return on the average actively managed dollar will be less than the return on the average passively managed dollar."[xxxii] The implication is that the manager who minimizes expenses—including both trading costs and management fees—on average, will outperform the manager who charges higher fees and attempts to outperform the market through superior asset allocation, trading, market making, or security selection.

Since publishing that paper, Professor Sharpe has largely been proven correct. Every year S&P publishes its SPIVA (which stands for S&P indexes versus active management) U.S. scorecard. In this annual report, S&P calculates nearly every U.S. fund manager return, net of fees (but excluding loads) alpha, versus their benchmarks and over various time periods. The results? Not good for active management. For the five-year period ending December 31, 2017, 84.2% of large-cap managers, 85.1% of mid-cap managers, and 91.2% of small-cap managers lagged their respective benchmarks. Similarly, for the 15-year period ending December 31, 2017, 92.3% of large-cap managers, 94.8% of mid-cap managers, and 95.7% of small-cap managers lagged their respective benchmarks. The results were similar but not quite as damning for active fixed-income managers. For the five-year period ending December 31, 2017, 52.6% of Barclays Global Aggregate managers, 40.9% of Barclays U.S. Government/Credit intermediate managers, and 85.7% of Barclays Emerging Markets managers lagged their benchmarks. Similarly, for the 15-year period, 69.4% of Barclays Global Aggregate managers, 73.5% of Barclays U.S. Government/Credit Intermediate managers, and 66.7% of Barclays Emerging Markets managers lagged their benchmarks. This study attempts to control for survivorship bias by including closed funds during each period of study.[xxxiii] Critics of this report are quick to point out that this study is comparing active managers versus their benchmarks, and not active managers versus their passive counterparts. This is relevant because over each time period, net of fees, passive managers underperform their benchmarks nearly 100% of the time! Additionally, this study does not speak to the relative magnitude of underperformance (i.e, who underperforms less—active or passive), nor does it demonstrate which asset classes are more appropriate for active management or passive management.

Nevertheless, given the lackluster performance of active management and the growing library of academic literature suggesting it is impossible to consistently outperform the market, it should be no surprise that flows into passively managed portfolios are outpacing flows into actively managed portfolios. According to the Morningstar Direct 2018 Asset Flows Commentary, flows into actively managed U.S. equity portfolios have been flat to negative in each calendar year from 2006 through 2017, while flows into passively managed U.S. equity portfolios have been flat to positive each year over the same period. According to Morningstar, this active-to-passive equity rotation peaked in 2016 when actively managed U.S. equity portfolios experienced approximately $250 billion in outflows while passively managed U.S. equity portfolios received slightly over $200 billion in inflows.[xxxiv] Investment Company Institute data tells a similar story. Figure 5.1 shows that since January 2008, actively managed equity mutual funds have experienced $1.3 trillion in cumulative outflows while passively managed equity mutual funds and exchange-traded funds (ETFs) have experienced nearly $1.6 trillion in cumulative inflows.[xxxv] This active-to-passive

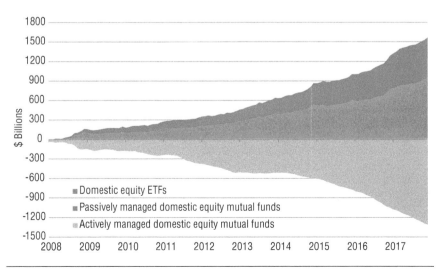

Figure 5.1   Cumulative flows into passively managed equity funds and out of actively managed equity funds. *Source*: Investment Company Institute

rotation seems to be largely confined to equity investments, however. Flows into actively managed taxable-bond portfolios have been positive in nine of the past 12 years ending in 2017, while flows into passively managed taxable-bond portfolios have been positive every calendar year from 2006 through 2017.[xxxvi]

Not everybody is convinced, however, that this migration to passive investing will ultimately benefit investors. In an interview on CNBC in 2017, Nobel Prize-winning economist Robert Shiller stated, "The problem is that if you are talking about passive indexing, that is something that is really free-riding on other people's work. So people say, 'I'm not going to try to beat the market. The market is all-knowing.' But how in the world can the market be all-knowing, if nobody is trying—well, not as many people—are trying to beat it?" Dr. Shiller went on to call indexing a pseudoscience.[xxxvii] Similarly, in March 2017, Ned Davis (founder of Ned Davis Research Group, a large institutional research provider) wrote a piece entitled *The Passive Investing Bubble*. In this report, Davis makes the case that passive flows have helped inflate equity prices that are *clearly in bubble territory*. Davis further makes the case that declining correlations between asset classes and individual equities will provide active stock pickers with an opportunity to outperform passive mandates.[xxxviii]

Separately, the March 2018 Bank of International Settlements (BIS) Quarterly Review included a paper entitled "The implications of passive investing for securities markets." In it, the authors make the case that an increase in the size of passive mandates may lead to "less security-specific information." This is another way of saying that price movements of securities may be increasingly driven by events such as the inclusion of a security in an index or a broader re-allocation of capital, and not a change in the fundamentals of a company. This further suggests that prices of companies may deviate from their intrinsic value due to capital flows. The authors conclude that while the current "effect on security prices and issuers may not be large . . . the effects could become significant if the passive fund management industry continues to expand." The authors of the paper further speculate that passive funds may help facilitate additional leverage, meaning large corporations are more leveraged today than would be the case had there been no passive funds. This is because "the largest issuers tend to be more heavily represented in bond indices. As passive bond funds mechanically replicate the index weights in their portfolios, their growth will generate demand for the debt of the larger, and potentially more leveraged, issuers."[xxxix]

In another related study,[xl] the Federal Reserve Bank of Boston examined the growth of the passive index industry. They concluded there are three channels through which passive index funds may pose a risk to financial stability. First, leveraged and inverse passive strategies could increase financial volatility. Both types of funds, because of their design and objectives, trade in the same direction as market movements earlier in the day. So, as equities rise, the funds buy the market, and they sell when equities fall. This type of high-frequency trading may exacerbate short-term market movements. Second, due to the rapid growth of index funds, the asset management industry is going through a consolidation that could lead to overconcentration of assets. Specifically, passive management assets are more concentrated than active management assets, and an idiosyncratic event at a single fund manager may lead to outsized flows and market disruption. Finally, the authors speculate that index funds are *price inelastic* investors because their sole objective is to meet the weights of the index rather than achieving a total return bogey. As a result, it is likely index funds have impacted the security valuations, volatility, and co-movement of assets included in indexes by causing liquid, on-the-run[1] securities to become overvalued.

REBALANCING STRATEGIES

Irrespective of whether an investor utilizes an active or passive strategy, or if a professional money manager hired by an investor utilizes fundamental or technical analysis, an investor's asset allocation will drift over time. Additionally, this drift will require investors to rebalance their portfolio in order to maintain given risk and return objectives. The drift in a portfolio's allocation is driven by the fact that not all holdings in the portfolio appreciate or depreciate by the same amount over a given period. For example, Mike is 50 years old and saving for his retirement. He currently has $200,000 saved, and after consulting with a financial planner, he determines that a balanced portfolio with 50% equities and 50% bonds is appropriate given his return objective and risk aversion. Imagine for a moment that not long after creating his 50%/50% policy portfolio, equities appreciate 20% while bonds remain unchanged and generate a 0% return. Mike's portfolio has appreciated to $220,000, but it is now 54.5% equities ($120,000) and 45.5% bonds ($100,000). Given the fact that his equity allocation is currently 4.5% higher than his initial allocation, what should he do, and when should he do it? And if he rebalances, should he fully rebalance (to a 50/50 portfolio) or partially rebalance (say, to 52/48—equities/bonds)?

The answers to these questions are not entirely straightforward. During the rebalancing process, which generally includes selling assets that have appreciated and purchasing assets that have depreciated, the investor will incur expenses that fall into three categories. The first expense category is the aggregate

---

[1] On-the-run describes the most recently issued security from an issuer that periodically issues debt. For example, the U.S. Treasury issues new 10-year notes once a quarter. Following the issuance of a new 10-year note, the newly issued security is considered on-the-run while the previous on-the-run security (and all other previously issued 10-year notes) are now considered off-the-run.

transaction costs associated with executed orders. Transaction costs may include fees levied on selling shares in funds and incurring bid/offer expenses when transacting securities, ETFs (exchange-traded funds), closed-end funds, or other instruments. The second expense category is the tax liability incurred while transacting; selling an appreciated asset may lead to capital gains or ordinary income taxes. The third category is the implicit cost of the investor's time should the investor actively monitor their portfolio and guide the rebalance herself.

But, not rebalancing can lead to other, albeit implicit, expenses. The first such expense is the portfolio's deviation from what might otherwise be considered *optimal*. In Mike's case, a 50/50 stock/bond portfolio is optimal given his return objective and his willingness to assume risk—plus, as academics might describe, it is most appropriate given the objective to maximize expected utility. So, any deviation from his 50/50 portfolio will come at an expected loss of investor utility because of a change in the ex-ante risk and return profile of the new portfolio. The second expense is the likely increase in portfolio volatility that is associated with failing to rebalance. A portfolio that has both equities and bonds will generally experience an upward drift in the allocation to equities, which will lead to higher portfolio volatility. In fact, a hypothetical portfolio that holds securities that are equally volatile and have identical expected returns will experience an increase in volatility over time if the securities are not rebalanced since positions will naturally become increasingly concentrated. The final implicit expense of failing to rebalance is a potential opportunity cost of not improving the return of the portfolio due to rebalancing. In 1982, Robert Fernholz and Brian Shay demonstrated mathematically that under certain circumstances (no transaction costs, no taxes, perfect liquidity, a random walk, etc.), a portfolio that is continuously rebalancing will outperform a portfolio with no rebalancing; the authors referred to this rebalancing premium as *excess growth*.[xli] Later, Leland (1999) demonstrated that a portfolio strategy that involves selling covered calls or is constantly rebalancing has a concave return profile. Because of the concave return profile, a constantly rebalancing portfolio has higher expected return for a given exposure to the equity market.[xlii] Separately, in a 2015 AQR white paper, Ilmanen and Maloney showed that for a simple two-asset portfolio (stocks and bonds) and five-asset portfolio (two equity, two bond, and one commodity), from 1972 to 2014, rebalancing both improved portfolio return and reduced portfolio volatility irrespective of the rebalancing strategy that was employed.[xliii]

In short, a rebalancing strategy can be viewed as an expense minimization exercise: an investor should attempt to minimize transaction costs, taxes, and their time on the one hand, while also attempting to minimize a deviation from optimal portfolio allocation, portfolio volatility, and a potentially higher returning portfolio owing to rebalancing. The key is setting an appropriate threshold for rebalancing. There is no one-size-fits-all threshold that is appropriate because each investor's situation is unique; however, there are a few options and rules-of-thumb that we'll review here.

Calendar Rebalancing

Also called *time dependent* rebalancing, this strategy involves rebalancing to a policy portfolio at a predetermined interval, irrespective of the portfolio's deviation at the time of the rebalance. The time interval might be monthly, quarterly, or annually. The benefit of this approach is that it provides the investor with a clearly defined risk management prescription. Additionally, it ensures that deviations from the policy portfolio will likely remain relatively small as portfolio drift over a quarter or even a year will remain relatively mild. The primary disadvantage to this strategy is that there might be unnecessarily high transaction expenses and tax impacts. This is because some trading might occur even if the portfolio's deviation from a policy portfolio may be relatively small.

Additionally, if the time interval is short (monthly or quarterly), the investor may forgo some return due to an elimination of a potential momentum effect. Hurst, Ooi, and Pederson (2017) find evidence that a variety of investments exhibit momentum over 3- to 12-month periods.[xliv] In fact, backtests suggest that rebalancing *too frequently* may reduce performance; two separate studies have shown the hypothetical performance of portfolios that were rebalanced monthly is slightly lower than portfolios that were rebalanced annually.[2] However, attempting to time the rebalancing in order to accommodate for momentum may be somewhat impractical, especially since momentum may not be determined by recent performance. Rather, Novy-Marx (2010) suggests momentum is not determined by recent performance but by performance from the previous seven- to 12-month period.[xlv] If that's right, then this suggests that an asset manager should wait longer than 12 months prior to rebalancing, and he should not sell assets that appreciated seven to 12 months ago but have not materially appreciated in the past six months. In that case, he should wait another six months or so to rebalance. We think most investors agree that this approach is confusing and not practical. Instead, to address the potential of incurring unnecessarily high transaction expenses and lowering portfolio return by inadvertently selling the momentum factor, an investor may choose to utilize a *percentage of portfolio* rebalancing approach.

---

[2] See Exhibits 3 and A1 of Antti Ilmanen and Thomas Maloney. December 18, 2015. "Portfolio Rebalancing, Part 1: Strategic Asset Allocation" as well as Figure 5 of Jaconettei, Colleen M., Francis M. Kinniry Jr., Yan Zilbering, 2015. "Best practices for portfolio rebalancing."

Percentage of Portfolio Rebalancing

Also called *deviation from policy rebalancing*, this strategy involves rebalancing to a policy portfolio when the existing portfolio deviates by a given threshold, irrespective of time. This threshold may be 1%, 5%, 10%, or something else. The benefit of the approach is that it avoids rebalancing at a predetermined time even if the portfolio drift has been relatively mild. A disadvantage of this approach is that an investor will have to identify an approximate threshold and then continuously monitor the portfolio. Additionally, selecting a threshold may be difficult; a portfolio with two investments (for example, a stock and bond mutual fund) might necessitate a higher threshold (say 5%), while a portfolio with twenty investments might necessitate a lower threshold (say 1%). Finally, continuously monitoring might be an unnecessarily high burden for investors, particularly individuals. To address these concerns, many professionals utilize a *calendar and threshold* approach.

Calendar and Threshold Rebalancing

This strategy attempts to balance all of the previously mentioned concerns and involves rebalancing the portfolio on a scheduled basis (quarterly, annually, etc.)—but only if the portfolio, at the time of its review, has deviated by a predetermined threshold (3%, 5%, etc.). If the portfolio has not deviated by its given threshold when reviewed, it is not rebalanced. Similarly, if the portfolio deviates more than a given threshold prior to the scheduled calendar review, the portfolio is not rebalanced. The benefit of this approach is that it combines the benefit of avoiding potentially expensive and taxing rebalances when deviations from the policy portfolio are small, while simultaneously reducing the time needed to determine if a rebalancing is warranted. The disadvantage to this approach is that deviations from the policy portfolio may remain beyond the predetermined threshold until the next rebalancing period.

So, what approach is the most appropriate for investors? While there is no one-size-fits-all strategy as each investor's policy portfolio, tax situation, investment vehicles, and ability to monitor their portfolio is different, the analysts at Vanguard Research make a strong case that annual or semi-annual monitoring with a 5% threshold reasonably balances all considerations. In their 2015 white paper "Best Practices for Portfolio Rebalancing," the authors review a hypothetical 50/50 stock/bond portfolio from 1926 through 2014. The authors then compare the portfolio given the three rebalancing approaches (calendar, threshold, and calendar + threshold) utilizing different thresholds and frequencies. The authors further calculate the cost of rebalancing (utilizing annual turnover and number of rebalancing events are proxies for this expense), and finally calculate the hypothetical portfolio returns and realized volatility. Over the reviewed period, there was no material reduction in portfolio volatility by rebalancing monthly or quarterly, or setting tight thresholds (like 1%) versus annual rebalancing at a 5% threshold. Additionally, annual rebalancing at a 5% threshold reduced the number of rebalancing events over this 88-year period to only 36 instances. Vanguard Research caveats their conclusion by stating that their analysis does not include all tax considerations that are unique to each investor.[xlvi]

Income Redirecting

An additional approach to rebalancing is redirecting dividend and interest income such that this income is used to continually purchase whatever asset would bring the portfolio closer in line with the policy portfolio. This approach is also appropriate for investors who are saving and making regular contributions to their accounts. For taxable investors, income redirecting is a tax-efficient strategy because no securities are sold and no capital gains taxes will be incurred. In the aforementioned Vanguard study, the authors demonstrate that this rebalancing approach generates a risk-and-return profile similar to rebalancing annually at a 5% threshold, but with no portfolio turnover. The primary caveat in this analysis is that future dividend and interest income will likely be lower than over the period in which the 89-year period ended in 2014; so, unless the investor also makes regular contributions to his or her portfolio, the realized benefit of this strategy may be lower in the future than in the past. Said another way, a portfolio constituted today may not generate sufficient income in the future to ensure that the portfolio that is utilizing only income redirecting does not materially drift over time.

Constant Proportion Portfolio Insurance (CPPI)

The notion of CPPI was first introduced by Andre Perold (1986)[xlvii] for fixed income instruments and by Fischer Sheffey Black and Robert Jones (1987)[xlviii] for equity instruments. The authors view a portfolio as containing an *active* asset and a *reserve* asset that has both a lower return and less volatility than the active asset. Black and Jones equate the active asset to equities and the reserve asset to bonds. The authors further assume that the investor has a floor or minimum value of their portfolio, below which they do not want their portfolio value to fall. The CPPI portfolio approach recommends that the investor sell the active asset as the portfolio value falls and purchases the active asset as the portfolio value rises. In doing so, the portfolio de-risks as its value approaches the investor's floor and re-risks as the portfolio value becomes increasingly far from the investor floor. Leland (1999) demonstrated that this strategy is akin to purchasing an equity asset and a basket of puts at various strikes. Furthermore, unlike rebalancing, which creates a concave return profile, this strategy creates a convex return profile.[xlix] While this strategy may be appropriate for some investors in certain circumstances, in practice it is difficult to execute since an investor needs to actively monitor the portfolio, trade in and out of the active and passive securities, incur significant transaction costs, and generate taxable events. Also, the convex return profile of the portfolio suggests that the portfolio will realize a lower return than a portfolio with a concave return profile (i.e., the return will be lower than if the investor had utilized a traditional rebalancing approach).

INSURANCE

An investment is an action of acquiring something that is expected to yield a future economic benefit, such as interest income or principal growth. But, is an insurance policy also an investment? Interestingly, the National Association of Insurance Commissioners (NAIC) explicitly prohibits the use of the word *investment* in the marketing materials for life insurance policies.[l] So, an insurance policy is not an investment in the traditional sense, although it certainly may have its place in an individual's portfolio. There are five broad categories of life insurance, including:

- *Term life insurance*: this insurance provides coverage for a prespecified term
- *Whole life insurance*: this insurance provides coverage for the life of the policyholder and can build cash value over time
- *Universal life insurance*: this insurance provides coverage for the life of the policyholder but has flexible premium payments and insurance coverage calculations
- *Variable life insurance*: this insurance offers fixed premiums and a minimum death benefit, but unlike whole life insurance, its cash value fluctuates with a portfolio that is selected by the policyholder
- *Variable universal life insurance*: this policy offers flexible premium payments (like universal life) and its cash value fluctuates with investment accounts (like variable life)

So, who might benefit from these products? Individual purchasers typically fall into two groups. The first group utilizes their death benefit to pay a one-time expense such as their final expenses or estate taxes. The second group wants to ensure that a dependent would be financially secure if the policyholder were to die. For example, the working parent of young children, or a retiree whose pension has a *life only* payment plan that will not transfer to a spouse, might benefit from a life insurance policy. So, while life insurance is not an investment in the traditional sense, it is a safety net. While these policies certainly have utility in certain circumstances, individuals considering these products should perform their due diligence prior to purchasing one. Questions worth asking include:

- Are returns guaranteed?
- If so, at what rate?
- Is it possible that some of the imputed net-of-fee returns are negative at some time while the policy is in effect?
- Does this policy require premium payments to increase if the policy value falls below a threshold?
- Is this the lowest cost plan, as measured by management fees, across plan providers?

SUMMARY AND INVESTMENT IMPLICATIONS

Summary

I can still remember how I felt nearly twenty years after I returned from school, logged into my brokerage account, and discovered that Recoton was trading down 30% in the after-hours. I looked at my brokerage account, glanced at the Recoton-made joystick on my desk, and thought—this is supposed to be easy! I suppose this memory has been ingrained, due in part to loss aversion—a heuristic which states that losses *feel* more negative than the equivalent gains *feel* positive (see Chapter 11). In hindsight, my failed first attempt at stock picking could not be attributed to a poorly developed investment thesis—how could I have known that the executives were committing fraud? Nevertheless, the experience drove home a few points regarding the strategies or approaches to developing buy and sell decisions. These points were:

- The process of developing trade ideas is complicated and time consuming if done right—and easy if done wrong
- Even if done correctly, there is no sure thing since even the most highly researched company and developed thesis still has idiosyncratic risk
- Despite my sincerest attempts to self-educate, I was far from an expert
- Unless I intended to dedicate myself to this passion of investing, outsourcing to a professional is likely more appropriate

Since those early days, I've learned a bit and can now differentiate between investing, speculating, and the different approaches to generating buy and sell decisions. Some additional closing thoughts follow regarding investment strategies and how investors might consider incorporating or avoiding them.

Investment Implications

- *Investing*: broadly speaking, investing is an activity in which cash is exchanged for a security or other legal claim and includes a reasonable expectation that principal and interest will be returned in the future. Two of the world's most famous investors, Graham and Buffett, consider fundamental analysis, which includes an estimate of a prospect's intrinsic value, to be inherent to investing. In other words, if fundamental analysis isn't performed, it isn't investing. In practice, few people have both the training and acumen necessary to conduct proper due diligence on a universe of investment opportunities; so, most people hire professionals by purchasing mutual funds or other investment products.

- *Speculating*: like investing, speculating involves the exchange of cash for a security or claim. However, unlike investing (as defined by Graham and Buffett), speculating does not involve the estimate of the intrinsic value of a security. Rather, speculating involves an estimate of the future price of the security or claim. Some speculators utilize technical analysis which involves the study of past price movements to extrapolate the likely future path of a security's price. Most academics are highly skeptical of this approach. However, most academics do concede that if a security exhibits positive price momentum (i.e., recently appreciated), the security is more likely to continue to appreciate in the near term.

- *High-frequency trading*: high-frequency trading is a form of algorithmic trading whereby computers process real-time market data to generate buy and sell orders. The most common type of high-frequency trading involves market making, whereby the firm running the trading algorithm buys and sells securities attempting to earn a spread, which is the difference between the price at which it buys and sells securities. Proponents of high-frequency trading suggest this is one of the reasons trading costs have materially declined over the past thirty years. Critics of high-frequency trading argue that smaller investors lose pennies every time they make a transaction and that high-frequency trading increases trading volume but leaves the system increasingly vulnerable. Following the Flash Crash of 2010, we know that high-frequency trading did not cause or materially exacerbate the rapid decline of equities. Rather, human error in the form of an inappropriate algorithm and spoofing (which is illegal) were the primary drivers of the Flash Crash. While high-frequency trading is not an activity that most people should attempt on their own, the utilization of algorithms to execute large orders is something institutional traders should strongly consider.

- *Active and passive*: investing (or speculating) while utilizing fundamental analysis or technical analysis is an active approach to investing.

Specifically, the investor is attempting to outperform a stated benchmark by developing and executing an investment thesis. However, it is exceptionally difficult to continually outperform benchmarks in highly efficient markets like developed equity markets; most managers fail to do this over 5-year and 15-year periods. As a result, investors are increasingly utilizing passive investment options in which the manager attempts to match a benchmark return (before fees) while minimizing transaction and management fees. Passive options are worth considering, especially for taxable accounts because these products, in addition to having lower fees, generally have fewer taxable events throughout the year.

- *Rebalancing*: rebalancing is necessary if an investor intends to maintain a desired asset class mix and/or a specific risk/return profile. Rebalancing can be thought of as a cost-minimization exercise. Explicit costs of rebalancing include transaction expenses, taxes, and the investor's time, while the implicit costs of not rebalancing is a drift in the risk-target of the portfolio. In general, directing portfolio contributions, dividend income, and portfolio interest payments to the most recent underperforming asset (bringing the portfolio closer to a targeted allocation) is the most efficient strategy. If this isn't possible, rebalancing annually if the portfolio has deviated by more than 5% from its targeted allocation is a reasonable approach.

CITATIONS

i. https://www.sec.gov/Archives/edgar/data/82536/0000899681-99-000125.txt.

ii. Dalio, Ray. (September 19, 2017). *Principles: Life and Work*. Simon & Schuster. p. 7.

iii. Recoton Files for Bankruptcy Protection. (April 8, 2003). *The Wall Street Journal*.

iv. Graham, B., and D.L. Dodd. (2009). *Security Analysis: Principles and Technique*. New York, NY: McGraw-Hill. Sixth Edition. p. 106.

v. Graham, Benjamin, 1894–1976. (1959). *The Intelligent Investor: A Book of Practical Counsel*. New York, NY: Harper. p. 36.

vi. http://www.berkshirehathaway.com/letters/1988.html.

vii. Gordon, M.J. and Eli Shapiro. (October 1956). "Capital Equipment Analysis: The Required Rate of Profit." Management Science, 3(1).

viii. Modigliani, Franco, and Merton H. Miller. (June 1958). "The Cost of Capital, Corporation Finance, and the Theory of Investment." A.E.R. 48: pp. 261–97.

ix.   Arnott, Robert D. and Clifford S. Asness. (January–February 2003). "Surprise! Higher Dividends = Higher Earnings Growth." *Financial Analysts Journal.*

x.   Brackenborough, Susie, Tom McLean, and David Oldroyd. (2001). "The Emergence of Discounted Cash Flow Analysis in the Tyneside Coal Industry c .1700–1820." 33 Brit. Acct. Rev. pp. 137–55.

xi.   Graham, Benjamin, 1894–1976. (1959). *The Intelligent Investor: A Book of Practical Counsel.* New York, NY: Harper. p. 513.

xii.   De La Merced, Michael J. (November 3, 2009). "Berkshire Bets on U.S. with a Railroad Purchase." *The New York Times.*

xiii.   https://www.sec.gov/Archives/edgar/data/934612/000119312509 259413/ddefm14a.htm.

xiv.   Nelson, Samuel Armstrong. (1903). "The A B C of Stock Speculation." S.A. Nelson. p. 39.

xv.   Malkiel, Burton Gordon. (2003). *A Random Walk Down Wall Street: The Time-Tested Strategy for Successful Investing.* New York, NY: W.W. Norton. p. 159.

xvi.   Lo, Andrew W., Harry Mamaysky, and Jiang Wang. (August 4, 2000). "Foundations of Technical Analysis: Computational Algorithms, Statistical Inference, and Empirical Implementation." *Journal of Finance, 2000,* Vol. 55. pp. 1705–1765.

xvii.   Carhart, Mark M. (March 1997). "On Persistence in Mutual Fund Performance," *Journal of Finance.* American Finance Association, Vol. 52(1). pp. 57–82.

xviii.   Asness Debunks Fama's Views on Momentum. (February 7, 2016). https://www.ai-cio.com/news/asness-debunks-famas-views-on -momentum/.

xix.   Aldridge, Irene. (2013). *High-Frequency Trading: A Practical Guide to Algorithmic Strategies and Trading Systems,* 2nd Edition. Wiley.

xx.   Office of the Comptroller of the Currency, Treasury (OCC); Board of Governors of the Federal Reserve System (Board); Federal Deposit Insurance Corporation (FDIC); and Securities and Exchange Commission (SEC). (December 10, 2013). "Prohibitions and Restrictions on Proprietary Trading and Certain Interests in, and Relationships with, Hedge Funds and Private Equity Funds." https://www.sec.gov/ rules/final/2013/bhca-1.pdf.

xxi.   Meyer, Gregory, Nicole Bullock, and Joe Rennison. (January 1, 2018). "How high-frequency trading hit a speed bump." *Financial Times.* https://www.ft.com/content/d81f96ea-d43c-11e7-a303-9060cb1e5f44.

xxii. French, Kenneth R. "The Cost of Active Investing." (April 9, 2008). Available at SSRN: https://ssrn.com/abstract=1105775 or http://dx.doi.org/10.2139/ssrn.1105775.

xxiii. Ro, Sam. (April 1, 2014). "Cliff Asness Explains How High-Frequency Trading Helps Us and Why Everyone Else Is Making a Big Stink About It." *Business Insider.* https://www.businessinsider.com/cliff-asness-on-high-frequency-trading-2014-4.

xxiv. Interview. Steve Kroft. (August 17, 2014). "Is the U.S. stock market rigged?" CBS News 60 Minutes. https://www.cbsnews.com/news/michael-lewis-stock-market-rigged-flash-boys-60-minutes/.

xxv. SEC Rule 11Ac1-1(a)(13). p. 140.

xxvi. https://www.nyse.com/publicdocs/nyse/markets/liquidity-programs/arca_lmm_fact_sheet.pdf.

xxvii. Browning, E.S. and Jenny Strasburg. (October 6, 2010). "The Mutual Fund in the 'Flash Crash.'" *Wall Street Journal.*

xxviii. U.S. Commodity Futures Trading Commission and U.S. Securities & Exchange Commission. (September 30, 2010). "Findings Regarding the Market Events of May 6, 2010." p. 14. https://www.sec.gov/news/studies/2010/marketevents-report.pdf.

xxix. AO 91 (Rev. 11/11) Criminal Complaint. DOJ Fraud Section Assistant Chief Brent S. Wible. Untied States of America v. Navinder Singh Sarao.

xxx. 1:15-cv-03398. CIVIL ACTION. U.S. DISTRICT COURT. U.S. Commodity Futures Trading Commission v. NA V Sarao Futures Limited PLC and NA Vinder Sing Sarao.

xxxi. Press Release. Office of Public Affairs. The United States Department of Justice. (November 9, 2016). "Futures Trader Pleads Guilty to Illegally Manipulating the Futures Market in Connection with 2010 'Flash Crash.'" https://www.justice.gov/opa/pr/futures-trader-pleads-guilty-illegally-manipulating-futures-market-connection-2010-flash.

xxxii. Sharpe, William F. (January/February 1991). "The Arithmetic of Active Management." *The Financial Analysts' Journal.* Vol. 47, No. 1. pp. 7–9.

xxxiii. S&P Dow Jones Indices. (2018). SPIVA U.S. Score Card.

xxxiv. Morningstar Direct Asset Flows Commentary: United States. (January 18, 2018). Morningstar Research.

xxxv. *2018 Investment Company Fact Book.* Investment Company Institute. Figure 3.14.

xxxvi. Morningstar Direct Asset Flows Commentary: United States. (January 18, 2018). Morningstar Research.

xxxvii. Landsman, Stephanie. (November 14, 2017). "Passive investing is a 'chaotic system' that could be dangerous, warns Robert Shiller." https://www.cnbc.com/2017/11/14/robert-shiller-passive-investing -is-a-dangerous-chaotic-system.html.

xxxviii. Davis, Ned. (March 22, 2017). "The Passive Investing Bubble." *Ned's Insights*. Ned Davis Research Group.

xxxix. Sushko, Vladyslav and Grant Turner. (March 11, 2018). "The Implications of Passive Investing for Securities Markets." *BIS Quarterly Review*, March 2018. Available at SSRN: https://ssrn.com/abstract =3139242.

xl. Anadu, Kenechukwu, Mathias Kruttli, Patrick McCabe, Emilio Osambela, and Chae Shin. (August 27, 2018). "The Shift from Active to Passive Investing: Potential Risks to Financial Stability?" https:// www.bostonfed.org/publications/risk-and-policy-analysis/2018/the -shift-from-active-to-passive-investing.aspx.

xli. Fernholz, R. and B. Shay. (May 1982). "Stochastic Portfolio Theory and Stock Market Equilibrium," *Journal of Finance*. Vol. 37, No. 2. pp. 615–624.

xlii. Leland, Hayne E. (1999). "Optimal Portfolio Management with Transactions Costs and Capital Gains Taxes." Research Program in Finance Working Paper No. 290. Berkeley, Calif.: Institute of Business and Economic Research. University of California.

xliii. Ilmanen, Antti and Thomas Maloney. (December 18, 2015). "Portfolio Rebalancing, Part 1: Strategic Asset Allocation." AQR white paper. https://www.aqr.com/Insights/Research/White-Papers/Portfolio -Rebalancing-Part-1-Strategic-Asset-Allocation.

xliv. Hurst, Brian, Yao Hua Ooi, and Lasse Heje Pedersen. (June 27, 2017). "A Century of Evidence on Trend-Following Investing." Available at SSRN: https://ssrn.com/abstract=2993026 or http://dx.doi .org/10.2139/ssrn.2993026. See table Exhibit 2.

xlv. Novy-Marx, Robert. (2012). "Is momentum really momentum?" *Journal of Financial Economics*. Elsevier. Vol. 103(3). pp. 429–453.

xlvi. Jaconettei, Colleen M., Francis M. Kinniry Jr., and Yan Zilbering. (November 2015). "Best practices for portfolio rebalancing." Valley Forge, PA: The Vanguard Group.

xlvii. Perold, André. (August 1986). "Constant Proportion Portfolio Insurance."

xlviii. Black, F., and R. C. Jones. (1987). "Simplifying Portfolio Insurance." *The Journal of Portfolio Management.* Vol. 14, No. 1. pp. 48–51.

xlix. Leland, Hayne E. (1999). "Optimal Portfolio Management with Transactions Costs and Capital Gains Taxes." Research Program in Finance Working Paper No. 290. Berkeley, Calif.: Institute of Business and Economic Research. University of California.

l. Model Regulation Service—2nd Quarter. (2015). Advertisements of Life Insurance and Annuities Model Regulation. Section 4B. https://www.naic.org/store/free/MDL-570.pdf.

6

EQUITY INVESTING

David E. Linton, CFA
Director, Portfolio Construction and Manager Research
Pacific Life Fund Advisors LLC

Di Zhou, CFA, FRM
Portfolio Manager and Managing Director
Thornburg Investment Management

Before class begins, students thumb through notes and get ready to *not* voluntarily answer questions while future Nobel laureate Professor Eugene Fama loads decades-old academic papers for use as *slides*. It's only the third week of the class and most of the students already feel behind. The lecture begins:

> So, as we've discussed, every morning all of Wall Street's traders and port-folio managers go outside, look up, the clouds part, and God reveals to all market participants the true covariance matrix of all financial assets. Then all the traders and portfolio managers go to work to construct the true tangency portfolio.

"Hey, Di, that's the third time he's said that. What the hell is he talking about?"

"I'll explain after class," Di reassured me. Three hours later over lunch, as we all waited for tension-type headaches to subside, Di explained to our study group, "I think Fama is alluding to the true relationship among asset returns. If everyone sees the true covariance matrix instead trying to best estimate it, we could all construct the most efficient portfolio that will eventually be the market portfolio."

"What's the market portfolio?"

Di continued, "It's the theoretical portfolio that includes every investible asset, with each one being weighted according to its relative value. It's also the tangency portfolio, which is the portfolio in which you invest when you combine a risk-free investment with the market portfolio. It's *tangential* to the efficient frontier. So, Fama thinks there is no bother trying to *beat the market* because none of us could ever outperform that portfolio on a risk-adjusted basis."

"But, the sky doesn't open and God doesn't really reveal the true covariance matrix, so what does that mean for us?" I asked.

"I think it means that the market is not efficient. Assets are not always priced to perfection. Even if there is consistent, perfect dissemination of information, which is a key criterion for efficient market hypothesis, investors' interpretation of that information often results in the realized covariance matrix. People always overshoot or undershoot when they price securities. Because the market portfolio most likely isn't the true tangency portfolio, there are opportunities to beat the market. But I don't think that's what Fama wanted us to take away from that analogy."

For full disclosure, if either of us were reading a book and this decade-old conversation was inserted, we would both be skeptical. But, as Fama's God-revealed covariance matrix is our witness, this conversation happened. So, how does one go about beating the market? Before we answer this question (which we will, to Fama's dismay), we will first introduce a variety of topics relevant to equity investors including:

- The history of equities and the development of equity exchanges,
- A review of equity valuation methodologies and stock selection approaches,
- A review of different approaches to equity portfolio construction, and
- The growth of passive equity investing.

After establishing this foundation, we will close with our philosophy on how to construct a portfolio that can outperform an equity benchmark. Finally, for those readers with an aversion to academic literature and who would like to learn more, we recommend *The Intelligent Investor* by Benjamin Graham, first published in 1949. Warren Buffett calls it "the best book on investing ever written." Another of our recommendations is *Investing: The Last Liberal Art* by Robert Hagstrom. This work builds on Charlie Munger's notion of a latticework of mental models and promotes the study of different subjects; this in turn opens our minds to ideas that could lead to investment excellence. Finally, *The Essays of Warren Buffett: Lessons for Corporate America* by Warren Buffett is a collection of Buffett's letters to Berkshire Hathaway shareholders that provides valuable insight on Buffett's way of investing.

BRIEF HISTORY OF EQUITIES, EQUITY EXCHANGES, AND INSTITUTIONAL INVESTING

As we described in Chapter 1, a stock is a claim of partial ownership of a corporation's equity. The holder of equity is the most junior participant in a corporation's capital structure, and the equity investor is entitled to all of a corporation's residual income after the corporation pays its suppliers, employees, bond holders, the government (taxes), and preferred stock holders. Equity holders have rights defined by U.S. corporate law that fall into four categories: *economic*, *control*, *information*, and *litigation*. In short, shareholders in corporations may sell their shares, receive dividends, elect a company's board of directors, receive information about a corporation's operations, and may sue the board of directors if it fails to act on behalf of shareholders. Equity shareholders can be divided into two categories: common and preferred. Common shareholders are the most subordinated stakeholders in the company and receive all residual income, whether that income is paid out via a dividend or retained. This class of shareholders is typically what is thought of as equity investors. Preferred shareholders are senior to common shareholders but junior to all other stakeholders. Preferred shares are considered equity, but they are more akin to a hybrid between equity and debt. Specifically, preferred shareholders receive a higher dividend than common shareholders, and they receive priority over common shareholders in the event of a corporate bankruptcy and liquidation. However, once their dividend has been paid, common shareholders continue to receive any residual. As a result, preferred shares typically have limited appreciation potential whereas common shareholders have (theoretically) unlimited appreciation potential.

The Origins of Equities and Equity Exchanges

The earliest known example of stocks, or equity-like investments, can be traced to around 200 BC in Rome. At the time, the Roman government would award contracts to provide services to state-recognized companies. Shares in these companies were called *partes* or *particule* and these shares could be sold and exchanged among other Romans.[i] Until the establishment of well-regulated exchanges, the trading of equities was primarily over-the-counter, a term used today to indicate a transaction without the use of an exchange. The earliest stock exchanges can trace their roots to 15th-century Antwerp, Belgium. City officials organized a *Bourse Market* (exchange) that originally was used as a central trading point for commercial goods, and originally this market hosted fairs when merchants, farmers, craftsmen, businessmen, and other participants would meet to trade and exchange goods.[ii]

Antwerp's rival, Amsterdam, built and opened its bourse in 1530 and in 1602 the Dutch East India Company became the first known company to utilize these bourses to issue stocks and bonds, leading to the creation of the first stock exchange.[iii] A central exchange helped facilitate both the secondary trading of equity as well as its primary (initial) issuance. In 1602, the Dutch East India Trading Company was established as a limited liability company (a novelty at the time) and the new entity raised 6,424,588 guilders from 1,815 investors in six cities, the majority of which was raised in Amsterdam.[iv] The use of these proceeds was to secure the necessary equipment, ships, supplies, and insurance to launch multiple trading expeditions to Southeast Asia. Additionally, the benefit of this arrangement is that both profits and losses were diffused among a sufficiently large number of investors, and capital was sufficient for multiple expeditions; together, the idiosyncratic risk of single expeditions was largely eliminated.

IPOs and the Growth in the Equity Market

While exchanges and corporations have significantly evolved since this time, the impetus for raising equity has remained largely unchanged. Whether it was the Dutch East India Company in 1602 or Facebook in 2012, corporations raise equity to expand operations, acquire capital, and engage in ventures that are expected to generate a return in excess of the cost of the capital raised. Further motivations for going public may also include ensuring that a family business can diversify its stakeholders and ensure succession. Sometimes early investors pressure management to engage in an initial public offering (IPO) as a means for them to exit their investment. Finally, conglomerates may utilize an IPO to *carve out* a business to achieve a higher level of valuation transparency.

Prior to a corporation issuing publicly traded equity, private entities regularly raise equity capital privately from its founders, angel investors, and venture capitalists. Once these avenues have been exhausted and the corporation has (usually) maintained operations for a few years, a corporation may issue public equity in an IPO. The process to IPO is generally an arduous one that involves a company enhancing corporate governance protocols, filing a prospectus, seeking and receiving approval from regulators and an exchange, hiring a syndicate of banks, conducting a road show, pricing the IPO, and finally raising capital with the help of the bank syndicate. Following the IPO, a corporation must now distribute accurate financials to the public, manage relationships with external investors, and adhere to Securities and Exchange Commission (SEC) reporting requirements.[v] Despite the headache associated with public issuance, this market has continued to grow and attract capital from those with excess capital to corporations capable of judiciously deploying that capital. In 2017, $189.7

billion in capital was raised by U.S. corporations between IPOs and secondary *follow-on* offerings.[vi] Meanwhile, by 2017, the U.S. equity market had grown to $32.1 trillion while the global equity market reached $85.3 trillion in 2017.[vii]

Trading Equities, Equity Exchanges, and Dark Pools

From their humble beginnings as outdoor markets, stock exchanges have grown and matured into major institutions where global equities are listed and traded. According to The World Bank, $77.6 trillion in shares traded in 2017,[viii] or nearly 91% of the market value of the global value of equities. These are enormous figures, so who are the institutions that facilitate this trading, and how does this trading occur?

To begin with, stock exchanges are locations, either physical or electronic, where people (or computers) acting on behalf of brokerage firms can buy and sell securities that have been listed on the exchange. Publicly traded companies are generally listed on at least one exchange and some companies are listed on multiple exchanges. Each exchange has its own requirements for a security to be listed on its exchange, and these requirements may include shareholder structure, the firm's profitability history, or the market capitalization of the firm. Trading on an exchange is limited to brokers who are also members of the exchange. Exchanges also have their own standards for who can be a member and are generally limited to institutions.

The process by which a security is transacted begins with a client order to buy or sell a security. This client may be an individual with a retail brokerage account or a large institutional investor who can speak with a trader directly at a brokerage firm. Once the brokerage firm receives an order for execution, the brokerage firm must then locate either a seller or buyer of that security. To do this, the brokerage firm utilizes its connection with the exchange on which the security is listed. On the exchange, securities are constantly being offered for sale or bid for purchase. The spread between where one can purchase or sell a security is known as the bid/ask spread. Once the broker has located the best price, it transacts (generally) electronically via the exchange. Once the trade is matched, the information related to this transaction is sent to a clearinghouse by the exchange. Custodians of both sides are then tasked with ensuring cash and securities are transferred between the two accounts.

The number of major stock exchanges varies based on what criteria are used to determine what qualifies as a major exchange. Currently, there are between 60[ix] and 79[x] such exchanges. However, listings and trading are heavily concentrated in the largest handful of exchanges. The largest of which is the New York Stock Exchange with a market capitalization of its listed companies being over $28 trillion as of mid-2018.[xi] A national historical landmark, its iconic building is located in lower Manhattan at 11 Wall Street. The large facility was intended to house over one thousand traders utilizing an *open outcry* process of finding the best price. Beginning in the mid 1990s, the NYSE began incorporating electronic trading, which now constitutes a majority of its trading volume; however, there are people present to trade some of its listed stocks. The second largest global stock exchange is Nasdaq, with a market capitalization of around $12 trillion as of early 2019.[xii] Nasdaq is an acronym for National Association of Securities Dealers Automated Quotations, and began in the early 1970s as a quotation system, merely publishing trading data but not matching buyers and sellers. Nasdaq does not have a physical location like the NYSE; all buyers and sellers are matched electronically. Rounding out the top five global exchanges includes the Japan Exchange Group, the Shanghai Stock Exchange, and the Shenzhen Stock Exchange.[xiii]

Beginning in the 1980s, volume has migrated away from these exchanges and trade on what is colloquially termed a *dark pool*. A dark pool is a private securities exchange in which generally large financial institutions trade anonymously and trades are reported on a delay. Unlike exchanges in which current prices and market depth are continuously reported, there is no such information made available in these exchanges. The rationale for this is that it allows large institutional investors to trade large blocks without moving the market or becoming the victim of front running. There are three types of dark pools: exchanges established by companies that utilize their own trading rules, broker-owned pools where brokers match their own clients, and dark pools set up by public exchanges that provide their clients with some degree of anonymity.

In 2017, the U.S. Committee on Capital Markets Regulation estimated that around 30% of U.S. equity share trading volume takes place off-exchange (in the dark), while another 15% takes place on-exchange, but is "hidden" in that the orders exist but are not displayed to the public.[xiv] Proponents of dark pools argue that these sources of liquidity offer investors the opportunity to gain better execution, generate less volatility while they trade, and trade with lower commissions. However, there are many skeptics that firmly disagree. One of the most vocal critics of dark pools is Michael Lewis, who in *Flash Boys* argues that these dark pools have become the playground for high-frequency traders with informational advantages that profit at the expense of individual investors. Additionally, with a lack of transparency, it is possible that large block trades are executed at prices away from the posted levels on exchanges, which would lead to worse rather than better execution. Due to the ongoing concerns of potential abuse, in 2018 the U.S. SEC adopted additional rules for alternative trading systems (ATSs) (i.e., dark pools). These rules require ATSs to disclose how orders interact, are matched, and are executed, among others.[xv]

ACTIVE INVESTMENT APPROACHES

So now that we've reviewed the basics of what equities are and how institutions trade these securities, the next questions are: how are investment decisions made and how are the prices of these securities determined? As John Burr Williams wrote in his 1938 piece *The Theory of Investment Value*, "The bid and asked quotations will reflect the opinions of the most optimistic non-owner and the least optimistic owner. . . . At the margin, opinion, mere opinion, will determine the actual price, even to the extent of values running into billions of dollars."[xvi] So, if the price is set based on the opinions of market participants, how are these opinions formed? To answer this question, we'll begin by reviewing three approaches by which participants formulate their views on the relative attractiveness of equities: *thematic* (or top-down), *fundamental* (or bottom-up), and *quantitative*.

Thematic or Top-Down Investing

Thematic, or top-down investing, begins by identifying trends and positioning the portfolio to benefit from those trends. There are generally two types of trends or themes: cyclical themes and structural themes. Cyclical themes focus on the short- to medium-term changes (typically over the next one to three years), such as changes in the business cycle, commodity cycle, or capital cycle. The identification of structural themes is popular among investors who seek to invest in long-term secular changes (typically three to ten years), such as changing demographics, shifts in consumer preference (i.e., e-commerce), changes in technology, and several others. Thematic investors conduct in-depth research to gain fundamental understanding of the impact of those economic, political, and social trends on regions and sectors, which reveals investable opportunities. Thematic investing's top-down approach provides a unique or alternative way to generate return, making it an attractive complementary strategy to fundamental investing.

While identifying themes—such as the adoption of green technology or an aging population in developed economies—are easy in theory, in practice, correctly recognizing macro trends alone won't guarantee profitable returns. For example, is the theme a secular trend (such as the use of blockchain technology) or a short-term fad (such as the rise of Bitcoin)? Even if we successfully identify a secular theme, the next question is: are we too late? Identifying changing demographics, e-commerce adoption, and the rise of fintech are themes that are arguably already well-known. Next, if the theme is emergent and not widely accepted, the next question is whether or not this theme will generate outsized returns for equity investors. Let's use solar industry as an example; the solar industry has been growing rapidly gaining market share from traditional base power generators. It has a lot of potential for future growth as the International Energy Agency (IEA) estimates that 16% of global electricity will be generated from solar power by 2050.[xvii] However, solar stocks have failed to generate attractive returns for several reasons including the Chinese government's heavy subsidies to its own industry, rapidly changing technology requiring high investments, and solar industry's unsustainably high level of leverage. Finally, once a theme is identified, the final question is: could we isolate companies that will benefit the most from the theme or trend? For example, in the electric vehicle penetration theme, investors have choices to buy lithium, cobalt, or copper mines; cathode companies; battery system makers; or original equipment manufacturers. It is not always clear where the best investments are along the value chain given the competitive dynamics, the evolution of technology, and the various levels of political support by different governments. In other cases, it could also be difficult to find target companies to express top-down views. For example, while a global freshwater shortage is a well-understood theme, investors tend to purchase companies in water treatment or water infrastructure as an adjacent investment idea due to lack of companies with direct exposure (to fresh water).

Fundamental or Bottom-Up Investing

In contrast to thematic investing focusing on identifying macro trends, bottom-up investing focuses on the analysis of an individual company to identify attractive investment opportunities. In Graham and Dodd's 1934 seminal work *Security Analysis*, they introduced an approach to value securities that is still relevant today. Specifically, investors are encouraged to calculate an estimate of the fair value of a company by conducting in-depth fundamental analysis. This fundamental analysis includes evaluating a company's competitive positioning, learning industry dynamics, incorporating economic and market forecasts to estimate future corporate sales and earnings, and much more. Graham and Dodd postulated that the actual market prices would often deviate from the fair value, which in turn would provide opportunity to buy or sell securities. Investors would generate excess returns over time as market prices converge with fair value of the companies.

Today's adherents to Graham and Dodd's style of fundamental investing follow similar processes. Specifically, investors focus their attention on understanding how businesses create value; they do this by evaluating companies' products and services, supply and demand trends, competitive analysis, supply chain analysis, industry dynamics, and much more. Based on business fundamentals, investors utilize different valuation methods to determine a fair value for the company; several of these valuation methods are discussed in upcoming sections. While companies that have competitive advantages and high-quality management teams along with operations in industries that are supported by secular growth are fundamentally attractive, everything has a price. Consistently overpaying for companies with the aforementioned characteristics is not a winning strategy. Rather, bottom-up investors would suggest that purchasing companies with an intrinsic value that is greater than its current price is the most important aspect of investing; a troubled company that is undergoing improvements may have more upside potential than a well-run company that is priced to perfection.

Quantitative (Factor) Investing

Quantitative investing relies upon mathematical models to identify patterns among decades of stock prices and other financial market data to generate investment decisions. A common quantitative modeling approach is called *factor-based* modeling, which we explore in more detail in Chapter 10. In summary, quantitative models are utilized to find *factors* that have statistically significant predictive power. Portfolio managers utilize this approach and then construct a portfolio of stocks that collectively exhibit targeted characteristics (or factors) in hopes that these exposures generate a positive risk premium. Factor models may incorporate fundamental information, such as cash flow multiples, price-to-earnings (P/E) ratios, price-to-sales (P/S) ratios, dividend-payout ratios, return on equity, and the like. Similarly, these models may also include macro information, such as industrial production, employment growth, and inflation, as well as sentiment information, such as analyst's earnings revisions, insider buying, and others.

Quantitative investors approach investing in an analytical, non-emotional, disciplined, and consistent manner. A lack of emotions that cloud investment decisions is a major benefit of quantitative investing: models aren't moody, do not get overly excited about shiny new products, do not have egos, and are not likely to be misguided by behavioral biases (behavioral biases are discussed in Chapter 11). By contrast, people are emotional and prone to behavioral biases. Discipline is another key benefit of quantitative investing that is consistent and repeatable. Quantitative models use a systematic investment methodology for security selection within the investable universe. Despite the benefits of quantitative-driven investing, there are also risks with the reliance of such models. Factor-based models, for example, use historical data to determine the relationship between factors and returns. However, these relationships may not continue into the future. Some factor relationships may have only appeared statistically significant because analysts tested thousands of factors thereby ensuring some factors would appear to be significant even if by chance. Some factors may generate positive risk premium, but they may do so over horizons (like 10 or 20 years)—much longer than a manager's typical horizon. Of additional concern, nonlinear relationships among the variables may go undetected. As a result, a portfolio may underperform in stress scenarios like the 2008–2009 global financial crisis. Quantitative models could also fail to capture the inflection point of changing market conditions. As an example, Long-Term Capital Management (LTCM) utilized model-based investing to take directional positions in currencies and bonds. When Russia devalued its currency, that event was beyond the normal range that LTCM had estimated; the loss on this currency trade (among several others) led to the fund's collapse.

EQUITY VALUATION

In his 2008 letter to shareholders, Warren Buffett famously wrote:

Long ago, Ben Graham taught me that, "Price is what you pay; value is what you get." Whether we're talking about socks or stocks, I like buying quality merchandise when it is marked down.[xviii]

Implied by this quote is that there may be a gap between a security or company's value and its price. This deviation is an opportunity for a shrewd portfolio manager. Through diligent research, an analyst might discover a company that may change the world for the better, experience an explosion in sales, and display a dramatic increase in household awareness—but, such an investment will not necessarily translate into outside portfolio returns if the investor overpays for the company's stock. Valuation is by far the most critical element to long-term investing. In this section, we will look at a few common methodologies that investors use to evaluate companies. However, we do note that valuation is as much art as science. As such, successful investors recognize the strengths and weaknesses of each valuation methodology and often triangulate different approaches to determine the value of a company. We will introduce several such approaches including the *dividend discount model, one-stage* and *two-stage Gordon growth models, discounted cash flow* (DCF) *models*, and *relative valuation* (RV) *models*.

Dividend Discount Model

As we first introduced in Chapter 5, the dividend discount model (DDM) is one of the most simple and intuitive models. If the only cash payments that investors receive from a company are dividends, the value of that company should be the present value of all future dividends:

$$\text{Value per share of stock} = \sum_{t=1}^{t=\infty} \left(\frac{E(DPS_t)}{1+k_e)^t} \right)$$

where:

DPS_t = expected dividends per share
k_e = cost of equity

There are two inputs to the model: expected dividends and cost of equity. Expected dividends are the product of forecasted future earnings and payout ratios. Cost of equity is the required rate of return that the market demands in exchange for owning the firm's equity. The general model is flexible and allows for changes in dividend growth rates and discount rates across time.

The Gordon Growth Model

There are many versions of DDM, the simplest of which is the Gordon growth model. This model values a stock by assuming its dividend grows at a constant rate to perpetuity:

$$\text{Value per share of stock} = \frac{D_1}{(r-g)}$$

where:

D_1 = expected dividends next period
r = cost of equity
g = the stable dividend growth rate, in perpetuity

The Gordon growth model is most suited for companies that exhibit two characteristics: first—growth rates that are similar or lower than the nominal gross domestic product growth rate, and second—a well-established dividend payout policy. A substantial portion of publicly traded companies, including all companies that operate in cyclical industries, do not meet these criteria. Additionally, while the Gordon growth model is easy to use, it is sensitive to the inputs for growth rate; valuation estimates change substantially as you alter any of the inputs.

Two-Stage Dividend Discount Model

For companies that have not reached the steady-growth stage, a two-stage DDM may be more appropriate than the Gordon growth model. This is because the two-stage DDM has the flexibility to account for companies whose growth rate is not currently stable but may soon reach a slower, steady state of growth:

$$\text{Value of stock} = \sum_{t=1}^{t=n} \frac{DPS_t}{(1+k_{e,hg})} + \frac{P_n}{(1+k_{e,hg})^n}$$

where:

$$P_n = \frac{DPS_{n+1}}{k_{e,st} - g_n}$$

where:

DPS_t = expected dividends per share in year t
k_e = cost of equity
P_n = price at end of year n
g = extraordinary growth rate for the first n years
g_n = growth rate after year n, in perpetuity
hg = extraordinary growth state
st = steady state

The two-stage DDM is best suited for companies that are currently in a high-growth stage, and they are expected to maintain an elevated growth rate for several years, after which the company will reach a more moderate steady state of growth. A challenge for an analyst who is utilizing this model is forecasting how long a firm will stay in the initial high-growth phase. In short, the longer the company stays in a high-growth phase, the more valuable that company is. Once the company reaches a steady state, whether that is in two years or twenty years from now, the terminal value of the company will then be determined by the Gordon growth model.

Irrespective of whether an analyst uses a one-, two-, or multi-stage DDM, these models rely on one critical input: dividends! What if a company pays no dividends and is not expected to pay dividends in the foreseeable future? A DDM can't value the company, and for this reason, an analyst must utilize a DCF model.

DCF Analysis

A DCF model values a business not on the dividends it is expected to pay, but rather the cash that the entity is expected to generate. These cash flows may be operating cash flow, free cash flow (FCF) to equity, or FCF to the firm.[1] Irrespective of which cash flow is chosen, each model will derive a similar value because the value of a business is the future expected cash flow discounted at a rate that reflects the riskiness of the cash flow:

$$Value = \frac{CF_1}{(1+r)^1} + \frac{CF_2}{(1+r)^2} + \cdots + \frac{CF_\infty}{(1+r)^\infty} = \sum_{n=i}^{\infty} \frac{CF_n}{(1+r)^n}$$

where:

CF = cash flow at period t
n = life of the asset
r = discount rate reflecting the riskiness of the estimated cash flows

Discounted CF valuation is comprehensive, captures all major assumptions about the business, and doesn't require comparable companies. The DCF approach is most appropriate if we can estimate a company's future cash flow with some degree of certainty and have a good proxy for a discount rate. By contrast, the DCF valuation methodology is less appropriate if future cash flow is unpredictable. For example, a troubled company that currently generates negative cash flow but has valuable assets is not a suitable candidate for a DCF valuation. Additionally, a DCF valuation is very sensitive to changes in assumptions, so a small change in the discount rate could impact the calculated value dramatically. Despite these shortcomings, many investors heavily rely on DCF models. This is because the alternative may be even worse; many investors fear reported earnings are (in part) a negotiated number between management, accountants, and auditors. In contrast, cash flow is less subject to manipulation and may be a better measure of corporate profitability.

Given the difficulties involved in arriving at a precise valuation number, scenario analysis tries to capture the expected value across different possible outcomes. Under scenario analysis, investors estimate cash flows and asset value under various scenarios (common ones are best-case scenario and worst-case scenario) with the intent of getting a better sense of the range and magnitude of the outcomes.

---

[1] The following are the definitions of each cash flow:

Operating cash flow (OCF): cash generated by a company's normal business operation. This figure does not include cash flows related to financing, including interest payments, nor does it include cash flows associated with investment.

FCF to firm (FCFF): cash generated by a company's business operations after depreciation expenses, taxes, and all working capital investments.

FCF to equity (FCFE): cash available for distribution to equity holders. This is FCFF plus net borrowings minus interest expenses.

Relative Valuation

The intrinsic value of a company refers to the estimate of its inherent value (not its price). Whether an analyst utilizes a DCF model, or estimates a company's value utilizing the liquidation approach,[2] an estimate of its replacement value,[3] or another intrinsic value methodology, each model or approach is sensitive to several underlying assumptions. This model sensitivity creates significant uncertainty when valuing an enterprise. Due to this uncertainty, some analysts search for opportunities to utilize the relative valuation method. What is this approach? We'll begin with a simple example: consider how a real estate agent may value your house. She may estimate the cash flow that a landlord may earn should he rent the home, then subtract the expected management expenses and taxes, and discount to estimated future cash flows to the end of the life of the house. Or, an agent may simply determine the average price per square foot for homes sold in your neighborhood and multiply that dollar value by your home's square feet. The former approach is similar to a DCF model, while the latter (and much more common) approach is similar to a relative valuation calculation. This methodology of identifying simple singular metrics (like square feet and average price per square foot) can be applied to valuing corporations as well. Relative valuation doesn't seek to estimate intrinsic value of the company; rather, it assigns valuation measures relative to its peer group.

At the core of the relative valuation methodology is the belief that comparable companies should be priced comparably. The multiples (like price per square foot) that analysts utilize in order to value comparable companies include P/E, enterprise value to earnings before interest tax depreciation and amortization (EV/EBITDA), FCF per share to stock price (FCF yield), and several others. If a stock with similar fundamentals as the comp group is valued substantially below its comp group, investors assume that there may be an error in the price of a security and this mispricing will be corrected over time. Returning to our real estate example, imagine all homes in a neighborhood are priced at $300 per square foot and one home is offered at $200 per square foot. You may have identified a materially underpriced home. (Or a home with a slab leak, mold, and a leaky roof!) See Table 6.1 for an example of a cross-sectional relative value analysis of Proctor & Gamble.

---

[2] The liquation valuation methodology values the company's assets by assuming the firm will cease operations and be liquidated via asset sales.

[3] The replacement valuation methodology values the company as the cost to replace all of a firm's assets.

Table 6.1   Cross-section analysis for Proctor & Gamble

		Market			Valuation (FY+1)	
	Price	cap ($ mil)	EV ($ mil)	P/Sales	EV/EBITDA	P/E
Procter & Gamble	$99.06	$247,782	$270,691	3.6x	14.9x	20.8x
US Comps						
Church & Dwight	$63.92	$15,742	$17,532	3.6x	16.9x	24.3x
Colgate Palmolive	$65.91	$57,165	$63,104	3.6x	14.4x	21.9x
Kimberly Clark	$115.92	$39,926	$47,148	2.2x	11.1x	16.6x
Clorox	$154.91	$19,855	$22,213	3.0x	15.8x	23.0x
Estee lauder	$153.25	$55,341	$56,358	3.6x	17.0x	27.5x
Average				**3.2x**	**15.0x**	**22.7x**
European Comps						
Reckitt Benckiser	£ 6,001	$5,723	$68,981	3.3x	13.9x	17.0x
Unilever	€ 49.13	$159,443	$184,228	2.6x	13.3x	17.7x
Henkel	€ 86.30	$40,903	$44,119	1.7x	9.6x	14.4x
Nestle	CHF 86.40	$262,882	$293,448	2.7x	13.8x	18.8x
Danone	€ 64.80	$50,251	$66,287	1.7x	11.3x	15.5x
Loreal	€ 224.50	$142,421	$139,403	4.2x	17.7x	27.5x
Average				**2.7x**	**13.3x**	**18.5x**
Asian Comps						
Kao	¥ 8,038.00	$35,543	$34,355	2.4x	12.3x	22.4x
Unicharm	¥ 3,466.00	$19,470	$19,305	2.7x	14.0x	26.6x
Hindustan Unilever	INR 1,794.50	$55,038	$54,090	8.6x	36.5x	52.6x
LG H&H	₩ 1,210,000	$16,840	$17,059	2.5x	13.3x	22.4x
Amorepacific	₩ 170,000	$8,855	$8,356	1.6x	10.0x	21.8x
Hengan	HKD 63.25	$9,719	$9,798	2.7x	10.1x	14.7x
Vinda	HKD 15.82	$2,408	$3,004	1.1x	9.5x	19.2x
Average				**3.1x**	**15.1x**	**25.7x**

Source: Bloomberg and author's calculations (as of 2/11/2019)

Cross-sectional analysis, like the one shown in Table 6.1, illustrates valuation differences of similar companies at a specific point in time. Investors make judgments whether a company should be priced higher or lower versus peers based on factors such as growth trajectory, profit margin, riskiness of the business, etc. By contrast, a time series comparison allows an investor to identify how corporate relative valuations have changed over time. Additionally, a time series may allow an investor to better judge if a company is trading *cheap* or *rich* to its historical valuation, or if the company's outlook has changed such that prior multiples are no longer appropriate.

Figure 6.1 is an example of this time-series comparison. From 2000 to 2010, Walmart stock price had been range bound; however, its P/E multiple de-rated from 40× to 13× during this period. What are we to assume from this? Perhaps investors correctly priced Walmart in 2000 with a high P/E multiple of 40× reflecting its promising growth potential. As Walmart delivered earnings growth and its EPS growth decelerated toward 2010, its P/E multiple de-rated and the stock price was left unchanged.

While comp multiples are easy to use and can provide an analyst with valuable insight, this approach has significant drawbacks. First, no two companies are exactly alike and identifying appropriate comparable companies may be difficult. Second, similar businesses may be utilizing different accounting methodologies, limiting the usefulness of utilizing a book value or earnings yield comp. Additionally, comp ratios may be subject to manipulation because management may recognize earnings early or capitalize expenses to make FCF from operations appear higher. Next, businesses that appear similar but have different

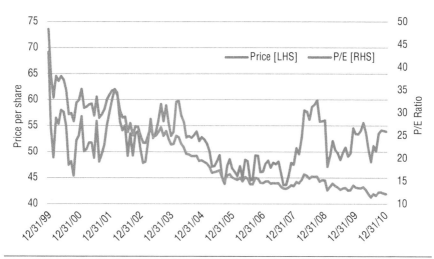

Figure 6.1   Walmart Inc. P/E time series. *Source*: FactSet

comps may in fact not be so similar—the market may know something you don't! Finally, market multiples are a reflection of the current market mood. That mood could change at any time, which would impact valuation. Due to these drawbacks, analysts often utilize relative value metrics to triangulate their estimation of stock valuations and identify undervalued companies.

PORTFOLIO CONSTRUCTION

Until now, we have covered a variety of approaches to stock selection including top-down thematic, bottom-up fundamental, and quantitative methodologies. However, identifying attractive stocks is only the first of a two-step process. The second step is to assemble stocks into a portfolio. While proper portfolio construction won't offset poor stock selection, poor portfolio construction and risk management may largely offset good stock selection. In this section, we will review two portfolio construction approaches: *mean-variance optimization* and *conviction-based portfolio construction*.

Mean Variance Optimization

Modern portfolio theory (MPT) was first introduced by Harry Markowitz in his paper, *Portfolio Selection*, published in the *Journal of Finance* in 1952.[xix] In its simplest form, MPT provides a framework to construct and select portfolios based on the expected return of the investments and the risk appetite of the investors. MPT is also commonly referred to as mean-variance analysis. This framework begins with an investor's estimates of the returns, volatilities, and correlations of an investment universe. Given these estimates, and depending on an investor's constraints (such as no leverage or short selling), an investor may then build an optimal portfolio. *Optimal* is defined as *the highest possible return for each unit of risk*. Conditional on a volatility target, there is a corresponding maximum potential return; when combining all optimal portfolios at each unit of risk the graph becomes an *efficient frontier*, as shown in Figure 6.2.

In his previously mentioned paper, *Portfolio Selection*, Markowitz begins by stating, "The process of selecting a portfolio may be divided into two stages. The first stage starts with observation and experience and ends with beliefs about the future performances of available securities. The second stage starts with the relevant beliefs about future performances and ends with the choice of portfolio."

We find this an interesting choice of words and speculate that there is a tacit admission of the limitation of this approach. Investors don't have the *true covariance matrix* despite how many times they look up into the sky. The best investors can do is to estimate it. Perhaps this is why the process starts with

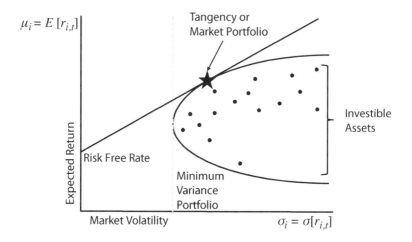

Figure 6.2   Mean variance optimization and the efficient frontier

observation, experience, and *beliefs.* Using observation and experience, each investor must form his or her own beliefs regarding the future return, its volatility, and the correlation of each security considered for inclusion in a portfolio. This means a thousand investors with an identical dataset may each derive a different covariance matrix estimate, and there is no way to know ex-ante which investor's matrix will best approximate the covariance of future returns. Additionally, the mean variance model is sensitive to inputs, particularly expected return estimates, which makes it subject to significant estimation error and input biases. For example, events that have not happened are not captured in the historical data, asset volatilities and correlations are time varying, and this model implicitly assumes that returns follow a normal distribution (returns rarely do). Despite these limitations, MPT has had a profound impact on how investors view risk, return, and portfolio management. At its heart, the theory demonstrates that portfolio diversification can reduce investment risk. In fact, the growing prevalence of passive investing is an indication of the ubiquity of modern price theory.

Conviction-Based Portfolio Construction and *Active Share*

In his 1993 Berkshire Hathaway shareholder letter, Warren Buffett wrote, "The strategy we've adopted precludes our following standard diversification dogma. Many pundits would therefore say the strategy must be riskier than that employed by more conventional investors. We disagree. We believe that a policy of portfolio concentration may well decrease risk if it raises, as it should, both the intensity with which an investor thinks about a business and the comfort level he must feel with its economic characteristics before buying into it."[xx] We believe the *standard diversification dogma*, to which Buffett is referring, is constructing an index-like portfolio and the utilization of the aforementioned mean optimization approach. By contrast, Buffett prefers a concentrated portfolio and weights his investments based upon his conviction of each company's outlook and the degree to which he is confident in that outlook.

This conviction-based approach is regularly employed by active bottom-up investors. High-conviction stocks have larger positions in the portfolio than low-conviction stocks. As a result, those portfolios look very different from indices and tend to have high *active share*.[xxi] Active share is the distance between a given portfolio and its benchmark. The value ranges from 0.0 (meaning the portfolio is identical to its benchmark) to 1.0 (meaning the portfolio holds no securities that can be found in its benchmark). There is an active debate as to whether or not active share is an indicator of the likelihood of outperforming a benchmark. Petajisto (2013) argues that active share is a good indicator of benchmark or *four-factor* alpha. To do this, he showed that from 1990 to 2009 *stock pickers* (managers with high active share) outperformed their benchmarks (net of fees) by +1.25% while *closet indexers* (managers with low active share) underperformed their benchmarks (net of fees) by 0.91%.[xxii] Portfolio managers at AQR disagree, however. Frazzini et al. (2015) argue that high active share funds are predominantly funds benchmarked to small- and mid-cap indices and that these benchmarks did poorly over the 1990–2009 sample period. When controlling for the specific benchmark, there was no statistical evidence that suggests high active share managers are likely to outperform low active share managers.[xxiii]

Owing to a rejection of mean-variance optimization but still needing a risk-management framework, it is common to see bottom-up investors manage portfolio risk by setting a few broad diversification parameters. These parameters may include a minimum number of stocks, maximum single stock position size, minimum and maximum weighting of any sector, and minimum and maximum weighting of any country. Thornburg Investment Management, in addition to the previously mentioned criteria, also utilizes a proprietary three-basket approach to further diversify the portfolio. These baskets include: basic value, consistent earners, and emerging franchises. Companies in basic value baskets are pro-cycle companies that benefit the most during economic expansions and experience the most downside during economic contractions. Companies we classify as cyclical companies include industrials, banks, or companies whose business models are not cyclical but are highly leveraged and therefore sensitive to economic cycles. Consistent earners are companies that are less sensitive to economic cycles with relatively higher visibility on future cash flows, such as consumer staples. Finally, emerging franchises are companies that are growing at a rapid rate and often trade at a high valuation but we believe they are still trading at a discount to their intrinsic value. Through a full market cycle, basic value, consistent earners, and emerging franchises tend to occupy around 40%, 40%, and 20% of the portfolio, respectively. However, basket weights could vary modestly depending on market environment. Since companies are classified into the three baskets based on their business models and sensitivity to economic cycles, stocks would perform differently in different parts of the cycle. For example, when the economy is in a cyclical upturn, basic value stocks tend to outperform. When the economy is in a recession, consistent earners generally outperform. Meanwhile, when investors value secular growth ideas, emerging franchise stocks benefit. Therefore, Thornburg believes the three-basket approach is another portfolio construction tool providing an additional layer of diversification.

RECENT DEVELOPMENTS IN EQUITY INVESTING

While the methodologies mentioned so far for valuing and identifying securities for inclusion in a portfolio are now widely recognized, it should be noted that these approaches have varied significantly over time. For example, each security valuation model requires the existence of company-specific financial information drawn from publicly available generally accepted accounting principles (GAAP) accounting data. However, GAAP accounting data, which ensures methodological consistency among firms and the inclusion of anything that may be deemed *material*, was not available in its current form until the 1970s following the creation of the Accounting Principles Board (APB) in 1959.[xxiv] As equity investors look to the future, two trends have shaped (and will continue to shape) the equity investment landscape. They are the growth of passive options and the growth of factor investing. We'll review the rationale for passive investing including its benefits, disadvantages, and the opportunities that the growth in passive investing may create for the traditional stock picker. A detailed discussion of factor investing can be found in Chapter 10.

Passive Stock Investing: Rationale and Early Adoption

As discussed in Chapter 5, passive equity portfolio management does not involve valuing a universe of securities to identify which securities should be included in a well-diversified portfolio. Active equity portfolio management assumes that a portfolio constructed from a subsection of an investible equity universe (its benchmark) can generate superior returns to its benchmark since a handful of securities are *cheap* at any given time. By contrast, passive investing begins with the assumption that while some securities may in fact be cheap because all information is already contained in the price of the security, there is no way to identify cheap securities ex-ante. Thus, the best-performing equity portfolio is most likely to be the portfolio that minimizes transaction costs and portfolio management costs. Over time, the compounding effect of lower fees and transaction costs will allow a passively managed portfolio to outperform a majority of higher-priced actively managed portfolios. Extending this philosophy to the actual management of a portfolio means that equity portfolio managers should not screen equities for inclusion in their portfolio. Rather, the optimal portfolio holds every security in an index (if possible) in proportion to each security's representation in the index. If this is not feasible, then a passive portfolio can be constructed using a sampling method. This approach is also called *indexing*.

The first passively managed index fund was launched in 1976 by The Vanguard Group; the 500 Index Fund's objective is to track the S&P 500. This fund, with over $400 billion in assets as of 12/31/18,[xxv] was initially called *Bogle's Folly* because it owes its existence to a culmination of market forces as well as John Bogle's vision and tenacity. Two years prior to the fund's launch, Vanguard founder John Bogle was fired as the Wellington Management Company chairman and CEO after 23 years at the firm. Bogle did not go quietly into the night, and the next day Bogle approached the board of directors for the Wellington Funds (see Chapter 2 for a discussion of the relationship between a fund board and the management company) and proposed that they create their own mutual fund company to manage the funds *at cost*. A seven-month battle ensued and Bogle was given permission to launch The Vanguard Group with the mandate of operating for the sole benefit of fund holders (as opposed to fund stakeholders, such as the traders, portfolio managers, and executives). As part of the agreement when The Vanguard Group was launched, it could only operate as a fund administrator and could neither manage nor distribute funds.

Not long after The Vanguard Group commenced their operations, Bogle proposed to its board that Vanguard launch the world's first index mutual fund. Bogle argued that an index fund was not *managed* and therefore did not violate its agreement with Wellington. The board agreed and Bogle assembled a team of underwriters with an IPO target of $150 million. Optimism was high; *Fortune* magazine wrote a piece on the IPO stating, "Index funds . . . now threaten to reshape the entire world of professional money management." The IPO flopped— it raised $11.3 million, which was insufficient to purchase 100 shares of each of the stocks in the S&P 500. The underwriters suggested they cancel the IPO. Bogle disagreed, and with little fanfare and much mocking, one of today's largest mutual funds was born.[xxvi]

Passive Stock Investing: Growth in Passive Investing and Their Potential Market Distortions

From this humble beginning, passive funds (also known as *index funds*) have gained widespread acceptance. As mentioned in Chapter 5, the S&P indexes versus active management (SPIVA) scorecard shows that most active managers have failed to outperform their benchmarks on a net-of-fee basis over the past five, 10, and 15 years.[xxvii] As a result, for the 12-year period that ended 12/31/2017, actively managed equity mutual funds experienced $1.3 trillion in cumulative outflows while passively managed equity mutual funds and exchange-traded funds (ETFs) experienced nearly $1.6 trillion in cumulative inflows.[xxviii] Despite these recent flows, the market share of index funds is still relatively small. According to the Investment Company Institute (ICI), as of 12/31/2017, domestic index equity passive funds and ETFs held 13% of the total equities outstanding, albeit up from 3% in 2002.[xxix]

However, there are two potential issues with the growth of passive investing: passive investors are less invested in corporate governance issues, and fewer active investors mean a stock price has less stock-specific information embedded in its price. With respect to the corporate governorship issues, less than two months before he passed away, John Bogle raised this issue in a November 28, 2018 op-ed in *The Wall Street Journal*. This piece notes that 81% of index mutual funds are held by only three fund managers. Additionally, if flows into passively managed index funds continues, these three fund managers may soon own 30% or more of the U.S. stock market and own over 50% of publicly traded stocks. In that case, these fund managers would have effective control of most, if not all, publicly traded corporations. In his words, "I do not believe that such concentration would serve the national interest." His piece points out problems with some of the already advanced policy prescriptions, such as eliminating the voting rights of passive managers or limiting the number of securities that a passive manager can hold. He does state that a constructive step would be, "Enact[ing] federal legislation making it clear that directors of index funds and other large money managers have a fiduciary duty to vote solely in the interest of the funds' shareholders."[xxx]

The second potential problem with the growth of passive fund management was highlighted in the March 2018 *BIS Quarterly Review*. Specifically, passive flows into equities mandates can distort the prices of equities, and this distortion, while likely small today, "could become significant if the passive fund management industry continues to expand."[xxxi] In their report, the Bank of International Settlements (BIS) is referring to the price discovery mechanism whereby active asset managers express their valuation view on individual securities through their buy and sell orders. Market prices reflect the equilibrium point of active investors' supply and demand. Unlike active asset managers, passive fund managers take security prices set by active asset managers and market makers *as given* and buy and sell securities based solely on the funds' inflows and outflows as well as the changing constituents of their benchmarks. As a result, the increasing share of passive assets means that there are fewer price sensitive investors, which blunts the price discovery mechanism whereby prices adjust to reflect views on relative security attractiveness.

Potential Future of Active and Passive Equity Investing

The debate between passive and active investing will not end any time soon—and both methods for portfolio construction will persist into the foreseeable future. Yet to be determined are the long-term respective shares that each investment approaches. In other words, will passively managed portfolios find a steady state once they control 25% of the equity market? Maybe 50% or 80%? Economists Lubos Pastor and Robert Stambaugh in their working paper, *On the Size of the Active Management Industry*,[xxxii] argue that the reason that active management has lost market share is due to poor relative performance—and additionally, that poor performance can be attributed to decreasing returns to scale. Specifically, as the asset management industry grew, managers' ability to outperform their benchmarks declined. However, as the relative size of active management shrinks, active managers may once again find more plentiful opportunities to outperform their respective benchmarks. Once this occurs, active management would also stop losing market share to passive funds; thus, a steady state will have been reached.

BEATING THE MARKET

At the beginning of this chapter, we promised that we would detail a philosophy on how to construct a portfolio that can outperform an equity benchmark, even if that meant we would earn the ire of our former professor, Eugene Fama. True to our word, we will leave our readers with our belief on the three most important disciplines necessary to outperform an equity benchmark. These are: build and work within your circle of competence, invest for the long term, and ensure that risk is properly managed.

Circle of Competence

Find your investing edge and build a portfolio around it. There is no single investing approach that ensures investing success versus peers and a benchmark. In fact, there are successful strategies in every style category from deep value, relative value, core, growth at reasonable price (GARP), and several more. However, once you have decided what investment strategy you will utilize, it is critical to build a *circle of competence*, and ensure that you are one of the best in the industry at applying a given investment strategy.

Turning our attention briefly to some of the most successful and famous investors, we can see that while each of them utilizes a different approach, they are all considered the best within their given niche or circle of competence. For example, Warren Buffett identifies companies that have wide moats and are cheap given traditional valuation metrics. Peter Lynch (Fidelity) was famous for investing in businesses with which he was intimate, both as an investor and as a consumer. Joel Greenblatt (Gotham Capital) advocates the use of a *magic formula*, which includes picking a concentrated portfolio of stocks of companies with higher earnings yields and return on capital.[xxxiii] Carl Icahn (Icahn Enterprises), Dan Loeb (Third Point), and Bill Ackman (Pershing Square Capital Management) take an active role in companies to unlock value for equity investors. David Tepper (Appaloosa Management) seeks opportunities in distressed companies.

No one is born with an investment circle of competency—and the development of this ability is time consuming and challenging. Additionally, once this competency is established, it should not remain static. Maintaining flexibility with respect to viewing the market and its opportunities will remain highly relevant. David Einhorn (Greenlight Capital), another highly successful activist, stated in *The Art of Value Investing*: "Some areas lend themselves better to our types of analysis than others. It is very hard for us to figure out how much brands are worth, for example. It's also hard for us to figure out how much future scientific developments are worth. We tend to stay away from those kinds of things. But at the right price, we'll consider anything."[xxxiv] In the same publication, John Burbank (Passport Capital) cautioned investors about staying too close to a given region, sector, or type of company when he said: "I have a problem with the concept of circle of competence as defined by many value investors, who won't invest in energy, won't invest in commodities, won't invest outside of the U.S. This business requires constant learning, even sometimes abandoning percepts about industries and geographies that no longer apply. If you're not willing or able to do that, I think the environment ahead means you're in for a very tough time."[xxxv]

Invest for the Long Term

While market pundits regularly discuss short-term political, industry, and company-specific concerns, we believe it is more appropriate to have a multiyear investment horizon. David Herro (Harris Associates) put it blatantly: "I would assert the biggest reason quality companies sell at discounts to intrinsic value is time horizon. Without short-term visibility, most investors don't have the conviction or courage to hold a stock that's facing some sort of challenge, either internally or externally generated. It seems kind of ridiculous, but what most people in the market miss is that intrinsic value is the sum of all future cash flows discounted back to the present. It's not just the next six months' earnings or the next year's earnings. To truly invest for the long term, you have to be able to withstand underperformance in the short term, and the fact of the matter is that most people can't."[xxxvi]

Regardless of the circle of competence you have chosen, company due diligence remains critical. Prior to making an investment, it is important to fully understand how the company works. An analyst should be able to answer these (and many more) questions: How does the company make money? In what industry does the company operate and what are the growth drivers for the industry? What is the competitive dynamic in the industry? What are the company's competitive advantages? Are the competitive advantages sustainable? How does the company allocate capital? The answers to each of these questions are most insightful (and relevant) when discussed over a multi-year horizon.

Controlling Risk

Risk, as defined by tracking errors versus as a benchmark, is neither inherently good nor bad. However, we do note that closet benchmarks, or portfolios that closely emulate their benchmark, have little tracking error and are almost certain to underperform a benchmark net-of-fee basis. Therefore, we believe that constructing a portfolio that has sufficiently concentrated positions, with a moderate tracking error, is highly appropriate. That said, we believe it is critical to ensure that a portfolio doesn't have one or more *unintended risks*. These may include size biases (large or small market cap bias), style biases (value or growth style), country/region biases, currency biases, or something else. Therefore, once all risks of a portfolio are identified, hedging unintended risks is a highly appropriate risk management process.

The processes for managing risk varies as much as the investment styles themselves; we admit this is little more than a cursory review of risk management approaches.[4] For example, hedge funds regularly utilize short positions and derivatives to hedge out unwanted risks. Meanwhile, fundamental investors may look through their portfolio to identify if themes are present and desirable.

---

[4] For investors who want more information on ways to monitor and manage equity portfolio risk, we recommend *Active Portfolio Management* by Richard C. Grinold and Ronald N. Kahn and *Financial Risk Manager Handbook* by Philippe Jorion

For example, investors in Norwegian banks must be aware that a decline in oil price impacts Norwegian banks' fundamentals because its economy is highly correlated with oil price. Margin of safety is another favorite tool used by fundamental investors to defend against the risk that the analyst is incorrectly valuing a company. In its simplest terms, Graham describes margin of safety as "a favorable difference between price on the one hand and indicated or appraised value on the other."[xxxvii] Investors often estimate upside and downside price targets using different assumptions in scenario analysis to assess whether the risk-reward trade-off is favorable. Jeffrey Ubben from ValueAct Capital stated: "People don't believe business quality is a hedge, but if your valuation discipline holds and you get the quality of the business right, you can take a 50-year flood, which is what 2008 was, and live to take advantage of it."

SUMMARY AND INVESTMENT IMPLICATIONS

To the best of our knowledge, the clouds have never parted to reveal to all market participants the *true* covariance matrix. As a result, no two analysts, traders, or portfolio managers will ever agree on an asset's worth, and the *market portfolio* will remain a hypothetical mathematical output. Thus, there remains opportunity for active equity managers because the consensus expected covariance (of all tradable assets) will never equate the realized covariance. This is not an attack on market efficiency as defined by the rapid incorporation of information into the price of securities. Rather, it is an acknowledgment that humans are imperfect analyzers of data and therefore are individually and collectively prone to estimation error.

Summary

The holder of equity is the most junior participant in a corporation's capital structure, and the equity investor is entitled to all of a corporation's residual income. Corporations regularly raise equity capital to expand operations, acquire capital, and engage in projects that are expected to generate a return in excess of the cost of the capital raised. The first time a corporation offers equity for purchase to the public is called an IPO. The process to IPO is arduous but viewed as necessary for most large multi-national corporations, after which its stock trades on an exchange. Depending on what constitutes a *major* exchange, there are currently between 60 and 79 exchanges. However, the lion's share of trading occurs on the New York Stock Exchange, Nasdaq, the Japan Exchange Group, the Shanghai Stock Exchange, and the Shenzhen Stock Exchange. More recently, trading volume has migrated away from exchanges and now around 30% of trading volume takes place in dark pools. Dark pools are private exchanges where securities are not bid and offered publicly; additionally, shares exchange anonymously. Proponents argue that this allows large institutions to transact in size without causing significant price movements. Critics argue that these pools are playgrounds for high-frequency traders that regularly front run investors.

Active investing strategies are many, and for the purpose of easily reviewing them, we categorize these strategies into *thematic* (or top-down), *fundamental* (or bottom-up), and *quantitative*. Thematic investing involves identifying long-term cyclical or secular trends (such as an aging population) and positioning the portfolio to benefit from these trends. Fundamental investing involves careful analysis of a company, placing a value on the enterprise, and purchasing companies (stocks) that are priced well below an analysts' assessment of the value of the security. Quantitative investing utilizes mathematical models to identify factors that are expected to generate a positive risk premium. Since factors cannot be purchased, a portfolio is constructed of stocks that are expected to have exposure to targeted factors. The process of valuing a security (i.e., engaging in fundamental analysis) varies depending on the company, its industry, and its stage of growth. Common models include the DDM, the Gordon growth model, the multi-stage DDM, and a variety of DCF models. Often used as a complement to these models are relative valuation models, which provide not a value of a company but its RV to peers given a variety of metrics.

Two regularly utilized portfolio construction methods include mean-variance optimization and conviction-based portfolio construction. Mean-variance optimization was first introduced in the 1950s and involves constructing a portfolio that generates the highest ex-ante return per unit of volatility. To calculate this, a portfolio manager must first generate an estimate of each holding's volatility (variance), correlation to each other asset, and expected return of each asset. This process is fraught with estimation error, so many managers instead utilize conviction-based portfolio construction models. Utilizing this approach, portfolio managers construct portfolios that are concentrated and are weighted based upon an analysts' conviction that a given security will outperform its peers or benchmark. Owing to difficulty with consistently outperforming a market-value-weighted benchmark net of fees, passive equity options have gained in popularity. Passively constructed portfolios attempt to match a given index, gross of fees, and attempt to minimize both transaction costs and management expenses. Proponents of passive investing believe that a low-fee product has the greatest likelihood of outperforming other managers over a multi-year period. Proponents of active investing raise concerns that passive funds may distort market prices and increase market volatility. A growth in passive funds may also increase the opportunity set for discerning active investors.

Investment Implications

- If you are engaged in active equity management, it is critical to build a circle of competence. Specifically, ensure that you are one of the best in the industry at applying a given investment strategy. Otherwise, it is unlikely you will be able to generate an excess performance net of fees.
- Ensure your investment horizon is sufficiently long. Corporations are going concerns, and the most well-run corporations are not managed to hit quarterly earnings targets. Rather, efficiently run corporations, and well-constructed portfolios, have multi-year horizons during which investments are anticipated to generate strong performance.
- Risk management, as defined by a moderate tracking error, is appropriate. Little or no tracking error is indicative of a closet benchmarked portfolio that will likely underperform its benchmark net of fees. Conversely, an excessively high tracking error indicates that a portfolio is either too concentrated or the benchmark against which the portfolio is being evaluated is not appropriate.

CITATIONS

i. William Smith, D.C.L., LL.D.: *A Dictionary of Greek and Roman Antiquities*. John Murray, London, UK, 1875. pp. 972–974.
ii. Kohn, Meir G. (July 2003). Organized Markets in Pre-Industrial Europe. Available at SSRN: https://ssrn.com/abstract=427764 or http://dx.doi.org/10.2139/ssrn.427764.
iii. Kellenbenz, H. (1967/1996). *Introduction to Confusion de Confusiones*. In M. Friedson (ed.) *Confusion de Confusiones* (pp. 125–146). New York, NY: Wiley.
iv. Wells, H. (2018). Research Handbook on the History of Corporate and Company Law. (2018). Research Handbooks in Corporate Law and Governance series. Edward Elgar Publishing Limited. p. 105.
v. Guide to going public. (2018). Strategic considerations before, during, and post-IPO. 2018 EYGM Limited. 2018 EYGM Limited.
vi. SIFMA *2017 Fact Book* www.sifma.org. p. 21.
vii. ———. www.sifma.org. p. 55.
viii. https://data.worldbank.org/indicator/CM.MKT.TRAD.CD.
ix. Comparing the World's Stock Exchanges. (2016). The Money Project.

    x. https://www.stockmarketclock.com/exchanges.

   xi. https://www.nyse.com/market-cap.

  xii. https://www.nasdaq.com/press-release/nasdaq-welcomes-new -fortress-energy-llc-nasdaq-nfe-to-the-nasdaq-stock-market-2019 0131-00943.

 xiii. Comparing the World's Stock Exchanges. (2016). The Money Project.

 xiv. The State of the U.S. Equity Markets. (September 2017). Committee on Capital Markets Regulation.

  xv. Press Release. (July 18, 2018). SEC Adopts Rules to Enhance Transparency and Oversight of Alternative Trading Systems. https://www .sec.gov/news/press-release/2018-136.

 xvi. Burr Williams, John. (2019). *The Theory of Investment Value*, by John Burr Williams. SERBIULA (sistema Librum 2.0). p. 34.

xvii. Technology Roadmap—Solar Photovoltaic Energy 2014. (September 15, 2014). International Energy Agency. p. 1.

xviii. http://www.berkshirehathaway.com/letters/2008ltr.pdf. p. 4.

 xix. Markowitz, H.M. (March 1952). "Portfolio Selection." *The Journal of Finance.* 7(1): pp. 77–91. doi:10.2307/2975974.

  xx. http://www.berkshirehathaway.com/letters/1993.html.

 xxi. Cremers, Martijn and Antti Petajisto. (2009). How Active Is Your Fund Manager? A New Measure That Predicts Performance.

 xxii. Petajisto, Antti. (January 15, 2013). Active Share and Mutual Fund Performance. Available at SSRN: https://ssrn.com/abstract=1685942 or http://dx.doi.org/10.2139/ssrn.1685942.

xxiii. Frazzini, Andrea, Jacques Friedman, and Lukasz Pomorski. (2016). "Deactivating active share." *Financial Analysts Journal.* 72. pp. 14–21.

xxiv. Zeff, Stephen A. (2019). Evolution of U.S. Generally Accepted Accounting Principles (GAAP).

 xxv. https://institutional.vanguard.com/web/c1/product-details/fund/ 0040.

xxvi. Bogle, John C. (2014). "Lightning Strikes: The Creation of Vanguard, the First Index Mutual Fund, and the Revolution It Spawned." *The Journal of Portfolio Management.* 40. 140913001535001. 10.3905/ jpm.2014.2014.1.044.

xxvii. S&P Dow Jones Indices. (2018). SPIVA U.S. Score Card.

xxviii. *2018 Investment Company Fact Book.* Investment Company Institute. Figure 3.14.

 xxix. ———. Investment Company Institute. Figure 2.8.

 xxx. Bogle, John C. (November 29, 2018). "Bogle Sounds a Warning on Index Funds." *The Wall Street Journal.*

xxxi. Sushko, Vladyslav and Grant Turner. (March 11, 2018). The Implications of Passive Investing for Securities Markets. BIS Quarterly Review,
March 2018. Available at SSRN: https://ssrn.com/abstract=3139242.

xxxii. Pástor, Luboš and Robert F. Stambaugh. (August 2012). *Journal of Political Economy*. Vol. 120, No. 4. pp. 740–781.

xxxiii. Greenblatt, Joel. (2010). The Little Book that Still Beats the Market.

xxxiv. Heins, John and Whitney Tilson. (2013). *The Art of Value Investing:
How the World's Best Investors Beat the Market*. Wiley. p. 56.

xxxv. ———. (2013). *The Art of Value Investing: How the World's Best Investors Beat the Market*. Wiley. p. 57.

xxxvi. ———. (2013). *The Art of Value Investing: How the World's Best Investors Beat the Market*. Wiley. p. 77.

xxxvii. Graham, Benjamin. (1973). *The Intelligent Investor*. Fourth Revised
Edition. New York, NY. p. 281.

7

FIXED INCOME INVESTING[1]

This chapter is not for the faint of heart because I attempt to condense a discussion of an immensely diverse asset class into a single chapter. In fact, after reviewing an early draft, a good friend and former colleague told me that I needed a "carrot or revelation at the end to justify the suffering." Note taken. So, if you have no interest in fixed income, feel free to skip ahead; perhaps the factor investing or behavioral finance chapters will have greater appeal. If, however, you find this asset class as fascinating as I do, I hope you enjoy both this chapter along with the carrot at the end.

The length of this chapter, as well as several other recommended readings (in a later paragraph) begs the question: why is it necessary to write so much about a single asset class? The answer is that the fixed income markets are enormous (larger than the equity markets), complex (the valuation of bonds goes well beyond calculating a single discount rate), issuers are variable (governments, corporations, agencies, and many others issue debt), and critical to the global economy (large institutions utilize this market to implement policy). This chapter begins with a cursory review of bonds, including what they are and how to calculate the current price for a bond. I then introduce other bond-related concepts including yield, duration (interest rate sensitivity), the yield curve, credit risk, and other sources of bond risk. I then pivot to the different types of bond issuers, and reference the aforementioned drivers of risk and return so that the reader can better understand how each issuer is unique. I next discuss potential sources of incremental return and relate these sources of return to both issuer types as well as credit and interest rate risk. And, finally—the carrot—I close with a discussion of how to construct an actively managed fixed income portfolio through the utilization of rank-ordering out of benchmark positions and the maximization of ex-ante information ratio.

---

[1] I would like to thank Stephen G. Moyer, CFA, Bharath Boggavaram, Yuri Garbuzov, and Bruce Brittain for their edits and feedback.

If at the end of this chapter you care to learn more, I recommend *The Strategic Bond Investor*, written by former colleague Anthony Crescenzi and/or Frank Fabozzi's *The Handbook of Fixed Income Securities* (the eighth edition of this work has 71 chapters and almost 1,800 pages!). Alternatively, Stephen Moyer, a friend and coauthor of the first chapter of this book, has a classic called *Distressed Debt Analysis* that is also a very well-written piece.

BRIEF REVIEW OF BONDS AND THE YIELD CURVE

As mentioned in Chapter 1, bonds are securities of indebtedness, or legal promises to make periodic payments for a predetermined time. These payments are typically *fixed*, contain indentures (legal agreements), are *senior* in the capital structure to equity investors, are often secured (have assets pledged to the bondholder), and typically contain covenants or rules that borrowers must follow prior to the bonds' repayment. In this section, I'll briefly review bond features, introduce the methodologies for valuing a bond, and describe bond risk measurements.

Bond Features

The following list defines some key features that are shared by all bonds:

- *Issuer*: this is the legal entity that is responsible for the payment of interest and repayment of principal. The issuer may be a corporation, government, agency, supranational, or an individual.
- *Principal*: this is the value that will be repaid at the maturity of the bond. This value is also called the par value or the face value.
- *Coupon*: this is the periodic interest payment made to owners of the security. The coupon rate is usually determined when the bond is issued.
- *Maturity*: this is the date when the issuer must repay the bond's principal.

There are several features that are common but not universal to all bonds. These features are:

- *Secured or unsecured*: secured bonds are collateralized by an asset such as plant, equipment, or income stream. Unsecured bonds are backed by *the full faith and credit* of the issuer, which means that the purchaser of the bond has no claim to a specific asset in the case of default.
- *Covenants*: these are binding agreements between a bond issuer and a bondholder that prohibit the issuer from engaging in an activity (like a merger or acquisition) or require the issuer to meet a criterion (such as maintain leverage below a threshold).

- *Seniority*: this is the order of repayment in the event of a sale or bankruptcy. Senior debt must be repaid prior to subordinated debt.
- *Call (or refunding) provisions*: this feature allows the issuer of the bond the right to retire a portion or the entirety of the debt prior to the scheduled maturity.
- *Put provisions*: this feature allows the holder of the bond to sell the issue back to the issuer (usually) at par on a designated date.
- *Sinking-fund provision*: this provision requires the issuer to retire a portion of the outstanding issue on a predetermined schedule, ahead of the final maturity of the debt.
- *Convertibility provision*: this provision allows the holder of a bond to exchange the bond for a specified amount of common stock.
- *Warrants*: a warrant is an option issued by a firm that permits the owner to purchase shares of common stock at a prespecified price. Sometimes warrants will be combined with bonds to enhance the investor's potential returns. If the warrant can only be executed by the bondholder, it is *nondetachable*. If the warrant can be sold separately from the bond, the warrant is *detachable*.

Bond Valuation: Present Value of Cash Flows

Like any financial instrument, the value of the security is equal to the present value of future cash flows. For bonds, this calculation is relatively straightforward since cash flows are known with a higher degree of certainty than with other financial assets, such as equities or options. The discount rate used to compute the present value of each individual cash flow depends on the nature of the bond, particularly whether the bond is subject to default risk. For a bond issued by the U.S. Treasury, the appropriate discount rate is the market interest rate for holding a zero- (or no-) coupon treasury bond that matures at a given period. For bonds that pay semi-annual cash flows, the formula to calculate the present value is:

$$P = \frac{C}{(1+i_1)^{1/2}} + \frac{C}{(1+i_2)^{2/2}} + \cdots + \frac{C}{(1+i_N)^{N/2}} + \frac{M}{(1+i_N)^{N/2}}$$

where:

P = market price of the bond
C = the bond semi-annual coupon
M = the value of the bond at maturity (also known as the bond face value)
N = each semi-annual period
i_N = the market interest rate of a zero-coupon security that matures at a given period

For readers who would like to see examples of this present value calculation, please see Appendix A at the end of this chapter.

SOURCES AND MEASUREMENTS OF RISK AND RETURN

Bond Return Metrics: Yield, the Yield Curve, and Total Return

Current yield is the annual bond coupon divided by the current price. Its primary utility is the simplicity of calculation and ease of understanding:

$$Current\ Yield = \frac{annual\ dollar\ coupon\ interest}{current\ price}$$

By contrast, yield to maturity (YTM) is the internal rate of return of an investment that will make the present value of the cash flows equal to the current price of the security. The formula to calculate YTM is nearly identical to the calculation of the present value of the bond with one exception: rather than using a time-period specific discount rate for each cash flow, the YTM calculation uses a single discount rate for all cash flows. Thus, formula that relates the price of a bond to its cash flows is:

$$P = \frac{C}{(1+YTM)^{1/2}} + \frac{C}{(1+YTM)^{2/2}} + \cdots + \frac{C}{(1+YTM)^{N/2}} + \frac{M}{(1+YTM)^{N/2}}$$

where:

P = market price of the bond
C = the bond semi-annual coupon
M = the value of the bond at maturity (also known as the bond face value)
N = each semi-annual period
YTM = the yield to maturity

As the YTM for Treasuries is conditional on each bond's price, coupon, and tenor, I can plot each bond's YTM given its tenor, as shown in Figure 7.1. This visual representation of bonds' collective yields given their times to maturity is called the *yield curve*. A normal yield curve is one in which each yield rises as the tenor increases, as was the case in February 2010. During this time, investors received a significant term premium in the form of a higher yield for owning longer-duration bonds vis-à-vis shorter-duration bonds. A flat yield curve is one when there is little term premium for owning longer-duration bonds, as is the case in December 2018. An inverted curve is one when there is a negative

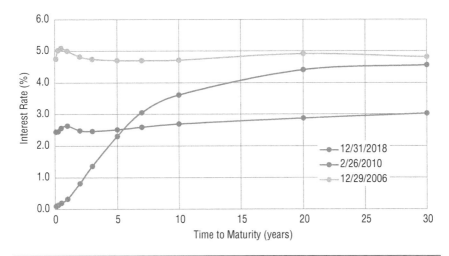

Figure 7.1   YTM and the yield curve. *Source*: U.S. Treasury[i]

term premium, usually measured as the spread between the 2-year and 10-year points on the curve. In December 2006, the yield on the 2-year Treasury was +0.3% higher than the yield on the 10-year point of the curve. An inverted yield curve is generally an indicator of a future recession (see Chapter 4).

So, conditional on an investor planning to hold a bond until maturity, and without concern for default risk, what bond should an investor purchase? In this case, an investor might be wise to purchase the U.S. Treasury with the highest YTM. So, is YTM a useful metric for the portfolio manager of an active bond portfolio? No. Professor Frank Fabozzi laments in Chapter 6 of *The Handbook of Fixed Income Securities*, "Unfortunately, some portfolio managers find comfort in *meaningless measures such as the yield-to-maturity* because it is not necessary to incorporate any expectations"[ii] (emphasis added). He goes on to recommend that investors use a total return calculation to compare bond investments. The total rate of return (TRR) of a security is the sum of the security's yield plus the incremental return derived from the security's expected price appreciation.

In Appendix A: Example 6, I show that the total return of a hypothetical 2.5 year Treasury with a six-month holding period is materially greater than the YTM of the same bond. This simple example suggests that prudent active bond management can add nontrivial return by purchasing bonds with the highest *total return* and not the bonds with the highest current yield or YTM. To be fair, nothing is certain, and a lower-yielding, higher total-return portfolio may experience periods of relative underperformance. However, over a sufficiently long period, the highest total-return portfolio wins. Yet, despite the benefit of utilizing total return in lieu of YTM, calculating bond-specific total returns is eschewed by some bond managers due to three concerns: first, there is no sin-gle defined holding period for a bond; second, the calculation is time and re-source intensive; and third, it is necessary to make assumptions regarding the future price of the bond at the time it is sold. Despite these concerns, I believe a well-resourced bond manager should utilize prudent assumptions and cal-culate the expected total return for all bonds held in client accounts, as well as potential bonds that may be added to a client account. This process will allow managers to rank order bonds that may be added or removed from a portfolio thereby ensuring that a portfolio offers the best possible risk-adjusted returns.

Bond Risks: Changes in Interest Rates

The primary risk that I have indirectly highlighted thus far is *interest rate risk*, which is represented by *duration* and *convexity*.[2] As yields rise (fall), the price of a fixed income security will fall (rise). In normal environments, the greater the sensitivity to interest rate movements (duration), the higher the security's yield. Interest rate risk can be subdivided into *level risk* and *curve risk*. Level risk is the risk that all points on a yield curve rise or fall in unison and by the same amount. Conversely, curve risk is the risk that some points on the yield curve rise or fall more than other points on the yield curve. Since the price of a bond is equal to the present value of all cash flows discounted independently, the increase of any one discount rate will cause the value of the bond to fall. There are two commonly utilized metrics to quantify the risk that specific points in the curve will move vis-à-vis other points on the curve. The first metric is *curve duration*. This metric is an estimate of the sensitivity of a bond's price to changes in the yield curve (such as the spread between a 2-year U.S. Treasury and a 10-year U.S. Treasury). The second metric is *key rate duration*, which measures the sensitivity of a bond's price to a change in a specific maturity point along the entirety of the yield curve. To reduce both level and curve risk, the purchaser of a bond can choose to purchase a bond with a short time to maturity, such as two years rather than 10 years. However, while this will reduce key rate duration and curve duration, the purchaser will likely give up some yield as well as increase reinvestment risk.

Reinvestment risk is the risk that interest rates may fall prior to or at the ma-turity of the bond. Should interest rates fall, the rate of the reinvested coupons,

---

[2] Duration and convexity are measures of the price sensitivity of a bond (measured as a percentage of the price) to changes in interest rates (again measured as a percentage change in the interest rate). For a given percentage change in interest rate, a bond with higher duration will have a larger percentage change in price.

sometimes referred to as interest-on-interest, will also fall. Similarly, if the holder of a bond intends to reinvest the proceeds of a bond's principal into another bond at maturity, reinvestment risk is the risk that the interest rate will be lower when the investor wants to reinvest the matured principal. To reduce reinvestment risk, an investor can purchase a bond with a longer tenor, such as 10 years rather than two years. Alternatively, an investor may also reduce reinvestment risk by purchasing a bond with a low coupon or no coupon at all. However, while this reduces reinvestment risk, it will also increase duration risk. So, what should a bond investor do when trying to balance duration and reinvestment risk? That depends on the investor's utility function as well as the current pricing of the bond term structure. In other words, to select an optimal bond or portfolio of bonds, an investor must first determine how much they are being compensated for assuming either duration risk or reinvestment risk (more on that later in this chapter).

The final interest rate risk that I will introduce is *prepayment* or *call risk*. For bonds that have an embedded call option, meaning the issuer may choose to purchase or refinance some or all of the bond at their discretion, the holder of such a bond is exposed to call risk. This risk manifests itself in two ways: first, should interest rates fall and the issuer exercises the call option, the holder of the bond is now exposed to reinvestment risk and will now need to reinvest its proceeds at a lower interest rate; second, call risk caps the upward potential of a bond price. Specifically, a bond will not appreciate significantly above the strike of a call; otherwise, the issuer will call the bond. In light of this risk, the holder of a callable bond is compensated with a higher yield than a bond without an embedded call option.

Bond Risk Metrics: Duration and Convexity with Option-Free Bonds

As discussed previously, the price of a bond is the present value of all future cash flows discounted at period-specific interest rates. For an option-free bond (i.e., without an embedded call or put option), the bond's price/yield relationship is nonlinear, as represented by the dark line in Figure 7.2. The tangency line at points p^* and y^* is the first derivative of the price-to-yield relationship of a hypothetical bond. This line, known as *interest rate duration*, provides an estimate for the price change of a bond for a given change in yield. An approximation of the duration of a bond is estimated as follows:

$$\frac{V_- - V_+}{2(V_0)(\Delta y)}$$

where:

V_- = bond price if yields decline by Δy
V_+ = bond price if yields rise by Δy
V_0 = initial bond price
Δy = change in yield in decimal

Note: this estimate of duration is also known as modified duration because I assume that the cash flows from the bond are *not* modified due to changes in interest rates. This assumption may not be appropriate for bonds with embedded options.

Returning to Figure 7.2, I note that for relatively small moves in the yield, the actual and estimated bond price change is quite similar. However, for larger movements in yields, the estimated price and actual price of the bond diverge. This divergence can be attributed to a bond's *convexity*. Bonds without embedded options are positively convex; this means that irrespective of the change in interest rates, the estimated price utilizing only the bond's starting price and its

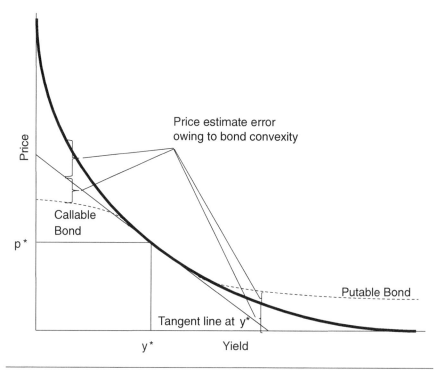

Figure 7.2   Price/yield relationship for bonds with and without optionality

duration will be too low. An approximation of the convexity measure of a bond is estimated as follows:

$$\frac{V_- + V_+ - 2V_0}{2(V_0)(\Delta y)^2}$$

where:

V_- = bond price if yields decline by Δy
V_+ = bond price if yields rise by Δy
V_0 = initial bond price
Δy = change in yield in decimal

See Appendix A for examples of the calculation and use of duration and convexity.

Bond Risk Metrics: Duration and Convexity for Bonds with Embedded Options

The duration and convexity measurements introduced thus far are appropriate to calculate approximate price changes for option-free bonds. However, these approximations are not suitable for bonds with embedded options such as calls or puts. If a bond is callable, the issuer can choose to repurchase the bond at a prespecified premium to par (say, a price of 104) irrespective of prevailing interest rates. Therefore, there is a limit to the appreciation potential of a callable bond because the bond will not appreciate significantly above its call price. Similarly, a puttable bond allows the purchaser of the bond to sell the bond to the issuer at a predetermined price. This feature is rare and is usually accompanied with a *change of control* or downgrade trigger. With such bonds, there is a reduction to the depreciation risk of the bond because the bond is unlikely to fall below the put price, as shown in Figure 7.2. Since the price of a bond can be heavily influenced by the embedded optionality, the previously introduced duration and convexity estimates break down. The methodology for calculating duration and convexity for bonds with imbedded options is beyond the scope of this chapter. However, it is helpful to know that the term given to a bond's duration that contains embedded optionality is *effective duration*. For example, a callable bond may have a modified duration of 5.0 but an effective duration of 3.0, indicating the callable bond is less price sensitive to changes in interest rates than would be the case without the embedded call option.

Bond Return Metrics: Credit Spread

While sensitivity to changes in the interest rate is the primary risk to bondholders, the assumption of credit risk can also be an important source of both return

1998	1999	2000	2001	2002	2003	2004	2005	2006	2007	2008	2009
UST 10.0	US HY 2.4	UST 13.5	US IG 10.3	UST 11.8	US HY 29.0	US HY 11.1	UST 2.8	US HY 11.8	UST 9.0	UST 13.7	US HY 58.2
US IG 8.6	US IG -2.0	US IG 9.1	UST 6.7	US IG 10.1	US IG 8.2	US IG 5.4	US HY 2.7	US IG 4.3	US IG 4.6	US IG -4.9	US IG 18.7
US HY 1.9	UST -2.6	US HY -5.9	US HY 5.3	US HY -1.4	UST 2.2	UST 3.5	US IG 1.7	UST 3.1	US HY 1.9	US HY -26.2	UST -3.6

2010	2011	2012	2013	2014	2015	2016	2017	5 Yr	10 Yr	15 Yr	20 Yr
US HY 15.1	UST 9.8	US HY 15.8	US HY 7.4	US IG 7.5	UST 0.8	US HY 17.1	US HY 7.5	US HY 5.8	US HY 8.0	US HY 9.0	US HY 6.8
US IG 9.0	US IG 8.1	US IG 9.8	US IG -1.5	UST 5.1	US IG -0.7	US IG 6.1	US IG 6.4	US IG 3.5	US IG 5.7	US IG 5.4	US IG 5.8
UST 5.9	US HY 5.0	UST 2.0	UST -2.7	US HY 2.5	US HY -4.5	UST 1.0	UST 2.3	UST 1.3	UST 3.3	UST 3.6	UST 4.6

Figure 7.3   Annual returns of U.S. Treasury, investment grade, and treasury indexes.[3] *Source: Bloomberg*

[3] Indexes shown are:
- Bloomberg Barclays U.S. Corporate Total Return Value Unhedged USD
- Bloomberg Barclays U.S. Treasury Total Return Unhedged USD
- Bloomberg Barclays U.S. Corporate High Yield Total Return Index Value Unhedged USD

and risk. In the U.S., because issuers other than the U.S. Treasury potentially could default on their payment obligations, they pay an interest premium, or spread, over the indicated rate of the U.S. yield curve. This spread is an incremental return to the bondholders for assumption of that credit or default risk. Assuming the issuer does not default on the obligation, these incremental returns accrue to the bondholder. For example, Figure 7.3 shows the returns for representative U.S. Treasury, U.S. Investment Grade, and U.S. High Yield indexes. While the returns generated by these indexes were partially impacted by the level and shape of the yield curve, the primary determinant of *relative* performance is relative credit exposure for these indexes. Because of this assumption of credit risk, the high yield index has generated the highest returns for the 5-, 10-, 15-, and 20-year periods that ended 12/31/17, while the U.S. Treasury index generated the lowest returns. However, I must recognize that higher return also comes with higher risk as measured by the realized volatility of the indexes. For example, in 2008 and 2009, the U.S. high yield index generated returns of −26.2% and +58.2%, respectively, while the U.S. Treasury index generated returns of +13.7% and −3.6%, respectively.

Bond Credit Risk

The credit risk of a bond can be subdivided into three categories: *default risk*, *downgrade risk*, and *credit-spread risk*. First, default risk is the risk that an issuer will default on an obligation. An investor in a bond with credit risk should be compensated with an incremental return over a treasury at least equal to the cumulative probability of default between the time the bond is purchased and when it matures, multiplied by the expected loss in the event of a default at each point in time. Second, downgrade risk is the risk that the bond will decline in price due to a deterioration in the credit quality leading to a downgrade in the credit-rating of the bond issuer. A downgrade of a bond, particularly if the rating falls below *BBB−* (which is the lowest investment grade rating), regularly leads to forced selling and a decline in the price of the bond.[4] The final risk assumed by an investor in a security not guaranteed by the U.S. Treasury is referred to as credit-spread risk. The credit spread is the incremental return that a credit investor expects to earn over the corresponding risk-free treasury rate. However, this spread can widen (increase) if the credit fundamentals of the issuer worsen, the economy deteriorates, or investors become increasingly risk averse. Thus, an investor assumes the risk that this premium increases leading to a decline in the bond's value. Figure 7.4 shows a time series of the credit spread

---

[4] A security that has been downgraded from an investment grade to a high yield rating is known as a *fallen angel*. Institutional investors are often forced to sell these securities due to portfolio guidelines that limit or restrict noninvestment grade securities.

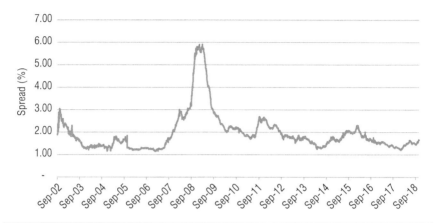

Figure 7.4   Average BBB-spread over comparable U.S. Treasuries (2002–2018). *Source*: Bloomberg

for holding a BBB-rated U.S. corporate bond. Since this spread is the product of estimated default probabilities and recoveries in the event of default (both of which can change), plus other premiums such as downgrade or illiquidity, it is impossible to determine at any point the market implied probability of default or market implied expected recovery in the event of a default. However, it is safe to assume that in instances when credit spreads widen dramatically, such as in 2007 and 2008, the market implied probability of default increased while the expected recovery in the event of default declined.

The two most regularly utilized measures of credit spread are zero-volatility spread (or Z-spread) and option-adjusted spread (or OAS). Z-spread is the constant spread added to each discount rate to arrive at a bond's price. The underlying curve is the treasury spot curve. The Z-spread is appropriate for bonds without embedded options. OAS is like a Z-spread; however, this spread accounts for embedded options.

Bond Credit Risk Metrics: Credit Spread Duration and Credit Rating

The two credit risk metrics by which both securities and portfolios are regularly measured is *credit-spread duration* and *credit rating*. Credit-spread duration is similar to duration in that it estimates the change of the price of a security given a change in the security's YTM. However, unlike duration, which is a measure of sensitivity to changes in interest rates, credit-spread duration measures the sensitivity of a bond's price to changes in the incremental credit spread. However, there is an inherent problem with utilizing credit-spread duration for a portfolio that has bonds with a variety of credit qualities—not all credit spreads are equal. What does that mean? Well, a 10-year AA-rated bond may have a similar credit-spread duration as a 10-year BBB-rated bond. So, does that mean the two bonds have similar credit risk? No! This is because while both bonds might appreciate or depreciate if their respective credit spreads widen or tighten by identical amounts, the typical magnitude of widening or tightening for an AA-rated bond is different from a BBB-rated bond. So, what is the solution? A regularly adopted methodology is to normalize credit-spread duration such that all bonds are viewed assuming an identical rating. There are many ways to do this— sometimes called (depending on the firm) adjusted credit-spread duration, market weighted spread, equivalent unit of spread duration, or some other name—but all of these approaches are beyond the scope of this introductory chapter.

Another common, less analytical, and simpler methodology for assessing the general credit risk of either a security or a portfolio of securities is the utilization of credit ratings (or weighted average credit rating, as in the case of a portfolio). Credit ratings are assigned by rating agencies and these ratings are intended to assess the risk of default. These ratings vary from AAA (highest quality) to D (in default), as shown in Table 7.1.

Table 7.1 Credit ratings across rating agencies

Long Term			Short Term			Summary
Moody's	S&P	Fitch	Moody's	S&P	Fitch	Description
Investment Grade						
Aaa	AAA	AAA	P-1	A-1+	F1+	Highest Quality
Aa1	AA+	AA+	P-1	A-1+	F1+	
Aa2	AA	AA	P-1	A-1+	F1+	High quality
Aa3	AA–	AA–	P-1	A-1+	F1+	
A1	A+	A+	P-2 or P-1	A-1 or A-1+	F1 or F1+	
A2	A	A	P-2 or P-1	A-2 or A-1	F1	Upper-medium quality
A3	A–	A–	P-2 or P-1	A-2 or A-1	F2 or F1	
Baa1	BBB+	BBB+	P-2	A-2	F2	
Baa2	BBB	BBB	P-3 or P-2	A-3 or A-2	F3 or F2	Lower-medium quality
Baa3	BBB–	BBB–	P-3	A-3	F3	

Continued

Long Term			Short Term			Summary
Moody's	S&P	Fitch	Moody's	S&P	Fitch	Description
Speculative Grade / High Yield						
Ba1	BB+	BB+	NP	B	B	
Ba2	BB	BB	NP	B	B	Low-grade
Ba3	BB–	BB–	NP	B	B	
B1	B+	B+	NP	B	B	
B2	B	B	NP	B	B	Highly speculative
B3	B–	B–	NP	B	B	
Caa1	CCC+	CCC+	NP	C	C	
Caa2	CCC	CCC	NP	C	C	Extremely speculative
Caa3	CCC–	CCC–	NP	C	C	
Ca	CC	CC	NP	C	C	Default likely imminent
	C	C	NP	C	C	
C	D	D	NP	D	RD/D	In Default

So, how are we to interpret this table? These ratings are a current assessment of the likelihood that a bond will be repaid in full. As the creditworthiness of issuers and issues change over time, so do the credit ratings. As such, ratings transition upward (toward AAA) when the credit quality improves, whereas they transition downward (toward D) when credit quality deteriorates. Each year, the rating agency Standard & Poor's (S&P) publishes a study of global corporate ratings (beginning in 1981) to assess the average transition rates for corporate bonds given the rating at the beginning of each year. Unfortunately, S&P did not give me permission to reproduce the results of the most recent study; so, I'll include some of the highlights: the data show that most of the time, bonds end the year with the same rating as they started with. For example, 87.0% of these bonds retained their AAA-rated bond for the year. 8.8% of the bonds were downgraded to AA, 1.1% of the bonds were downgraded below AA, no bonds defaulted, and 3.2% of the bonds lost their rating (usually because the issuer chose not to renew its contract with S&P). Alternatively, for bonds rated between CCC and C, 43.5% of these bonds continued to be rated between CCC and C after one year, 14.1% of these bonds were upgraded (usually to B), 15.6% of these bonds lost their rating, and 26.8% of the bonds defaulted.[5] One word

---

[5] For more information, see Table 23 of the S&P *2017 Annual Global Corporate Default Study and Rating Transitions Report.*

of caution on using credit ratings exclusively to assess credit risk—they can be a lagging indicator. Kou et al. (2008)[iii] showed that movements in credit spreads often precede ratings migrations. In other words, if a credit spread widens significantly, this is likely an indicator that the creditworthiness of a company has fallen and its rating will migrate downward in the future. The reason for this is that investors are constantly monitoring a security's credit fundamentals and their assessments of changes in fundamentals will be reflected in market prices (and hence spreads) well before the rating agencies formally react.

Other Sources of Bond Return and Risk

In addition to interest rate and credit risk, bondholders are exposed to several other risks for which the bondholder should be compensated. These additional risks include liquidity, inflation, and volatility.

Liquidity Risk

This is the risk that an investor is unable, at a moment in time, to sell a bond at or near its inherent value or is unable to sell a bond in a reasonably short period of time. For example, a holder of $10 million U.S. Treasuries can safely assume that because of the tremendous liquidity in the U.S. Treasury market they could sell their stake at any time without meaningfully impacting the price of the securities. However, a holder of $10 million worth of a $100 million bond issued by a relatively unknown CCC-rated issuer might find that if forced to sell, they could cause the price to decline significantly. It is difficult to identify the exact liquidity premium any bond receives because liquidity risk is positively correlated with credit risk. However, this premium can be inferred by examining the typical bid/offer spread for the bond. The bid/offer spread is the difference in price between where a dealer will buy or sell a given security. In general, the wider the bid/offer spread, the more illiquid the security, and the higher an illiquidity premium the holder of that instrument should receive.

Inflation Risk

Also known as *purchasing-power risk*, this is the risk that inflation rises by an amount greater than the market implied inflation rate at the time the investor purchases the bond. For example, if at the time the investor purchases the bond, the bond yield is 3% and market implied inflation is 2%, the implied real yield (yield ex inflation) is 1%. Inflation risk is the risk that inflation exceeds 2% during the bondholding period and thus the purchasing power of the bond's cash flow is reduced. Inflation-linked bonds[6] appreciate with inflation, meaning the holders of these instruments are not exposed to inflation risk. Floating-rate bonds are also less exposed to inflation risk because these instrument's interest rates rise with a short-term reference rate that is positively correlated to inflation expectations.

Volatility Risk

This risk is that the price of the bond will decline as a result of an increase in an implied volatility (generally interest rate volatility). Bonds that are short call and put options generally decline in value when implied volatility rises. This is because the likelihood that the bond will be called (such as a mortgage-backed security) to the detriment of the bondholder increases as implied volatility rises. This risk is also referred to as *vega*.

Other risks include *exchange-rate risk*, which is the risk that a bond held in a foreign currency declines in value because of a depreciation of that foreign currency versus the U.S. dollar. *Event risk* is the risk that an idiosyncratic event occurs that impairs the issuer's ability to service the debt, such as a natural disaster, activist investor, takeover, or corporate restructuring. *Legal risk* involves any legal ruling that impacts the economics of the trade; for example, a government may declare that a bond is taxable when it was originally expected to be tax-exempt. Finally, *sector risk* is the risk that different sectors (such as financials, industrials, or health care) will underperform other sectors owing to a sector-specific development.

TYPES OF BOND ISSUERS

While interest rate risk is common to all bonds, credit, illiquidity, event, volatility, and several other risks are unique to the bond's issuer. For this reason, it is important for a fixed income investor to understand each of the major bond issuers so that she may be able to identify the drivers of each bond's risks and ensure that she is being adequately compensated for the assumption of those risks. The six issuer categories of U.S. bonds that I will cover are: treasury, municipal, federal agency, corporate, mortgage-related, and asset backed securities (ABS). As shown in Figure 7.5, issuers in the U.S. collectively have over $40 trillion in outstanding debt in 2017, which has more than doubled since 2003. While the value of corporate and municipal bonds as a percentage of total

---

[6] In the U.S., inflation-linked bonds are commonly called TIPS for Treasury Inflation-Protected Securities. Abroad, these bonds are regularly called *linkers* as in the bond payout is *linked* to an inflation rate.

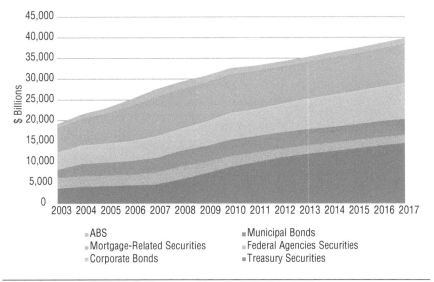

45,000

Legend:

ABS   Municipal Bonds
Mortgage-Related Securities Federal Agencies Securities
Corporate Bonds   Treasury Securities

Figure 7.5   U.S. debt outstanding. *Source*: Securities Industry and Financial Markets Association (SIFMA)

bonds outstanding has remained relatively constant over that period, the same is not true for treasury, federal agency, mortgage-related, or ABS. Between 2007 and 2017, as a percentage of debt outstanding, federal agency debt has fallen from 10.5% to 4.9%, ABS debt has fallen from 7.1% to 3.6%, and mortgage-related debt has fallen from 34.1% to 23.3%. Conversely, treasury debt has risen from 16.4% to 36.3% on the heels of wider U.S. fiscal deficits.[iv]

Treasury Securities

U.S. Treasury securities are obligations of the U.S. federal government and issued by the Department of the Treasury. These securities are issued for two reasons: first, the U.S. Treasury issues debt when the federal government outlays exceed revenue in the form of individual, corporate, and other taxes. Thus, debt is issued to plug the hole created by a fiscal deficit. The second reason is that when existing debt matures, the U.S. Treasury regularly issues new debt, providing investors the opportunity to roll their obligations into new securities. The stock of these securities is expected to exceed $16 trillion by 2019 (79% of U.S. GDP) and will continue to grow over the next several years. The U.S. Congressional Budget Office forecasts U.S. federal government debt held by the public will increase, due to growing fiscal deficits, to $27.1 trillion by 2027 (94.5% of U.S. GDP).[v]

The U.S. Treasury sells five types of securities including: bills, notes, bonds, Treasury inflation-protected securities (TIPS), and floating rate notes (FRNs) as shown in Figure 7.6.[vi] Treasury bills are securities that mature in one year or less with original maturities of one month, three months, six months, and one year. Occasionally, the U.S. Treasury issues cash management bills (CMBs) that cover temporary cash shortfalls and have maturities ranging from seven days to 50 days. A feature unique to bills and CMBs is that they are issued at a discount (a price less than par) and do not pay coupons; all other treasury securities pay coupons, generally semi-annually. Treasury notes are securities with original maturities between one year and 10 years. Treasury bonds have maturities between 10 and 30 years. In 1997, the Treasury began selling TIPS; these securities have the unique feature that their principal is adjusted for inflation using the consumer price index. As such, purchasers of these securities are protected from inflation surprises and they lock in a "real yield" when they purchase these bonds. Finally, in 2014 the Treasury began selling FRNs. These two-year securities pay quarterly interest payments based on the three-month T-bill auction rate.

The issuance of securities is announced at least a month in advance by the U.S. Treasury, although in practice the issuance schedule rarely changes. In general, 3-, 10-, and 30-year notes and bonds are auctioned and settled mid-month, while 2-, 5-, and 7-year notes are auctioned and settled near month-end. Bills with various tenors are auctioned weekly, while TIPS are generally auctioned and settled mid-month and FRNs are auctioned and settled near month-end.[vii] The settlement of these securities corresponds with the maturity of existing securities, so both security holders and the U.S. Treasury do not experience short-term cash shortfalls or excess cash as they *roll* positions. While the U.S. Treasury ultimately decides what tenors it will issue, treasury officials are influenced by

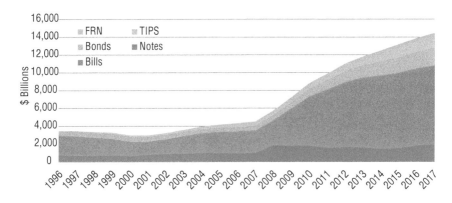

Figure 7.6   U.S. Treasury securities outstanding. *Source*: SIFMA

the Treasury Borrowing Advisory Committee (TBAC). The TBAC is an advisory committee comprised of senior representatives from investment firms and banks. In addition to advising treasury officials on the strength of the U.S. economy and discussing technical details of the treasury market, this committee may recommend to the treasury an optimal mix of treasury instruments to best balance the competing objectives of minimizing rollover risk (to do this, the treasury should primarily issue long-term securities) while minimizing the U.S. Treasury's average interest expense (to do this, the treasury should issue primarily short-term securities).

In general, U.S. Treasuries (and potentially German Bunds) are considered the lowest-risk securities available for purchase. These instruments are backed by the full faith and credit of the United States government, and for this reason are considered to have no credit risk. These markets are exceptionally liquid and trade with narrow bid-offer spreads. The volatility of these instruments is primarily driven by movements in interest rates. Owing to their low-risk, high-liquid nature, these instruments are commonly held by foreign investors and their central banks ($6.2 trillion as of June 2018), other U.S. government accounts ($5.3 trillion as of June 2018), and the U.S. Federal Reserve ($2.8 trillion as of June 2018).[viii]

Agency Debt Securities

These securities are direct obligations of U.S. government-sponsored enterprises (GSEs) or federal government agencies. Federal government agencies are public instrumentalities of government policy such as the Federal Housing Administration (FHA) and the Government National Mortgage Association (Ginnie Mae). Their debt is also backed by the full faith and credit of the U.S. government. GSEs, in contrast, are structured as publicly chartered but privately owned and operated entities. GSEs include the Federal National Mortgage Association (Fannie Mae) and the Federal Home Loan Mortgage Corporation (Freddie Mac). Because GSEs are not explicitly backed by the U.S. government, they have a modest degree of credit risk. However, their debt is considered *implicitly* guaranteed, meaning that the government will protect bondholders and ensure that the entities remain going concerns. This was the case in September 2008 when Fannie Mae and Freddie Mac were placed in a conservatorship; as part of its involvement, the U.S. Treasury would purchase preferred shares from each GSE (thereby injecting cash) in the event that either enterprise's liabilities exceeded its assets. Because of this action, Fannie Mae and Freddie Mac shareholders suffered major price declines; however, bondholders were fully protected.

Like the U.S. Treasury, these agencies offer predicable issuance at regularly scheduled and reoccurring dates. Longer dated agency securities are called debentures and have maturities between one and thirty years. Short-dated agency securities which have tenors of one year or less are called discount notes. As the name implies, they are issued at a discount to par and like a U.S. Treasury bill, a discount note does not pay a coupon. The largest issuers of agency debt issue securities with identical maturities as treasury notes and bonds, creating a robust yield curve of issues. This is intended to attract purchasers of debt that might otherwise purchase a U.S. Treasury. Government agencies that are engaged in securitizing mortgages (such as Fannie Mae, Freddie Mac, and Ginnie Mae) regularly issue callable longer-term debt to allow them to better manage their interest rate exposure. In general, agency debt is a highly liquid market with low credit risk and narrow bid-offer spreads. This market peaked in outstanding issuance in 2008 at $3.2 trillion but fell to around $1.9 trillion by 2017.[ix]

Municipal Bonds

Municipal bonds (or *munis*) are securities issued by states, municipalities, or counties generally to finance large capital expenditures such as airports, schools, hospitals, highways, or other public works projects. These securities are considered tax-exempt because interest from these bonds is exempt from *federal* income taxes; these securities may still be taxed at the state and local level. Conversely, U.S. Treasury securities are exempt from state and local taxes; however, these securities are taxable at the federal level. Thus, it's important to note that when a bond is referred to as tax-exempt, the security is exempt from federal taxes. There are two primary types of municipal bonds: general obligation and revenue bonds. General obligation bonds are secured by the issuer's taxing power. Revenue bonds, by contrast, are secured by the anticipated revenue from a project linked to the bond's issuance. For example, an airport-revenue bond may be secured by anticipated revenue from airport fees, while a toll-road bond may be secured by anticipated toll revenue.

A regularly cited feature of municipal bonds is their equivalent taxable yield, which is calculated with the following formula:

$$Equivalent\ taxable\ yield = \frac{tax\ exempt\ yield}{(1-marginal\ tax\ rate)}$$

Why is this relevant? Imagine an investor is considering two AA-rated, 5-year bonds: one a corporate (taxable) and one a muni (tax-exempt). The AA-rated corporate bond YTM is 4.0% while the muni YTM is 3.0%. Additionally, the investor's marginal federal tax rate is 35%. All other things being equal (credit risk, illiquidity risk, etc.), which bond is more appealing, assuming both bonds will be held in taxable accounts? To answer this question, I need to calculate the muni bond equivalent taxable yield:

$$Equivalent\ taxable\ yield = \frac{3.0\%}{(1-35\%)} = 4.62\%$$

Thus, the muni with an equivalent taxable yield of 4.62% is more appealing than the corporate bond with a 4.0% YTM. It's worth noting that this analysis has its limitations, as the YTM calculation does not assume either bond is callable and all cash flows will be reinvested at the same rate; however, it's still a useful yardstick to compare bonds with disparate tax treatment.

Munis are generally investment-grade securities (modest credit risk) but are less liquid than treasuries and agency debentures. They are most appropriate for individual taxable investors. According to the Municipal Securities Rulemaking Board (2018), in 2007, approximately 59% of munis were held directly by individuals while 32% of munis were held by mutual funds, ETFs (exchange-traded funds), and other professionally managed products (likely held by individuals). That combined figure of 92% direct and indirect individual holdings has declined to 81% in 2017. By contrast, depository institutions have increased their share of the muni market from 7% in 2007 to 18% in 2017 as the low-yielding environment and lack of investment opportunities elsewhere has led them to increase their muni holdings.[x]

Corporate Bonds

Large corporations regularly issue bonds. The use of proceeds for these securities vary and include sales, general, and administrative expenses (SG&A), major capital expenditures, acquisitions, or the retirement of existing debt which may soon mature. SIFMA estimated in 2018 that the U.S. corporate bond market was roughly $9.0 trillion outstanding, as shown in Figure 7.7.[xi] The corporate bond for market can be subdivided into several categories, but I will focus on four:

- *Commercial paper (CP)*: these are short-term promissory notes, issued at a discount to par by corporations. Their maturity is up to 270 days and the average CP issuance is around 30 days.[xii] These securities are not collateralized and for this reason, typically only the most creditworthy companies issue these securities. CP issued with a maturity no greater than 270 days is exempt from Security and Exchange Commission registration requirements,[xiii] making CP appealing to corporations.
- *Investment grade (IG)*: these are securities that are rated between AAA and BBB- or Baa3 by one or more credit rating agencies. The typical tenor of an IG corporate bond at issuance is between three and 30 years, and a majority of them have fixed coupons at issuance. A minority of three- and five-year IG corporate bonds also have floating rate coupons.

When issued, IG corporate bonds generally are larger than $300 million because this is the minimum issue size to be included in the Bloomberg Barclays U.S. Aggregate Index.[xiv]

- *High yield (HY)*: these are securities that are rated BB+ or Ba1 or lower by one or more credit rating agencies and considered below investment grade. These bonds are typically issued with terms of 10 years or less and are often callable after four or five years. The comparatively short tenor of these issues can be attributed to the higher default risk of these issuers, which reduces the attractiveness of long-duration high-yield bonds. When issued, HY corporate bonds generally are larger than $150 million because this is the minimum issue size to be included in the Bloomberg Barclays U.S. High Yield Corporate Index.[xv]

- *Leveraged loan*: these are loans made to companies with credit ratings that are below investment grade. Additionally, these loans are generally syndicated with ten or more nonbank issuers, are the most senior debt in the borrower's capital structure, and are only issued by large corporations. *Syndicated* means the security is a single loan with universal terms but with multiple lenders. Leveraged loans often contain covenants; however, from 2014 through 2017, more than 70% of new leveraged loans were considered *covenant-lite* by rating agencies.[xvi] When issued, these securities are usually larger than $50 million because this is the minimum issue size in order to be included in the S&P/LSTA U.S. Leveraged Loan 100 Index.[xvii]

Corporate bonds, or bonds that have credit risk more broadly, generally offer higher returns than government bonds with little to no default risk. However,

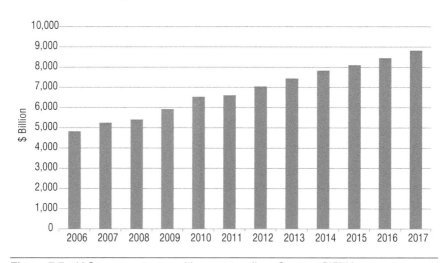

Figure 7.7   U.S. corporate securities outstanding. *Source*: SIFMA

this additional income comes with the potential for underperformance and higher volatility. The primary purchasers of corporate bonds are large institutions including pension funds, insurers, sovereign wealth funds, and hedge funds. To gain exposure to corporate bonds, individuals generally purchase mutual funds that invest in part or exclusively in corporate debt. While private bankers or individuals utilizing a brokerage account may purchase or sell corporate bonds, generally only institutions transact in these securities, and they are usually traded over-the-counter or without the utilization of an exchange. Corporate bond liquidity varies significantly by rating, issuer, and issue size. In general, the higher-rated, larger issues are more liquid than poorly-rated, smaller issues.

Mortgage-Related Securities

Mortgage-related securities are securitized products. Securitization is the process of pooling hundreds or thousands of individual loans into a single legal structure or security that is tradable. The cash flows an investor receives are generated by the underlying loans, aggregated, and then redirected to the investor according to a predetermined schedule. With respect to mortgage-backed securities (MBSs), potentially thousands of home mortgages are sold by a mortgage originator or bank to a trust or special-purpose vehicle (SPV), which in turn is sold to investors. As of 2017, as shown in Figure 7.8, the U.S. mortgage-related market was over $9.3 trillion in outstanding securities, which is slightly larger than the U.S. corporate bond market. This industry, which was at the epicenter of the 2008/2009 financial crisis, has evolved considerably in the past 10 years. In 2007, the mortgage-related securities market totaled $9.4 trillion outstanding, which was 34% of the entire U.S. bond market. At that time, non-agency

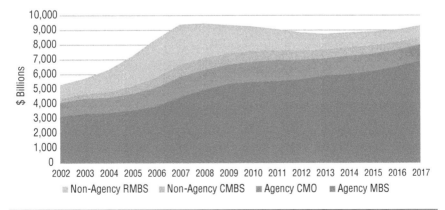

Figure 7.8   U.S. mortgage-related securities outstanding. *Source*: SIFMA

(i.e., *not* Fannie Mae, Freddie Mac, Ginnie Mae, or other) securities constituted $3.6 trillion of this market, or 38% of the entire mortgage-related market. By 2017, non-agency securities outstanding have shrunk to $1.3 trillion, or 14% of the entire mortgage-related market.[xviii]

The largest subgroup of the mortgage-related securities are agency MBSs; this group of securities is guaranteed by one of the aforementioned government agencies. As a result of this guarantee, investors in these instruments assume only interest rate risk. A loan is considered eligible to be securitized by an agency (such as Fannie Mae or Freddie Mac) if it is a conventional loan that confirms to the maximum size set by the Federal Housing Finance Agency (FHFA)[xix] and other funding criteria set by Fannie Mae and Freddie Mac. These requirements generally include: stable employment, a FICO score above 620, between 5% to 20% down payment, loans limited in size to $484,350 (with some high-price areas up to $726,525) for single-unit homes, and several others. Conforming loans are regularly sold by banks and mortgage brokers to Fannie Mae and Freddie Mac. Conversely, Ginnie Mae guarantees the loans that have originated from government agencies including the FHA, Department of Veterans Affairs, and others. During the securitization process, loans with similar tenors (10-, 15-, 30-year, etc.) and interest-rate type (fixed or adjustable rate) are packaged together; conversely, loan pools are generally disparate with respect to FICO score and region. In the event that an agency security is structured such that the cash flows from the underlying loans are directed to the investor (minus a servicing charge), the securities are considered *pass-throughs*. The size of the pass-through market is over $6.9 trillion as of 2017 and it constitutes 74% of the entire mortgage-related market, up from 48% in 2007.[xx]

Agency collateralized mortgage obligations (CMOs) are like MBSs in that the underlying drivers of cash flow are also home mortgages, and these mortgages are guaranteed by an agency so there is essentially no credit risk. However, with CMOs the cash flows are redirected from mortgage payers to investors according to a schedule and hierarchy. The utilization of tranches adds another layer of complexity to an already complex security. So why is this so popular? Well, the holder of an MBS will receive some interest and principal on a monthly basis. But how much principal and interest? There is significant uncertainty with respect to the timing of cash flows because homeowners with mortgages regularly refinance their mortgage when interest rates fall, while the rate of refinancing declines and the weighted average life of mortgage loans increases when interest rates rise. Some investors are comfortable with the uncertainty of cash flow timing while others are not. The CMO attempts to address this by creating tranches that are more appealing to investors than a traditional pass-through MBS; the CMO is designed so that some tranches have highly predicable cash flows while other tranches assume most of the uncertainty with respect to the timing of cash flows. For example, planned amortization class (PAC) tranches utilize a *companion tranche* to smooth principal repayment cash flows. Z-tranches pay neither interest nor principal for a lockout period. Principal-only (PO) securities pay only principal, while interest-only (IO) securities pay only interest generated from the underlying collateral.

So, what happens if a loan that was originated by a bank or mortgage broker is larger than the maximize size set by the FHFA, or certain other underwriting criteria (e.g., borrower FICO, loan-to-value ratio). In this case, the mortgage, which is characterized as *nonconforming* may still be securitized; however, the loan will be a pooled in a *non-agency* or *private-label* MBS. Like their agency MBS counterparts, these non-agency MBSs are sold to investors after an intermediary pools underlying non-conforming loans are placed into an SPV. However, unlike an agency MBS, the underlying loans are not guaranteed by an agency. Therefore, if a homeowner defaults on a mortgage and the loan exceeds the value of the home, a holder of a non-agency MBS will incur the loss. As a result, these products have credit risk in addition to interest rate risk. But, since not all MBS purchasers are willing or able to assume credit risk, banks utilize the CMO structure to tranche investments and create credit protection for most of the non-agency MBS investors. How is this accomplished? Like an agency CMO, cash flows are redirected according to a schedule; the difference is that with a non-agency CMO, principal and interest is first paid to the most senior tranche investors, as shown in Figure 7.9. Once that tranche has been paid in full, the next most senior tranche receives interest and principal payments, and

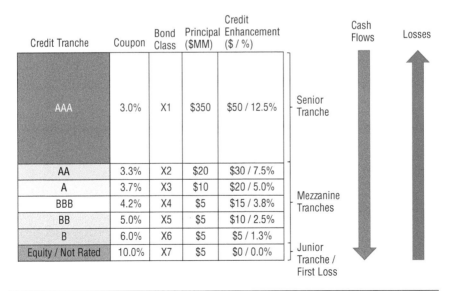

Figure 7.9   Hypothetical CMO

so on. This is also known as a *waterfall*. Alternatively, losses are first assumed by the most junior tranche, and only once that tranche has been *wiped out* from losses will the second most junior tranche assume any losses. Because the historical principal loss rate for mortgage pools is fairly low, a majority of tranches receive AAA- or AA-ratings.

Finally, mortgage-backed securities that are secured by mortgages on commercial properties, instead of residential real estate, are known as commercial mortgage-backed securities (CMBS). These securities also generally involve tranching and the utilization of a waterfall schedule. The non-agency residential mortgage-backed securities (RMBS) and CMBS markets collectively are $1.3 billion, or 14% of the mortgage-related securities market. This is down significantly from their 2007 peak of $3.6 billion, or 38% of the mortgage-related securities market.[xxi] It is worth noting that the non-agency RMBS market was at the epicenter of the financial collapse of Bear Stearns, Lehman Brothers, Countrywide, and several other banks and broker dealers.

Asset Backed Securities

As of 2017, the size of the U.S. ABS market is $1.5 trillion, down from a peak of $2.0 trillion in 2007, as shown in Figure 7.10.[xxii] The ABS market shares similarities with the MBS market in that the creation of securities involves securitization and typically the use of tranches and SPVs. However, all the instruments' underlying loans are nonmortgage financial assets, including student loans, equipment loans, credit card receivables, automobile loans, and even other bonds. The latter includes collateralized debt obligations (CDOs)

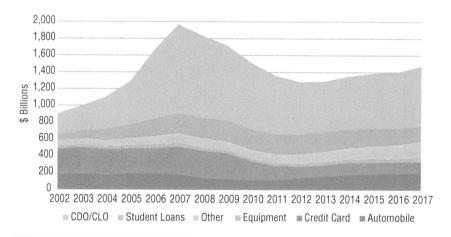

Figure 7.10   U.S. ABS outstanding. *Source*: SIFMA

and collateralized loan obligations (CLOs). The underlying collateral for CLOs are exclusively bank loans (leveraged loans), while the underlying collateral for CDOs includes a variety of typically high-yield instruments including high-yield bonds, leveraged loans, and the below investment grade tranches of RMBS, CMBS, and other CDOs. It is generally believed that the ABS market began in 1985[xxiii] with the creation of a roughly $200 million AAA-rated note paying 11.24% (a +0.49% spread to a Treasury) backed by computer leases, issued by Sperry Corporation and underwritten by First Boston.[xxiv] In the mid-1980s, Sperry Corporation was a well-known computer corporation where the core business involved the production and sale of computing equipment and software. Its customers regularly financed their purchases and in 1984, Sperry Corporation decided to eliminate the computer leases from its balance sheet. This would eliminate interest rate risk to its corporation, allow the computer business to access credit markets more easily, and free up executive resources to focus on growing its computer business. The launch of these notes was a success and the market grew rapidly thereafter.

While the assets that are used as collateral for an ABS are highly variable, corporate motivations to securitize these loans are quite similar. In general, corporations that securitize loans or receivables benefit from diversifying their sources of funding, reducing their interest rate sensitivity, transferring risk to entities that could better assume that risk, potentially improving capital ratios by reducing the size of a balance sheet, and increasing firm resources to focus on their core businesses. The banks that facilitate these transactions benefit from the fees they collect by originating the original security and by engaging in secondary market making (trading) once the securities have been issued. Investors in the securities benefit by having the opportunity to invest in high-quality assets with diversified structures, yields, collateral, and maturities.

While there are no doubt benefits to this market, there are problems as well. One concern is that ABS issuers may *shop* their structure to the rating agencies, and then hire the agency that will give the proposed ABS structure its most favorable rating. Another concern, as discussed in Chapter 1, is that securitization may reduce originators' incentives to carefully screen and monitor borrowers since these activities are costly and the originators bear no risk of default once the loans have been sold. Additionally, lenders may select the riskier loans to securitize and keep the safer loans on their balance sheet.[xxv] Another potential concern for this market is secondary market liquidity. According to a 2017 Financial Industry Regulatory Authority (FINRA) analysis of ABS market liquidity, the combined average daily volume for auto loan, credit card, and student loan ABS was only $1.2 billion. Additionally, only an average of three dealers actively transact in any given security. In contrast, the average daily volume for forward settle agency MBS (known as the TBA or to-be-announced market) was $200 billion with 17 counterparties able to transact.[xxvi] Meanwhile the average daily volume for U.S. Treasuries is generally around $500 billion[xxvii] with over 20 counterparties able to make markets. Because of these concerns, this is a market that is dominated by institutional investors that have the ability to perform significant due diligence as well as manage client liquidity.

Global and Emerging Markets

Finally, I will briefly introduce the market for bonds outside of the U.S. As of 2017, the U.S. bond market collectively was around $40 trillion, or roughly 40% of the global bond market, which left another $60 trillion issued by entities domiciled outside of the U.S., as shown in Figure 7.11.[xxviii] A bond issued in local currency (non-U.S. dollar) is called a *local currency* bond, while a bond issued in a G7 currency (such as the U.S. dollar, European euro, British pound, or Japanese yen) is called a *hard currency* bond. From the perspective of a U.S. investor, these bonds present additional risks as well as rewards. However, buyer beware: global bond market liquidity varies significantly by issuer, local currency bonds present additional legal risk, and many issuers do not produce audited financial statements that adhere to generally accepted accounting principles, or GAAP standards. Due to these risks, as well as several other difficulties associated with investing in these markets, generally, only central banks and large institutional investors (including actively managed mutual funds) are engaged in this market.

Of note, when a foreign entity issues a hard currency bond, such as when Argentina issues a dollar-denominated bond or Croatia issues a euro-denominated bond, the issuing entity agrees to adhere to the law of the country in

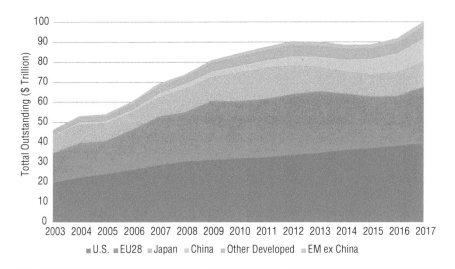

Figure 7.11   Global bond market outstanding. *Source:* SIFMA

whose official currency the bond is denominated. This provides bondholders with more legal protection in the event of default. For example, in 2005, Argentina defaulted on $81.8 billion in hard-currency bonds which had been issued in eight different jurisdictions including New York. Dollar-denominated bondholders who did not settle with the country brought claims against Argentina in New York courts, resulting in judgments with attachment orders. An attachment order means that courts can seize the country's assets or cash flow from future international debt transactions. This effectively blocked Argentina's access to the international credit markets until all defaulted debt was settled with creditors and the attachment orders lifted.[xxix] So, why would a country or corporation issue debt in a foreign currency and voluntarily adhere to the laws of a foreign jurisdiction? One motivation could be if the issuing entity is running a trade deficit in that foreign currency. For example, if Brazil purchased $2 billion more in goods and services from foreign countries than it sold to those countries, the government of Brazil may choose to issue $2 billion in dollar-denominated debt. Thus, while the United States issues debt when it runs a fiscal deficit, foreign countries with whom the United States trades may issue dollar-denominated debt if they run a trade deficit. Another motivation for a foreign entity issuing debt in the United States is that the government or corporation may be able to issue debt at a lower real interest rate in the U.S. (or other) market than in their domestic market.

SOURCES OF INCREMENTAL FIXED INCOME RETURN

Armed with the knowledge of bond return estimates, issuer types, their structures, and their risks, how should an active fixed income portfolio manager construct a portfolio that has a high probability of outperforming a fixed income benchmark? Asked another way, how did Bill Gross consistently outperform the Barclays Aggregate Index for all of those years,[7] and while doing so, grow the PIMCO Total Return Bond Fund to $292 billion at its peak? The first clue is in the name: Total Return. The Total Return fund was designed to maximize both the income and appreciation potential of its underlying assets (total return), given a targeted level of active risk or tracking error. The sources of this tracking error were generally from an assumption of additional duration, credit, or illiquidity risk for which investors are compensated for the assumption of those risks. With this in mind, I will begin by reviewing each

---

[7] The PIMCO Total Return Bond Fund outperformance from May 11, 1987 (inception) through September 30, 2013 was 1.14%, net of fees, for the institutional share class. *Source*: page 8: https://www.sec.gov/Archives/edgar/data/810893/000119312513461838/d598247dncsrs.htm#tx505962_2a.

one of these risks and provide a lens through which each risk's premium is measured. I will then discuss other premiums available to active bond managers. Then, in this chapter's final section, I will describe a framework by which an active bond manager can construct a portfolio and maximize the ex-ante likelihood of outperforming a benchmark.

Illiquidity Premium

The liquidity of a security is a measure of the ease by which it can be purchased or sold. This can further be measured by the time necessary to transact, the *cost* to trade such as bid/offer spreads or roundtrip cost, and the number of willing market makers. The most liquid fixed income security by these metrics are Treasury repurchase agreements with an overnight term (also known as Treasury overnight general collateral repo), in which a dealer and investor, or two dealers, exchange cash for U.S. government Treasuries at a 1-2 basis point bid/offer spread. This transaction settles one day and is unwound the following day. At the opposite end of the spectrum are esoteric fixed income products that require significant due diligence and rarely transact, such as certain CDOs. These instruments may not trade for months or years, may have only one or two dealers willing to act as a market maker, and the bid/offer spread may be several percentage points.

All things being equal, more illiquid assets should offer higher yields and higher returns. This higher return for illiquid assets can be rationalized two ways: first, illiquidity may be viewed as an implicit reduction in value. When valuing an asset, its value should be reduced by the expected cost of trading over the course of the security's lifetime. Second, holding an illiquid asset is akin to selling an option. Specifically, illiquid assets tend to become increasingly illiquid when the market value for that asset has declined. Therefore, the holder of the illiquid instrument should be compensated for the risk that they will be unable to sell the security, or its price will depreciate by more than a liquid asset when general risk premia rise. As a result, all assets other than overnight Treasury repos should receive some sort of liquidity premium since the holder of the asset is assuming some degree of illiquidity risk. Of note, there is a positive correlation between a bond's liquidity and its credit quality: the poorer the credit quality, in general, the less liquid the bond.[xxx] So, it's often difficult to decompose the compensation a credit investor is receiving between the risk of a bond default and the risk of the cost to transact the bond.

In general, an active bond portfolio manager may be able to outperform its benchmark by allocating some portion of their portfolio to illiquid (or at least *less* liquid) assets, thereby harvesting a liquidity premium. Commonly utilized benchmarks, such as the Barclays U.S. Aggregate Index, are composed almost exclusively of highly liquid bonds. As mutual fund assets are generally *sticky*, meaning only a small portion of investors redeem on any given day, an allocation to fewer liquid bonds may be manageable because there should be ample, more liquid assets that can be sold to fund normal redemption activity.

Credit Premium

As described earlier in this chapter, bonds other than those issued or guaranteed by the U.S. Treasury (or German federal government) have credit risk. The incremental return that a bond investor earns by holding such a bond is called a *credit spread* or *credit premium*. This premium should be roughly the expected loss for holding a bond with credit risk. Thus, if a bond is yielding 1% over a U.S. Treasury with a similar maturity, an investor might expect that this 1% spread is compensation for a hypothetical 2% likelihood of default and a 50% loss to the bondholder conditional on default. However, empirically, this hasn't been the case. Rather, on average, investors have been overcompensated for holding securities with credit risk. This phenomenon was highlighted by the Bank of International Settlements (2001), which showed that the incremental yield pickup for corporate bonds at given tenors and credit ratings was consistently above the average yearly loss from defaults.[xxxi] Since this study was published, the outperformance of credits versus underlying Treasuries has persisted, as shown in Figure 7.3. Specifically, investors in credit indices have outperformed investors in U.S. Treasuries over 5-, 10-, 15-, and 20-year periods that ended in 2017. If the credit premium that corporate bond investors earned was equal to the loss associated with credit defaults, these credit index returns would be roughly that of the Treasury indices. Other studies suggest that some of the incremental credit return can be partially attributed to less favorable tax treatment of corporate bonds (which are taxable at the state level, while Treasuries are not). Some speculate that this credit premium is partial compensation for a negative skew of returns as well as a high correlation of those returns with other credits. Said another way, a default will only lead to lower returns and not higher returns (negative skew), and conditional on one company defaulting, the likelihood of other defaults rises.

Regardless of the source of a credit premium, the persistence of this premium means an active bond portfolio manager may be able to outperform its benchmark over a multi-year period by harvesting this premium. To do this, the portfolio manager should construct a portfolio with a slightly lower credit quality than its benchmark by allocating more of their portfolio to bonds of lower credit quality than the benchmark's average credit quality. Because this is already well understood among active fixed income managers, high-yield, emerging market, or leveraged loans can be regularly found in portfolios benchmarked against the Bloomberg Barclays U.S. Aggregate Index.

Duration Premium

One theory that is used to explain the term structure for interest rates is the *expectations hypothesis*. This hypothesis states that the long-term interest rate is determined by the market's expectation of the short-term rate over the holding period of the long-term asset, plus a constant risk premium. For example, if an investor can purchase a one-year U.S. Treasury yielding 1% or a two-year U.S. Treasury yielding 2%, the expectations hypothesis states that the one-year forward year for a one-year yield on a bond should be about 3%. In this case, an investor should be agnostic as to whether they invest in a one-year bond at 1% then roll the proceeds into a one-year bond at 3%, or they purchase a two-year bond at 2%, because the total returns are nearly identical at the end of two years. The 3% rate is the one-year rate, one-year forward, or just the *forward* rate. The implication of the expectations hypothesis is that the current (or *spot*) interest rate should drift toward the forward rate. However, Campbell and Shiller (1991)[xxxii] and more recently Sarno, Thornton, and Valente (2005)[xxxiii] demonstrate this isn't the case. Rather, spot interest rates are more likely to follow a random walk (Duffee 2002).[xxxiv] This observation is profound because it allows bond managers to calculate a bond's total return without needing to estimate a future spot interest rate curve. Rather, a manager can simply assume interest rate curves will remain unchanged for the life of a bond, thereby allowing the manager to calculate the total return of a bond at any given point in the future. Additionally, this observation is important because it suggests that, all things being equal, a higher yielding bond (owing to its higher duration) will earn a higher return than a lower yielding bond. As a result, on average, an active portfolio manager should be able to add excess return by extending the duration of the portfolio over its benchmark.

Other Sources of Incremental Return

In addition to the three primary sources of excess return (duration, illiquidity, and credit premium), there are a plethora of additional sources of incremental return. One of these is a new-issue premium (or discount). In general, when an issuer issues a new security, this bond is sold to investors at a slight discount to where this bond will trade in the secondary market. As a result, purchasers will experience modest price appreciation in the security as soon as it begins trading. Therefore, when a new-issue premium exists (sometimes when bonds are in demand there is no premium), active bond managers can add incremental return by sourcing bonds in the primary market.

An additional source of incremental return is selling volatility. More accurately, this strategy involves purchasing securities that are callable or whose duration may be extended (as is the case with mortgage-backed securities). By purchasing these securities, the investor is collecting a premium for selling optionality to the issuer. The value of that option is a function of the likelihood that this option will be exercised, which in turn is impacted by the implied volatility of interest rates. When examining S&P 100 index contracts, Christensen and Prabhala (1998) demonstrated that equity implied volatility was higher than realized volatility.[xxxv] This result is relatively intuitive; if implied volatility was equal to realized volatility, nobody would sell volatility because there would be no incremental gain for selling *insurance*. This paper provided a framework to empirically test whether implied volatility was greater than realized volatility in other markets, such as interest rates. As it turns out, like its equity counterpart, interest rate implied volatility tends to be higher than realized volatility. Therefore, an active manager may generate excess returns over long periods of time by purchasing agency mortgage-backed securities in lieu of U.S. Treasuries.

Another source of incremental return may be attributed to purchasing securities that are *structurally cheap*, or that historically generate a higher return than similar securities for reasons unrelated to the securities' duration, liquidity, and credit risks. For example, Fama (1984) first highlighted the oddity that in the U.S. Treasury bill market, bills with eight- and nine-month maturities outperformed shorter and longer term Treasury bills. So, in other words, eight- and nine-month Treasury bills were structurally cheap versus one- to seven- and 10- to 12-month Treasury bills, and due to this structural cheapness the eight- and nine-month bills tended to outperform other Treasury bills in subsequent months.[xxxvi] Another security that was structurally cheap for years was the fifth Eurodollar (also known as *ED5*) contract. This contract allowed investors to speculate or hedge the three-month U.S. dollars London Interbank Offered Rate (LIBOR) on a given date. The fifth contract is the contract that references the three-month LIBOR rate 15 months forward. This contract was structurally cheap to the fourth Eurodollar contract (*ED4*), which references the three-month LIBOR rate 12 months forward. In view of this structural cheapness, ED5 contracts were often a major position in Gross's Total Return portfolios. Looking for opportunities further out on the curve, I regularly noticed that three- and seven-year credits were structurally cheap as compared to five-year credits; therefore, while working on the credit desk, I often purchased bonds with these tenors. So, what causes these structural oddities? While it is impossible to know with certainty, most practitioners attribute this cheapness to large institutions that are restricted (whether from client guidelines or government rules) from purchasing bonds outside a given tenor. For example, U.S. money market funds cannot purchase securities that mature in greater than 13 months (397 days). Thus, when ED5 contracts begin trading, money market funds are ineligible to purchase them. However, once ED5 rolls down to ED4, this contract is now eligible for purchase by money market funds. This marginal bid at ED4, and lack of bid at ED5, creates a structural premium that an active manager can harvest.

The final source of incremental return that I will cover here can be categorized as a relative value trade. These trades, which are too many to detail here, offer incremental return by owning one security versus another similar security. For example, a credit basis trade may involve an investor purchasing a corporate bond and then purchasing credit protection, synthetically creating a position free of credit risk (akin to a Treasury). This trade can generate positive returns if there is significant incremental return over a Treasury with a similar duration to the corporate bond. In another potential relative value trade, a manager may choose to purchase U.S. Treasury futures in lieu of U.S. Treasuries if the implied financing of such a position is sufficiently low. Or, perhaps a manager can engage in a fixed-for-float interest rate swap in lieu of purchasing a Treasury, and in doing so pick up a swap-spread premium. Active managers may also look to engage in relative value trades between similar credits or mortgages. For example, a manager may choose to sell their Verizon 2023 corporate bond and purchase equal parts of Verizon 2022 and 2024 bonds. There are thousands of such relative value trades, and maintaining a systematic approach to sourcing and reviewing these trades is critical to ensuring these cheap securities are quickly identified and added to an actively managed portfolio.

ACTIVE FIXED INCOME PORTFOLIO MANAGEMENT: OPTIMIZATION AND OUTPERFORMANCE

Given the plethora of sources of potential excess return, how should a bond portfolio manager construct his portfolio to maximize its risk-adjusted returns versus a benchmark? To do this a portfolio manager must be able to rank order all potential out-of-benchmark paired trades to then select the options that offer the highest risk-adjusted return subject to other risk guidelines (like portfolio credit quality, minimum portfolio liquidity, or maximum tracking error). This process is highly iterative, as most optimizations are. In this section, we'll demonstrate a fixed income portfolio optimization process with a simple example that utilizes many of the aforementioned fixed income sectors.

Steps One, Two, and Three: Total Return and Marginal Carry Calculation

The first step involves the portfolio manager calculating the expected total return for their portfolio benchmark. There is no universal method for calculating bond or bond portfolio total return; but, conditional on not having a high conviction on the future path of either interest rates or credit risk premium, I recommend assuming credit and interest rate curves remain unchanged over the next three months. Then, calculate the total return of each benchmark security over that period and annualize the returns. Finally, aggregate the weighted total returns for each benchmark security to arrive at the expected benchmark total return (henceforth referred to as *carry*).

Step Two involves calculating the carry of all out-of-benchmark securities that will be considered for inclusion in the portfolio. In Table 7.2, examples of out-of-benchmark securities include five-year U.S. Treasury futures, seven-year BBB-rated asset backed securities, BB-rated bank loans, and several others. Step Three involves the estimation of the additional marginal carry associated with a given security substitution equal to 1% of the portfolio market value (PMV). For example, I might consider selling hypothetical benchmark *Security A* which has an estimated carry of 300 basis points (bps) per year and purchasing hypothetical out-of-benchmark *Security B* with an estimated carry of 500 bps per year. The marginal pickup in carry with a 1% portfolio substitution is (500 bps – 300 bps) × 1%, or 2 bps.

Steps Four and Five: Tracking Error and Rank Order of Trades

Step Four involves calculating the additional marginal tracking error associated with a security substitution. For example, a hypothetical portfolio manager is considering selling 1% of a three-year U.S. Treasury note (held in the portfolio) and purchasing 1% of a five-year U.S. Treasury note. In Table 7.2, I show this hypothetical trade would add 0.7 bps in marginal carry (indicating the five-year U.S. Treasury will out-carry the three-year U.S. Treasury by 70 bps). However, following this trade, the active portfolio will now overweight the five-year key rate duration and underweight the three-year key rate duration. Additionally, the portfolio will have a higher overall duration than the benchmark. Therefore, this trade will add incremental tracking error.[8] For this analysis, let's assume that the portfolio manager is starting with their previous benchmark (i.e., she holds a portfolio exactly mirroring their benchmark) meaning the current portfolio has zero tracking error at this time. After the substitution of 1% market value three-year U.S. Treasury notes for 1% market value five-year U.S. Treasury notes, the portfolio tracking error is now 0.4 bps. Thus, the marginal tracking error for the portfolio substitution is 0.4 bps.

---

[8] The process by which a fixed income manager can estimate this tracking error is beyond the scope of this chapter; the estimation of a fixed income portfolio's ex-ante tracking error involves a complex analytical exercise that may involve the estimation of a robust covariance matrix of fixed income portfolio factors.

Table 7.2   Active fixed income management first pass optimization

		Steps 1–3	Step 4	Step 5
Sell	Buy	Marginal Carry (bps)	Marginal Tracking Error (bps)	Marginal Carry / Marginal TE
ED4 Contract	ED5 Contract	0.20	0.10	2.00
5-yr. UST	5-yr. UST futures	0.20	0.10	2.00
3-yr. UST	5-yr. UST	0.70	0.40	1.75
5-yr. UST	5-yr. Agency Debenture	0.20	0.15	1.33
5-yr. UST	5-yr. A-Rated Corps	1.70	1.30	1.31
7-yr. BBB-Rated Corps	7-yr. BBB-rated ABS	1.40	1.10	1.27
5-yr. VZ Corp	3-yr. and 7-yr. VZ Corp	1.10	0.90	1.22
5-yr. UST	30-yr. Agency MBS	1.10	1.00	1.10
3-yr. UST	3-yr. BB-rated EM Bond	3.00	2.90	1.03
3-month U.S. bill	BB-Rated Bank Loan	6.00	5.90	1.02
5-yr. A-Rated Corps	5-yr. BBB-Rated corps	1.30	1.50	0.87
5-yr. UST	10-yr. UST	1.10	1.40	0.79
30-yr. Agency MBS	5-yr. A-Rated Corps	0.50	0.90	0.56
5-yr. BBB-rated Corps	5-yr. BB-rated Corps	1.00	2.20	0.45
5-yr. A-Rated Corps	5-yr. A-Rated Munis	0.20	0.80	0.25
10-yr. UST	10-yr. German Bund	(0.50)	2.00	(0.25)
10-yr. UST	10-yr. UST futures	(0.10)	0.05	(2.00)

Active Portfolio Management Impact. First Run	
Additional Carry vs Benchmark (bps)	15.6
Additional Tracking Error vs Benchmark (bps)	13.9
Ex-ante Information Ratio	1.13

Trade	Position Size (% PMV)	Total Marginal Carry (bps)	Total Marginal Tracking Error (bps)	
Structural RV Trade	1%	0.20	0.10	
Treasury RV Trade	1%	0.20	0.10	
Adding duration and yield curve RV trade	1%	0.70	0.40	
Adding credit and illiquidity risk	1%	0.20	0.15	
Adding credit and illiquidity risk	1%	1.70	1.30	Add trade. Bring each trade to 1% PMV.
Adding illiquidity risk	1%	1.40	1.10	
Credit RV Trade	1%	1.10	0.90	
Selling volatility	1%	1.10	1.00	
Adding credit and illiquidity risk	1%	3.00	2.90	
Adding credit and illiquidity risk	1%	6.00	5.90	
Adding credit and illiquidity risk	0%	-	-	
Adding duration and yield curve RV trade	0%	-	-	
Substituting volatility for credit premium	0%	-	-	Do not add out of benchmark position.
Adding credit and illiquidity risk	0%	-	-	
Substituting source of credit risk	0%	-	-	
Diversifying source of duration	0%	-	-	
Treasury RV Trade	0%	-	-	
Sigma		**15.6**	**13.9**	

Step Five involves the calculation of the ratio of marginal carry to marginal tracking error for each paired trade. This ratio is sufficiently like the information ratio (IR) so that I will use this descriptor going forward. At this point, the portfolio manager (PM) can now rank order all potential security substitutions by their estimated ex-ante IR. In the hypothetical example in Table 7.2, I assume that the PM will incorporate any active position that has an ex-ante IR greater than 1.0. Thus, of the 17 considered positions, the PM will add 10 of these positions. The total impact to the portfolio's carry is an aggregation of the marginal carry from each trade. However, the impact to the portfolio's tracking error will not exactly equal an aggregation of the marginal tracking error from each trade. This is because newly added active positions will interact with each other. However, this interaction effect is sufficiently small that I will not consider it here in an initial iteration of an optimization. Following this first pass, this now actively managed hypothetical fixed income portfolio includes 10% out-of-benchmark positions, the portfolio out-carries its benchmark by 15.6 bps/yr, and the portfolio has an estimated tracking error of 13.9 bps/yr as shown in Table 7.2.

Step Six and Beyond: Portfolio Iteration

In the initial iteration, I added out-of-benchmark positions, each weighted 1% of the PMV. However, in an optimal portfolio, some positions should be larger than 1%. Meanwhile, some positions that were initially rejected for inclusion may add sufficient incremental return once out-of-benchmark security interactions are included in the tracking error calculation. Therefore, the optimization process should continue until one of these two conditions is met:

1. There are no additional paired trades that warrant inclusion in the existing portfolio given an IR target
2. The portfolio has reached one or more binding constraints, such as maximum tracking error, minimum credit quality, minimum liquid assets, maximum or minimum duration, or something else

In Table 7.3, I continue with our hypothetical portfolio optimization exercise. In this instance, I rerun the portfolio optimization and add an additional 1% PMV to positions that have an information ratio of more than 1.0. Note that the marginal carry for each paired trade will remain unchanged as the portfolio optimization process continues. This is because the paired-trade incremental carry is calculated by subtracting an out-of-benchmark position carry from an in-benchmark position, and the total carry of the existing portfolio is not a consideration. What will change, however, is the estimated tracking error of each paired position. In our hypothetical example, the tracking error for most paired trades increases following the initial pass. As a result, four positions were not upsized while six positions were upsized from 1% to 2% PMV. Additional carry versus the benchmark has increased to 20.0 bps from 15.6 bps, while portfolio tracking error has increased to 17.6 bps from 13.9 bps. In practice, this optimization would continue until either of the two previously mentioned conditions are met.

Continuous Optimizations and High Conviction Forecasts

The optimization process that was mentioned earlier is dynamic and should be rerun on a weekly, monthly, quarterly, and annual basis. If done correctly, as sources of alpha emerge or are eliminated, an actively managed and regularly optimized total-return-focused fixed income portfolio will be continually repositioned so that its sources of tracking error offer the highest possible risk-adjusted incremental return. For example, in the aforementioned example, the PM substituted three-year U.S. Treasury notes for five-year U.S. Treasury notes because it was estimated at that time that the five-year U.S. Treasury out-carried the three-year U.S. Treasury by 70 bps/yr. This calculation is driven almost exclusively by the shape of the yield curve, which at the time of this hypothetical example was relatively *steep*. If in the future, the yield on the three-year point of the curve rises so that it is above that of the five-year, then this trade would no longer add incremental carry; rather, this paired trade would subtract incremental carry while still adding tracking error. So, an active PM would consider *going the opposite direction*, or selling the five-year U.S. Treasury note in favor of purchasing the three-year U.S. Treasury note. This trade would be highlighted to the PM if she rank-orders trades during the optimization process. Separately, if a PM has a high conviction regarding the forward outlook of the shape of the yield curve, a change in credit or illiquidity premium, a change in volatility, or any other potential source of risk and return, these views can be incorporated into this portfolio optimization framework. For example, if the PM believes credit spreads will tighten (decline) over the next quarter, this estimation can be incorporated into the portfolio carry calculation. Alternatively, if the PM believes the economy will soon enter a recession, the PM can utilize a recession scenario covariance matrix when estimating tracking error.

Table 7.3   Active fixed income management second pass optimization

Sell	Buy	Marginal Carry (bps)	Marginal Tracking Error (bps)	Marginal Carry / Marginal TE
ED4 Contract	ED5 Contract	0.20	0.14	1.43
5-yr. UST	5-yr. UST futures	0.20	0.14	1.43
3-yr. UST	5-yr. UST	0.70	0.55	1.27
5-yr. UST	5-yr. Agency Debenture	0.20	0.17	1.18
5-yr. UST	5-yr. A-Rated Corps	1.70	1.50	1.13
7-yr. BBB-Rated Corps	7-yr. BBB-rated ABS	1.40	1.29	1.09
5-yr. VZ Corp	3-yr. and 7-yr. VZ Corp	1.10	1.11	0.99
5-yr. UST	30-yr. Agency MBS	1.10	1.12	0.98
3-yr. UST	3-yr. BB-rated EM Bond	3.00	3.05	0.98
3-month U.S. bill	BB-Rated Bank Loan	6.00	6.20	0.97
5-yr. A-Rated Corps	5-yr. BBB-Rated corps	1.30	1.58	0.82
5-yr. UST	10-yr. UST	1.10	1.47	0.75
30-yr. Agency MBS	5-yr. A-Rated Corps	0.50	0.95	0.53
5-yr. BBB-rated Corps	5-yr. BB-rated Corps	1.00	2.31	0.43
5-yr. A-Rated Corps	5-yr. A-Rated Munis	0.20	0.84	0.24
10-yr. UST	10-yr. German Bund	(0.50)	1.80	(0.28)
10-yr. UST	10-yr. UST futures	(0.10)	0.05	(2.00)

Active Portfolio Management Impact. Second Run	
Additional Carry vs Benchmark (bps)	20.0
Additional Tracking Error vs Benchmark (bps)	17.6
Ex-ante Information Ratio	1.13

Trade	Position Size (% PMV)	Total Marginal Carry (bps)	Total Marginal Tracking Error (bps)	
Structural RV Trade	2%	0.40	0.24	Upsize trade. Bring each trade to 2% PMV.
Treasury RV Trade	2%	0.40	0.24	
Adding duration and yield curve RV trade	2%	1.40	0.95	
Adding credit and illiquidity risk	2%	0.40	0.32	
Adding credit and illiquidity risk	2%	3.40	2.80	
Adding illiquidity risk	2%	2.80	2.39	
Credit RV Trade	1%	1.10	0.90	Do not upsize. Maintain each trade at 1% PMV.
Selling volatility	1%	1.10	1.00	
Adding credit and illiquidity risk	1%	3.00	2.90	
Adding credit and illiquidity risk	1%	6.00	5.90	
Adding credit and illiquidity risk	0%	-	-	Do not add out of benchmark position.
Adding duration and yield curve RV trade	0%	-	-	
Substituting volatility for credit premium	0%	-	-	
Adding credit and illiquidity risk	0%	-	-	
Substituting source of credit risk	0%	-	-	
Diversifying source of duration	0%	-	-	
Treasury RV Trade	0%	-	-	
Sigma		**20.0**	**17.6**	

SUMMARY AND INVESTMENT IMPLICATIONS

Summary

Bonds are legal promises to make periodic payments for a predetermined time, and these legal promises can be traded between entities. These securities specify the issuer, coupon, and maturity, and they often contain covenants and other legal provisions. Like all financial instruments, the value of a bond is equal to the present value of its future cash flows. The value of a credit-risk-free instrument is equal to each cash flow, discounted at the appropriate treasury interest rate. If a bond has credit risk, a spread is added to each discount rate; this spread is commonly referred to as the Z-spread. The YTM of a bond is the single discount rate that equates the bond's cash flows and the current price of the security.

Interest rate duration risk is an estimation of the price sensitivity of a bond to changes in interest rates. Convexity is the second-order estimation of the price sensitivity of a bond to changes in interest rates, and it accounts for the non-linearity in bond price changes with respect to changes in interest rates. In general, longer-term bonds without embedded options have higher duration and convexity. In addition to interest rate risk, bonds have credit risk, liquidity risk, inflation risk, interest rate volatility risk, and they may have exchange-rate risk, event risk, legal risk, and sector risk.

In the United States, the issuers of bonds include the U.S. Treasury, U.S. agencies, municipalities, corporations, as well as intermediaries that create mortgage-related securities and ABSs. Global and emerging market issuers also issue both local and dollar-denominated securities available for purchase by U.S. investors.

So how should a fixed income PM synthesize this plethora of issuers, risks, and returns to generate a portfolio that is superior to its benchmark? To accomplish this task, a PM should follow an iterative process that ensures that all of the aforementioned sources of potential return and risk are constantly being reconsidered. Out-of-benchmark trades should be rank ordered and included into the portfolio if they meet a minimum threshold of ex-ante expected return to its marginal additional tracking error. The incorporation of a total return calculation, as well as a reasonable estimate of bond factor covariance, is essential to this process.

Investment Implications

A well-managed fixed income portfolio:

- Sources incremental return from a variety of asset classes
- Maintains a structural bias toward higher-carry securities

- Incorporates expectations for forward rates, spreads, and covariances when conviction is high
- Utilizes total return calculations to estimate *carry*
- Continually optimizes the portfolio so that high-information ratio trades are constantly being rotated into the portfolio while low-information ratio trades are being rotated out

Finally:

- Fixed income PMs should be able to identify each risk and ensure that they are being adequately compensated for each risk when evaluating a bond
- Potential sources of incremental returns can occur in any fixed income class; so, considering all fixed income sectors and asset classes maximizes the likelihood that a manager is utilizing the most opportune out-of-benchmark securities when spending a tracking error budget

APPENDIX A: BOND MATH EXAMPLES

In the following examples, I will assume that all bonds are U.S. Treasuries. As such, they have no credit risk and pay semi-annual coupons.

Example 1: Calculate the market implied interest rate of a six-month U.S. bill priced at 99.504. Use this formula:

$$P = \frac{C}{(1+i_1)^{1/2}} + \frac{C}{(1+i_2)^{2/2}} + \cdots + \frac{C}{(1+i_N)^{N/2}} + \frac{M}{(1+i_N)^{N/2}}$$

where:

P = market price of the bond
C = the bond semi-annual coupon
M = the value of the bond at maturity (also known as the bond face value)
N = each semi-annual period
i_N = the market interest rate of a zero-coupon security that matures at a given period

$$99.504 = \frac{100}{(1+i_1)^{1/2}}$$

Solving for i_1, the annual interest rate is 1.00%.

Example 2: Calculate the one-year market interest rate (i_2). Assume the six-month annualized interest rate is 1.0%, the current price of a one-year note is 99.968, and the note pays a 1% coupon, paid semi-annually.

$$99.968 = \frac{0.5}{(1+1.00\%)^{1/2}} + \frac{0.5}{(1+i_2)^{2/2}} + \frac{100}{(1+i_2)^{2/2}}$$

Solving for i_2, the annual interest rate for a security that matures in exactly one year and pays no coupons is 1.035%.

Example 3: Calculate the price of a 2.5-year U.S. Treasury note with a 3.0% annual coupon. Assume the zero-coupon yield curve is:

$i_1 = 1.000\%$
$i_2 = 1.035\%$
$i_3 = 1.070\%$
$i_4 = 1.100\%$
$i_5 = 1.200\%$

$$P = \frac{1.50}{(1+1.000\%)^{1/2}} + \frac{1.50}{(1+1.035\%)^{2/2}} + \frac{1.50}{(1+1.070\%)^{3/2}} +$$

$$\frac{1.50}{(1+1.100\%)^{4/2}} + \frac{1.50}{(1+1.200\%)^{5/2}} + \frac{1.00}{(1+1.200\%)^{5/2}}$$

Solving for P, I calculate 104.439.

Example 4: Calculate the current yield of a 2.5-year U.S. Treasury note with a 3.0% coupon and a price of 104.439. Utilize this formula:

$$Current\ Yield = \frac{annual\ dollar\ coupon\ interest}{current\ price}$$

Solving:

$$Current\ Yield = \frac{3.0}{104.439} = 2.87\%$$

Example 5: Calculate the YTM of a 2.5-year U.S. Treasury note with a 3.0% annual coupon priced at 104.439. Use this formula:

$$Yield\ equation\ 2:\ P = \frac{C}{(1+YTM)^{1/2}} + \frac{C}{(1+YTM)^{2/2}} + \cdots + \frac{C}{(1+YTM)^{N/2}} + \frac{M}{(1+YTM)^{N/2}}$$

where:

P = market price of the bond
C = the bond semi-annual coupon
M = the value of the bond at maturity (also known as the bond face value)
N = each semi-annual period
YTM = the yield to maturity

$$104.439 = \frac{1.5}{(1+YTM)^{1/2}} + \frac{1.5}{(1+YTM)^{2/2}} + \cdots + \frac{1.5}{(1+YTM)^{N/2}} + \frac{100}{(1+YTM)^{N/2}}$$

Solving, YTM = 1.196%.

Example 6: Calculate the annualized total return of a 3.0%, 2.5-year U.S. Treasury bond priced at 104.439 and held for six months. Assume the yield curve is unchanged.

Step 1: Calculate the expected future price of a 3.0%, 2-year U.S. Treasury bond in six months. Assume the zero-coupon interest rate curve is unchanged.

i_1 = 1.000%
i_2 = 1.035%
i_3 = 1.070%
i_4 = 1.100%

$$P = \frac{1.50}{(1+1.000\%)^{1/2}} + \frac{1.50}{(1+1.035\%)^{2/2}} + \frac{1.50}{(1+1.070\%)^{3/2}} + \frac{1.50}{(1+1.100\%)^{4/2}} + \frac{1.00}{(1+1.100\%)^{4/2}}$$

Solving, P = 103.757.

Step 2: Calculate future cash flows.

$$Total\ Future\ Dollars = Future\ Sale\ Price + Future\ Coupon$$

Solving, Total Future Dollars = 103.757 + 1.50 = 105.257

Step 3: Calculate annualized TRR.

$$Annualized\ Total\ Rate\ of\ Return = \left(\frac{total\ future\ dollars}{current\ bond\ price}\right)^2 - 1$$

Solving, *annualized TRR* = $(105.257 / 104.439)^2 - 1$ = 1.572%.

Example 7: Calculate the duration of a 3.0%, 2.5-year U.S. Treasury bond priced at 104.439. Use this formula:

$$\frac{V_- - V_+}{2(V_0)(\Delta y)}$$

where:

V_- = bond price if yields decline by Δy
V_+ = bond price if yields rise by Δy
V_0 = initial bond price
Δy = change in yield in decimal

$$Duration = \frac{104.690 - 104.189}{2(104.439)(0.001)}$$

Solving, *duration* = 2.40. Thus, for every 100 bps (increase) in yield, the bond will appreciate (depreciate) by about 2.40%, as shown in the following equation:

Bond Price Change Estimate (%) = *Duration* × *Change in yield* (%)

Example 8: Calculate the convexity of a 3%, 2.5-year Treasury bond priced at 104.439. Use this formula and solve for a 0.10% move in yield:

$$\frac{V_- + V_+ - 2V_0}{2(V_0)(\Delta y)^2}$$

where:

V_- = bond price if yields decline by Δy
V_+ = bond price if yields rise by Δy
V_0 = initial bond price
Δy = change in yield in decimal

$$Convexity\ measure = \frac{104.690 + 104.189 - 2(104.439)}{2(104.439)(0.001)^2}$$

Solving, *convexity* = 4.787. The convexity adjustment, which is the adjustment in our price estimate for a new bond given a change in rates, is shown by the following formula:

Convexity Adjustment Estimate (%) = *Convexity measure* × Δy^2

Example 9: Combine the duration and convexity equations to calculate the new price of a 3%, 2.5-year Treasury bond initially priced at 104.439 for a −1.0% decline in yield. Use the following formula:

$$V_1 = V_0(1 + D(-\Delta y) + C(\Delta y^2))$$

where:

V_1 = new bond price
V_0 = initial bond price
D = duration
C = convexity
Δy = change in yield in decimal

Solving for a −1.0% decline in yield:

$$V_1 = 104.439(1 + 2.4(0.01) + 4.787((-0.01)^2))$$

where:

V_1 = new bond price
V_0 = 104.439
D = 2.40
C = 4.787
Δy = −0.01

Solving each component separately:

Estimated bond price change owing to duration:	+2.400%
Estimated bond change owing to convexity:	+0.048%
Total estimated price change:	+2.448%

Therefore, the estimate of V_1 is 104.439 × (1.02448) = 106.996; the actual price of the bond following a −1.0% decline in interest rates is 106.990.

CITATIONS

i. https://www.treasury.gov/resource-center/data-chart-center/.
ii. Fabozzi, F.J. (2001). *The Handbook of Fixed Income Securities*. New York: McGraw Hill. p. 114.
iii. Kou, Jianming and Simone Varotto. (June 2008). "Timeliness of Spread Implied Ratings. European Financial Management." Vol. 14, Issue 3. pp. 503–527. Available at SSRN: https://ssrn.com/abstract=1132531 or http://dx.doi.org/10.1111/j.1468-036X.2007.00362.x.
iv. SIFMA. *Fact Book 2018*. p. 29.

v. Congress of the United States Congressional Budget Office. *The Budget and Economic Outlook: 2018 to 2028.* p. 81.

vi. https://www.sifma.org/resources/research/us-marketable-treasury-issuance-outstanding-and-interest-rates/.

vii. https://www.treasury.gov. Resource Center. Quarterly Refunding Auction Schedule. (https://www.treasury.gov/resource-center/data-chart-center/quarterly-refunding/Pages/default.aspx).

viii. United States Treasury. Bureau of the Fiscal Service. (December 2018). Treasury Bulletin. Ownership of Federal Securities. Tables 1 and 2.

ix. SIFMA. *Fact Book 2018.* p. 29.

x. Municipal Securities Rulemaking Board. 2018. Trends in Municipal Bond Ownership. Chart 1.

xi. SIFMA. *Fact Book 2018.* p. 29.

xii. https://www.federalreserve.gov/releases/cp/about.htm.

xiii. Hicks, J. William. (1976). "Commercial Paper: An Exempted Security Under Section 3 (a) (3) of the Securities Act of 1933." Articles by Maurer Faculty. Paper 1015.

xiv. Bloomberg Barclays Index Methodology. (March 2017). Bloomberg Barclays Indices. p. 31.

xv. ———. (March 2017). Bloomberg Barclays Indices. p. 31.

xvi. International Monetary Fund. (April 2018). "Global Financial Stability Report: Bump Road Ahead." Figure 1.9.

xvii. S&P Dow Jones Indices: S&P/LSTA U.S. (February 2018). Leveraged Loan 100 Index Methodology. p. 4.

xviii. SIFMA. (November 1, 2018). U.S. Mortgage-Related Securities Outstanding. Excel download: "Mortgage-Related Outstanding" tab.

xix. https://www.fhfa.gov/DataTools/Downloads/Pages/Conforming-Loan-Limits.aspx.

xx. SIFMA. (November 1, 2018). U.S. Mortgage-Related Securities Outstanding. Excel download: "Mortgage-Related Outstanding" tab.

xxi. ———. (November 1, 2018). U.S. Mortgage-Related Securities Outstanding. Excel download: "Mortgage-Related Outstanding" tab.

xxii. ———. (November 1, 2018). U.S. ABS Issuance and Outstanding. Excel download: "ABS Outstanding" tab.

xxiii. Fabozzi, Frank J. Editor. (2012). *The Handbook of Fixed Income Securities.* Chicago, IL: McGraw-Hill Eduation. Print. p. 727.

xxiv. Rosenthal, James A. and Juan M. Ocampo. (1998). Securitization of Credit. Crockett, TX. Print. pp. 158–159.

xxv. The Joint Forum Report on asset securitization incentives. (July 2011). Bank for International Settlements. pp. 45–47.

xxvi. He, An and Bruce Mizrach. (June 2017). "Analysis of Securitized Liquidity." FINRA Office of the Chief Economist. Research Note. Tables 4 and 9.

xxvii. SIFMA. https://www.sifma.org/resources/research/us-treasury-trading -volume/.

xxviii. ———. *Fact Book 2018.* p. 51.

xxix. Hornbeck, J.F. (February 6, 2013). "Argentina's Defaulted Sovereign Debt: Dealing with the 'Holdouts.'" Congressional Research Service. pp. 1, 5–6.

xxx. Van Loon, P., A. Cairns, A. McNeil, and A. Veys. (2015). "Modelling the Liquidity Premium on Corporate Bonds." Annals of Actuarial Science, 9(2), pp. 264–289. doi:10.1017/S1748499514000347.

xxxi. Amato, Jeffery D. and Eli M. Remolona. (December 1, 2003). "The Credit Spread Puzzle." *BIS Quarterly Review.* Available at SSRN: https://ssrn.com/abstract=1968448 or http://dx.doi.org/10.2139/ssrn .1968448.

xxxii. Campbell, John Y. and Robert J. Shiller. (1991). "Yield Spreads and Interest Rate Movements: A Bird's Eye View." *Review of Economic Studies.* 58(3). pp. 495–514.

xxxiii. Sarno, Lucio, Daniel Thornton, and Giorgio Valente. (2005). The Empirical Failure of the Expectations Hypothesis of the Term Structure of Bond Yields. Federal Reserve Bank of St. Louis, Working Papers. 42. 10.1017/S0022109000002192.

xxxiv. Duffee, G. (2002). "Term Premia and Interest Rate Forecasts in Affine Models." *Journal of Finance.* 57(1). pp. 405–443.

xxxv. Christensen, Bent Jesper and N.R. Prabhala. (1998). "The relation between implied and realized volatility." *Journal of Financial Economics.* 50(2). pp. 125–150.

xxxvi. Fama, Eugene F. (December 1984). *Journal of Financial Economics.* Volume 13, Issue 4. pp. 529–546.

8

REAL ASSET INVESTING

Bob Greer
Scholar in Residence, J.P. Morgan Center for Commodities at the
University of Colorado Denver Business School
Senior Advisor, Core Commodity Management

David E. Linton, CFA
Director, Portfolio Construction and Manager Research
Pacific Life Fund Advisors LLC

INTRODUCTION

In 1995, before there had been any conferences devoted just to commodities, there was a conference in California on the broader subject of *real assets*. One of the speakers was renowned commodity investor Jim Rogers, who participated remotely while on an extended world tour. Jim is one of the cofounders of the Quantum Fund, run by Soros Fund Management, and he is well-known among commodity investors as the creator of the Rogers International Commodity Index (RICI®). This index was established in 1997 and began tracking the total return of investing in a basket of commodities in 1998.[i] Jim was quite bullish on commodities, so much so that he exclaimed, "Buy oats. If I weren't traveling, I would buy oats!" Of course, he wasn't suggesting investors buy bushels of actual oats and store them in a grain elevator. He was instead advocating the purchase of futures contracts on oats.

Bob, who was sitting in the audience at the time, opened his *Wall Street Journal* to check the futures prices of oats. "The market must agree with Jim," Bob commented to a colleague also in attendance. "The price of the nearby oats futures contract is $1.80 per bushel, while the price of oats for delivery six months later is $2.00. So oats would have to appreciate by more than 10% in six months for Jim to make money buying oats. Good luck with that."

Some eleven years later, David, then a product associate at PIMCO covering their *absolute return* strategies, was reviewing a monthly holdings report. "What's this line item?" he asked his manager. "It's got a strange alphanumeric identifier, and part of that identifier corresponds to wheat. I've never seen anything like it."

"Go ask Bob."

"Who?"

"Bob Greer, our commodities expert. He knows his stuff. You should really get to know him."

After a brief introduction, Bob explained, "Yeah, that's a trade we put on in some of our commodity accounts. Looks like your portfolio manager put this on as well. We've taken physical delivery of wheat in several elevators and will be reselling it in three months at a price 3% higher than when we purchased it. It's close to a 10% annualized return after storage costs."

"Huh."

We highlight these stories because we believe commodity investors should appreciate that there are two different ways to invest in commodities: either with a derivative whose price is determined by the underlying commodity (such as a futures contract) or by taking or delivering the physical commodity. Both approaches have costs and benefits, and either approach may or may not be practical given the investor or hedger's objectives and abilities.

In this chapter we will review the history of real asset investing; describe the major commodities, their producers, consumers, and investors; and finally we will explain common ways in which investors may gain exposure to or hedge price movements of these assets. For investors who would like to read more on commodities and commodity investing, we have several recommendations. This broader category of inflation assets is described in *The Handbook of Inflation Hedging Investments*, edited and cowritten by Robert J. Greer. Another recommended book specifically on investing in commodities is *Intelligent Commodity Investing*, edited by Hilary Till and Joseph Eagleeye. Within this category of commodities, and with a similar title, another worthwhile reference is *Intelligent Commodity Indexing*, by Robert Greer, Nic Johnson, and Mihir Worah. This book details the most common ways to invest in commodities. Specifically, it explains how a manager might gain commodity exposure by purchasing commodity futures contracts and fully collateralizing those contracts with an actively managed fixed income portfolio.

BRIEF HISTORY OF REAL ASSETS, COMMODITY EXCHANGES, AND COMMODITY INVESTING

Real assets are physical—you can see and touch them like an office building, a bushel of wheat, or a bar of silver. These assets contrast with financial assets, which were discussed in detail in Chapter 1. Real assets are *investible assets*, meaning you can purchase them with the expectation that you will gain utility from its consumption, the ability to resell it in the future, or the return of capital via future cash flows.

Real assets and all other investible assets can be further subdivided into three super-classes: *capital assets, consumable/transformable (C/T) assets*, and *store-of-value assets*. Capital assets, like stocks or bonds, derive their value from a claim to future cash flows. Real estate such as apartments, office buildings, or bridges, are examples of such capital assets. C/T assets like wheat, copper, or oil have value due to their ability to generate utility during consumption. The price of these assets is generally set by typical supply/demand dynamics. Finally, store-of-value assets include items like precious metals or artwork. These too have a price determined primarily from their supply and demand. Another lens through which we can view commodities is whether they are *renewable* or *depletable*. Soft commodities generally are grown (like wheat, sugar, and coffee) and may spoil. Hard commodities are taken from the ground, like metals and oil, and they generally do not spoil. For this reason, hard commodities have been used as stores of value by different cultures throughout modern history. Our brief historical review of real assets will focus on C/T (soft) commodities and store of value (hard) commodities.

Brief History of Real Assets

Hunter/gatherers may have begun cultivating and harvesting crops as early as 23,000 years ago while the appearance of agricultural habitats first appeared around 12,000 years ago.[ii] Meanwhile, coins made of precious metals first appeared around the seventh century BC and were minted by the Kingdom of Lydia in modern day Turkey.[iii] The reasons vary (and are speculative) as to why humans developed into agrarian societies after millennia of successful hunter-gathering; however, the effects of this transition include societies that were larger, more specialized, and sedentary.[iv] The rationale for the adoption of a coin-based economy, and away from a barter economy, is more apparent— coins utilized as a store of value solve the problem of a *double coincidence of wants*.[1,v] A baker, farmer, jeweler, and scribe may all have goods and services

---

[1] This expression is attributed by economist Ross M. Starr (Starr 1972) to an 1875 unpublished manuscript found at the University of Minnesota.

that they want to sell or buy; however, unless they each have what the other wants, no transactions will occur. Furthermore, should they all offer their goods and services for a price set in a common unit and with the ability to transact for a store of value (such as a coin), then all four individuals can buy and sell goods without any two people selling to and buying from the other. Coins were often minted from precious metals such as gold or silver. These metals are malleable, making them poor metals for use in the forging of a tool. However, they are considered attractive, meaning the coins could be relatively easily repurposed as jewelry. They are also relatively scarce.

Development of Commodity Exchanges and Incorporation of Commodity Speculation

Commodities have been produced, bought, and sold for centuries. Many civilizations established markets where producers and consumers could transact. However, prior to the advent of a futures market, a farmer would have to wait until his crop was harvested and then bring it to a market where consumers and processors would offer to buy it—along with the crops of other farmers who had also recently harvested the same crop. If weather had been favorable during the growing season then products would be abundant and prices low. However, if the growing season had been poor, there could be a shortage and, while the farmers might enjoy a high price on the crops they were able to harvest, the consumers and processors would suffer by having to pay a high price. Both sides had a great amount of business risk based on the uncertain price of the product.

In response to this inefficiency, markets were developed for *future* delivery of a crop. In that marketplace, a standard form of contract would specify a quantity of a crop, say wheat, and also specify price premiums and discounts based on the specific quality of wheat. The place(s) where the wheat could be delivered was specified. Then, very important, the contract would specify the time at which the transaction would take place. There were multiple months in which a load of wheat might be delivered, so there was a contract for each of these months. Now in this marketplace, a farmer, in advance of his wheat harvest, could find a miller who needed the wheat at a certain time, and the farmer and miller could enter into a contract to deliver the specified quantity for a specified price. To ensure that both sides of this contract would perform on their obligation, each would post some earnest money with a trusted third party, which evolved into posting *margin* with an exchange. The first known such exchange opened in 1530 in Amsterdam. The Amsterdam Bourse (Amsterdam Stock Exchange) was established as an open-air market and commodity exchange. It was later rebuilt in 1608, six years after the establishment of the Dutch East India Company.[vi] In this market, grains, herring, spices, whale oil, and even tulips were exchanged.[vii]

Producers and consumers could transact, agree to terms for future delivery, and take delivery of the products at this exchange.

The development of this and other similar exchanges was a major step forward in reducing risk to both the consumer and producer of a commodity. However, the liquidity risk remained. Specifically, the farmer might not always find a miller to bid on his crop delivery, much less find multiple millers, which would collectively provide a competitive price discovery. Likewise, a miller might not be able to locate a farmer who would deliver crops on the specific date desired. Additionally, a miller might want multiple suppliers to ensure the best price. The organic solution was the inclusion of commodity speculators into the commodity futures market. A speculator was a person or entity that neither produced nor consumed the commodity but might still be able to provide a valuable service or assume the risk that neither a producer nor consumer could alleviate. One risk that a speculator is willing to assume is the risk of price changes between the time a contract for delivery was signed and the time of the delivery of the commodity. Additionally, the speculator may be willing to sign a contract guaranteeing delivery of a commodity at a certain time, knowing she will need to find a willing seller of the commodity as well prior to the delivery of the commodity. Speculators therefore provide the market with liquidity and make money by venturing that they would be able to sell (buy) commodities to another at a higher (lower) price than what was paid when purchasing the commodity.

The final step in evolution of the commodities market was the centralization for trading and re-trading of futures contracts. As exchanges grew and matured, some began intermediating themselves between the buyer and seller of a commodity. For this to work, whenever a buyer and seller enter into a futures transaction, they report that trade to the exchange, which would then step into the middle of the transaction. At the initiation of the futures contract, the exchange requires margin from both seller and buyer. Because of this agreement, both seller and buyer shed the risk of nonperformance by the other party. This risk is assumed by the exchange. Meanwhile, the exchange does not have price risk, since its book was always neutral—as many buyers as sellers. Additionally, to minimize the risk of one party's nonperformance, the exchange demands collateral at the initiation of the contract while further demanding or returning additional collateral as prices move daily.

THE ADOPTION OF COMMODITY INVESTING

The development of commodity markets, the incorporation of commodity speculators, and the establishment of commodity futures exchanges dramatically increased the efficiency of commodity production and reduced the cost of producer and consumer risk management. Without futures markets, a producer would have to invest significantly more capital in his business to protect from a potential slide in prices. Likewise, without a futures market, consumers would need to hold large inventories of commodities (that might spoil) to ensure that they had a sufficient quantity of a commodity when needed. The final and most recent development of commodities markets has been the incorporation of the commodities *investor*. Like a speculator, an investor neither produces nor consumes the underlying commodity. However, unlike the speculator who attempts to profit from matching buyers and sellers (at different times) for a profit, the investor chooses to gain exposure to commodity prices because of a long-term view and with the expectation of futures price appreciation. In fact, it was not until 1978 that we saw the first description of a commodity investing strategy utilizing commodity futures (Greer 1978).[viii]

Until the late 1970s, commodities had a reputation for high-risk speculation because initial margin was low and this allowed speculators to utilize tremendous leverage. Greer challenged this approach and demonstrated that this asset class has utility in a person's well-diversified portfolio. In his often-cited paper, Greer demonstrated that commodity prices are no more volatile than stocks; commodities are positively correlated to inflation (and inflation changes) so they offer investors a valuable inflation hedge; and finally, a rules-based strategy[2] can be utilized to track a hypothetical index of commodities. It took over 20 years from the initial publication of that article before investors began to embrace this new type of asset class and investment. However, once both institutional and retail investors realized the value that commodity exposure can bring to a well-diversified portfolio, collectively they allocated several hundred billion dollars to the asset class. Early adopters generally were content to passively track a published index, but that has changed. Over the past ten years, larger institutional investors have begun demanding their hired teams of portfolio managers add value to a passive benchmark. Some institutional investors also view the commodity markets as a potential source of absolute return from a diversified set of risk factors in addition to inflation hedging, diversification, and positive returns. Other (mainly institutional) investors have also begun to take delivery of certain physical commodities in addition to maintaining more liquid positions in the futures markets. Investing in the physical markets, though, does typically require institutional-sized investments and reliance on skilled specialized managers.

---

[2] The rules utilized in his paper, still relevant today, include: (1) holding only long positions, (2) fully collateralizing those positions with fixed income instruments (i.e., there is no leverage), (3) allocating to liquid futures contracts in available commodities in proportion to their importance to world trade, and (4) rolling contracts so the investor would never take physical delivery of a commodity.

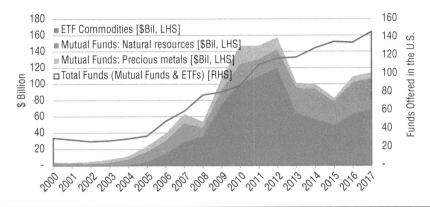

Figure 8.1 Mutual fund and ETFs offered in the U.S.: assets under management and number of funds. *Source*: Investment Company Institute[ix]

The Investment Company Institute (ICI) publishes data on publicly offered commodity-related U.S. mutual funds and exchange-traded funds (ETFs). By 2000, there were a mere 30 funds offered to U.S. investors that took positions in natural resources and precious metals with a combined $4 billion in assets. That figure has grown to 146 funds and $114 billion in assets by year-end 2017, as shown in Figure 8.1. We do not have publicly available information on the commodity-related investments of institutional investors, which generally utilize private vehicles and separate accounts. However, we are confident that the size of this market is larger than the commodity-related retail market.

COMMODITIES: ENERGY, METALS, AND AGRICULTURE

Energy

Energy is the most popular sector of commodity investing because energy is the single largest commodity sector in the global economy; the U.S. alone in 2016 consumed $1 trillion in energy and energy-related products, according to the U.S. Energy Information Administration.[x] Energy's primary uses include applications in residential, commercial, industrial, and transportation activities. The sources of energy include nuclear, coal, biomass, and others; however, the two markets most relevant to energy investors are by far the largest: crude oil (and its derivative products) and natural gas.

Because of crude oil's application in energy production and transportation, the relative ease of extraction, the global location of wells, and having over a hundred years for this market to mature, crude oil is very much a *global* market.

U.S. oil production troughed in 2008 at around five million barrels per day but has since increased to around 12 million barrels per day by the end of 2018. The U.S. Energy Information Administration projects that U.S. oil production will exceed 15 million barrels per day by the early 2020s.[xi] When considering crude oil in the United States, the relevant blend is West Texas Intermediate (WTI). WTI, also known as Texas light sweet, is the crude oil referenced by the CME Group (a global markets company) commodity futures contracts. Oil delivery for these contracts is in Cushing, Oklahoma[xii]—a small town of less than 10,000 inhabitants but through which runs a concentration of the U.S. oil pipelines and rail lines. By contrast, Brent Crude is the crude oil used by the European Intercontinental Exchange (ICE), which is delivered to four European markets (Brent, Forties, Oseberg and Ekofisk).[xiii] Brent is used to price about two-thirds of global oil contracts.[xiv] Both products are petroleum products and, to some degree, are fungible—meaning they can both be refined into the products that we use, such as gasoline. However, the products are not identical. WTI is *sweeter*—meaning it has less sulfur (this is relevant when refining the product) and even more important, it's on the other side of the Atlantic Ocean. There are also many other grades (e.g., sour or heavier) which typically trade at discounts to these benchmark contracts.

The price of crude oil, like any commodity, is largely determined by supply and demand. The Organization of Petroleum Exporting Countries (OPEC) is a 14-nation intergovernmental organization (a cartel) of oil-producing nations that produce around 40% of the world's crude oil.[xv] This organization became infamous in October 1973 when in response to Western assistance to Israel during the Yom Kippur war, the cartel reduced global oil supply. As a result of this disruption, in the United States, the price of imported oil rose from $2.75 per barrel in January 1973 to $11.10 in March 1974.[xvi] More recently, OPEC's influence has begun to wane as the United States has retaken the position as the world's largest crude oil producer. The growth in U.S. production is largely attributable to a growth in production from shale. Shale oil is a crude oil that lies between layers of shale rock. Oil companies produce shale oil by fracturing (or *fracking*) the rock by forcing water, sand, and chemicals deep into the formation. This allows the oil to seep into the wells. Also, the technology for horizontal drilling improved so that one drilling rig can go beneath the earth and then run horizontally to cover a larger area for oil (or natural gas) production. This form of drilling has the added benefit that it can respond more quickly to changes in the price of oil than larger and more expensive projects, such as offshore or deep-water drilling. However, the production from a shale well declines faster than production from a larger conventional field, so shale producers rely on a steady stream of capital to keep drilling. Also, the typical light sweet crude that shale wells produce is not always desired by many U.S. refineries that are engineered to process the heavier crude that they purchase from foreign producers. In response to this increased U.S. production, Russia has begun to cooperate with OPEC to form *OPEC+* in an attempt to manage crude oil prices.

In contrast, despite the size of its market, natural gas is one of the *least global* commodities (i.e., a primarily regional market) since natural gas is difficult to transport. The United States has about three million miles of pipelines that link natural gas production, storage facilities, and consumers according to the U.S. Energy Information Administration.[xvii] Despite this seemingly large network, if a pipeline isn't adjacent to a petroleum well that also produces natural gas, the gas may be discarded or pumped back into the ground, as it is more difficult to transport than a liquid petroleum products that can be easily moved by rail car or truck. Additionally, overseas transportation of natural gas is not feasible unless it is first cooled and liquified and converted to Liquid Natural Gas (LNG). Once the LNG reaches its destination port, it must be converted back to gaseous form and transported by pipeline. Despite these headwinds, due to its abundance, low carbon emissions when burned, and cheap cost to source, natural gas exports from the United States are expected to rapidly grow in the coming decades. The U.S. Energy Information Administration forecasts that natural gas exports may grow to over 25 billion cubic feet per day by 2030.[xviii] Additionally, by the mid-2030s, U.S. natural gas consumption is forecasted to roughly equal that of petroleum in terms of energy equivalence.[xix] Thus, we may expect natural gas to become more *global*, akin to WTI and Brent oil.

Metals: Industrial and Precious

As mentioned in the chapter's introduction, both industrial and precious metals are C/T commodities owing to their value being derived from their transformation into something else. Additionally, precious metals may also function as stores of value. In 2016, Visual Capitalist estimated the total size of the metals market to be around $660 billion; this includes precious metals such as gold and silver, as well as industrial metals including iron and copper, and several others. By contrast, the oil market (value of all oil consumed in a year) was estimated to be $1.7 trillion.[xx]

Industrial (base) metals with liquid futures contracts include copper, aluminum, zinc, nickel, and lead. But there are several others. For instance, iron ore is generally considered the most important base metal due to its use in the production of steel. China is the world's largest producer and consumer of iron,[xxi] and in 2017 China produced 49% of the world's steel, or 831 million metric tons.[xxii] Base metals are heavily utilized in building and manufacturing; for this reason, their demand is highly correlated to global economic conditions. However, their supply is on a cycle that is well in excess of a typical business cycle.

For example, it may take as long as 10 years from the discovery of an ore body until the mine's supply reaches the global market. Additionally, once a mine is developed, the mine's rate of production cannot be readily adjusted to meet changing short-term demand for its ore. For this reason, base metals may experience significant price volatility since there is generally little excess capacity available to absorb growing demand and little ability for producers to reduce production if demand declines.

Unlike base metals in which demand is largely driven by economic growth, precious metal demand may also be driven by its use as a store of value. Its utility as a store of value increases as real interest rates (the interest earned minus inflation) fall since the opportunity cost of foregone interest also falls. Gold is the most important precious metal, although platinum, palladium, and silver also have similar uses. Since 2000, gold has been primarily utilized for jewelry production; global central banks were primarily net sellers of gold before 2009 but net buyers thereafter. Additionally, there continues to be modest demand for gold for use in electronics, and following the 2009 global financial crisis, there was a multi-year spike in gold for use as a stand-alone investment.[xxiii] Due to its value, nearly all gold that has been mined remains in circulation, in some form or another, today. Typically, when prices rise, the market reaction function is to increase not the production of new gold, but rather the production of scrap gold (think selling gold to your local pawn shop). Finally, because gold can easily be stored with little storage cost and no wastage, investors may take physical delivery of gold when originally purchased in the futures market. This is unique in commodities; by contrast, investors and speculators that utilize the futures market rarely take delivery of cattle, oil, or wheat.

Agriculture

In contrast to industrial and precious metals, agriculture commodities are renewable—or commodities that are grown rather than extracted. This includes grains (corn, wheat, and soybeans), sugar, cotton, coffee, cocoa, timber, livestock, and several others. While few people in developed countries work in the agriculture industry, in 2016 globally, 27% of people work in this industry, down from 41% in 1995. The total value globally of all agriculture products produced reached $2.3 trillion, up from $1.4 trillion in 1995.[xxiv] For a majority of agriculture products, demand is relatively stable while supply is more volatile. This volatile supply can be attributed to seasonality (which is known), or idiosyncratic causes such as unusual weather, pestilence and crop failures, war, or other environmental and political causes. As a result, it is generally surprises in supply (whether they be positive or negative) that largely determine the short-term direction of agricultural commodity prices. Supply responses vary by commodity, and longer-term supply responses may exacerbate price swings. We'll now briefly cover some of these agricultural commodities, ordered roughly in terms of their production cycle (and thus their ability to respond to supply shocks).

Many grains (such as corn and wheat) have a production cycle of a year and for this reason, can be substituted for other crops subject to soil conditions and local weather patterns. Other agriculture products have multi-year production cycles, such as coffee, cocoa, and sugar. For this reason, supply disruptions can lead to spot price gyrations that are more dramatic and longer term as producers are less able to increase short-term supply (or work down a glut of supply). Livestock (cattle and hogs) also have multi-year production cycles, with the cycle for hogs being less than two years, while for cattle it is closer to 10 years. Timber is unique within agricultural investing. Timber is a crop, but one that has more flexibility with respect to its harvest schedule than any other agriculture product. If a timber manager delays harvesting a tree, that tree will continue to grow and produce more board feet of timber until it fully matures, at which point it is harvested.

Commodity futures were first developed for agriculture products and continue to be used today by a variety of investors, speculators, producers, consumers, and hedgers. Food manufacturers such as processors and millers utilize these contracts to lock in the price at which they purchase their inputs, which reduces the volatility of their profit margins. Farmers regularly utilize futures to ensure that they can harvest some or all of their crop at a profit. Feedlot managers who raise livestock can protect themselves against rising feed costs, while grain elevator operators can utilize futures to ensure that their inventory doesn't materially depreciate. Finally, investors can utilize these markets to hedge against rising inflation or because they believe one or more commodities will appreciate during their investment horizon.

DRIVERS OF COMMODITY INVESTING RETURN

A complicating factor in commodity investing using liquid futures (and not taking delivery of the physical product) is that the total return to the commodity investor is not equal to the change in the commodity spot price. On the contrary, the two returns may significantly diverge. For example, if an investor had held natural gas futures rather than owning the gas, and had rolled her position forward each month, she would have experienced a 90% cumulative loss for the 15-year period that ended December 2009. In contrast, the price of natural gas rose by 118% over the same period![xxv] Before we can answer the question how this could be, we will first define several key terms. We will then decompose the total return of a commodity investment into its constituent parts to highlight how market dynamics and portfolio management decisions can generate such an investment outcome.

Key Terms: Spot, Futures, Contango, and Backwardation

The *spot* price is the current price of a commodity that can be purchased or sold for either immediate delivery or the next available delivery date (up to three months away depending on the commodity). When people are discussing the direction of the price of a commodity (generally in the media), they are often referring to the commodity's spot price. The *spot market* refers to the price of immediate delivery of a physical asset that will often be settled with cash. Therefore, the *spot market* is also referred to as the *cash market* for a commodity. By contract, the *futures price* is the price at which a commodity can be purchased or sold for delivery at some point in the future, often greater than three months. The futures price can be viewed as the market-implied forward spot price. That is, if the spot price of a commodity is $80, and the futures price of a commodity for delivery 1-year from now is $100, the market is forecasting that the spot price will rise by $20 to $100 in one year. In practice, the futures and spot prices are each determined by their own supply and demand dynamics; so, it may not always be appropriate to assume the spot price will drift to the futures price prior to a futures contract becoming the spot contract. We will discuss that principle in more detail later.

The futures market can be in either *contango* or *backwardation*. As shown in Figure 8.2, a contango market is when the forward price of future delivery of a commodity is higher than (or at a premium to) the current spot price. By contrast, backwardation occurs when the forward price of future delivery is

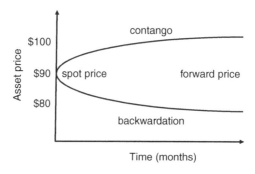

Figure 8.2   Hypothetical commodity market: spot, forward, contango, backwardation

lower than the current spot price. The shape of the forward curve of prices is commodity-dependent and can change based on the seasonal production or demand of a commodity. A curve in backwardation might indicate there is currently a low inventory or tight supply of a commodity that is expected to reverse in the future. Conversely, commodities that have high storage costs often trade at contango because consumers are willing to pay a premium to avoid incurring storage costs.

Commodity Investment Total Return

As previously mentioned, our natural gas investor who began buying and rolling futures contracts in 1994 might have been shocked to learn that her investment had depreciated by 90% over the next fifteen years despite the increase in the spot price of natural gas. So, to what can we attribute this negative total return? Let's first decompose an individual commodity investment utilizing futures contracts into its three numerical parts:

Total return = change in spot price + roll yield + collateral yield[3]

The first component of the commodity total return formula is the most intuitive; if the spot price of a commodity appreciates, the holder of the futures contract will eventually realize that price appreciation. For example, imagine a Brent Crude oil futures curve that is flat at the time a futures contract is purchased. If the spot price of Brent were to rise by $5 and remain there, eventually all futures contracts would realize a $5 gain as their contract eventually becomes the spot contract.

The second component of this equation is roll yield. This figure can be further decomposed into its constituent parts, which are:

Roll yield = (spot price − futures price) / spot price

We can observe each of these prices to calculate the roll yield. For example, if the futures price of Brent in one year is $105 and the current spot price is $100, then the roll yield for holding a Brent contract is ($100 − $105) / $100 = −5.0% / year. Owing exclusively to this roll yield, if spot prices did not move for a year, then an investor that gained exposure to Brent by purchasing a futures contract with delivery in one year would realize a 5% annual *loss*. Also, it is worth pointing out that this hypothetical curve is in contango as the futures price is higher than the spot price; curves in contango generally reduce the total return to commodity investors who utilize the futures market.

---

[3] While this equation is accurate and appropriate for calculating the total return for a single commodity investment, it does not provide an accurate estimate of the total return for a basket of commodities. We will discuss this often-overlooked portfolio component of return later in this section.

Continuing with the discussion of roll yield, we can also decompose this driver of returns into its constituent parts, which are:

Roll yield = convenience yield − (storage cost + financing cost) / $P_{Current}$

Storage costs vary by commodity while financing costs vary by counterparty and are determined by their creditworthiness and the prevailing market interest rates. Continuing with our Brent Crude example, let's assume the cost of storage is 7% per year, while the financing cost of the average market participant is 3% per year. Building on our earlier example, we can now solve for a convenience yield. The convenience yield is the additional *cost* that a commodity consumer is willing to assume for the convenience of holding the physical commodity as opposed to holding a contract that will allow the consumer to take delivery at a future date. Plugging these data points into the previous equation gives us:

$$-5\% = \text{convenience yield} - (7\% + 3\%).$$

Solving for the convenience, we find the *value* to a consumer holding a physical commodity in lieu of a futures contract is +5% per year.

The final component of the commodity total return equation is collateral yield. This is the return on the collateral held by the futures investor. When an investor purchases a futures contract, he must post collateral to an exchange, which usually consists of Treasury bills. However, the investor is entitled to the interest earned on that collateral while that collateral has been posted to the exchange. Additionally, only a small initial margin is generally posted by the investor (around 5% to 10% in most cases). So, the investor is free to invest the remaining 90% to 95% of the unencumbered capital in low-duration, high-quality collateral that can be posted to the exchange or quickly converted to cash or a Treasury bill to then post to the exchange.

Let's return to our natural gas investor one final time to highlight how the spot price and her total return could so materially diverge. We will assume that she invested her collateral in Treasury Bills that earned an average annual return of 4% from 1994 through 2009. We also know that on average the spot price of natural gas appreciated 5% per year, while the investor averaged a 14% *loss* on her investment per year. Plugging these figures into the total return equation, we find that roll yield of the natural gas contract was −23% per year! This means that the futures investor, on average, paid a futures price 2.2% higher than the spot price each month, only to see the spot price appreciate about 0.4% each month, meaning the futures investor lost 1.8% each time she rolled her monthly contracts. So, what was the source of this premium for the near futures delivery date? We can attribute this persistent premium to utility companies that are willing to pay for insurance to ensure they have the natural gas available to them exactly when they need it. Our hypothetical investor was forced to incur this premium as well because of her selection of the nearby futures contract and her trading strategy. In short, her portfolio management approach was suboptimal. Had this investor chosen to roll contracts 12 months ahead—from January to January—she could have avoided a majority of the negative roll yield and realized a positive return from her natural gas investment. It should be noted that, unlike natural gas, in most commodity markets it is the producer who has a stronger need to hedge than the ultimate buyer. The producer may have higher inventories and more concentrated exposure to just that one commodity price. That's why, for instance, a cattle producer is more likely to hedge his cattle price exposure than is the consumer who buys beef at the supermarket. Due to this strong pressure to hedge, the future price of a commodity will often be lower than the spot price, leading to backwardation in the future curve, as previously discussed. The exception is when supplies (inventory) are abundant, meaning the buyer has less need to hedge.

In a footnote earlier in this section, we mention there is another component of return to commodity investing which relates, not to the return components of an individual commodity investment, but rather to the allocation to a portfolio of commodities. This component of return is relevant to investors because most commodity investors purchase a portfolio, or basket, of individual commodities. This return component is driven by the rebalancing that naturally and necessarily occurs when an investor commits to this asset class. Please see Chapter 5 for a detailed discussion of rebalancing methodologies, benefits, and potential costs.

With respect to a commodity portfolio, to maintain a consistent percentage of exposure to a set of assets, the investor must periodically rebalance to target weights—sell what goes up and buy what goes down. Following the publication of his investment thesis (and one of the most heavily cited papers in finance) titled *Portfolio Selection* in 1952,[xxvi] Harry Markowitz is credited as having said diversification is "the only free lunch in finance." For commodity investors, this rebalancing return, or *free lunch*, is greater than it is for stock investors because individual commodities are less correlated to each other than stocks. So, how meaningful is the marginal return to a commodity portfolio that is attributable to minimally correlated individual commodities? The answer depends on the index and the period reviewed, but for two of the most widely utilized indexes, the Bloomberg Commodity Index and Credit Suisse Commodity Benchmark, over different time periods the annual return attributable just to rebalancing was an additional 2.5 to 3.0%.[xxvii] Put another way, if each individual commodity total return had been zero, a commodity portfolio (the index) would still have a significant positive return.

ACTIVE MANAGEMENT OF COMMODITY FUTURES INVESTMENTS

We chose the example of a natural gas investment to highlight our belief that there are many ways in which a skilled commodity manager can add value versus a passive benchmark. In fact, many managers that operate within this space regularly argue that there are *more* opportunities to add value to an actively managed commodity portfolio vis-à-vis a passive portfolio than are available to active equity and bond managers. We do not mean to disparage active equity and bond managers, nor do we mean to argue whether active equity and bond managers can or do add value versus their benchmarks. However, we feel it appropriate to briefly highlight some of the challenges and opportunities that active equity and bond managers regularly face simply to contrast this with the challenges and opportunities faced by active commodity managers.

We will start by briefly discussing how well active managers have performed. As highlighted in Chapter 5, the annual SPIVA (which stands for S&P Indexes versus Active management) U.S. Scorecard has shown for the five-year period that ended 12/31/17, a majority of active equity managers and active bond managers underperformed their respective benchmarks net of fees.[xxviii] To our knowledge, there is no SPIVA equivalent for commodity managers. However, an unpublished study by CoreCommodity Management in 2017 reviewed the annualized since-inception performance of 32 commodity mutual funds that were not passive ETFs. The study found only 11 funds underperformed their benchmarks net of fees while 21 funds outperformed their benchmarks net of fees. Admittedly this was a much smaller sample size, and the results are period dependent. However, this small sample indicates that a passive approach may be suboptimal.

Regarding the opportunity sets within these respective asset classes, the challenges that active equity managers face include returns that are largely driven by equity beta (meaning stocks are more highly correlated to each other), highly efficient markets with difficulty sourcing information that is not already priced into the security, and many sophisticated players ensuring general market efficiency. With respect to bonds, managers must contend with a highly efficient rates market that is the primary driver of returns. Additionally, like in the equity markets there are many sophisticated investors that quickly identify security-level mispricing and ensure the market remains efficient. In contrast to stocks and bonds, commodities represent a robust and diverse set of opportunities for a skilled manager to add value. Because each commodity is largely driven by the supply/demand characteristics of its own unique market, commodities have a lower correlation to each other than do stocks or bonds. Additionally, there are fewer price-sensitive active investors in this asset class, and there are several idiosyncratic components to each commodity that may be identified and exploited by a sophistical, active commodity manager. As a result, we believe there will almost always be good investment opportunities in one or more of those diverse markets.

To be fair, this does not mean there are $20 bills lying on the proverbial ground; nor does it mean active commodity investors are picking up nickels in front of a steamroller. However, a sophisticated manager with a deep understanding of the supply/demand fundamentals of the markets being traded has the potential to add value. We will briefly cover some of the unique opportunities here. For ease of discussion, we have categorized each of these opportunities as *curve, relative value (RV) and substitution,* or *other opportunities.*

Commodity Curve Opportunities

As mentioned previously, the commodity curve is a graphical representation of the current and forward price of a given commodity at a given time until delivery. As highlighted in the natural gas example, the shape of the curve is highly relevant to the total return of a commodity investor in light of the commodity's embedded roll yield. With this in mind, we highlight two examples of opportunities available to active commodity investors, given the shape and composition of this curve.

First, indexes tend to hold their positions at the front of the forward curve, but an active manager can choose to hold positions in the same commodity further out on the curve. Especially in a contango market, the curve is typically steepest at the front, which means the index will be facing a larger headwind of negative roll yield. Positions further out on the curve can still capture most of the rise and fall of the commodity's price, but with less of a negative roll yield. As a result, by purchasing positions further out on the curve, an active manager can minimize a negative roll yield, which is accretive to the total return of the investor. If managers have a high conviction that the shape of the curve will change, they may also trade spreads on the curve, which may benefit if the curve moves in the manager's favor.

Separately, a published benchmark rolls its positions from the nearby to a distant contract on a predetermined schedule described in the published handbook for that index. A manager can choose to roll positions on a different schedule, based on observations of short-term liquidity or for some other rationale. Doing so can enable the active manager to gain superior (read cheaper) pricing on rolled positions than would otherwise be the case if the manager followed the same schedule as the benchmark.

RELATIVE VALUE AND SUBSTITUTION OPPORTUNITIES

The next group of investment opportunities that are unique to active commodity investors is what we broadly define as RV trades. By RV, we mean commodities that are unique and that are not fungible (able to replace the other), but they can be substituted or transported so that they serve a similar purpose to the ultimate consumer. For example, Robusta coffee is derived from the Coffea canephora plant and constitutes roughly 40% of the world's coffee production. Separately, Arabica coffee is derived from the Coffea arabica plant and constitutes roughly 60% of the world's coffee production.[xxix] No doubt some readers who are also coffee connoisseurs would balk at the idea that these two coffee beans are highly substitutable; but, for the casual coffee drinkers like us, they are. For this reason, the price of the two beans should not materially diverge. In instances when one bean appreciates significantly versus another, an active manager can purchase one bean and sell the other anticipating the price of the two beans will converge.

Another example of an RV trade is WTI versus Brent Crude oil. As mentioned previously, WTI has slightly less sulfur than Brent. More important, for a U.S. producer to sell in a European market, the producer must ship the product across the ocean. So, while the two products should not have identical prices, they should be highly correlated. In fact, the maximum price deviation from one product to the next should be the cost to transport the oil from one delivery point to another plus the difference in the cost to refine one product so that it is identical to the other. As shown in Figure 8.3, these products are highly correlated and while the difference between the two oils may diverge, there is an upper limit to their long-term divergence. This maximum divergence (or delta) is time varying and depends on idiosyncratic items such as pipeline availability, oil field production, and refinery demand; however, a discerning commodity investor should be able to identify and profit when this delta has extended beyond the value that is appropriate given its fundamentals.

Another variation of RV trades looks at the economics of processing one commodity into another. For instance, crude oil is processed into gasoline and heating oil (along with other products). The *crack spread* is roughly the profit margin that a refinery can earn from *cracking* hydrocarbons into petroleum products. The crack spread may be derived from the spread between crude oil contracts and one or more of its derivative products, such as gasoline or heating oil. A commodity analyst with a deep understanding of refinery economics and operating schedules may be able to trade those three products by purchasing (selling) a position in crude oil and selling (purchasing) a position in gasoline and heating oil. Similarly, the *crush spread* is roughly the spread

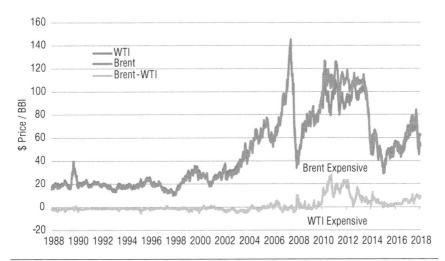

Figure 8.3   Relative pricing of WTI and Brent Crude Oil. *Source*: Bloomberg

earned by *crushing* soybeans into soybean meal and soybean oil. Thus, a trader who wants to profit from a wide (narrow) crush spread may purchase (sell) soybean futures and sell (buy) soybean meal and soybean oil. An even more exotic spread trade would involve trading live cattle versus feeder cattle, corn, and soybeans.

A final strategy we will highlight is *substitution* trades. For example, an index may use Chicago wheat, but an active manager might substitute wheat traded on another exchange. For instance, Kansas City wheat has a higher protein content, making it more valuable than the wheat traded on the CME contract in Chicago. But that higher valuation may not, at times, be reflected in the difference in the two futures contracts, since so many investors gravitate to the liquidity of the Chicago contract.

Other Opportunities

Other opportunities for an active commodity manager are many and we will do little more than introduce them here for the sake of brevity. Many individual commodity futures now have options traded on them, which gives a manager a way to express a view on volatility of a market that he follows. Therefore, if the implied volatility of a particular commodity rises, he may sell options and profit if the realized volatility of the commodity is below the implied volatility at the time the derivatives are sold. Separately, some managers may judiciously use equity of commodity producers as an alternative way to get exposure to a particular commodity or to get exposure to a commodity which is not actively traded on a futures exchange. To do this, an analyst can estimate the amount of revenue the company derives from producing the relevant commodity. Finally, some managers will actively manage the fixed income portfolio that collateralizes their commodity positions with an attempt to outperform T-bills or another highly liquid, high-quality, low-duration pool of assets.

REAL ESTATE

When considering an investment in a real asset, we wonder: what could be more *real* than real estate? But what does that term really (no pun intended) encompass? At its most basic level, real estate can be divided into *land* and *improvements*. While the land can't be moved, a development can be made on the land, and this development and its use will affect the value of the total asset. Real estate may also be decomposed into both capital assets and stores of value. Specifically, the development (i.e., improvement) is a capital asset since a building will be expected to generate future cash flows (rents) and therefore the value of the asset can be valued using a traditional discounted cash flow model. Alternatively, the land may be considered a store of value. Mark Twain is credited with saying, "Buy land—they're not making it anymore." Regardless of whether Mark Twain did state that, the sentiment is factual. By reason of its finite supply, land can function as a store of value akin to a precious metal or artwork. So, what is the real estate market's size, how does one evaluate real estate as an investment, and how can one invest in real estate? We'll address those questions here.

Real Estate Overview

When most people think of real estate, they initially think of housing; this is sensible, as a person's house is generally their largest investment and only real estate investment. In 2019, Seattle-based real estate website and marketplace Zillow estimated the total U.S. housing stock to be valued at $33.3 trillion as of year-end 2018.[xxx] Meanwhile, the Federal Reserve Bank of St. Louis estimates that household equity in real estate (the value of their properties minus loans taken against these properties) totals $15.4 trillion as of Q3 2018.[xxxi] Despite these immense figures, these sizes are only a small fraction of the global value of real estate. In 2015, Savills, a publicly traded global real estate services provider, calculated the global value of all real estate. Their estimate? $217 trillion, including residential, commercial, and agriculture property.[xxxii] By comparison, Savills estimated global financial assets (stocks and bonds) at the time to be $149 trillion while the World Bank estimated 2015 global GDP to be $74.9 trillion.[xxxiii] While only $81 trillion of the $217 trillion is considered by

Savills to be *investible*, it is nevertheless helpful to recognize the sheer size of this investible asset.

This $217 trillion worth of total (or $81 trillion worth of investible) real estate can be divided into *developed* and *undeveloped* real estate. As the name implies, undeveloped real estate is merely an investment in land and this land may have no improvements (buildings). Investments in this type of land may be for speculative purposes (a city may expand into a vicinity in the next several years), as a store of value, or with the objective of harvesting a natural resource such as timber or oil. Developed real estate is land that has some improvement or building; this building (or buildings) has value that can be calculated using a traditional cash flow model. Developed real estate can broadly be divided into four categories including retail, office, multi-family, and industrial. Additionally, each of these categories can be further subdivided. For instance, retail includes regional malls, strip centers, *big box* centers, or stand-alone buildings. Office includes single-tenant buildings, multi-tenant buildings, or office complexes. Multi-family generally indicates an apartment building, though a single project could be multi-use, including retail and office. Industrial includes large single-tenant warehouses, manufacturing properties, mini-storage projects, and multi-tenant industrial parks. Finally, each of these subcategories can be categorized by the property's quality, ranging from high quality (stable cash flows) to speculative quality (uncertain cash flows; potential redevelopment).

Investment Considerations

The primary metric by which real estate investments are measured is by a capitalization rate, or cap rate. The cap rate is equal to the property's net operating income (NOI) divided by the current market value of the property. The NOI is calculated by first estimating the annual revenue the property will generate (such as rental income) and then subtracting all the operating expenses incurred for managing and maintaining the property. These expenses include building maintenance, taxes, insurance, and management fees. For example, if a property costs $1,000,000 and is expected to generate an NOI of $50,000 in the first year, its cap rate will be 5% ($50,000 / $1,000,000).

One advantage of this ratio is that it offers investors a simple, single metric for comparing properties. All other things being equal, the higher the cap rate, the more attractive the investment. In this respect, a cap rate is similar to a stock's dividend yield or bond yield. Despite this ratio's utility, it has several drawbacks. One disadvantage of utilizing only a cap rate is that this ratio is an initial snapshot and it doesn't include an expectation for the future path of the property value or the property's future NOI. For example, a property with a forecasted cap rate of 0% for two years but 10% thereafter may be a much more attractive investment opportunity than a property with an expected 5% cap rate to perpetuity. Cap rates also don't account for liquidity. In general, a highly liquid property (one that could be sold in a reasonably short period of time and at a fair market value) should demand a lower cap rate than a property that is illiquid. Finally, cap rates don't incorporate the quality of the property or creditworthiness of the tenants. A property in a declining city or with tenants that are experiencing closures (such as a mall) demands higher cap rates than a property in a growing city and with highly creditworthy tenants.

Cap rates in the United States are strongly correlated with bond yields. This makes intuitive sense because bonds are a potential substitute investment for a property. As bond yields fall, property cap rates look increasingly attractive on a relative basis. So, investors respond to the change in the relative attractiveness by *bidding up* the price of properties, which lowers the future cap rates. As shown in Figure 8.4, the rolling 1-year average yield on the 10-year U.S. Treasury, as well as the cap rates for each of the four major property types, have both fallen roughly in tandem since the mid-1990s. We would expect cap rates to always trade at a premium to the yield on a 10-year U.S. Treasury note because real estate is illiquid and has some degree of default risk (your tenants could fail to pay you). So, for illustrative purposes, we created an additional index to act as a proxy for cap rates. Specifically, we equally blended the rolling four-quarter average yields on the Bloomberg Barclays U.S. Aggregate Bond Index and the Bloomberg Barclays U.S. Corporate High Yield Index. This blended benchmark contains a moderate degree of default risk as well as bonds that are less liquid than U.S. Treasuries. This blended yield tracks cap rates well; the one

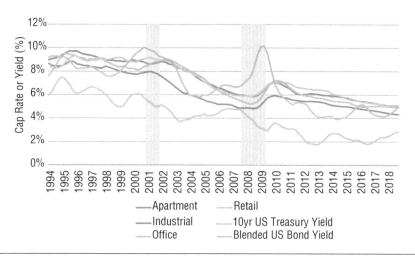

Figure 8.4   Commercial real estate cap rates and U.S. fixed income yields.
Source: NCREIF, Bloomberg

exception was during the 2008–2009 recession during which the yields on our proxy index increased ahead of the cap rates on properties. This may be explained by the bond index re-pricing more quickly due to the bonds being more liquid than real estate.

Investment returns for property have been competitive with equities from the perspective of a U.S. investor, as shown in Table 8.1. For the 20-year period that ended 12/31/2018, U.S. home prices as estimated by the S&P Core Logic Case-Shiller U.S. National Home Price Index have appreciated at an annualized rate of +4.1%. By comparison, U.S. equities and U.S. bonds have returned +5.6% and +4.5%, respectively. Of note, most U.S. homeowners are leveraged (meaning they have a mortgage), so the average total returns to homeowners have been higher than the simple price appreciation of their properties. Meanwhile,

Table 8.1   U.S. real estate returns and Sharpe ratios ended 12/31/2018. Utilizes quarterly data

			Annualized Returns			
Period	Risk Free	S&P 500	U.S. Aggregate (Bonds)	NCREIF Property Index	FTSE NAREIT All Equity REITS	Case-Shiller U.S. National Home Price Index
1-yr.	1.9%	−4.4%	0.0%	7.0%	−4.0%	5.1%
3-yr.	1.0%	9.3%	2.1%	7.3%	4.2%	5.6%
5-yr.	0.6%	8.5%	2.5%	9.4%	8.3%	5.3%
10-yr.	0.4%	13.1%	3.5%	7.5%	12.5%	3.1%
20-y.r	1.9%	5.6%	4.5%	9.0%	9.9%	4.1%
10-yr. ended 12/31/08	3.4%	−1.4%	5.6%	10.5%	7.4%	5.1%

			Sharpe Ratios			
Period	Risk Free	S&P 500	U.S. Aggregate (Bonds)	NCREIF Property Index	FTSE NAREIT All Equity REITS	Case-Shiller U.S. National Home Price Index
1-yr.	—	(0.39)	(0.92)	22.02	(0.48)	1.52
3-yr.	—	0.77	0.34	11.30	0.34	2.19
5-yr.	—	0.81	0.64	5.73	0.68	2.08
10-yr.	—	0.90	0.99	1.52	0.58	0.62
20-yr.	—	0.23	0.79	1.61	0.40	0.49
10-yr. ended 12/31/08	—	(0.29)	0.61	1.73	0.20	0.37

Sources: S&P, Bloomberg Barclays, NCREIF, FTSE, S&P Core Logic, and Bloomberg

the returns on U.S. commercial real estate have been even higher according to the National Council of Real Estate Investment Fiduciaries (NCREIF). The NCREIF property index measures the investment performance of a large pool of individual commercial real estate properties acquired in the private market for investment purposes only. This index estimates the total return of such investments, which includes both the income return (rents minus expenses) and capital return (property appreciation) while assuming no leverage.[xxxiv] This index has outperformed U.S. equities and bonds and has impressive 10-year and 20-year Sharpe ratios in excess of 1.0. The Financial Times Stock Exchange (FTSE) National Association of Real Estate Investment Trusts (NAREIT) All Equity REITs Index also paints a similar picture. This market capitalization-weighted index of U.S. equity REITs has generated returns over the past 10 and 20 years of +12.5% and +9.9%, respectively. Of note, REITs are generally leveraged, which is why this index has higher returns but lower Sharpe ratios than either the NCREIF property index or the Case-Shiller U.S. home price index.

Investment Vehicles

Investors can get exposure to real estate in a variety of ways. One of the most popular is to buy shares of REITs. REITs were first created in 1960 when President Eisenhower signed into law the REIT Act title contained in the Cigar Excise Tax Extension of 1960.[xxxv] The objective of this legislation was to provide individuals with a mechanism through which they could invest in large-scale, income-producing real estate without needing to purchase the physical property. The solution was to allow investors to purchase shares in a REIT; a REIT is a company that owns and usually operates income-producing real estate or related assets (such as loans against properties). To qualify as a REIT, at least 75% of total assets must be in real estate assets or cash, at least 75% of income must be derived from real estate sources, 95% of income must be passive, and at least 90% of income must be distributed to shareholders each year. Most REITs distribute 100% of their income annually to avoid incurring corporate taxes.

There are three categories of REITs: *Equity, Mortgage,* and *Hybrid.* Equity REITs own and operate income-generating real estate, while mortgage REITs are generally leveraged and own mortgage-backed securities. Hybrid REITs invest in both assets. As the market has evolved since the early 1960s, REIT products have diversified and investors can now purchase REITs that invest in specific asset classes, such as a retail REIT, an office REIT, an industrial REIT, a multi-family REIT, and even a timber REIT. Investors can also now invest in funds of REITs, which purchase shares of other REITs. Publicly offered REITs are registered with the Securities and Exchange Commission (SEC) and most trade on an exchange. However, a small portion of REITs do not trade on an exchange; these

REITs have limited liquidity and an investor may incur large transaction fees if he chooses to sell his shares to the REIT manager.[xxxvi] Qualified and institutional investors may also have the opportunity to invest in a nonregistered REIT. This product is comingled like a registered REIT; but it is neither registered nor publicly offered. The benefit of this product is that it can be more bespoke or opportunistic since it is not beholden to the Internal Revenue Service or SEC rules. Large institutional investors also invest in separate account real estate. That would be an account that buys, holds, and manages the bricks and mortar itself, perhaps including redevelopment and eventual sale of the portfolio assets. In this instance, usually an institutional investor is represented by an asset manager who understands the specific nature of the portfolio and is responsible for most or all of the management of the property.

SUMMARY AND INVESTMENT IMPLICATIONS

Summary

Real assets are physical, unlike financial assets that are contractual. Real assets and other investible assets can be further subdivided into three super-classes: capital assets, which derive value from cash flows; C/T, which derive value during their consumption; and store of value. Separately, renewable commodities generally are grown while depletable commodities are taken from the ground. Due to inefficiencies that are created by matching producers and consumers with agricultural goods, markets developed whereby producers and consumers could agree in advance of a harvest for the future delivery of a crop. Exchanges later developed, thereby eliminating the risk of one party not adhering to the terms of that contract. These exchanges further allowed speculators to enter the market, thereby increasing the depth of the market and solving for the problem that there may not be a willing buyer or seller of a commodity, to a certain date, at that time. Finally, in the late 1970s, investors began evaluating commodities as an investible asset class worth including in a well-diversified portfolio.

Commodity investing opportunities, that don't involve physical delivery, include the purchase of futures contracts. The commodity markets that are available through futures include energy, metals, and agriculture. Energy is the second largest commodity sector in the global economy (behind agriculture), and oil and natural gas contracts play a critical role in ensuring that global markets are functioning efficiently. Metals collectively are smaller than energy and agriculture in terms of the size of the market, and this category of commodities can be subdivided into industrial and precious. The price of industrial metals is largely driven by global economic conditions; prices may be volatile as production cycles for mines may exceed 10 years. Precious metals have applications in electronics and may be used for jewelry; but, they are primarily viewed as a store of value. Finally, agriculture is the largest of these three commodity assets. Agricultural products have relatively short production cycles, but their supply remains volatile because of weather conditions that cannot be fully hedged.

The total return of a commodity investment that utilizes futures can be subdivided into three constituent parts: change in spot price, roll yield, and collateral yield. The change in spot price is the change in price for the next delivery of that commodity. Roll yield, depending on the commodity, may be a more critical component of total return; should the curve remain in contango (meaning the future price is higher than the spot price), futures purchasers will continue to experience a negative roll yield as their positions season. The collateral yield is the return generated on the fixed income portfolio used to collateralize the futures positions. A final component of total return involves the benefit of regularly rebalancing, which is material since individual commodities exhibit little correlation with each other. We believe that actively managed commodity strategies have the potential for outperformance. Sources of potential alpha for active commodity managers include commodity curve trades and RV trades.

The final real asset that warrants consideration in a portfolio is real estate. Real estate can be divided into land and improvements, the latter is the capital, such as buildings that have utility and can be expected to generate rents in the future. Globally, the real estate market is immense and may exceed $250 trillion by the time this book is published. Undeveloped land may be utilized as a store of value or utilized in the future to harvest resources, while developed real estate is generally expected to yield a product or some form of rent. Developed real estate can be subdivided into four categories including retail, office, multi-family, and industrial. A cap rate, or the net operating income divided by the current market value of the property, is the most common metric for evaluating the attractiveness of real estate investments. Most investors gain exposure to real estate through their homes, rental properties, or REITS. Institutional investors may purchase assets and hire managers to run and maintain their properties.

Investment Implications

- As characterized by the opening story of Jim Rogers, an investor in real assets must know what they are buying. Specifically:
  - Is the investment in physical commodities or commodity futures?
  - If it is physical, can it spoil and what is the storage cost?
  - If it is futures, what is the roll yield?

◻ Is the investment in real estate, and if so, what type of real estate?
◻ Is the investment asset actively managed, and if so, what is the investment process of the manager?
• These are all important questions because a single asset manager cannot be an expert in all the real assets that are available for investment
• Active commodity managers that utilize futures should employ strategies to minimize the expenses of commodity investments, such as a negative roll yield
• Finally, commodity investors should be mindful of the investment objectives of real assets in the overall portfolio, which is to provide inflation protection, diversification, and an acceptable risk-adjusted return in the context of its impact on the portfolio.

CITATIONS

i. Rogers International Commodity Index (RICI®) Composition Adjustments. (February 2, 2018). *PR Newswire*.
ii. Snir, A., D. Nadel, I. Groman-Yaroslavski, Y. Melamed, M. Sternberg, O. Bar-Yosef et al. (2015). "The Origin of Cultivation and Proto-Weeds, Long Before Neolithic Farming." *PLoS ONE* 10(7): e0131422. https://doi.org/10.1371/journal.pone.0131422.
iii. https://www.britishmuseum.org/explore/themes/money/the_origins _of_coinage.aspx.
iv. Pryor, Frederic L. (2004). "From Foraging to Farming: The So-Called 'Neolithic Revolution.'" in (ed.) *Research in Economic History*, Vol. 22. Emerald Group Publishing Limited. pp. 1–39.
v. Starr, Ross M. (May 1, 1972). "The Structure of Exchange in Barter and Monetary Economies." *The Quarterly Journal of Economics*. Vol. 86, Issue 2. pp. 290–302. https://doi.org/10.2307/1880564.
vi. Stringham, Edward Peter. (December 18, 2001). "The Extralegal Development of Securities Trading in Seventeenth Century Amsterdam." *Quarterly Review of Economics and Finance*, Vol. 43, No. 2. p. 321. 2003. Available at SSRN: https://ssrn.com/abstract=1676251.
vii. Kellenbenz, H. (1957/1996). "Introduction to Confusion de Confusiones." In M. Friedson (ed.) *Confusion de Confusiones* (pp. 125–146). New York, NY: Wiley.
viii. Conservative Commodities: A Key Inflation Hedge. (July 1978). Robert J. Greer. *The Journal of Portfolio Management*, 4(4). p. 26–29. doi: 10.3905/jpm.1978.408649.

ix. *2018 Investment Company Fact Book*. Investment Company Institute. Table 11 (p. 218), Table 12 (p. 219), Table 54 (p. 261), and Table 55 (p. 262).

x. Table E15. Total Energy Price and Expenditure Estimates, Ranked by State. (2016). U.S. Energy Information Administration (www.eia.gov).

xi. Annual Energy Outlook 2019. (January 24, 2019). U.S. Energy Information Administration. p. 55.

xii. https://www.cmegroup.com/trading/energy/crude-oil/light-sweet-crude_contract_specifications.html.

xiii. ICE Crude & Refined Oil Products. https://www.theice.com/public docs/ICE_Crude_Refined_Oil_Products.pdf.

xiv. Mike Davis—Director Market Development, ICE Futures Europe. (April 7, 2011). "Oil Price Benchmarks, Fundamentals & Implications. ICE Global Markets in Clear View. Presentation." p. 34.

xv. https://www.eia.gov/finance/markets/crudeoil/supply-opec.php.

xvi. "The 1973 oil crisis: One generation and counting. The Federal Reserve Bank of Chicago." (October 1994). No. 86.

xvii. https://www.eia.gov/energyexplained/print.php?page=natural_gas_pipelines.

xviii. Annual Energy Outlook 2019. (January 24, 2019). U.S. Energy Information Administration. p. 83.

xix. ———. (January 24, 2019). U.S. Energy Information Administration. p. 27.

xx. Desjardins, Jeff. (October 14, 2016). "The Oil Market Is Bigger than All Metal Markets Combined." https://www.visualcapitalist.com/size-oil-market/.

xxi. Commodity Special Feature from World Economic Outlook. (October 2015). International Monetary Fund.

xxii. Steel Statistical Yearbook. (2018). Worldsteel Association.

xxiii. Commodities at a Glance. (March 2015). Special Issue on Gold. United National Conference on Trade and Development.

xxiv. World Food and Agriculture Statistical Pocketbook. (2018). Food and Agriculture Organization of the United Nations. p. 46.

xxv. Greer, Robert J. (2013). *Intelligent Commodity Indexing: A Practical Guide to Investing In Commodities*. New York, NY. McGraw Hill. p. 32.

xxvi. Harry Markowitz. (March 1952). Portfolio Selection. *The Journal of Finance*. Vol. 7, No. 1. pp. 77–91.

xxvii. Greer, Robert. (Spring 2016). "Portfolio Rebalancing and Commodities: The Whole Is Greater Than the Sum of the Parts." Global Commodities Applied Research Digest, published by the J.P. Morgan Center for Commodities at the University of Colorado Denver Business School.

xxviii. S&P Dow Jones Indices. (2018). SPIVA U.S. Score Card.

xxix. "Coffee: World Markets and Trade." (December 2018). United States Department of Agriculture—Foreign Agricultural Service. p. 5.

xxx. Lloyd, Alcynna. (January 4, 2019). "U.S. housing market value climbs to $33.3 trillion in 2018." www.housingwire.com.

xxxi. Board of Governors of the Federal Reserve System (U.S.). (January 26, 2019). Households; Owners' Equity in Real Estate, Level [OEH-RENWBSHNO], retrieved from FRED, Federal Reserve Bank of St. Louis; https://fred.stlouisfed.org/series/OEHRENWBSHNO

xxxii. Around the world in dollars and cents. (2016). Savills World Research. Figure 1.

xxxiii. https://data.worldbank.org/indicator/NY.GDP.MKTP.CD?end=2015.

xxxiv. NCREIF: National Council of Real Estate Investment Fiduciaries. Frequently Asked Questions about NCREIF and the NCREIF Property Index (NPI). https://www.ncreif.org/public_files/Users_Guide _to_NPI.pdf.

xxxv. Section 10(a) of Public Law no. 86–779, 74 Stat. 998, 1003–1008 (September 14, 1960), enacting Internal Revenue Code sections 856, 857, and 858.

xxxvi. Investor Bulletin: Real Estate Investment Trusts (REITs). (December 2011). SEC Office of Investor Education and Advocacy. https://www .sec.gov/investor/alerts/reits.pdf.

9

HEDGE FUNDS

David E. Linton, CFA
Director, Portfolio Construction and Manager Research
Pacific Life Fund Advisors LLC

Andrew Ross, CFA, FRM, CAIA
Senior Director, Investment Risk and Structured Products
Pacific Asset Management

In fall 2009, one of the Chicago Booth Investment Management conference cochairs joined me and a small group of students at lunch, noticeably excited, and asked, "Hey guys—you know who David Einhorn is, right?"

"Isn't he the guy who shorted Lehman?" I asked.

"I thought he was the hedge fund manager that nearly won the World Series of Poker a couple of years ago," another classmate said.

"You're both right. He agreed to come speak to the Investment Management Club next month."

"No way—how'd you set that up?" I asked.

"I just emailed him. I introduced myself and asked him if he wanted to present at the Chicago Booth Investment Management Conference. He said he had another commitment, but would speak to our club."

David Einhorn is the cofounder of Greenlight Capital, an equity long/short hedge fund based in New York City; its assets under management (AUM) peaked in 2014 at around $12 billion.[i] Einhorn initially made a name for himself by engaging in a public battle with Allied Capital, whom he argued was defrauding the Small Business Administration. In May 2008, at the Ira W. Sohn Investment Research Conference, Einhorn detailed how the investment bank Lehman Brothers seemed to have re-categorized assets between Level 2 and Level 3 within its financial statements, resulting in a recorded gain of $722 million in value. Despite accounting statements that suggested otherwise, Lehman denied that it had written up its Level-3 assets. Skeptical, Einhorn shorted Lehman and made his short position public.[ii] Only months later, Lehman folded and its assets were sold at fire-sale prices to London-based investment bank Barclays plc.

Many students, myself included, were thrilled to have Einhorn speak at our club. Einhorn had become a household name within the investment management community, and here was an opportunity to have an intimate conversation with someone who was considered one of the world's best.

After a brief introduction in front of a room with about 100 eager students, Einhorn explained that he wanted to keep the conversation casual and mostly Q&A.

"How'd you come up with your name, Greenlight?" someone asked.

"Well, I had a sit-down with my wife and told her I wanted to start a hedge fund. We talked about the pros and cons, and I admitted most funds fold and I might very well fail. Despite that, she told me she'd support me and gave me the *green light*. So, I ran with *Greenlight*."

"How'd you know Lehman was a powder keg?" another student asked.

"So, after looking at Lehman's financials, we couldn't figure out why they didn't have significantly larger write-downs. Their disclosure of CDO holdings simply didn't add up. So, we had a call with their CFO Erin Callan. I had about twenty questions for her, none of which she answered well. We were on the second-to-last question, and she said she had to leave but the head of Lehman risk would answer any remaining questions. So, we started over at the first question and ran through every question a second time. We got different answers on almost every question! So, we knew things were not good at Lehman."

"How do you source your investment ideas?" was the final question of the day. Most students (myself included) naturally assumed there was some financial mathematical wizardry that had made Greenlight so successful to date.

"Simple, I buy good companies that are cheap, and I short bad companies that are expensive. Everything we need we can find by speaking to managers, reviewing financials, talking to suppliers and customers, and doing other due diligence."

We all thought, "*That's it? Wow.*"

Since its inception, the hedge fund industry has evoked an aura of mystery and excitement associated with it because investors became mesmerized by the large personalities and cocktail party fodder that certain investments are thought to bring. However, what people will find if they start to peel back the onion just a little bit is something far more comprehensible. With the application of the lessons learned in this book so far, combined with some general pointers here in this chapter, investors should find it much easier to break through much of this mystique.

In this chapter, we will review the past, the present, and the potential future for hedge funds. Additionally, we will review four of the most common hedge fund categories: *equity hedge, event-driven, global macro,* and *relative value.* Specifically, we will review how these categories are defined, how portfolios within these categories are constructed, how these funds have performed, and the utility derived from each strategy's inclusion in a well-diversified portfolio. We will then close with our thoughts on the future of this industry, a chapter summary, and list the investment implications. Finally, for readers that would like to further read about this topic, we recommend *When Genius Failed* by Roger Lowenstein. It's the story of Long-Term Capital Management (LTCM), which when it launched was the largest start-up at that time—at $1.25 billion;[iii] meanwhile, its failure was so stunning and unexpected that the Federal Reserve Bank of New York was forced to organize a $3.625 billion bailout by LTCM's creditors.[iv] For those who wish to get into more of the nuts and bolts of hedge fund investing, we recommend Mark Anson's *Handbook of Alternative Assets.* Anson provides valuable real-world insight into the subject developed over the course of his career, which at the time of its publication had included stints as the CIO of British Telecom and the CIO of CalPERS, and now includes stops as the CIO of Commonfund, the CIO of the Bass Family Office, and the President of Nuveen.

HEDGE FUNDS: OVERVIEW AND BRIEF HISTORY

A hedge fund is a commingled vehicle that is not a Securities and Exchange Commission (SEC)-registered mutual fund. In Chapter 2, we laid out the requirements for investment managers who manage mutual funds. A hedge fund is a legal fund structure that intentionally does not meet the requirements for mutual funds. This gives a hedge fund the ability, if it chooses, to invest in all asset types, restrict client redemptions, invest in highly illiquid assets, both purchase and short securities, charge performance fees, and deploy leverage. A more suitable name for the structure might simply be *unregistered fund* instead of *hedge fund.* In fact, the use of the nomenclature *hedge fund* has led to considerable confusion among many investors in these funds who may have assumed that their investments in hedge funds were, in fact, *hedged.* Indeed, many of the earlier iterations of these unregistered funds did utilize their ability to short to hedge market risk. Today, there remains a subset of managers who are focused on continuing to generate *absolute return* stream profiles for their clients that do not derive any benefit from equity or credit market beta. However, these absolute-return types of hedge funds are more the exception than the rule. As the industry has evolved over the past two decades, the notion of hedge funds in general being hedged to the market has been debunked except for a few very successful firms (most of whom are closed to new capital).

So, how did hedge funds get to this point? As with many of the topics discussed in this book, we will begin with the history of the subject to ensure that our readers have a solid understanding of the present status of the industry. We will then speculate with respect to the hedge fund industry's future trajectory.

Brief History of Hedge Funds

If hedge funds are just a legal structure, what do hedge fund managers do? Generally speaking, hedge fund managers, like active mutual fund managers, construct portfolios of types of securities that we have previously covered: stocks, bonds, derivatives, commodities, etc. However, hedge fund managers generally are less focused on outperforming specific benchmarks, which results in their typically taking more concentrated positions within specific securities or within a subset of a universe. Nevertheless, much of what drives the hedge fund manager to make an investment in any given security is the same valuation metrics utilized by their mutual fund counterparts.

It is generally agreed that the first modern hedge fund was founded in 1949 by Alfred Winslow Jones, an editor of *Fortune Magazine* and writer for *Time Magazine*. While conducting research for his article, "Fortunes in Forecasting," he became acquainted with the inner workings of Wall Street, and several months prior to publishing his article, Jones established an investment partnership that would evolve into the first modern hedge fund.[v] Jones's partnership is the first well-known instance where an investment manager employed both short sales and leverage to create a framework that aimed both to limit market exposure and to amplify stock selection skill (i.e., alpha). Additionally, Jones incorporated an incentive fee structure, which, like short selling and leverage, were not new concepts but the inclusion of it in this framework was. Jones additionally agreed to keep nearly all of his own investment capital in the fund, a commitment that many hedge fund investors still expect of hedge fund managers today. Jones later hired additional managers to oversee portions of the portfolio with significant autonomy; this is a business model used by many of the largest hedge funds today to diversify a portfolio's stream of alpha.[vi]

In 1966, *Fortune Magazine* published "The Jones Nobody Keeps up With," which detailed Jones' investment framework, outsized returns, and 20% performance fee. Prior to the publication of this article, the nascent hedge fund industry remained relatively a niche player and generally maintained a low profile. However, following the publication of the aforementioned article, many copycats entered the market. At least 140 hedge funds were estimated to have launched in the three years after the publishing of that article. Many of these new funds, however, did not embrace the short side of the Jones framework, and when the broad market declined by 70% from 1966 to 1974, most hedge funds folded and the industry retreated from the limelight.[vii] Exactly 20 years after the *Fortune*

Magazine article, *Institutional Investor Magazine* spotlighted Julian Robertson, founder and manager of Tiger Management Corp. The article titled, "The Red-Hot World of Julian Robertson," noted that Robertson's Tiger Fund had compounded returns of +43% for six years running, vastly outpacing the S&P which annualized +18.7% over that same time span. The article further compared and contrasted Robertson's investment approach to that of Alfred Jones and noted that his investment universe was much wider, including commodities, currencies, and bonds.[viii] Like the *Fortune Magazine* article before it, the *Institutional Investor* article sparked a new wave of interest in hedge fund investing.

No review of the history of hedge funds would be complete without a mention of the failure in 1998 of LTCM. LTCM was launched in 1994 by John Meriwether, a former bond trader and the founder of the bond arbitrage group at the investment bank Salomon Brothers. LTCM would primarily trade fixed income instruments and derivatives, and it would engage in spread strategies whereby it would earn profits if the prices of two instruments converged. Meriwether formed an all-star team of academic and Wall Street professionals including former vice chairman of the Federal Reserve, David Mullins, and future Nobel Laureates Bob Merton and Myron Scholes.[ix] Because of its pedigree, LTCM received extraordinary amounts of leverage from Wall Street, which allowed the fund to generate annualized returns in excess of +40% between 1994 and 1997. The fund seemed to be an unstoppable Wall Street force until August 1998, when Russia defaulted on its domestic debt and devalued its currency.[x] By the end of August, the fund was down more than 50% for the year. By September, its fund was down 90% with capital dwindling to just $400 million on over $100 billion in assets. Shortly thereafter, after several meetings at The Federal Reserve Bank of New York, which provided the facilities for the discussion to take place, 14 banks injected $3.6 billion into LTCM in exchange for a 90% stake of its assets. Following the bailout, all remaining LTCM positions were liquidated at a small profit to the banks involved in the bailout.[xi]

The LTCM saga received significant amounts of negative press, and not surprisingly, most observers resented the Fed's role in the bailout of LTCM and its well-to-do partners. However, as significant as the experience was for those who went through it, the hedge fund industry trend had gained enough significance that the pullback in momentum from the LTCM debacle proved to be only temporary; in early 2000, the tech bubble popped and the hedge fund industry began another period of outperformance.

Recent Growth and Maturation of the Industry

The strong performance of the hedge fund industry in the 1990s and into the early 2000s led to the notion that hedge fund strategies were capable of generating equity-like returns with bond-like volatility. So, it is with this backdrop that flows into hedge funds were strong and assets grew from just over $100 billion in assets in 1997 to approximately $2.3 trillion in 2007, as shown in Figure 9.1. During the global financial crisis (GFC) in late 2008 and 2009, due to poor performance and significant investor liquidity needs, hedge fund managers experienced a nearly 50% decline in assets. However, industry assets quickly recovered and were around $3 trillion by the end of 2018.

Overall industry assets have stagnated at roughly $3 trillion as recent performance has been disappointing and investors have become increasingly frustrated with the higher fees and lower liquidity that is common to hedge funds. Of concern for this industry, the ability of hedge fund managers to generate equity-like returns with low correlation to equities and bonds seems to have declined in the past 10 years. Meanwhile, in light of high fees and low transparency, some investors have eschewed these products in favor of more traditional investment strategies. Other institutional investors have re-evaluated their allocation to hedge funds and, more commonly, now view hedge fund allocations as components within their long-only asset allocations; for example, including equity hedge funds as part of the equity allocation and credit hedge funds as part of the credit allocation. Over the coming years, we would expect this trend to continue.

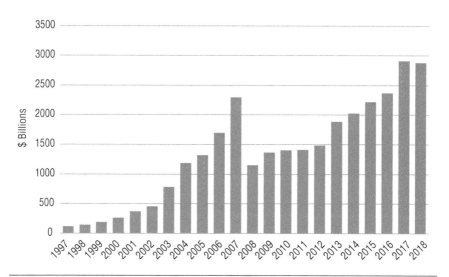

Figure 9.1   Value of assets managed by hedge funds worldwide. *Source:* statistica[xii]

Who Invests in Hedge Funds?

Hedge funds are restricted investments, which means only *qualified* investors may invest with them (see Chapter 2). As a result, for much of their early history, hedge fund investors were primarily high net worth and ultra-high net worth individuals. On the institutional side, the hedge fund history has historically generated significant interest from endowments and foundations that typically have been close to the forefront of investing in nontraditional formats. Defined benefit plans, with long horizons and low short-term liquidity needs, eventually became major investors in hedge funds as well. Interestingly, many individuals who would not be able to invest in hedge funds directly are in fact exposed to them through their defined benefit plans. This is because their qualifying power is aggregated together within their pension plans. Of note, the inclusion of a hedge fund allocation within institutions' portfolios rapidly accelerated after 1999. That year, California Public Employees' Retirement System (CalPERS), the largest pension fund in the U.S., announced it would invest up to $11.25 billion into hedge funds. That amount constituted up to one quarter of the $45 billion liquid securities' investments, and 7% of its total portfolio.[xiii] Interestingly, in 2014, CalPERS reversed course and announced it would exit its hedge fund investments, citing high fees and lackluster returns.[xiv] Today, the industry continues to count assets from institutional and high net worth investors alike.

Different Types of Hedge Funds

There are many different types of hedge funds, and there are many ways to group them. Perhaps the most recognizable and prominent taxonomy of hedge funds is the one created by Hedge Fund Research, Inc. (HFR). Established in 1992, HFR is a significant aggregator of hedge fund information with over 2,000 separate asset managers managing nearly 6,700 separate products voluntarily reporting to HFR monthly.[xv] HFR data is often cited in the media and their global quarterly hedge fund report is widely regarded as the most comprehensive in the industry. Like most categorizations, HFR's methodology and definitions are somewhat subjective, but they are also the market standard and have proven to be robust. Therefore, we will utilize HFR data and definitions in this chapter, but the reader should be aware that there are several other ways to categorize hedge funds (as there are with stocks) and no one way is necessarily superior to the others.

Figure 9.2 illustrates that when market pundits and observers discuss the performance of hedge funds for any given period, they are in fact describing the performance of a composite of many different strategies and asset classes. Although we frequently hear aggregate hedge fund performance cited and quoted, it is worthwhile to note that we have not yet heard on CNBC a discussion

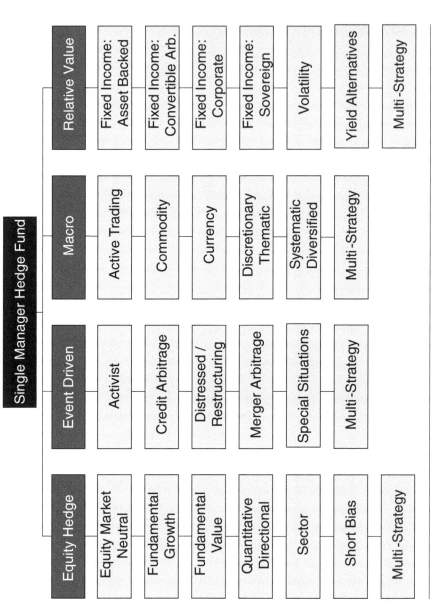

Figure 9.2 Hedge Fund Research strategy classification. *Source:* Hedge Fund Research

regarding the performance of the mutual fund industry from the prior month. One could in fact argue that the entire mutual fund industry is far more homogenous than the hedge fund industry; while most people would not think to aggregate fixed income mutual fund performance with equity mutual fund performance, most are fine with aggregating the strategies of equity hedge, event-driven, macro, and relative value, and all of their subcomponents. This is in no small part due to the marketing by hedge fund managers themselves; those who, despite their different strategies, asset classes, and market exposures, often tout the same target returns, risk, and correlation numbers. This would imply that aggregating the performance, the funds would be sensible given they seemingly share the same benchmark. To be clear, we do not support this type of aggregation. Let's now turn to the main strategies as outlined by HFR and visually represented in Figure 9.2.

EQUITY HEDGE

We will begin our discussion of hedge fund subcategories with the equity hedge category. As the name implies, equity hedge managers invest primarily within the equity markets, generally seeking to generate excess returns on both their long and their short positions through either superior fundamental research or from superior quantitative analysis. The first subcategories we will briefly discuss are *fundamental growth, fundamental value, sector-focused,* and *short-biased.* Fundamental growth managers typically identify as having an expertise in discerning which companies stand to generate the highest future earnings growth. Fundamental value managers seek to find companies with strong balance sheets and cash flows that they view as cheap. Fundamental growth and value managers will short stocks that exhibit the opposite characteristics of their long portfolios. Meanwhile, sector-focused managers confine themselves to picking stocks (taking both long and short positions) within a sector in which they feel they maintain an edge in analyzing. Most fundamental equity hedge funds run with moderate to high (30% to 70%) exposure to equity markets although others do aim for a more reduced market profile. Short-biased hedge fund managers, as their name implies, aim to maintain a consistently negative exposure to broader equity markets and seek to emphasize short positions in companies with the worst forward outlooks.

On the other side of the spectrum are *quantitative* equity hedge managers, whose investment processes are quantitatively driven, as their name implies. *Equity market neutral* strategies seek to deliver steady returns from positioning that is either informed by multifactor analysis, statistical arbitrage, or trade flow analysis. *Multifactor* model-driven managers utilize many of the techniques described in detail in Chapter 11 to purchase securities that exhibit desirable factor exposures and to short those that exhibit undesirable factor exposures. To distinguish themselves, multifactor model-driven managers pursue more complex and exotic factors to deliver alpha above what has become readily available in the market. *Statistical arbitrage* managers focus on trading pairs or groups of related stocks—a concept best illustrated with the basic example of trading Coke against Pepsi based on how the spread of the two stocks compare today to prior history. *Quantitative directional* managers employ the same techniques as described previously with the exception that they do not aim to maintain a market-neutral profile. *Multi-strategy* equity market hedge funds employ any of the aforementioned methodologies and typically do not use any one approach to constitute more than 50% of their positions. Finally, trade flow analysis is a primary input for *high-frequency traders* (HFTs) who aim to exploit tiny pricing differences that appear in infinitesimal time periods often due to trade flow data. Most HFTs are funded proprietarily and do not accept outside investments; so, they are typically not included in hedge fund categorizations. But, they are noted here for the reference of our readers (see Chapter 5 for more detail on HFTs).

Who's Who in the Equity Hedge Category

Located 60 miles east of Manhattan in East Setauket, New York, Renaissance Technologies (RenTech) is widely regarded as one of the world's most successful hedge funds. Founded in 1982 by James Simons, RenTech has been referred to as "the commercial version of the Manhattan Project"[xvi] and is best known for its flagship Medallion Fund. This fund, which was closed to outside investors in 1993, generated an astounding gross of fee +71.8% annualized return between 1994 through mid-2014.[xvii] It returned all outside capital to investors in 2005 and the current cap for fund assets is between $9 and $10 billion. Annual net returns were more modest (around 40% per year since inception through 2018) since the fund charges fees of 5% management plus a 44% performance fee. In 2018, RenTech founder James Simons remained atop the Institutional Investor highest-paid hedge fund managers list, earning $1.7 billion in 2017, up from $1.6 billion in 2016.[xviii] In 2018, Forbes estimated Simons's net worth to be $20 billion, making him the wealthiest fund manager in the world.[xix]

RenTech currently manages around $97 billion as of 2018 and employs roughly 300 people of which about 90 have PhDs.[xx] Renaissance is an early pioneer of quantitative trading, which relies on statistical analysis to identify opportunities and computers to execute its trades. RenTech uses big data to identify statistically significant drivers of market return that can be exploited. One such example was a study that showed French equities were more likely to appreciate if it was sunny in Paris.[xxi] Mathematics and academic rigor is infused in Renaissance's DNA. Prior to founding Renaissance, James Simons was chair of the department of mathematics at Stony Brook University, had been a professor at MIT and Harvard, received the Oswald Veblen Prize in Geometry, and cocreated the Chern-Simons theory. In 1977, he left academia to try to make money trading commodities. In the 1980s, Renaissance began attracting mathematicians and other researchers from academia, the private sector (including IBM), and even from the nonprofit sector (which includes the Institute for Defense Analyses).[xxii] Since that early time, RenTech has consistently focused on hiring people with backgrounds in the fields of science, technology, engineering, and mathematics. According to James Weatherall in *The Physics of Wall Street*, Renaissance "avoids hiring anyone with even the slightest whiff of Wall Street bona fides." PhDs in finance need not apply—nor should traders who got their start at traditional investment banks or even other hedge funds. The secret to Simons's success has been steering clear of the financial experts."[xxiii]

In contrast to RenTech, whose emphasis is on mathematical and statistical analysis, is Dallas-based Maverick Capital. Maverick is one of the most successful true *stock picking* hedge funds as defined by their performance, longevity, and asset base—seeking to generate alpha by picking better stocks on the long and the short side by knowing the companies. Founded by Lee Ainslie in 1993, Maverick Capital portfolios hold around 150 long and short positions and carry between 30% and 60% net long exposure to the market.[xxiv] Maverick's approach eschews mathematical modeling in favor of fundamental analysis. Maverick's analysts meet management teams, analyze markets, speak with customers, distributors, competitors, and corporate stakeholders. Maverick's flagship fund generated an annualized return around +11.5% from 1995 through mid-2018[xxv] versus the +9.7% of the S&P 500 over the same period.[1] Its founder Lee Ainslie is one of the original *Tiger Cubs*, a name given to hedge fund managers who worked for Julian Robertson at Tiger Management.[2]

---

[1] Period used: 12/30/1994 through 6/29/2018. Source: Bloomberg. Ticker: SPTR Index

[2] Julian Robertson founded Tiger Management in 1980 with $8.8 million. By 1998, the firm had grown to $21 billion and generated +31.7% annualized net of fee returns for investors. Poor performance in 1998 and 1999 led to significant investor withdraws, and the firm was shut in 2000 and all capital was returned to investors. Despite the poor performance at the end of its run, overall figures were still stellar. According to Robertson in his final letter to shareholders "Since inception, an investment in Tiger has grown 85-fold net of fees; more than three times the average of the S&P 500 and five-and-a-half times that of the Morgan Stanley Capital International World Index." *Source*: Julian Robertson. (March 30, 2000). Letter to Shareholders. https://money.cnn.com/2000/03/30/mutualfunds/q_funds_tiger/sidebar.htm.

Ainslie had attracted enough capital that by 1997 he closed the core fund at Maverick.[xxvi] For the past decade, Maverick has managed approximately $10 billion worth of capital. Ainslie has given several interviews in the past that have offered significant insight into Maverick's investment process and philosophy. In an interview with management consulting firm McKinsey & Company, Ainslie explained, "Our goal is to know more about every one of the companies in which we invest than any non-insider does. On average, we hold fewer than five positions per investment professional . . . We spend an inordinate amount of time trying to understand the quality, ability, and motivation of a management team . . . [I]t's our job to find the best and worst performers. In the end, our success is driven by making many good decisions rather than depending upon a few big home runs."[xxvii] Although Ainslie is the clear face of the organization and ultimate decision maker, he leans heavily on a group of six senior sector heads with whom he meets extensively and who generate the bulk of the investment ideas, along with the team of three to five people that works for each. Ainslie maintains a *no holds* concept in his investment style. As he puts it, "[I]t is critical to attempt to identify the best possible use of capital continuously . . . When somebody tells me that they don't think we should sell a stock, but that they wouldn't buy more at the current price either, then that investment probably does not represent one of our very best uses of capital."[xxviii]

Equity Hedge Performance

Given the level of equity market exposure that fundamental equity hedge funds typically carry, performance should be evaluated within the context of how equity markets have fared throughout the performance period. Over the course of the past 20 years, equity hedge funds have outperformed both stocks and bonds. However, the evaluation period has been a tale of two halves (see Appendix Figures 9.3 and 9.4 at the end of this chapter). As shown in Table 9.1, performance from 1999 to 2008 was outstanding. Despite carrying exposure to the U.S. equity market, which generated an annualized -1.4% return, equity hedge funds managed to generate robustly positive returns at $+6.9\%$ annualized. However, in the 10-year period that ended in 2018, equity hedge fund performance slipped to $+5.7\%$ annualized despite the backdrop of U.S. stock markets having generated $+13.1\%$ annualized returns over the same period. Equity hedge fund returns have outperformed U.S. bonds, although it should be noted that the quality of these returns, as measured by the Sharpe ratio, has generally been worse across observation periods.

Equity market neutral hedge funds collectively improved the quality of their returns between the 10-year period ending 12/31/2008 to the 10-year period ending 12/31/2018 as evidenced by their Sharpe ratio improving from 0.42 to

Table 9.1   Equity hedge index and sub-index annual returns and Sharpe ratios*

Annualized Returns

Period	Risk Free	S&P 500	U.S. Aggregate (Bonds)	HFRI Equity Hedge	HFRI Equity Market Neutral	HFRI Quantitative Directional	HFRI Sector-Tech/Healthcare	HFRI Fundamental Growth	HFRI Fundamental Value	HFRI Multi-Strategy	HFRI Equity Hedge (Asset Weighted)
1-yr.	1.9%	-4.4%	0.0%	-6.9%	-1.0%	-4.8%	3.3%	-9.7%	-8.8%	-6.4%	-5.9%
3-yr.	1.0%	9.3%	2.1%	3.6%	2.0%	3.4%	6.7%	3.8%	3.5%	2.5%	2.4%
5-yr.	0.6%	8.5%	2.5%	2.3%	2.7%	3.2%	7.0%	1.6%	2.2%	1.9%	2.3%
10-yr.	0.4%	13.1%	3.5%	5.7%	2.5%	4.8%	9.7%	5.9%	6.7%	4.9%	5.8%
20-yr.	1.9%	5.6%	4.5%	6.3%	3.6%	6.2%	8.7%	–	–	–	–
10-yr. ended 12/31/08	3.4%	-1.4%	5.6%	6.9%	4.8%	7.5%	7.7%	–	–	–	–

Sharpe Ratios

Period	Risk Free	S&P 500	U.S. Aggregate (Bonds)	HFRI Equity Hedge	HFRI Equity Market Neutral	HFRI Quantitative Directional	HFRI Sector-Tech/Healthcare	HFRI Fundamental Growth	HFRI Fundamental Value	HFRI Multi-Strategy	HFRI Equity Hedge (Asset Weighted)
1-yr.	–	(0.43)	(0.64)	(1.28)	(0.99)	(1.13)	0.16	(1.61)	(1.32)	(1.20)	(1.12)
3-yr.	–	0.76	0.37	0.43	0.42	0.51	0.70	0.39	0.35	0.26	0.24
5-yr.	–	0.72	0.68	0.29	0.98	0.53	0.81	0.14	0.23	0.22	0.29
10-yr.	–	0.94	1.09	0.72	0.87	0.69	1.27	0.59	0.78	0.66	0.81
20-yr.	–	0.26	0.79	0.51	0.61	0.39	0.48	–	–	–	–
10-yr. ended 12/31/08	–	(0.32)	0.58	0.36	0.42	0.29	0.23	–	–	–	–

Source: Authors' calculations and Hedge Fund Resources, Inc. (HFRI)
*Periods ended 12/31/2018 unless otherwise specified

0.87. However, the annualized return over these periods declined from +4.8% to +2.5%, which was lower than U.S. bonds over this period despite historically low bond yields. Suffice to say that investors who viewed equity market neutral products as a substitute for equities within their portfolios would have been disappointed by the results.

As expected, equity hedge funds maintain a nontrivial equity beta to the S&P 500, as shown in Table 9.2. For the category, the average equity beta is around 0.50—although this varies depending on the category and period reviewed. Due to this equity beta, the correlation between these strategies and equities remains high (see Appendix Table 9.9). Once we strip away performance in these strategies considering their equity betas, it becomes apparent that most of these strategies have not added value over the past 10 years. Additionally, there has been a notable decline in equity beta-adjusted excess returns, as shown in Table 9.2.

Equity Hedge Pros and Cons

The role that an equity hedge fund plays in an investment portfolio varies drastically depending on the targeted market exposure from the manager. One advantage of investing in equity hedge funds is the increased liquidity profile of the underlying positions. Because equity hedge funds typically confine themselves to publicly listed equity securities, the depth of the market for the positions can be readily ascertained by analyzing the nature of the markets in which they invest and the ownership level (i.e., the percentage of the float that the managers own) of the positions. As an example, a long/short equity manager who invests in small cap stocks will have a liquidity profile that resembles that of any investor in small cap stocks with a similar ownership level. Another advantageous aspect of equity hedge funds is the relative simplicity of the strategy. Fundamental equity hedge funds aim to pick better stocks than equity mutual funds do. As we saw in the Greenlight example, there is no real alchemy; just the use of the increased toolbox that hedge funds have at their disposal to amplify the alpha component of returns. Finally, these products may serve as a complement to traditional benchmark-focused public equity investments given their differentiated portfolio construction methodology.

Yet the simplicity of picking securities in a liquid market can also serve as a detriment because many efficient market proponents argue that it is not possible to simply outperform the market. Quantitative and equity market neutral funds that utilize a multifactor approach carry the additional risk of *factor crowding*. Factor crowding may occur when managers are invested in the same factors, which can both lower the potential returns of those factors as well as increase the volatility of those factors should one or more managers choose to

9.2 Equity hedge equity betas and equity beta-adjusted excess returns*

Period		U.S. Aggregate (Bonds)	HFRI Equity Hedge	HFRI Equity Market Neutral	HFRI Quantitative Directional	HFRI Sector-Tech/ Healthcare	HFRI Fundamental Growth	HFRI Fundamental Value	HFRI Multi-Strategy	HFRI Equity Hedge (Asset Weighted)
	Equity Betas (to S&P 500)									
3-yr.		(0.04)	0.50	0.09	0.41	0.56	0.54	0.60	0.46	0.47
5-yr.		(0.03)	0.47	0.09	0.40	0.48	0.53	0.55	0.47	0.45
10-yr.		(0.01)	0.47	0.11	0.44	0.39	0.57	0.53	0.44	0.42
20-yr.		(0.02)	0.46	0.06	0.59	0.58	—	—	—	—
10-yr. ended 12/31/08		(0.02)	0.47	0.01	0.75	0.76	—	—	—	—
	Equity Beta-Adjusted Excess Returns									
3-yr.		1.4%	-1.5%	0.2%	-0.9%	1.1%	-1.6%	-2.4%	-2.3%	-2.4%
5-yr.		2.1%	-2.0%	1.4%	-0.6%	2.6%	-3.1%	-2.8%	-2.4%	-1.9%
10-yr.		3.2%	-0.7%	0.7%	-1.1%	4.3%	-1.8%	-0.5%	-1.1%	0.1%
20-yr.		2.7%	2.7%	1.5%	2.0%	4.6%	—	—	—	—
10-yr. ended 12/31/08		2.1%	5.8%	1.4%	7.7%	7.9%	—	—	—	—

Source: Authors' calculations and HFRI
*10-year period ended 12/31/2018. Monthly returns used.

rapidly exit those factors.[3] Additionally, factor investing, as we will see in the next chapter, can go out of favor for several years and with no indication of when the factors will return to favor, or more precisely, generate positive risk premium. The final and most obvious drawback to equity hedge funds is the market exposure that many carry. Although this is typically very transparent to investors, the benefits of having equity hedge funds can be muted due to a lower diversification effect of investing in a strategy that carries a significant equity beta. Nevertheless, relative to many other strategies, the measurements of market exposure and beta for equity hedge funds tend to be stable; as a result, this strategy is less likely than other strategies to materially underperform expectations during market downturns.

EVENT-DRIVEN FUNDS

HFR's event-driven category is perhaps the most diverse of their four main categories. Event-driven managers, as a group, invest across the asset class and liquidity spectrums. What binds the group together is an investment thesis that is typically centered around some form of corporate *activity, event,* or *catalyst.* The nature of the corporate activity is what differentiates the individual subcategories of event-driven hedge fund managers. These corporate events include mergers, acquisitions, spin-offs, divestitures, security issuance, buybacks, restructurings, and distressed situations. Events can be broadly categorized as *hard,* which means there is an event that is publicized or announced—or *soft,* which means the possibility of an event that is as yet unannounced by the media or management. Trading around hard events typically resembles a tightly hedged absolute return strategy where a position is taken on a narrowly defined spread with a defined catalyst. Meanwhile, managers who invest in soft events aim to benefit when anticipated corporate events are eventually announced, which can lead to outsized gains for investors. Typically, managers who trade in hard events aim to hit a lot of singles, while managers who trade in soft events aim to hit home runs even if it means striking out from time to time when anticipated events do not materialize.

The main subcategories within the event-driven category that we will discuss briefly here are *merger arbitrage, special situations, activist, distressed,* and *credit arbitrage.* Merger arbitrage managers invest in announced mergers and

---

[3] Between August 7 and August 9, 2007, many equity long/short funds experienced exceptionally large losses. Amir E. Khandani and Andrew W. Lo estimate that *contrarian* strategies experienced (on average) an unleveraged return of −6.85%, which constitutes a 12-standard deviation event! For more information, please see their paper *What Happened To The Quants In August 2007?*

acquisitions. Their main strategy is to invest in the target of an acquisition and to short the acquirer against the long position.[4] The result is a tightly hedged, liquid trade that generates a modest profit in the case that the deal closes at the expense of higher losses if the deal *breaks*. Merger arb—or *risk arb* as it is sometimes referred to—tends to run muted exposure to the equity market. In contrast, special situations managers position themselves primarily in *soft catalyst* equities that they feel are poised for a breakout based on an as-yet unannounced corporate action from the underlying company. Activist managers also position themselves in soft catalyst positions, but they are not content to simply wait for a catalyst that leads to an outsized gain. Rather, the manager attempts to unlock the value of these positions by employing different strategies of shareholder activism, ranging from launching media campaigns and proxy fights to occasionally securing board representation to directly impact the direction of the companies in which they invest. Distressed managers specialize in the investments into the debt of stressed, distressed, defaulted, restructuring, and liquidating companies. Like activist managers, distressed managers often become involved with the management of the company. Distressed managers benefit from buying securities cheaply from traditional bond investors who seek liquidity from their positions prior to becoming encumbered in a protracted and complicated bankruptcy process. Credit arbitrage resembles an equity hedge strategy in that managers aim to invest in undervalued corporate credits and hedge them with overvalued corporate credits or index exposure. Because of the lower volatility that is inherent in corporate debt, credit arb managers will typically look to events to unlock outsized gains for their portfolios. Finally, some event-driven managers are categorized as *multi-strategy* because they utilize several of the previously mentioned strategies.

Who's Who in the Event-Driven Category

Event-driven managers are often typified by a *go-anywhere* mentality for investing. Two managers that capture this ethos are Paulson & Co and Sculptor Capital Management, formerly known as Och-Ziff. Paulson & Co., headquartered in New York City, was founded in 1994 by John Paulson who had previously worked at Bear Stearns in the mergers and acquisitions department and as a mergers arbitrager at Gruss & Co. Paulson's fund was initially a merger arbitrage fund, yet Paulson also was known at times for both buying and shorting corporate bonds. Managing around $500 million in 2002, Paulson & Co. was a comparatively small and little-known firm that shot to prominence in 2008 because

---

[4] The trade is possible because the announced price for the transaction almost always exceeds the target's current price. The price for the target converges to the agreed-upon price when the deal closes and the shareholders receive a certain portion of the acquirer's stock.

of successful bets against the U.S. housing market. It's believed that Paulson personally made between $3 and $4 billion in 2007 alone, which was the largest single-year payday for a hedge fund manager.[xxix]

In 2005, Paulson began to build short positions against U.S. housing by utilizing derivatives including swaps on the ABX index and other CDOs (collateralized debt). In 2006, he launched the first of two funds that were focused on shorting the housing market, which he marketed to investors as catastrophe insurance. Paulson's timing proved to be prescient. After starting the year with approximately $7 billion of capital, Paulson & Co. would make $15 billion for its clients in 2007 and another $5 billion in 2008. By the end of 2007, on the back of this performance plus approximately $6 billion in investor subscriptions, Paulson & Co.'s AUM surged to $28 billion.[xxx] True to the *go-anywhere* mentality of event-driven managers, Paulson began launching new strategies that included gold funds and corporate special situations funds. As early as 2009, Paulson had shifted his attention to gold, hypothesizing that the U.S. and other developed countries would encounter severe inflationary pressures because of the extraordinary simulative measures taken by central banks in response to the GFC.[xxxi] Paulson's assets peaked at $38 billion by 2011, the same year that the price of gold peaked. On the back of poor performance in some of his funds, Paulson's assets began to decline quickly; by 2013, his assets had dropped to $18 billion, and by 2018, they had dropped to $9 billion—the majority of which was Paulson's own fortune.[xxxii]

Sculptor Capital Management (Sculptor) is also based in New York City and is another large and highly relevant hedge fund. The first Sculptor fund, like Paulson's, focused on relative value and merger arbitrage. Also like Paulson, Sculptor would eventually widen the universe in which it invested and expanded its offerings to include convertible and derivative arbitrage, long short equity, real estate, energy, and special situations.[xxxiii] Founder Dan Och began his career at Goldman Sachs (GS) as a risk arbitrager and was later named head of proprietary trading in GS's equity division and cohead of U.S. Equities Trading.[xxxiv] Och founded Sculptor in 1994 with a $100 million investment from the Ziff family, the founders of Ziff Davis Media. Sculptor currently manages around $33.0 billion between credit, multi-strategy, and real estate funds, and the flagship Master Fund has returned an annualized +8.7% net of fees from its inception (1/1/98) through September 30, 2018[xxxv] versus +7.5% for the S&P 500. Sculptor went public in 2007, making it one of only a handful of hedge funds that are publicly listed. As a result, its financial statements are public, which offers investors a rare glimpse into the inner financial workings of a major hedge fund. Also because of the IPO, Och was estimated to have made $1.1 billion; after the sale, he still owned 48% of the company.[xxxvi]

As Sculptor put it in their 2009 10K, "Since our inception, we have managed our business with a global perspective, taking advantage of investment opportunities wherever they arise. We have been among the pioneers of the hedge fund industry in building our global investment platform."[xxxvii] After the 2008/2009 GFC, Sculptor looked to take advantage of an expected rebound in U.S. housing to buy what they perceived as oversold mortgage assets; the investment paid off and the firm continued to grow, ultimately peaking at $47.5 billion by the end of 2014.[xxxviii] Amidst this success, Sculptor began to diversify from their core event-driven multi-strategy offerings into credit-focused and real-estate focused funds. Additionally, the company's London office began to push into Africa for opportunities through the Sculptor subsidiary, Sculptor Africa Management. However, the envelope was pushed a bit too far, and in 2016, the unit pled guilty to a conspiracy charge related to an accusation from the SEC that Sculptor paid more than $100 million worth of bribes in Africa to secure natural resource deals and other investments. As part of the settlement, Sculptor paid more than $400 million in fines and Och himself had to pay a $2.2 million fine.[xxxix] The settlement combined with unspectacular performance lead to significant investor concern, and Sculptor faced $13 billion worth of investor withdrawals in 2016 and into the first months of 2017.[xl] Although Sculptor has lost some of the luster it enjoyed in the earlier part of the decade, the firm continues to manage in excess of $30 billion today, and remains a considerable force in the industry. After the bribery scandal, Och took a step back from the firm he founded, moving into the typically more symbolic role of chairman until March 2019, allowing for a new set of leaders to take over the firm. In September 2019, the firm changed its name from Och-Ziff to Sculptor Capital Management in an attempt to further distance itself from its founder.

Event-Driven Performance

Like fundamental equity hedge funds, event-driven hedge funds should generally be assessed within the context of how equities have performed given the amount of market exposure that the strategy typically carries. Like equity hedge funds, event-driven hedge funds have outperformed both equities and bonds for the 20-year period ending in 2018. However, also like equity hedge funds, this outperformance was driven by outstanding performance during the first half of the observation, when event-driven hedge funds generated +7.8% annualized performance for the 10-year period ending in 2008. By comparison, the S&P 500 generated −1.4% annualized performance and U.S. bonds generated a +2.5% annualized performance over the same period, as highlighted in Table 9.3. For the 10-year period ending in 2008, the event-driven quality of returns also was better than both stocks and bonds, as measured by the Sharpe ratio.

For the 10-year period ending in 2018, event-driven hedge fund performance has been +6.5% per annum while the S&P 500 returned +13.1% per annum over the same period. Interestingly, although the absolute level of the category's

Table 9.3   Event-driven index and sub-index annual returns and Sharpe ratios*

Annualized Returns

Period	Risk Free	S&P 500	U.S. Aggregate (Bonds)	HFRI Event-Driven	HFRI Distressed/ Restructuring	HFRI Merger Arbitrage	HFRI Activist	HFRI Credit Arbitrage	HFRI Multi-Strategy	HFRI Special Situations	HFRI Event-Driven (Asset Weighted)
1-yr.	1.9%	-4.4%	0.0%	-2.3%	-1.6%	3.2%	-11.3%	2.1%	-4.4%	-5.0%	-0.6%
3-yr.	1.0%	9.3%	2.1%	5.1%	6.4%	3.7%	1.1%	6.6%	1.9%	5.9%	4.4%
5-yr.	0.6%	8.5%	2.5%	2.5%	1.8%	3.2%	2.2%	3.6%	1.2%	2.8%	2.6%
10-yr.	0.4%	13.1%	3.5%	6.5%	6.8%	4.1%	7.2%	7.9%	5.3%	7.0%	7.0%
20-yr.	1.9%	5.6%	4.5%	7.1%	7.5%	5.3%	—	—	—	—	—
10-yr. ended 12/31/08	3.4%	-1.4%	5.6%	7.8%	8.1%	6.6%	—	—	—	—	—

Sharpe Ratios

Period	Risk Free	S&P 500	U.S. Aggregate (Bonds)	HFRI Event-Driven	HFRI Distressed/ Restructuring	HFRI Merger Arbitrage	HFRI Activist	HFRI Credit Arbitrage	HFRI Multi-Strategy	HFRI Special Situations	HFRI Event-Driven (Asset Weighted)
1-yr.	—	(0.43)	(0.64)	(1.10)	(0.81)	0.48	(1.43)	0.09	(1.74)	(1.27)	(0.65)
3-yr.	—	0.76	0.37	0.96	1.12	1.14	0.01	1.54	0.23	0.85	0.72
5-yr.	—	0.72	0.68	0.43	0.23	1.07	0.18	0.84	0.14	0.38	0.39
10-yr.	—	0.94	1.09	1.17	1.14	1.62	0.61	1.86	0.79	1.03	1.13
20-yr.	—	0.26	0.79	0.85	0.92	1.14	—	—	—	—	—
10-yr. ended 12/31/08	—	(0.32)	0.58	0.62	0.72	0.88	—	—	—	—	—

Source: Authors' calculations and HFRI
*Periods ended 12/31/2018 unless otherwise specified

average return has slightly declined, the quality of returns has improved as quantified by the Sharpe ratio. In addition, event-driven hedge funds have also shown an ability to outperform bonds over both periods in terms of both return and Sharpe ratio. It bears noting, however, that the return for the five-year period ending in 2018 has been challenged with the category performing in line with bonds and significantly lagging equities. Among the substrategies, merger arbitrage funds have managed to continue to outperform bonds over most time periods while generating impressive Sharpe ratios.

Event-driven hedge funds also tend to have positive equity betas; we estimate those generally hover around 0.30, although this varies by sub-strategy with activist funds carrying the highest equity beta (around 0.60) and merger arbitrage funds carrying the lowest equity beta (around 0.10). Like equity hedge strategies, event-driven hedge funds remain highly correlated to U.S. equities and for this reason offer little diversification benefit (see Appendix Table 9.10). When adjusting for the equity beta of these strategies, as shown in Table 9.4, we note that most strategies have generated positive excess returns over the past five and 10 years, with credit arbitrage funds generating the most impressive excess returns while activist strategies have generated negative excess returns for investors.

Event-Driven Pros and Cons

Event-driven strategies are not for the faint of heart. The events upon which managers intend to capitalize bring both upside volatility and downside volatility that can be further magnified in volatile market conditions. The reason event-driven strategies become increasingly volatile when equities become increasingly volatile is that the targeted events often are correlated with the market. For example, merger arbitrage managers seek opportunities that may *break* if the equity market significantly declines. When this occurs, the planned merger may no longer look as attractive to the acquirer. Similarly, once a company becomes aware of the presence of an activist investor, its management may engage in a public fight with the activist and in doing so, cause the price of the target company's stock to fall. Even distressed managers who look to take advantage of the opportunities created in market downturns are exposed to market sentiment and may carry a high equity beta. Once the target of a distressed manager has completed its restructuring, the value of the restructured company will be significantly higher in a *good* market than a *bad* market; therefore, the upside to this strategy may be heavily influenced by overall market sentiment.

Further complicating this profile for activist and distressed managers is that managers are often restricted from selling their investments while they are

Table 9.4 Event-driven index equity betas and equity beta-adjusted excess returns*

Period	U.S. Aggregate (Bonds)	HFRI Event-Driven	HFRI Distressed/ Restructuring	HFRI Merger Arbitrage	HFRI Activist	HFRI Credit Arbitrage	HFRI Multi-Strategy	HFRI Special Situations	HFRI Event-Driven (Asset Weighted)
				Equity Betas (to S&P 500)					
3-yr.	(0.04)	0.31	0.28	0.11	0.62	0.19	0.26	0.43	0.31
5-yr.	(0.03)	0.30	0.27	0.12	0.59	0.17	0.27	0.40	0.34
10-yr.	(0.01)	0.30	0.27	0.10	0.63	0.16	0.33	0.37	0.31
20-yr.	(0.02)	0.31	0.25	0.11	—	—	—	—	—
10-yr. ended 12/31/08	(0.02)	0.33	0.24	0.13	—	—	—	—	—
				Equity Beta-Adjusted Excess Returns					
3-yr.	1.4%	1.6%	3.1%	1.8%	−5.0%	4.0%	−1.2%	1.4%	0.9%
5-yr.	2.1%	−0.5%	−1.0%	1.7%	−3.1%	1.7%	−1.5%	−0.9%	−0.7%
10-yr.	3.2%	2.3%	3.0%	2.4%	−1.2%	5.4%	0.7%	1.9%	2.8%
20-yr.	2.7%	4.1%	4.6%	3.0%	—	—	—	—	—
10-yr. ended 12/31/08	2.1%	6.0%	5.8%	3.7%	—	—	—	—	—

Source: Authors' calculations and HFRI
*Periods ended 12/31/2018 unless otherwise specified

engaged with company management. This lack of liquidity can be problematic during market downturns should investors attempt to redeem from the managers. Activist and distressed managers also carry significant *headline risk* relative to other hedge fund strategies. This can be a significant concern for institutional investors who may not want to be associated with a high-profile corporate fight. Additionally, activist managers who push companies to rationalize costs or to unload unprofitable businesses can be viewed harshly in the public domain.

This risk, however, does come with increased upside over time, as evidenced by this strategy's strong performance relative to other hedge fund strategies. It should be noted though that this performance generally comes with elevated market exposure and thus the diversification effects of investing in the strategy can be somewhat limited. However, like equity hedge funds, event-driven hedge funds can make useful additions to investment positioning within asset classes. For example, equity heavy special situations and activist investments can be used to complement traditional benchmark-focused equity exposure. Similarly, credit arbitrage and distressed strategies can be used to complement traditional credit exposures. Finally, event-driven hedge funds led by consistent teams may be able to generate consistent returns over time. This is because the process-based techniques that these teams employ to unlock value are generally seen as more repeatable than other investment judgment-based strategies.

GLOBAL MACRO

The HFR definition for global macro hedge funds includes strategies in which "the investment process is predicated on movements in underlying economic variables and the impact these have on equity, fixed income, currency, and commodity markets . . . rather than realization of a valuation discrepancy between securities."[xlii] Fund managers can employ teams of analysts or be run by a single trader and portfolio manager. Regardless of resources, the funds seek to position their portfolios to benefit from global trends, such as one region's stock market outperforming another or a general appreciation or depreciation of a basket of currencies. Often these portfolios have dozens of positions that may express a single theme (such as accelerating global growth) or its positions may be country or region-specific and express no theme at all. Managers generally utilize a broad range of financial instruments to implement their views including the use of futures, forward, options, and swaps on a variety of equity, bond, currency, and commodity indices. Positions are regularly both long and short.

Within the global macro category, there are six generally accepted sub-categories: *active trading, commodity, currency, discretionary thematic, systematic diversified,* and *multi-strategy.* Active trading strategies generally have high turnover and a quantitative analysis of macroeconomic variables. Commodity strategies may focus on trading one specific type of commodity, such as agriculture, energy, or metals, or the strategy may blend trading of all types of commodities. Currency strategies attempt to benefit from the relative appreciation of one currency (or basket of currencies) to another. These funds may be discretionary, whereby the portfolio manager utilizes a fundamental or technical approach but is not bounded by the model's rules, or they may be systematic whereby the investment process is driven by mathematical models. Discretionary thematic strategies attempt to identify and profit from global developments (or themes) such as global growth convergence, emerging markets disinflation, increasing developed market risk premia, or increasing regional political instability. Investment processes are primarily top-down. Systematic diversified strategies, like active trading, have investment process-driven models and involve little human overlay. These strategies generally focus on identifying and benefiting from trends, such as appreciating equities, depreciating commodities, or rising interest rates. Finally, multi-strategy macro products employ more than one of the previously mentioned processes and therefore do not clearly fit into another subcategory.

Who's Who in the Global Macro Category

Bridgewater Associates is based in Westport, Connecticut, and is the world's largest hedge fund with around $125 billion in assets under management as of 2018.[xliii] Within the spectrum of hedge funds, if Renaissance Technologies is at one extreme (relative value and quantitative, secretive, nonexistent employee turnover), Bridgewater is at the other extreme (macro, radical transparency, high employee turnover). Founded in 1975 by Ray Dalio, Bridgewater is best known for its Pure Alpha and All Weather strategies as well as its unique corporate culture. Bridgewater also publishes its "Daily Observations," which includes daily research pieces provided to its investors or by paid subscription. Bridgewater Pure Alpha invests in more than 150 markets, across asset classes and geographies,[xliv] and with the objective of identifying "uncorrelated alpha return streams." This product has returned around 12% per year, net of fees, for around 30 years and posted only three years of negative returns.[xlv] In addition to being one of the world's largest hedge funds, the Bridgewater Pure Alpha strategy has more net total gains for its investors than any other fund in the world: $49.7 billion.[xlvi] The All Weather product, originally launched in 1996, attempts to "perform well across all environments." Now considered a pioneer of *risk parity*,[5] the strategy allocates an equal amount of risk to each of four quadrants that will perform well in rising or falling growth or inflation.[xlvii]

In addition to being known for its size and stellar returns, Bridgewater Associates is also regularly in the news for its corporate culture. In his 2017 book, *Principles: Life and Work*, which was a New York Times Best Seller, Ray Dalio details the principles he believes are essential to personal, professional, and organizational success.[xlviii] One of his guiding philosophies is *radical transparency* which is a term that Dalio regularly uses to describe complete openness and real-time feedback. In 2017, *The New York Times* interviewed nearly 50 current and former employees and published an eye-opening article on the Bridgewater culture. According to the article, employees are regularly tested and graded on their knowledge of the "Principles." They constantly evaluate peers and supervisors on iPads, and these ratings generate an employee's permanent record called the "baseball card." All conversations are videotaped and those recordings are accessible by any employee at any time. The corporation has "captains" to enforce corporate rules and "overseers" who monitor department heads and report to Dalio. Employees may be publicly berated for "below-the-bar" thinking.[xlix] Perhaps not surprisingly, turnover is high among those who are newly hired, with about a third leaving within two years. While this corporate environment is clearly not for everybody, to be fair, some employees love it. In a *Business Insider* interview, one Bridgewater manager described how, on his second day as an employee, he learned in front of a 200-person meeting that he had been ranked as the worst manager at the firm. He then introduced himself to the group in attendance and described how this ranking had energized him to improve.[l]

Another high-profile global macro-focused firm is the New York City based *Soros Fund Management*. One of the world's most influential investment management firms, Soros Fund Management is best known as the adviser for the Quantum Group Funds; however, it is worth noting that the management firm also is known to work closely with nongovernment organizations, support philanthropies, and donate to political groups and campaigns. The Quantum Group Funds invest in equities, fixed income, and currencies, as well as private

---

[5] *Risk parity* is an investment strategy whereby managers allocate *risk* and not *capital*. For example, a manager that allocates capital equally to stocks and bonds will be allocating a majority of their risk to stocks because stocks are more volatile than bonds. A risk parity approach to a stock and bond allocation would target a portfolio that has an equal amount of risk derived from each of the two asset classes. The capital allocation would be driven by the relative riskiness and the correlation of those asset classes. Thus, to obtain risk parity among a stock and bond portfolio, a majority of the capital would be allocated to bonds. The expression *risk parity* has been attributed to a 2005 white paper authored by Dr. Edward Qian, of PanAgora Asset Management, titled *Risk Parity Portfolios: Efficient Portfolios through True Diversification*.

equity and venture capital funds. George Soros and the Quantum Group Funds became famous (or infamous) in 1992 when George Soros, along with several other managers including Paul Tudor Jones and Bruce Kovner, placed large currency positions betting that the British pound would devalue against the German mark. At that time, England was a member of the European Exchange Rate Mechanism (ERM), which required the pound to trade within a range against the mark. Soros and several others were correct that the Bank of England (BOE) would be forced to devalue its currency and on September 16, 1992 (known as Black Wednesday), the BOE withdrew from the ERM. The large position netted Soros and his funds $1.5 billion in a single month. Additionally, the publicity and outsized return allowed his funds to grow from $3.3 billion in mid-October 1992 to $11 billion by year-end 1993.[li]

The Quantum Group of Funds collectively held around $27 billion in assets as of year-end 2017.[lii] While this may seem small in comparison to Bridgewater's roughly $125 billion in AUM, it is worth noting that the Quantum Fund is believed to have generated the second-most returns for investors since inception at roughly $43.9 billion through 2018.[liii] In 2011, all outside investor capital was returned to avoid SEC registration; the funds currently exclusively manage capital for George Soros and his family.[liv]

Global Macro Performance

While Bridgewater's Pure Alpha and Soros Fund Management's Quantum Fund have generated stellar returns for several decades, unfortunately the same cannot be said for all managers. As shown in Table 9.5, for the 20-year period ending on 12/31/2018, the S&P 500 and Bloomberg Barclays U.S. Aggregate Bond Index generated annualized returns of +5.6% and +4.5%, respectively. Meanwhile, the HFRI Macro index generated an annualized net of fee return of +4.9%, so, roughly in line with stocks and bonds. However, late adopters to this strategy have not been the beneficiaries of stock- and bond-like returns. Note that for the 10-year period ending on 12/31/2008, the HFRI Macro Index significantly outperformed stocks while generating bond-like Sharpe ratios. By contrast, for the 10-year period ending on 12/31/2018, the S&P 500 and Bloomberg Barclays U.S. Aggregate Bond Index generated annualized returns of +13.1% and +3.5% respectively, while the HFRI Macro index generated an annualized net of fee returns of +1.1%. Additionally, the 10-year Sharpe ratio for HFRI Macro fell from 1.50 to 0.25. In short, investors would have been much better off to have purchased bonds as global macro strategies barely outperformed a risk-free asset. The sub-classes of global macro strategies also performed poorly during the 10-year period ending on 12/31/2018 with annualized returns ranging from +2.6% to +0.3%.

Table 9.5 Global macro index and sub-index annual returns and Sharpe ratios*

Annualized Returns

Period	Risk Free	S&P 500	U.S. Aggregate (Bonds)	HFRI Macro	HFRI Systematic Diversified	HFRI Macro (Asset Weighted)	HSFRI Active Trading	HFRI Commodity	HFRI Currency	HFRI Discretionary Thematic	HFRI Multi-Strategy
1-yr.	1.9%	-4.4%	0.0%	-3.6%	-6.0%	1.6%	0.3%	-3.1%	0.3%	0.5%	-4.5%
3-yr.	1.0%	9.3%	2.1%	-0.2%	-1.8%	2.0%	1.4%	0.5%	2.6%	0.3%	1.3%
5-yr.	0.6%	8.5%	2.5%	0.7%	0.5%	2.4%	2.2%	0.7%	2.0%	0.0%	1.5%
10-yr.	0.4%	13.1%	3.5%	1.1%	0.3%	3.2%	2.1%	1.0%	1.0%	1.6%	2.6%
20-yr.	1.9%	5.6%	4.5%	4.9%	5.9%	—	—	—	—	—	—
10-yr. ended 12/31/08	3.4%	-1.4%	5.6%	8.9%	11.7%	—	—	—	—	—	—

Sharpe Ratios

Period	Risk Free	S&P 500	U.S. Aggregate (Bonds)	HFRI Macro	HFRI Systematic Diversified	HFRI Macro (Asset Weighted)	HSFRI Active Trading	HFRI Commodity	HFRI Currency	HFRI Discretionary Thematic	HFRI Multi-Strategy
1-yr.	—	(0.43)	(0.64)	(1.10)	(0.91)	(0.08)	(0.26)	(0.98)	(0.42)	(0.44)	(1.40)
3-yr.	—	0.76	0.37	(0.29)	(0.39)	0.32	0.08	(0.13)	0.48	(0.33)	0.07
5-yr.	—	0.72	0.68	0.02	(0.03)	0.44	0.38	0.01	0.43	(0.25)	0.21
10-yr.	—	0.94	1.09	0.16	(0.02)	0.64	0.42	0.13	0.18	0.31	0.55
20-yr.	—	0.26	0.79	0.58	0.51	—	—	—	—	—	—
10-yr. ended 12/31/08	—	(0.32)	0.58	0.92	1.02	—	—	—	—	—	—

Source: Authors' calculations and HFRI
*Periods ended 12/31/2018 unless otherwise specified

Long equity beta exposure for these strategies has mostly been low (generally around 0.10) and has varied by strategy and time period, as shown in Table 9.6. When adjusting for the slight equity beta, two observations from the past ten years become apparent: first, global macro investors generally would have outperformed had they invested 10% of their capital in long stocks and 90% of their capital in a risk-free investment. Second, performance has materially deteriorated over the past 10-years, vis-à-vis the 10-year period ending in 2008.

Global Macro Pros and Cons

To decide if Global Macro strategies have a place in a personal or institutional portfolio, like any investment, this strategy must be evaluated holistically. The questions regarding the investor's return target, liquidity target, investment horizon, and existing portfolio, must all be considered. Additionally, each global macro strategy is different with respect to its return and volatility objective, the asset classes in which it invests, and the expertise of the portfolio management team. So, the following analysis is highly general and may not be applicable given the aforementioned considerations.

Unless an institutional investor has a high degree of confidence in the process of the portfolio management team, they may be disappointed by the results. Most global macro strategies are little more than go-anywhere spread products that attempt to source risk and return from nontraditional geographies (like frontier markets) and utilize less-liquid and more exotic instruments (including a variety of derivatives). Sourcing equity-like returns with bond-like volatility and correlation is a noble goal; but, the return profile of global macro strategies from the pre-global financial crisis era is unlikely to be repeated. As noted previously, global macro funds performed well prior to the GFC and took in an outsized portion of flow in subsequent years. While performance tends to be mean reverting, these flows may have also contributed to the poor performance in the 10-year period ending on 12/31/2018.

Of additional concern is that global macro products are broad in their risk exposure, often directional, and typically difficult to model. As global macro managers add or remove positions in a short period, it is difficult for asset allocators who utilize global macro funds to know at any given time what the primary drivers of risk are in their portfolios. By contrast, equity long/short and relative value funds typically have stable exposures to risk spreads, rates, equity betas, and other metrics. Owing to these concerns, it may be wise to allocate a modest amount to this strategy and to view these products as bond substitutes and not equity substitutes within a diversified portfolio. Investors with

Table 9.6 Global macro index equity betas and equity beta-adjusted excess returns*

Equity Betas (to S&P 500)

Period	U.S. Aggregate (Bonds)	HFRI Macro	HFRI Systematic Diversified	HFRI Macro (Asset Weighted)	HSFRI Active Trading	HFRI Commodity	HFRI Currency	HFRI: Discretionary Thematic	HFRI: Multi-Strategy
3-yr.	(0.04)	0.11	0.14	0.00	0.14	0.16	(0.10)	0.01	0.20
5-yr.	(0.03)	0.12	0.13	0.07	0.14	0.11	(0.05)	0.09	0.18
10-yr.	(0.01)	0.11	0.08	0.07	0.03	0.16	0.00	0.18	0.17
20-yr.	(0.02)	0.08	0.15	—	—	—	—	—	—
10-yr. ended 12/31/08	(0.02)	0.07	0.23	—	—	—	—	—	—

Equity Beta-Adjusted Excess Returns

Period	U.S. Aggregate (Bonds)	HFRI Macro	HFRI Systematic Diversified	HFRI Macro (Asset Weighted)	HSFRI Active Trading	HFRI Commodity	HFRI Currency	HFRI: Discretionary Thematic	HFRI: Multi-Strategy
3-yr.	1.4%	-2.1%	-4.0%	1.0%	-0.8%	-1.8%	2.4%	-0.8%	-1.4%
5-yr.	2.1%	-0.8%	-1.2%	1.2%	0.5%	-0.8%	1.7%	-1.4%	-0.6%
10-yr.	3.2%	-0.8%	-1.2%	2.0%	1.2%	-1.4%	0.5%	-1.0%	0.1%
20-yr.	2.7%	2.7%	3.4%	—	—	—	—	—	—
10-yr. ended 12/31/08	2.1%	5.8%	9.4%	—	—	—	—	—	—

Source: Authors' calculations and HFRI
*Periods ended 12/31/2018 unless otherwise specified

moderate cash-plus return targets may find this strategy more appropriate than investors with more aggressive return targets.

Relative Value

As previously mentioned, global macro strategies are structured to benefit from the movements of broad markets (such as stocks, currencies, or interest rates) and not the realization of valuation discrepancies between securities. By contrast, the relative value category of hedge funds is the exact opposite. HFR defines relative value strategies as "predicated on the realization of valuation discrepancies between securities."[lv] These strategies are often agnostic with respect to economic variables, such as the relative performance of stock and bonds, switches in economic regimes, or other macroeconomic considerations. Several relative value sub-strategies involve fixed income securities, including asset-backed, corporate, and sovereign. In all cases, analysts or portfolio managers attempt to harvest an incremental return between like issuers and securities. Long and short positions are often utilized to isolate specific sources of return while hedging the portfolio from adverse movements in credit spreads or interest rates.

Within the relative value category, the six subcategories we will briefly review here are *asset-backed, corporate, convertible arbitrage, volatility, yield alternatives,* and *multi-strategy*. Asset-backed relative value strategies focus on harvesting incremental returns between securities that are backed by loans, mortgages, receivables, student loans, or other sources of collateralization. Similarly, corporate relative value strategies source return from differences in corporate issues, often within the same issuer. Positions are often hedged such that a long corporate bond may be paired with a credit default swap, ensuring the combined position will not suffer an adverse movement in the event of a corporate default. In contrast, the convertible arbitrage relative value strategy focuses on harvesting a premium from pricing discrepancies between a corporate bond, a corporate bond that is convertible into equity, and the price of equity options. Volatility strategies trade volatility as though it were an asset class and attempt to purchase volatility (often via derivatives) that is *cheap* and sell volatility that is *rich*. This strategy benefits if purchased (or sold) implied volatility is less (or greater) than realized volatility. This strategy may utilize derivatives across a wide spectrum of asset classes including stocks, interest rates, currencies, and commodities. Yield alternatives strategies harvest incremental yield from securities in which returns contain exposure to assets including energy and real estate. Finally, multi-strategy relative value products derive returns from several of the formerly mentioned sources of premium. HFR defines a strategy as multi-strategy if the strategy is designed to maintain greater than 30% of exposure to two or more distinct strategies.

Who's Who in the Relative Value Category

Citadel LLC (formerly Citadel Investment Group), based in Chicago, Illinois, is relatively small in comparison to some of the other firms mentioned in this chapter, with around $30 billion in AUM as of early 2019.[lvi] However, we've included it here for several reasons. First, Citadel's flagship multi-strategy Wellington fund has reportedly delivered an impressive +19.1% annual net of fee return since its launch in 1990 through mid-2018.[lvii] Second, Citadel has expanded its capabilities and now runs separate segments including an asset management group and Citadel Securities, which is a market maker and high-frequency trading division that acts as the designated market maker for over 1,400 listed equities.[lviii] According to its website, Citadel Securities is now responsible for a whopping 21% of the U.S. equities volume across 8,000 listed securities, and trades over 16,000 securities.[lix] Finally, Citadel's founder Ken Griffin, in addition to being one of the America's wealthiest individuals with an estimated net worth of $11.7 billion,[lx] is well known among investors, politicians, and philanthropists.

Griffin first began investing in 1986 as a freshman at Harvard University trading convertible bonds. To secure real-time stock quotes, he subscribed to a service called Comstock that required the installation of a satellite dish; he convinced the building supervisor to allow him to install the dish, which at the time was prohibited because Harvard did not allow students to run businesses from their dormitories.[lxi] The next year Griffin started a fund to manage outside capital, which began with $265,000.[lxii] Griffin graduated from Harvard in 1989 and in 1990 started the Wellington Financial Group, which changed its name to Citadel in 1994. Assets reached $1 billion in 1998 and $30 billion by 2019.

Based in New York City, another (loosely categorized) relative value firm of similar size to Citadel is Millennium Management, which managed approximately $38 billion as of early 2019.[lxiii] Founded in 1989 by Israel "Izzy" Englander with $35 million, it has since grown into one of the world's largest multi-strategy hedge funds while Englander's net worth has grown to over $6 billion,[lxiv] according to Forbes. Since its inception, its flagship fund has generated an annualized return of around +14% through 2017, well ahead of the average hedge fund over that period.[lxv] While we're highlighting Millennium in the relative value section, Millennium's flagship fund is more akin to a multi-strategy fund. In fact, the portfolio is run by around 200 largely independent teams who received capital to manage and whose returns and capital aggregate to the larger fund. This structure is known as a *master feeder*. Individual strategies and their sleeves are highly variable and include relative value equity, merger arbitrage, fixed income relative value, and various commodity strategies. Reportedly one commonality between these strategies is they all remain highly liquid.[lxvi]

Another highly successful quantitatively driven firm based in New York City is Two Sigma. Like Renaissance Technologies, Two Sigma heavily utilizes quantitative models, machine learning, artificial intelligence, and the analysis of big data. Two Sigma was founded in 2001 by John Overdeck, David Siegel, and (now retired) Mark Pickard. Prior to founding Two Sigma, Siegel was the Chief Information Officer at D.E. Shaw and Chief Technology Officer at Tudor Investment Corporation. Siegel earned a PhD in computer science from MIT where he studied artificial intelligence.[lxvii] John Overdeck also worked at D.E. Shaw where he rose to the position of managing director prior to leaving and he then worked two years at Amazon where he codeveloped Amazon's personalization and targeted marketing features. Overdeck has an affinity for mathematics and earned a masters degree in statistics from Stanford University.[lxviii] Two Sigma has grown rapidly in the past 10 years, managing around $6 billion in 2011 and over $50 billion by 2017. Its two largest hedge funds, an equity fund and a global macro fund, are currently closed to outside investors.[lxix]

Relative Value Performance

While the performance generated by Citadel, Millennium, and Two Sigma have been out of reach for most investors, relative value hedge funds on average have generated respectable performance for the 10- and 20-year periods ending on 12/31/2018, as shown in Table 9.7. The 10-year annualized performance has been +6.9%, well ahead of U.S. bonds at +3.5%, but behind U.S. equities at +13.1%. The 10-year Sharpe ratios for these products have been in excess of 1.0 and generally ahead of both U.S. bonds and equities. Additionally, unlike the global macro category, the average performance of relative value funds has been in-line or better in the 10 years following the GFC than the 10 years prior.

Perhaps one source of strong relative value performance over the past 10 years has been its positive correlation with equities. The relative value index has a 0.63 correlation with equities for the 10-year period ending on 12/31/18 (see Appendix Table 9.12). Separately, the consistency of performance can also be observed in the equity beta-adjusted returns (our simple estimate of alpha), as shown in Table 9.8. There may be two ramifications of this performance of which investors should be cognizant. It is possible that relative value opportunities are structural and more likely to continue to be a source of alpha in the foreseeable future. It also could be possible that the relative strength of the relative value hedge fund category (no pun intended) and its recent outperformance, particularly from an excess return perspective, will draw a disproportionate amount of flows in the coming years, thereby eliminating much of the return potential of this category. Indeed, it is worth noting that the three- and five-year performance figures are not as strong as the 10-year figures.

Table 9.7 Relative value index and sub-index annual returns and Sharpe ratios*

Annualized Returns

Period	Risk Free	S&P 500	U.S. Aggregate (Bonds)	HFRI Relative Value	HFRI Yield Alternatives	HFRI FI Convert Arb.	HFRI FI-Asset Backed	HFRI FI-Corporates	HFRI RV Multi-Strategy	HFRI RV Volatility	HFRI Rel. Val. (Asset Weighted)
1-yr.	1.9%	-4.4%	0.0%	-0.2%	-3.9%	-3.5%	2.9%	-0.8%	-0.1%	-2.0%	0.5%
3-yr.	1.0%	9.3%	2.1%	4.1%	4.0%	3.4%	5.2%	5.7%	3.4%	2.4%	3.6%
5-yr.	0.6%	8.5%	2.5%	3.2%	0.5%	2.7%	5.3%	3.2%	2.8%	3.3%	3.3%
10-yr.	0.4%	13.1%	3.5%	6.9%	7.1%	8.7%	9.5%	7.3%	6.3%	3.7%	7.5%
20-yr.	1.9%	5.6%	4.5%	6.6%	6.0%	6.0%	8.3%	5.2%	5.3%	–	–
10-yr. ended 12/31/08	3.4%	-1.4%	5.6%	6.3%	5.0%	3.3%	7.1%	3.2%	4.3%	–	–

Sharpe Ratios

Period	Risk Free	S&P 500	U.S. Aggregate (Bonds)	HFRI Relative Value	HFRI Yield Alternatives	HFRI FI Convert Arb.	HFRI FI-Asset Backed	HFRI FI-Corporates	HFRI RV Multi-Strategy	HFRI RV Volatility	HFRI Rel. Val. (Asset Weighted)
1-yr.	–	(0.43)	(0.64)	(0.74)	(0.55)	(1.60)	0.46	(1.01)	(0.93)	(0.99)	(0.51)
3-yr.	–	0.76	0.37	1.12	0.29	0.73	1.82	1.40	1.08	0.47	1.07
5-yr.	–	0.72	0.68	0.95	(0.02)	0.68	2.20	0.79	1.00	0.77	1.21
10-yr.	–	0.94	1.09	1.88	0.77	1.37	3.27	1.60	1.75	0.82	2.23
20-yr.	–	0.26	0.79	1.18	0.51	0.59	1.85	0.04	0.81	–	–
10-yr. ended 12/31/08	–	(0.32)	0.58	0.65	0.21	(0.02)	0.96	(0.00)	0.18	–	–

Source: Authors' calculations and HFRI
*Periods ended 12/31/2018 unless otherwise specified

Table 9.8 Relative value index equity betas and equity beta-adjusted excess returns*

Period	U.S. Aggregate (Bonds)	HFRI Relative Value	HFRI Yield Alternatives	HFRI FI Convert Arb.	HFRI FI-Asset Backed	HFRI FI-Corporates	HFRI RV Multi-Strategy	HFRI RV Volatility	HFRI Rel. Val. (Asset Weighted)
				Equity Betas (to S&P 500)					
3-yr.	(0.04)	0.20	0.59	0.22	0.11	0.20	0.15	0.20	0.14
5-yr.	(0.03)	0.18	0.58	0.19	0.08	0.19	0.14	0.20	0.12
10-yr.	(0.01)	0.16	0.38	0.24	0.06	0.20	0.15	0.09	0.12
20-yr.	(0.02)	0.17	0.31	0.24	0.07	(0.34)	0.17	–	–
10-yr. ended 12/31/08	(0.02)	0.17	0.26	0.23	0.06	(0.74)	0.18	–	–
				Equity Beta-Adjusted Excess Returns					
3-yr.	1.4%	1.5%	–1.9%	0.6%	3.3%	3.0%	1.1%	–0.3%	1.4%
5-yr.	2.1%	1.1%	–4.7%	0.6%	4.0%	1.1%	1.1%	1.1%	1.8%
10-yr.	3.2%	4.4%	1.8%	5.2%	8.3%	4.4%	4.1%	2.2%	5.6%
20-yr.	2.7%	4.1%	3.0%	3.2%	6.1%	4.6%	2.8%	–	–
10-yr. ended 12/31/08	2.1%	3.7%	2.8%	1.0%	4.0%	–3.8%	1.7%	–	–

Source: Authors' calculations and HFRI
*10-year period ended 12/31/2018. Monthly returns used.

Relative Value Pros and Cons

In general, relative value strategies have offered investors impressive returns as evidenced by Sharpe ratios greater than 1.0 over the last 10- and 20-year periods. For this reason, an investor selecting an alternatives manager would be wise to at least consider managers that operate within this strategy. Additionally, the strategy group has relatively stable risk metrics, meaning an investor should be able to model these portfolios and ensure that their portfolios' aggregate risk is well managed. Of concern is that this strategy's strong performance may attract outsized flows that will limit the potential for future returns if the demand for idiosyncratic spread rises while its supply remains unchanged. Additionally, the spreads that these strategies target will likely widen (and the strategies underperform) in the event that the equity market performs poorly. This would result in the strategies having increased beta to very negative market events; in other words, the beta becomes elevated at the worst possible time for an investor. Despite this, these strategies in general do offer the potential for modest diversification and strong risk-adjusted performance, but the downside protection potential should be appropriately discounted.

FUTURE OF HEDGE FUNDS

In 2005, Warren Buffett included in his annual letter to Berkshire Hathaway investors an allegory titled "How to Minimize Investment Returns" where he lamented the several layers of fees that many investors end up paying for their investment exposure.[lxx] Buffett then publicly wagered $500,000 that no investment professional could select five hedge funds and collectively outperform the Vanguard S&P 500 index fund. As Buffett summed it up in his 2016 letter, "In Berkshire's 2005 annual report, I argued that active investment management by professionals—in aggregate—would over a period of years underperform the returns achieved by rank amateurs who simply sat still. I explained that the massive fees levied by a variety of 'helpers' would leave their clients—again in aggregate—worse off than if the amateurs simply invested in an unmanaged low-cost index fund."

In December 2007, Buffett found his counterpart in Ted Seides of Protégé Partners—each put up $500,000 for a $1 million prize to the winner's charity. The returns of the five unnamed funds, along with the S&P 500 index fund, can be found in the 2016 Berkshire Hathaway letter. The results? As Buffett explained, "The compounded annual increase to date for the index fund is +7.1%, which is a return that could easily prove typical for the stock market over time . . . In it, the five funds-of-funds delivered, through 2016, an average of only +2.2%, compounded annually. That means $1 million invested in those funds would have gained $220,000. The index fund would meanwhile have gained $854,000." Buffett ended his 2016 commentary regarding the bet with the comment, "The bottom line: When trillions of dollars are managed by Wall Streeters charging high fees, it will usually be the managers who reap outsized profits, not the clients. Both large and small investors should stick with low-cost index funds."[lxxi]

Yet, ironically, more than 50 years prior in 1962, Warren Buffett himself rolled up several investment partnerships totaling $7.2 million in capital into the Buffet Partnership, Ltd. I say *ironically*, because the investment partnership was not registered under the Investment Act of 1940, meaning that today it would fall under the classification of a hedge fund. The funds that Buffet managed even included several features that characterize hedge funds today, including a performance fee of 25% and a hurdle for that performance fee of 4% (although he did not charge a management fee, which is a staple cost of nearly every hedge fund today); limited redemptions by investors from the partnership, who could only redeem annually; and heavy position level concentration. Buffett's fund could even be thought of as one of the first activist hedge funds, given the involvement Buffett would take with the management of the companies in which he invested. In 1969, Buffett closed his investment partnership after extraordinary success in order to focus his career on the firm he radically transformed and still manages today, which has likewise been extraordinarily successful—Berkshire Hathaway.[lxxii]

Yet how do we reconcile Buffett's contempt for hedge funds today with the fact that he, in fact, was a very successful hedge fund manager himself at one time? We speculate that Buffett would argue that he did not directly *hedge* any of his performance, did not short, did not use leverage, and did not set himself out as more than an extremely well-studied stock picker. Yet his fund fits what would be called a hedge fund today. Once again, we assert that the term *hedge fund* literally refers to an unregistered investment vehicle, regardless of whether the market exposure is hedged. Because the hedge fund structure allows managers unfettered access to a variety of portfolio management tools, this legal vehicle can be extremely helpful for managers who have the skill to generate alpha—returns in excess of market exposure. For example, Buffett likely would not have been able to take similar positions in his partnership if he faced the prospect of daily redemptions.

Alphas, Betas, and the Wisconsin/New Mexico Model

The fact remains that the hedge fund vehicle is a much better vehicle to generate alpha in certain circumstances. Specifically, the flexibility offered in terms of asset classes, leverage, and shorting, when used appropriately, can create a stream of alpha that is not replicable in the mutual fund format. The issue of course is that not all hedge fund managers have the ability to generate strong returns. We posit that the feature of hedge fund strategies that carry varying levels of market exposure are unsustainable because they do not allow a proper evaluation of performance by most investors. Nevertheless, in the long run, the investment industry will always have a place for alpha, and the hedge fund structure provides skilled managers with the flexibility needed to amplify that source of alpha. We expect that going forward, hedge fund investors, to a greater degree than exists today, will disaggregate the returns of hedge fund managers between the betas and the alphas. This in turn will allow for a more direct comparison to other investments. Specifically, if a hedge fund is running a long equity exposure, its returns should be net of its equity exposure; then, this residual net of fees can be properly evaluated. Managers who fail to deliver alpha that is both net of fees and its underlying beta exposures will fade from existence.

Furthermore, we anticipate that investors will no longer classify hedge funds as an asset class to which an efficiently constructed portfolio should allocate capital. Rather, as stated previously, investors will become increasingly comfortable viewing hedge funds as vehicles rather than asset classes. Whereas the other asset classes that are included in the Markowitz framework are mutually distinct and represent components of the market portfolio, a *hedge fund asset class* invests in the other asset classes and the exposures overlap the other exposures within the framework. Additionally, perhaps one day, the term *hedge fund* will finally be replaced with a non-misleading term to describe it, such as *flex fund*, or as suggested earlier in the chapter, simply *unregistered fund*.

One investor who is at the forefront of the disentangling of hedge fund alpha from beta philosophy is the CIO of New Mexico's pension plan, Dominic Garcia. Garcia began his career in the investment department of the Public Employees Retirement Association of New Mexico (New Mexico PERA) before heading north to work at the State of Wisconsin Investment Board (SWIB). SWIB is arguably the most advanced and well-run pension plan in the United States, and a 2018 Pew Research report noted that Wisconsin's pension plan was the best funded in the country.[lxxiii] With respect to hedge funds, in a 2016 interview with *Institutional Investor*, SWIB CIO David Villa explained, "We define true value added as the excess return after subtracting the embedded market returns and adjusting for leverage."[lxxiv] In 2017, Garcia was tapped by the New Mexico PERA to come home to the state. Since that time, he began the process of molding the New Mexico plan into the Wisconsin model by re-categorizing PERA's allocation into a portfolio divided between alpha and beta.[lxxv] If portfolios to which PERA is allocating do not carry a full exposure to the benchmark, then the exposure will be adjusted to get it there. An example of the framework at work is the 2.9% excess return requirement for illiquid, private portfolios over global high-yield bonds to compensate for the excess risk they take by investing in less liquid positions.[lxxvi] As we round our vision for the future utilizing this framework, one could easily imagine a Warren Buffett-style fund being given an S&P 500 benchmark with an excess return requirement to compensate for the lower liquidity profile. Garcia sums up his views succinctly: "I think hedge funds are probably the most efficient active managers—period. But I think what's important for investors is that you treat them as alpha . . . you can't put them into your policy portfolio. They're not a total return strategy."[lxxvii]

SUMMARY AND INVESTMENT IMPLICATIONS

Over a decade ago, David Einhorn of Greenlight Capital surprised a room of eager Chicago Booth students when he explained that his investment process was buying good companies that are cheap and selling bad companies that are rich. That's it. There was no black box or super computer. While we wouldn't go so far as to say hedge funds should not be included in a well-diversified institutional portfolio, we do want our readers to appreciate that hedge funds, their managers, styles, and approaches to portfolio construction, are not unique. Rather, hedge funds invest in asset classes accessible to investors utilizing mutual funds; the primary differences between hedge and mutual funds are the legal structure, the use of leverage, performance fees, the ability to short, and volatility. Below is a summary of the chapter as well as some investment implications for those considering making an investment with one or more hedge funds.

Summary

A hedge fund is a commingled vehicle that is not registered with the SEC and that has the ability to invest in all asset types, restrict client redemptions, invest in illiquid assets, both purchase and short securities, charge performance fees, and utilize leverage. Despite their name, hedge funds are often not *hedged*, in that they do have exposure to equity, bond, or commodity markets. The first modern *hedge fund* was launched in 1949 but remained a bit of an oddity; except for a brief period of interest in hedge funds in the late 1960s and early 1970s, investor interest remained limited. Following strong performance in the 1990s, however, capital surged from around $100 billion to nearly $2.5 trillion in 2008; assets today are around $3 trillion. Hedge funds are restricted investments that are open only to qualified investors, including high net worth individuals and institutional investors such as foundations, endowments, pension plans, and family offices.

Hedge funds operate in a variety of asset classes and deploy several different strategies. The four categories we briefly covered are equity hedge, event-driven, macro, and relative value. Equity hedge products attempt to outperform a given equity index and regularly utilize leverage as well as both long and short positions. Event-driven managers invest in securities after developing an investment thesis that includes an event or catalyst that will unlock value and generate an outsized return. Global macro funds seek to benefit from global trends, such as the outperformance of one region versus another, changes in currency valuations, or convergence or divergence of interest rates. Relative value products invest in (usually) paired securities, which should lead to positive returns once the value of the two securities converges. Despite our sincerest attempt to classify managers into each of these four buckets, most managers have products that exist in several buckets, while many of those products have elements of several categories.

The hedge fund industry experienced rapid growth from the late 1990s through 2007, which roughly corresponded to the period when hedge funds, on average, outperformed both equities and fixed income instruments. Since that period, hedge fund returns have been lackluster, with most fund strategies significantly underperforming equities while global macro strategies, once the darling of the hedge fund universe, underperformed both stocks and bonds for the 10-year period ending in 2018 (see Figures 9.3 and 9.4 in the Appendix at the end of this chapter).

This decline in performance begs the question: has the increase in hedge fund assets directly caused the decline in hedge fund performance? One theory that would support this causality would be if we assumed that the positive alpha that is available in the market is finite and zero-sum. As markets have moved into the 21st century and have become more transparent and its participants more sophisticated, the ability to profit from another market participant's misguided bets could be declining. Thus, we have an increasing pool of capital that is chasing what is, at best, a finite pool of alpha and is more likely a declining pool of alpha. Another theory that could support the causality would be if we assumed that what many hedge funds hold out as alpha are returns derived from esoteric betas, of which there is also a finite (and possibly decreasing) supply. When the hedge fund industry was a mere $110 billion in 1997, there was little demand for these esoteric betas, which could lead to outsized returns for the demand side (i.e., investors). Regardless of the cause, as the industry has grown, the ability of hedge funds to generate outsized returns appears to have significantly diminished.

We believe that our presentation of the data behind the four main hedge fund strategies as stand-alone asset classes shows that investing in hedge funds as an asset class leaves much to be desired since their return generation and portfolio diversifying quality have subsided. Furthermore, some institutions are beginning to eschew the industry due to high fees and lackluster returns, while others are beginning to focus on stripping out manager betas from performance and more closely measuring performance net of fees and (all) betas to isolate *pure* alpha streams that can be layered onto more basic market exposures, known in the industry as *portable alpha*. We anticipate that these trends will continue.

Investment Implications

We believe hedge funds are not an asset class, but a vehicle through which managers gain exposure to other asset classes. As such, they should be viewed as complements to an allocation to stocks and bonds, as opposed to a substitute to such an allocation. Additionally, while this industry will continue to be large and relevant in the future, the heyday of hedge funds generating equity-like returns with bond-like volatility is likely behind us since it appears that the low-lying fruit (alpha) has been sourced. Thus, going forward, any allocation to these products should be done with the expectation that they will generate equity-lite returns.

We will leave our readers with some final closing thoughts on each of the four main hedge fund categories:

- *Equity hedge*: these products often maintain a positive exposure to the equity markets. Thus, their Sharpe ratios have generally lagged that of the S&P 500 and Barclays Aggregate for the 10-year period ending in 2018—and they will likely continue to do so. Additionally, these products have high correlations to equity markets; thus, they only add a modest diversification benefit. For these reasons, investors must believe their managers truly possess a secret sauce before allocating to products in this sector.
- *Event-driven*: these products have generated the impressive Sharpe ratios for the 10-year period ending in 2018, but exhibit positive correlation to the S&P 500. While future flows into these strategies may inhibit their ability to continue to generate outsized returns, they are likely well-positioned to earn strong risk-adjusted returns into the future. The one

caveat is that these products often invest in highly illiquid instruments and may experience increased correlation with the equity markets during corrections; thus, they offer less downside protection than other strategies.

- *Macro*: macro funds, once the darling of the hedge fund industry, have generated poor performance for the 10-year period ending in 2018. There are a select number of funds that continue to be successful in this endeavor; however, most funds have underperformed lower risk, lower fee fixed income instruments. Thus, buyer beware of macro strategies that claim to be able to consistently forecast and position portfolios ahead of major economic developments.

- *Relative value*: these strategies have generated the most impressive Sharpe ratios for the 10-year period ending in 2018. Additionally, these strategies have the second lowest correlation to equities (behind macro), meaning their inclusion does add modest diversification benefits. These products also have relatively stable risk metrics enabling clients to aggregate and manage their portfolio risk. Of concern, once everybody becomes aware of an asset class that offers outsized risk-adjusted returns, investor flows generally lead to the elimination of many investment opportunities. Thus, we would recommend investors in this space carefully monitor flows into it; should it become crowded, it is likely that this subcategory will lose its luster. These strategies also are exposed to increased correlations with the market during downturns in the market.

CHAPTER APPENDIX

Appendix Table 9.9 Equity hedge index and sub-index correlations*

Index	S&P 500	U.S. Aggregate (Bonds)	HFRI Equity Hedge	HFRI Equity Market Neutral	HFRI Quantitative Directional	HFRI Sector-Tech/Healthcare	HFRI Fundamental Growth	HFRI Fundamental Value	HFRI Multi-Strategy	HFRI Equity Hedge (Asset Weighted)
S&P 500	1.00									
U.S. Aggregate (Bonds)	(0.05)	1.00								
HFRI Equity Hedge	0.88	(0.10)	1.00							
HFRI Equity Market Neutral	0.60	(0.10)	0.68	1.00						
HFRI Quantitative Directional	0.93	(0.05)	0.91	0.71	1.00					
HFRI Sector - Tech/Healthcare	0.73	(0.14)	0.83	0.49	0.74	1.00				
HFRI Fundamental Growth	0.82	(0.03)	0.98	0.62	0.88	0.76	1.00			
HFRI Fundamental Value	0.90	(0.14)	0.99	0.66	0.90	0.81	0.94	1.00		
HFRI Multi-Strategy	0.88	(0.13)	0.97	0.67	0.89	0.81	0.92	0.96	1.00	
HFRI Equity Hedge (Asset Weighted)	0.84	(0.13)	0.97	0.70	0.89	0.85	0.94	0.96	0.95	1.00

Source: Authors' calculations and HFRI
*10-year period ended 12/31/2018. Monthly returns used.

Appendix Table 9.10 Event-driven index and sub-index correlations*

Index	S&P 500	U.S. Aggregate (Bonds)	HFRI Event-Driven	HFRI Distressed/Restructuring	HFRI Merger Arbitrage	HFRI Activist	HFRI Credit Arbitrage	HFRI Multi-Strategy	HFRI Special Situations	HFRI Event-Driven (Asset Weighted)
S&P 500 Return	1.00									
BCAG	(0.05)	1.00								
HFRI Event-Driven	0.78	(0.12)	1.00							
HFRI Distressed/Restructuring	0.65	(0.10)	0.95	1.00						
HFRI Merger Arbitrage	0.61	(0.04)	0.69	0.56	1.00					
HFRI Activist	0.76	(0.13)	0.82	0.69	0.65	1.00				
HFRI Credit Arbitrage	0.54	0.02	0.85	0.88	0.44	0.62	1.00			
HFRI Multi-Strategy	0.71	(0.06)	0.90	0.84	0.62	0.75	0.78	1.00		
HFRI Special Situations	0.78	(0.14)	0.98	0.91	0.67	0.79	0.81	0.85	1.00	
HFRI Event-Driven (Asset Weighted)	0.71	(0.15)	0.94	0.90	0.67	0.75	0.80	0.86	0.91	1.00

Source: Authors' calculations and HFRI
*10-year period ended 12/31/2018. Monthly returns used.

Appendix Table 9.11   Global macro index and sub-index correlations*

Index	S&P 500	U.S. Aggregate (Bonds)	HFRI Macro	HFRI Systematic Diversified	HFRI Macro (Asset Weighted)	HFRI Active Trading	HFRI Commodity	HFRI Currency	HFRI Discretionary Thematic	HFRI Multi-Strategy
S&P 500	1.00									
U.S. Aggregate (Bonds)	(0.05)	1.00								
HFRI Macro	0.35	0.30	1.00							
HFRI Systematic Diversified	0.16	0.37	0.94	1.00						
HFRI Macro (Asset Weighted)	0.21	0.32	0.87	0.84	1.00					
HFRI Active Trading	0.11	0.19	0.60	0.58	0.48	1.00				
HFRI Commodity	0.44	0.11	0.77	0.59	0.56	0.37	1.00			
HFRI Currency	0.02	0.15	0.46	0.39	0.52	0.31	0.27	1.00		
HFRI Discretionary Thematic	0.59	(0.00)	0.61	0.34	0.56	0.24	0.62	0.37	1.00	
HFRI Multi-Strategy	0.57	0.13	0.84	0.68	0.70	0.53	0.67	0.33	0.70	1.00

Source: Authors' calculations and HFRI
*10-year period ended 12/31/2018. Monthly returns used.

Appendix Table 9.12 Relative value index and sub-index correlations*

Index	S&P 500 Return	BCAG	HFRI Relative Value	HFRI Yield Alternatives	HFRI FI Convert Arb.	HFRI FI-Asset Backed	HFRI FI-Corporates	HFRI RV Multi-Strategy	HFRI RV Volatility	HFRI Rel. Val. (Asset Weighted)
S&P 500	1.00									
U.S. Aggregate (Bonds)	(0.05)	1.00								
HFRI Relative Value	0.63	0.03	1.00							
HFRI Yield Alternatives	0.60	(0.04)	0.78	1.00						
HFRI FI Convert Arb.	0.54	(0.01)	0.89	0.57	1.00					
HFRI FI-Asset Backed	0.31	0.03	0.77	0.47	0.65	1.00				
HFRI FI-Corporates	0.63	0.11	0.95	0.69	0.84	0.72	1.00			
HFRI RV Multi-Strategy	0.59	0.02	0.95	0.67	0.87	0.71	0.88	1.00		
HFRI RV Volatility	0.29	(0.01)	0.47	0.34	0.30	0.26	0.38	0.33	1.00	
HFRI Rel. Val. (Asset Weighted)	0.50	0.02	0.93	0.63	0.88	0.83	0.88	0.92	0.35	1.00

Source: Authors' calculations and HFRI
*10-year period ended 12/31/2018. Monthly returns used.

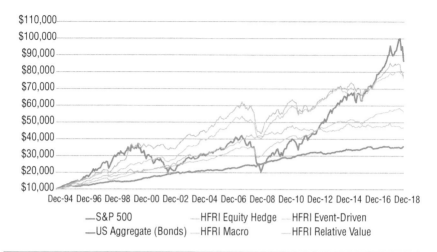

Appendix Figure 9.3 Growth of $10,000 by strategy—December 1994 to December 2018. *Source:* Authors' calculations and HFRI

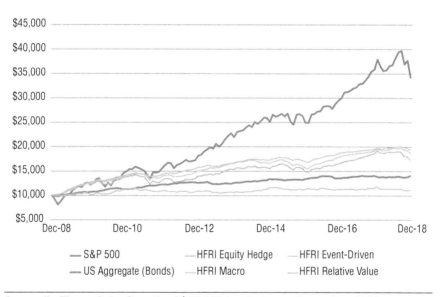

Appendix Figure 9.4 Growth of $10,000 by strategy—December 2008 to December 2018. *Source:* Authors' calculations and HFRI

CITATIONS

i. Zuckerman, Gregory. (July 4, 2018). " 'This Is Unbelievable': A Hedge Fund Star Dims, and Investors Flee."

ii. Sohn, Ira W. (May 21, 2008). Investment Research Conference. Einhorn, David. Greenlight Capital. "Accounting Ingenuity."

iii. Lowenstein, R. and Long-Term Capital Management (Firm). (2000). *When Genius Failed: The Rise and Fall of Long-Term Capital Management*. New York, NY: Random House. p. 39.

iv. ———. (2000). *When Genius Failed: The Rise and Fall of Long-Term Capital Management*. New York, NY: Random House. p. 207.

v. Hedge Funds: Investment and Portfolio Strategies for the Institutional Investor. (1995). Jess Ledermann and Robert A. Klein (eds.) Irwin Publishing Company. Chapter 1: Written by Ted Caldwell, President, Lookout Mountain Capital, Inc. pp. 6–7.

vi. ———. (1995). Jess Ledermann and Robert A. Klein (eds.) Irwin Publishing Company. Chapter 1: Written by Ted Caldwell, President, Lookout Mountain Capital, Inc. pp. 7–8.

vii. Hedge Funds: Investment and Portfolio Strategies for the Institutional Investor. (1995). Jess Ledermann & Robert A. Klein (Eds.) Irwin Publishing Company. Chapter 1: Written by Ted Caldwell, President, Lookout Mountain Capital, Inc. p. 9.

viii. Mallaby, Sebastian. (2010). *More Money than God: Hedge Funds and the Making of a New Elite*. Penguin Books; Reprint edition (May 31, 2011). p. 112.

ix. Lowenstein, R. and Long-Term Capital Management (Firm). (2000). *When Genius Failed: The Rise and Fall of Long-Term Capital Management*. New York, NY: Random House. p. 116.

x. ———. (2000). *When Genius Failed: The Rise and Fall of Long-Term Capital Management*. New York, NY: Random House. p. 134–46.

xi. "Hedge Funds, Leverage, and the Lessons of Long-Term Capital Management." (April 1999). Report of The President's Working Group on Financial Markets. Department of the U.S. Treasury. pp. 12–14.

xii. https://www.statista.com/statistics/271771/assets-of-the-hedge-funds-worldwide/.

xiii. CalPERS enters hedge funds. (August 31, 1999). https://money.cnn.com/1999/08/31/markets/calpers/.

xiv. Hartley, Jon. (September 22, 2014). "Why CalPERS Is Exiting the Hedge Fund Space." www.forbes.com.

xv. https://www.hedgefundresearch.com/about.

   xvi. Burton, Katherine. (November 22, 2016). "Inside the Medallion Fund, a $74 billion money-making machine like no other." https://www.afr.com/.

   xvii. Rubin, Richard and Margaret Collins. (June 16, 2015). "How an Exclusive Hedge Fund Turbocharged Its Retirement Plan." www.bloomberg.com.

  xviii. Taub, Stephen. (May 29, 2018). "The Rich List." *Institutional Investor*.

   xix. Kroll, Luisa and Kerry A. Dolan. "The 2018 Forbes 400." https://www.forbes.com/forbes-400/#e5ed907e2ffb.

   xx. Burton, Katherine. (November 22, 2016). "Inside the Medallion Fund, a $74 billion money-making machine like no other." https://www.afr.com/.

   xxi. ———. (November 20, 2016). "Inside a Moneymaking Machine Like No Other." www.bloomberg.com.

   xxii. ———. (November 22, 2016). "Inside the Medallion Fund, a $74 billion money-making machine like no other." https://www.afr.com/.

  xxiii. Weatherall, James Owen. (2013). *The Physics of Wall Street: A Brief History of Predicting the Unpredictable*. Houghton Mifflin Harcourt. New York, NY. p. xii.

  xxiv. Interview. (Winter 2014). Published in Graham & Doddsville. "An investment newsletter from the students of Columbia Business School." p. 22.

   xxv. Parmar, Hema. (October 12, 2018). Maverick's Short Bets Misfire, Eating into Main Fund Gains. *Bloomberg*.

  xxvi. Williamson, Christine. (June 11, 2007). "A calm exterior: Face to Face with Lee Ainslie." *Pensions & Investments*.

 xxvii. Dobbs, Richard and Timothy Koller. (April 2006). "Inside a hedge fund: An interview with the managing partner of Maverick Capital." www.mckinsey.com/.

xxviii. Interview. (Winter 2014). Published in Graham & Doddsville. "An investment newsletter from the students of Columbia Business School." p. 22–24.

  xxix. Zuckerman, Gregory. (January 15, 2008). "Trader Made Billions on Subprime." *The Wall Street Journal*.

   xxx. Ibid.

  xxxi. ———. (March 31, 2009). "Profiting from the Crash." *The Wall Street Journal*.

 xxxii. Parmar, Hema, Katherine Burton, and Katia Porzecanski. (March 21, 2018). "John Paulson Returns Money from Gold, Special Situations Funds." *Bloomberg*.

xxxiii. Och-Ziff Capital Management Group LLC Reports 2011. Fourth Quarter and Full Year Results.

xxxiv. https://www.ozm.com/about-oz/leadership/daniel-och.

xxxv. Oz Management Reports Third Quarter of 2018 Results. Exhibit 6, item 2.

xxxvi. Jones, Sam. (November 1, 2007). Och IPO nets Daniel a cool billion. ftalphaville.ft.com.

xxxvii. FORM 10-K. For the Fiscal Year Ended December 31, 2008. Och-Ziff Capital Management Group LLC. p. 54.

xxxviii. Och-Ziff Capital Management Group LLC Reports 2016 Fourth Quarter and Full Year Results. Exhibit 6.

xxxix. Stevenson, Alexandra. (September 29, 2016). Och-Ziff to Pay Over $400 Million in Bribery Settlement. *New York Times*.

xl. Copeland, Rob. (February 15, 2017). "Record $13 Billion Pulled from Biggest Public U.S. Hedge Fund Och-Ziff." *Wall Street Journal*.

xli. https://www.bloomberg.com/news/articles/2019-08-12/goodbye -och-ziff-hello-sculptor-hedge-fund-tries-on-new-name.

xlii. HFRX Hedge Fund Indices. (2019). Defined Formulaic Methodology. www.hfrx.com. p. 19.

xliii. The Hedge Fund 100. Institutional Investor (2018). https://www .institutionalinvestor.com/research/.

xliv. Taub, Stephen. (January 15, 2019). "Here's What Ray Dalio Made in Bridgewater's Impressive 2018." *Institutional Investor*.

xlv. Picker, Leslie. (January 6, 2019). "The world's largest hedge fund posted a 15% gain last year after calling global economic slowdown." www.cnbc.com.

xlvi. Taub, Stephen. (January 15, 2019). "Here's What Ray Dalio Made in Bridgewater's Impressive 2018." *Institutional Investor*.

xlvii. "The All Weather Story." Bridgewater. https://www.bridgewater.com/ resources/all-weather-story.pdf.

xlviii. Dalio, Ray. (2017). *Principles: Life and Work*. New York, NY: Simon & Schuster. Print.

xlix. Stevenson, Alexandra and Matthew Goldstein. (September 8, 2017). "Bridgewater's Ray Dalio Spreads His Gospel of 'Radical Transparency.'" *The New York Times*.

l. Lebowitz, Shana. (March 2, 2018). "The world's largest hedge fund told an employee he was a bad manager in front of 200 people—and he found it 'energizing.'" www.businessinsider.com.

li. Schaefer, Steve. (July 7, 2015). "Forbes Flashback: How George Soros Broke the British Pound and Why Hedge Funds Probably Can't Crack the Euro." www.forbes.com.

lii. Williamson, Christine. (January 23, 2018). "Hedge fund investment gains rise nearly 50% in 2017 to $181 billion." *Pensions & Investments*.

liii. Taub, Stephen. (January 23, 2018). "The Top-Earning Hedge Fund Firms of All Time." *Institutional Investor*.

liv. Burton, Katherine. (July 26, 2011). "Soros Returns Client Money to End Four-Decade Hedge-Fund Career." *Bloomberg*.

lv. HFRX Hedge Fund Indices. (2019). "Defined Formulaic Methodology." www.hfrx.com. p. 26.

lvi. Parmar, Hema and Melissa Karsh. (January 8, 2019). Citadel Hedge Fund Gains 9% in Strong Multi-Strategy Year. www.Bloomberg.com.

lvii. Flood, Chris. (August 12, 2018). Citadel converts $10,000 investment in 1990 into $1.3m. www.ft.com.

lviii. Chaparro, Frank. (July 21, 2018). "Citadel Securities, a massive Wall Street trader, has made an unusual bet on humans, and it could help the firm tap into an $800 billion market." www.businessinsider.com.

lix. https://www.citadelsecurities.com/products/equities-and-options/. Retrieved 2/17/2019.

lx. https://www.forbes.com/profile/ken-griffin/#6e0939ca5079. Retrieved 2/17/2019.

lxi. https://www.youtube.com/watch?v=NftzVC4JthM.

lxii. https://www.bloomberg.com/billionaires/profiles/kenneth-c-griffin/.

lxiii. https://www.mlp.com/home/. Retrieved 2/17/2019.

lxiv. https://www.forbes.com/profile/israel-englander/#69c0f7161462. Retrieved 2/17/2019.

lxv. Kishan, Saijel. (January 24, 2017). "After Bond Chief's Exit, Millennium's Englander on His Own." www.Bloomberg.com.

lxvi. Butcher, Sarah. (January 22, 2019). "Inside Millennium Management: The portfolio managers' hedge fund." news.efinancialcareers.com.

lxvii. Bloomberg profile: https://www.bloomberg.com/research/stocks/private/person.asp?personId=12207489&privcapId=127126990.

lxviii. https://www.twosigma.com/about/.

lxix. Wigglesworth, Robin. (October 23, 2017). "Two Sigma rapidly rises to top of quant hedge fund world." *Financial Times*.

lxx. Berkshire Hathaway Letter to Shareholder. Fiscal year 2005. pp. 18–19.

lxxi. ———. Fiscal year 2016. pp. 22, 24.

lxxii. Lowenstein, Roger. (April 29, 2008). *Buffett: The Making of an American Capitalist*. Random House Trade Paperbacks; Reprint edition. pp. 62–114.

lxxiii. The State Pension Funding Gap: 2016. (April 12, 2018). www.pewtrusts.org.

lxxiv. Denmark, Frances. (April 19, 2016). "Wisconsin CIO David Villa Brings Asset Management In-House." www.institutionalinvestor .com.

lxxv. Rundell, Sarah. (August 9, 2018). "N. Mexico PERA adopts Wisconsin model." www.top1000funds.com.

lxxvi. Kramer, Leslie. (October 3, 2018). "New Mexico Funds Fashion Private Debt Benchmarks that Fit." http://institutional-allocator.com/.

lxxvii. New Mexico PERA CIO Expanding Alpha, Beta Strategies at Plan Level. (May 3, 2018). Chief Investment Officer. Downloaded from NMPERA.org on 3/16/2019.

Part III

Recent Advances in Finance and Investing

10

FACTOR INVESTING
AND SMART BETA

David E. Linton, CFA
Director, Portfolio Construction and Manager Research
Pacific Life Fund Advisors LLC

Daniel Villalon, CFA
Managing Director, Portfolio Solutions Group
AQR

"What do you think about this?" the subject of the e-mail read that was sent to me by my manager. In the body of the e-mail was a link to an *Institutional Investor* article entitled "Smart Beta Is Making This Strategist Sick." Just months earlier I had created and presented an internal educational piece; the topics were *smart beta* and *factor investing*. The conclusion of the presentation was that factor investing has utility and smart beta portfolios have a place in an institutional investor's portfolio. My team and I questioned whether smart beta is an investing panacea; but, the lower-fee nature of the product and the growing library of academic research that indicates factor investing is a highly efficient form of portfolio construction suggest that we should continue to evaluate smart beta managers as searches arise.

The article that was forwarded to me was critical of smart beta and included numerous comical but well-reasoned arguments; the author stated that smart beta has become the E. coli of institutional investing.[i] I couldn't argue with several of the author's points: there are now over 300 published factors, 4,200 smart beta indexes, and a growing belief that excess returns may be earned by capturing risk premia inherent to uncorrelated factors. But, with so many factors and indexes, how could they all deliver on the goal of superior risk-adjusted performance? Many of these factors offset one another, others are highly correlated. Throw every factor into a portfolio and you end up with the market portfolio; but a market portfolio can't outperform the market, so what's wrong with this picture? Before we tackle these critiques, let's start at the beginning: what is factor investing?

FACTOR INVESTING

What exactly is a factor, and how does one go about buying it? A *factor* is a fundamental characteristic inherent to a security or a measure derived from the price of a security. The characteristics may include relative pricing (e.g., price-to-book value), recent price change (e.g., whether the change in price of the security over the past 12 months has been greater than, equal to, or less than the broader market's), sensitivity to a macroeconomic event (such as a surprise in inflation), or any number of other characteristics. Unlike stock returns that can be directly observed, factors cannot be directly observed; they can only be indirectly estimated utilizing statistical tools and assigned to each security.

The three main categories of factors include: macroeconomic, statistical, and fundamental. Macroeconomic factor models utilize observable economic time series, like inflation, industrial production, gross domestic product, and credit risk spreads, to explain security returns. Statistical factor models utilize principal-components-based analysis to determine if there are factors common to a dataset that have explanatory power. The utility of this approach may be limited by not specifying in advance what the factors are, or if these factors exist outside of the mathematical model. Finally, fundamental factor models incorporate measurable attributes of a company, such as its size, dividend yield, price-to-book, or recent price changes (i.e., momentum) to explain a portion of the stock's return. Despite their different approaches, these models are not necessarily inconsistent with one another and may all hold simultaneously. However, this does not mean that all models are equally useful in explaining excess returns. Additionally, some models may be more appropriate for different asset classes or specific securities. For instance, Connor (1995)[ii] demonstrates that in equities, fundamental models generally have the highest explanatory power. Additionally, most of the work done by academics has centered around fundamental models, and market practitioners primarily utilize fundamental models when constructing smart beta portfolios. For this reason, a majority of this chapter will focus on this type of model.

So, now that we know what a factor and factor model are, what is factor investing? Factor investing involves constructing a portfolio with desired characteristics by selecting securities that fit within given parameters. So, factor investing does not involve buying factors, per se; rather, it involves assembling a portfolio of securities that capture desired factors. For example, an equity investor may believe that high dividend-paying stocks outperform the broader market over long periods. So, the investor may choose to construct an equity portfolio with a bias toward, or a positive exposure to, the *dividend factor*. To do this, the investor may begin by calculating the dividend yield for every stock in their investible universe, which is the equivalent to calculating each security's dividend factor exposure. The investor may then eliminate any security that does not have a dividend factor in, for example, the top quartile of this universe.[1] With this remaining pool of companies, the investor may then construct their portfolio. This process will ensure that their portfolio's dividend yield is above the broader market dividend yield and the portfolio's exposure to the dividend factor is positive. Finally, it is important to note that while a factor is something that explains returns, not all factors have an inherent risk premium. In other words, some factors (like the *liquidity* factor) may be desirable for the investor, but holding a portfolio with securities that are more liquid than their peers does not in itself mean that this portfolio will earn or lose a risk premium owing to its liquidity factor exposure. Therefore, factor investing generally includes identifying and purchasing (or shorting) not just for factors, but factors that are expected to generate a positive (or negative) risk premium.

Commonly Utilized Factors

One source of confusion with respect to factor investing is that there are no universal definitions for factors. Rather, each manager or academic may define, measure, and construct factors somewhat differently. As a result, there has been a proliferation of published factors; Campbell R. Harvey, Yan Liu, and Heqing Zhu, in their 2016 paper—". . . and the Cross-Section of Expected Returns"—identify 315 factors within 312 published works and various working papers.[iii] However, there are seven factors that are more popular among both academics and practitioners, of which the latter group regularly utilize these factors for constructing portfolios or selling factor-specific smart beta products. These commonly utilized factors are: *value, growth, size, momentum,* and *low-risk* or *low-volatility, dividend, quality,* and *multi-factor*. A brief description of each factor can be found in Table 10.1.[iv]

---

[1] Some managers construct their factor portfolios with hard cut-offs; however, most managers will utilize a more nuanced ranking approach whereby securities are *scored* based on their estimated factor exposure. Once all securities in an investible universe are scored, each security can then be added to a portfolio (or potentially shorted) in proportion to their score.

Table 10.1　Common factors utilized by smart beta products

Factor	Definition	Common Measurements
Value	The excess return attributable to stocks that are "cheap" relative to either their fundamental value or their peers.	Price-to-book, price-to-earnings (or its inverse, earnings yield), price-to-sales, price-to-enterprise value, price-to-cash flow.
Growth	The excess return attributable to stocks that are not "cheap" but instead have outsized growth potential. Note, growth and value stocks are defined by many index providers as binary (a stock is either a "growth" or a "value" stock). However, some participants define it using other metrics.	Similar to "value," measurements may include price-to-book, price-to-earnings, price-to-sales, etc. Utilizing a different cross section, "growth" stocks may be identified using an earnings or sales growth rate.
Size	The excess return attributable to a firm's smaller size relative to their larger counterparts.	Market capitalization (full or free-float).
Momentum	The excess return attributable to the continuation of past performance.	Return versus a peer group. This is usually over the prior 3, 6, or 12 months, sometimes with the most recent month excluded.
Low-Risk or Low-Volatility	The excess return attributable to stocks with lower than average volatility, equity beta, or idiosyncratic risk.	Stock return standard deviation (annualized from the prior 1, 2, or 3 years), downside standard deviation, standard deviation of idiosyncratic returns.
Dividend	The excess return attributable to securities with dividend yields that are higher than the average dividend yield of a given universe of securities.	Dividend yield, dividend growth rate, dividend yield stability.
Quality	The excess return attributable to companies that are considered of "high quality" and are characterized by low debt, stable earnings growth, stable revenue growth, and other similar metrics.	Earnings stability, dividend growth stability, balance sheet strength which includes low leverage, stability of executive management, stability of cash flows, high ROE and ROA, high return on invested capital.
Multi-Factor	The excess return attributable to multiple factor exposures.	Some or all of the above.

Factor Returns

The primary appeal of constructing portfolios with specific factor characteristics is the positive risk premium that a manager may be able to generate versus his benchmark. For example, consider a U.S. large-blend manager who has a

Russell 1000 benchmark. An increasingly popular approach to generate returns in excess of that benchmark is to construct a portfolio with one or more factor tilts, or positive exposure to factors including size, quality, or value. Assuming these factors earn a premium over a period relevant to the portfolio manager, then this manager will appear to be skilled and capable of generating positive risk-adjusted excess returns. Alternatively, many new products—such as those offered by Dimensional, AQR, QS, and others—focus on constructing portfolios with targeted factor exposures. These portfolios have little if any proprietary top-down or bottom-up analysis and instead are driven primarily by models that are intended to construct a portfolio with exposure to one or more factors. Both approaches have had varying degrees of success, which partially explains the growing popularity of factor-driven investing. As shown in Figure 10.1, investors who are exposed to six of the seven previously mentioned factors have earned a positive factor premium over the period shown (the S&P 500 is also shown for comparison).

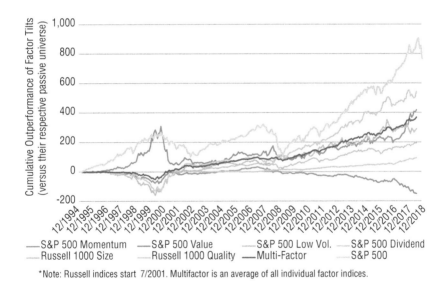

*Note: Russell indices start 7/2001. Multifactor is an average of all individual factor indices.

Figure 10.1   Cumulative excess returns of common factors[2] *Source*: Morningstar and authors' calculations

---

[2] *Source*: Morningstar. Factor indices are cumulative returns in excess of their relevant passive benchmark. Indices used include S&P 500 Momentum TR USD, S&P 500 Value TR USD, S&P 500 Low Volatility TR USD, S&P 500 Dividend Aristocrats TR USD, Russell 1000 Size Factor TR USD, and Russell 1000 Quality Factor TR USD. Time periods: S&P Indices, January 1995 to December 2018. Russell Indices, July 2001 to December 2018. Multi-factor return is the simple average monthly return of all the previously mentioned indices.

It should be noted that exposure to any of the aforementioned factors does not ensure that a portfolio will outperform its benchmark over a period relevant to most managers (typically one to three years). On the contrary, some factors have generated negative premiums for periods well beyond common investment horizons. For example, in Figure 10.1, from 1995 until early 2000, the low volatility, dividend, and value factors (as defined by the Morningstar methodology) all generated significant negative returns. Meanwhile, an investor who purchased this specific *momentum* factor in March 2000 had to wait nearly 17 years to recoup because of underperformance. More recently, the value factor highlighted in Figure 10.1 has detracted from performance for 20 years (underperformance has been particularly acute in the past 10 years). Furthermore, factors exhibit nontrivial volatility as shown in Figure 10.2. For example, for each calendar year from 2009 to 2018, the average difference in return between the highest and lowest previously mentioned factors is 11.7%. Therefore, exposure to factors can generate significant portfolio tracking error to a benchmark and must be scaled appropriately.

Fortunately for investors who utilize factors in the portfolio construction process, factors generally exhibit a low correlation to each other. For this reason, when constructing a portfolio, managers will typically target, or gain exposure to, more than one factor. The rationale is that a portfolio with several factors is more likely to generate positive excess returns than a portfolio with a single factor tilt. Additionally, the low correlation among factor total returns, as shown in Table 10.2, serves to reduce the factor exposures' collective contribution to portfolio tracking error.

So, now that factors have been identified and a whole industry established to gain positive exposure to factors that generate a risk premium, will this premium persist? Only time will tell. Melas, Briand, and Urwin (2011) argue that as investors increasingly purchase securities with desired factors, factor risk premiums may decline over time.[v] Others argue that factor premiums will likely persist indefinitely owing to *systematic risks* inherent to securities, which manifest themselves through factors. Others argue that factor premium will continue due to *systematic errors* that investors will continue to make. The case for factor risk premium persistence will be covered in greater detail later in this chapter.

Figure 10.2 Calendar year excess of benchmark factor returns[3] *Source:* Morningstar and authors' calculations

Rank	1997	1998	1999	2000	2001	2002	2003	2004	2005	2006	2007	2008	2009
1	Momentum 4.5	Momentum 28.5	Momentum 26.8	Low Vol. 34.1	Dividend 22.7	Low Vol. 14.9	Size 14.5	Low Vol. 6.8	Momentum 11.8	Value 5.0	Quality 5.8	Low Vol. 15.6	Size 13.3
2	Dividend 2.1	Dividend -11.8	Value -8.3	Dividend 19.2	Low Vol. 16.3	Dividend 12.2	Value 3.1	Size 6.6	Size 4.8	Low Vol. 3.9	Momentum 4.4	Dividend 15.1	Dividend 0.1
3	Low Vol. -3.0	Value -13.9	Dividend -26.4	Value 15.2	Value 0.2	Momentum 5.9	Dividend -3.3	Value 4.8	Quality 1.3	Dividend 1.5	Size -2.3	Quality 6.5	Quality -1.7
4	Value -3.4	Low Vol. -20.5	Low Vol. -28.8	Momentum -11.5	Momentum -14.8	Size 5.8	Quality -5.7	Dividend 4.6	Value 0.9	Quality -1.2	Value -3.5	Momentum 2.4	Value -5.3
5						Quality 2.0	Low Vol. -5.9	Momentum 0.2	Dividend -1.2	Size -1.2	Low Vol. -4.9	Size 0.0	Low Vol. -7.2
6						Value 1.2	Momentum -6.1	Quality -0.9	Low Vol. -2.7	Momentum -6.2	Dividend -7.6	Value -2.2	Momentum -9.2

Rank	2010	2011	2012	2013	2014	2015	2016	2017	2018	5-Yr Avg	10-Yr Avg	15-Yr Avg	20-Yr Avg
1	Size 11.7	Low Vol. 12.7	Size 2.8	Size 3.5	Low Vol. 3.8	Momentum 4.2	Value 5.4	Momentum 6.4	Low Vol. 4.7	Momentum 1.2	Size 2.4	Size 3.1	Dividend 2.6
2	Dividend 4.3	Quality 7.0	Value 1.7	Dividend -0.1	Dividend 2.1	Low Vol. 3.0	Size 3.9	Quality 6.4	Momentum 4.3	Low Vol. 1.1	Quality 1.5	Dividend 1.8	Low Vol. 2.2
3	Momentum 3.7	Dividend 6.2	Momentum 1.3	Value -0.4	Quality 0.1	Quality 1.2	Dividend -0.1	Dividend -0.1	Quality 2.1	Quality 1.0	Dividend 1.4	Quality 0.9	Momentum 0.7
4	Value 0.0	Momentum -0.5	Dividend 0.9	Momentum -1.0	Value -1.3	Dividend -0.5	Quality -1.3	Size -3.4	Dividend 1.7	Dividend 0.6	Momentum 0.1	Low Vol. 0.9	Value -0.1
5	Quality -1.6	Value -2.6	Quality -0.3	Quality -1.5	Size -1.9	Size -3.2	Low Vol. -1.6	Low Vol. -4.4	Size -3.6	Size -0.2	Low Vol. -0.5	Momentum 0.9	
6	Low Vol. -1.7	Size -2.7	Low Vol. -5.7	Low Vol. -8.8	Momentum -2.5	Value -4.5	Momentum -6.3	Value -6.5	Value -4.6	Value -2.3	Value -1.8	Value -0.9	

[3] *Source:* Morningstar. Indices used include S&P 500 Momentum TR USD, S&P 500 Value TR USD, S&P 500 Low Volatility TR USD, S&P 500 Dividend Aristocrats TR USD, Russell 1000 Size Factor TR USD, and Russell 1000 Quality Factor TR USD. Time periods: S&P Indices, January 1995 to December 2018. Russell Indices, July 2001 to December 2018. Annualized performance is the 5-, 10-, 15-, and 20-year periods ended December 2018.

Table 10.2   Correlations of monthly factor returns (excess of benchmark, July 2001 to December 2018)[4]

	S&P 500 Momentum	S&P 500 Value	S&P 500 Low Vol.	S&P 500 Dividend	Russell 1000 Size	Russell 1000 Quality
S&P 500 Momentum	1.00					
S&P 500 Value	(0.39)	1.00				
S&P 500 Low Vol.	0.28	(0.04)	1.00			
S&P 500 Dividend	(0.02)	0.27	0.64	1.00		
Russell 1000 Size	0.00	0.29	(0.20)	(0.01)	1.00	
Russell 1000 Quality	0.42	(0.60)	0.45	0.19	(0.46)	1.00

Source: Morningstar and authors' calculations

History of Factors within Academia

While factor investing and smart beta are catchphrases that have been popularized in the past decade; the utilization of statistical tools to measure portfolio factor exposure can trace their roots to academic research in the 1950s and 1960s. In 1952, while still a student at the University of Chicago and an employee at the RAND corporation, Harry Markowitz published "Portfolio Selection" in the *Journal of Finance*.[vi] This seminal paper laid the foundation of Modern Portfolio Theory, and has since become one of the most heavily cited publications in finance (39,062 citations as of July 2019, according to Google). This paper provided the mathematical framework for assembling a portfolio and maximizing the expected return of that portfolio per unit of risk. The paper then argues that investors who are risk-averse and rational will select a portfolio that maximizes their utility. Building off Markowitz's work, William Sharpe (1964),[vii] John Lintner (1965),[viii] and Jan Mossin (1966)[ix] each put forward an equation that relates a portfolio's expected return to a risk-free rate and sensitivity to the overall market. As explained by Markowitz in 1990 at a lecture at Baruch College, "My work on portfolio theory considers how an

---

[4] *Source*: Morningstar. Indices used include S&P 500 Momentum TR USD, S&P 500 Value TR USD, S&P 500 Low Volatility TR USD, S&P 500 Dividend Aristocrats TR USD, Russell 1000 Size Factor TR USD, and Russell 1000 Quality Factor TR USD. Time period: July 2001 to December 2018.

optimizing investor would behave, whereas the work by Sharpe and Lintner on the Capital Asset Pricing Model (CAPM for short) is concerned with economic equilibrium assuming all investors optimize in the particular manner I proposed."[x]

The CAPM equation put forward by the aforementioned economists is:

$$E(R_p) = R_f + \beta_p(E(R_m) - R_f)$$

where:

$E(R_p)$ is the expected return on the portfolio

R_f is the risk-free rate

β_p is beta, or a measure of sensitivity of a portfolio to the factor that follows it in the model

R_m is the return of the equity market

$E(R_m) - R_f$ is the excess return of the equity market over the risk-free rate (i.e., the equity risk premium)

Thus, $\beta_p(E(R_m) - R_f)$ is the return of a portfolio that can be attributed both to the equity risk premium and the portfolio's sensitivity to the equity risk premium.

In this context, we can view the CAPM as the first factor investing equation. The theory at the time was that there is one factor, which is the market factor, or more specifically, the equity market risk premium factor. However, eight years after Sharpe introduced the CAPM model, Black, Jenson, and Scholes (1972) tested this model with data beginning in the 1930s.[xi] They showed that portfolios constructed with zero covariance to the equity market (i.e., an equity beta of 0), still had positive and statistically significant returns greater than the risk-free rate. This suggests that the CAPM model was in some way incomplete.[5] Three years after that (1976), Wharton Professor Stephen Ross published *The Arbitrage Theory of Capital Asset Pricing,*[xii] in which he argued there may be more than one factor that can be used to explain returns. These factors don't necessarily have to include the equity market factor; he suggested, for example, that a relevant factor could be changes in gross national product. Additionally, there can be any number of factors that explain the return of an asset, and the expected

---

[5] The following year, future Nobel laureate Robert Merton wrote, "An Intertemporal Capital Asset Pricing Model" (1973), which extended the *single period* CAPM to become a multi-period model, thereby allowing for a changing investment opportunity set. Citation: Merton, Robert C. (1973). "An Intertemporal Capital Asset Pricing Model," Econometrica, Econometric Society, vol. 41(5). pp. 867–887. September. The implication is that time, in general, and an investor's time-varying wealth and utility function can impact the optimal portfolio construction and thus may be considered another factor.

return of an asset can be decomposed into factor returns and factor-specific beta coefficients. Ross's theory is now known as arbitrage pricing theory (APT), and the mathematical formula that he proposed is:

$$E(R_a) = R_f + \beta_{F1}R_{F1} + \beta_{F2}R_{f2} + ... + \beta_{Fn}R_{fn}$$

where:

$E(R_a)$ is the expected return on the asset
R_f is the risk-free rate
β_{Fn} is beta, or a measure of sensitivity of a portfolio to each factor
R_{Fn} is the expected return of each factor

This model does not necessarily contradict the CAPM model; rather, CAPM is a specific instance of APT whereby the only factor that is relevant to the pricing of an asset is the equity market factor. In 1986, working with Nai-Fu Chen at the University of Chicago and Richard Roll at the University of California, Los Angeles, Ross put forward evidence that macroeconomic variables including industrial production, expected and unexpected inflation, the spread between long and short interest rates, and the spread between high- and low-grade bonds, are relevant sources of risk premium.[xiii]

Returning to extrapolations and tests of the CAPM model, in 1977, Sanjoy Basu at McMaster University published a paper indicating that securities with higher earnings yields (the inverse of the price-to-earnings ratio) have higher risk-adjusted returns than randomly selected securities.[xiv] This was insightful for two reasons: first, it further called into question the CAPM model's descriptive ability in that it suggests the CAPM model was missing "something." Second, it challenges the notion of market efficiency because if all data is already included into the price of a security, sorting on a basic commonly known metric shouldn't yield excess performance. Other academics suggested in subsequent publications that the market can still be efficient and the earnings yield anomaly may be attributed to model misspecification. Simply put, the markets can be efficient but CAPM isn't complete. In 1981, Rolf Banz published his University of Chicago dissertation "The Relationship between Return and Market Value of Common Stocks."[xv] In the words of Banz: "This study contributes another piece to the emerging puzzle. It examines the relationship between the total market value of the common stock of a firm and its return. The results show that, in the 1936–1975 period, the common stock of small firms had, on average, higher risk-adjusted returns than the common stock of large firms."

In 1992, with these stock return anomalies already established, Eugene F. Fama and Kenneth R. French at the University of Chicago published their seminal paper "The Cross-Section of Expected Stock Returns."[xvi] They would later summarize the main findings in an equally important paper the following year:

"The bottom-line result is that two empirically determined variables, size and book-to-market equity, do a good job explaining the cross-section of average returns on NYSE, Amex, and NASDAQ stocks for the 1963–1990 period." The translation is that the equity risk premium is not the only factor that explains stock returns; rather, two other factors that they define as *size* and *book-to-market* also explain stock returns. The size factor was simply the difference between the returns of the smallest 30% of securities from the return from the highest 30% of securities (the authors refer to this as SMB, or small minus big). The book-to-market factor, which is now known as the value factor, is the return difference between the highest 30% and lowest 30% of securities sorted on the book-to-price ratio (the authors refer to this as HML, or high book-to-market minus low book-to-market). The empirical evidence produced by Fama and French indicate that, on average, smaller firms have higher stock returns than larger firms, and cheaper firms (as estimated by the book-to-price ratio of securities) have higher common stock returns than richer firms. Additionally, when accounting for these variables (SMB and HML) simultaneously, common stock returns can be better explained than using a single-factor model (such as the CAPM). And following the publication of these papers, the three-factor model quickly became the standard multi-factor model within academia.

The following year, Narasimhan Jegadeesh and Sheridan Titman, both from the UCLA Anderson School of Management, published "Returns to Buying Winners and Selling Losers: Implications for Stock Market Efficiency."[xvii] In this paper the authors examine, among other things, a stock selection strategy whereby the authors purchase the stocks with the top decile returns over the prior six months, sell the stocks with the bottom decile returns over the prior six months, and then hold these positions for six months. According to the authors, this strategy generated compounded excess returns of +12.01% per year between 1965 and 1989. Additionally, the authors conclude (our emphasis): "evidence indicates that the profitability of the relative strength strategies are *not due to their systematic risk.*" This insight was unique because this strategy seemed to contradict the notion that all relevant information is already incorporated into the price of securities.

In 1997, Mark Carhart at the University of Southern California made another material contribution to the explanation of stock performance, although his initial objective was to explain mutual fund performance. In his paper *On Persistence in Mutual Fund Performance*,[xviii] Carhart demonstrates that common risk factors explain most of equity mutual fund performance, but not the "hot hands" of star mutual fund managers. Building off of Jegadeesh and Titman's findings, Carhart noted that exceptionally strong fund manager performance can be partially attributed to the presence of the funds' positive exposure to a *momentum* factor. The momentum factor (later referred to as *up*

358 Foundations of Investment Management

minus down, UMD) chosen by Carhart was the return difference between the 30% of stocks with the best trailing performance versus the 30% of stocks with the worst trailing performance, where performance is measured over the past year skipping the most recent month.[6] In this paper he added the UMD factor to the Fama-French 3-factor model, and *voila*, the model did an even better job explaining stock returns! Although, you had to take Carhart's word on that highly relevant point. In the paper Carhart wrote, "I find that the 4-factor model substantially improves on the average pricing errors of the CAPM and 3-factor model. . . . These results are not included for the sake of brevity, but are available from the author upon request." No doubt many readers in academia did request his results, and momentum was generally included in factor modeling thereafter.

Not to be outdone, in September 2013, Fama and French wrote *A Five-Factor Pricing Model*.[xix] We're sure by now you see where this is going. While the paper has not yet been published in a major journal, it has nevertheless been downloaded over 44,000 times as of 2018. In this paper, Fama and French drop the momentum factor and add a *profitability* factor, which is defined as *robust minus weak* (RMW) profitability. Additionally, the authors add an *investment* factor, which is defined as *conservative minus aggressive* (CMA) investment. As you'd expect by now, the authors find that this 5-factor model does a better job explaining returns than the prior 1-, 3-, or 4-factor models.

History of Factor Investing Outside Academia (i.e., Today's Major Practitioners)

While the quantity of academic papers concerning security factor measurement and stock returns can now fill a small library, this research is only relevant to investors if it can be applied to form and manage real portfolios. Fortunately, several former University of Chicago students (and a couple educated elsewhere) chose to not pursue academic careers and instead opted to apply the knowledge of factor investing and founded their own firms. One promising PhD student who ventured outside the realm of academia is Dimensional Fund Advisors (Dimensional) founder David Booth. Booth graduated from the University of Kansas in 1969 with an MS in business and then enrolled at the University of Chicago Graduate School of Business as a PhD candidate.[xx] Booth's first class at Chicago was taught by Fama, who was impressed by Booth. In a 2008 interview, Fama said "Every year I ask the best PhD students in my class to be

---

[6] This is the *12-2* momentum factor. What does it measure? Imagine an investor is calculating stock momentum on 2/1/2019. The relevant period to measure equity returns for the 12-2 momentum factor is 12/31/2017 to 12/31/2018, which is 12 months, but the month of January is not considered.

research and teaching assistants. David Booth was the best of his group." However, after two years, Booth came to Fama and explained he did not want to continue to pursue a career in academia. Fama responded "Fine, there are a lot of rich and famous people who don't have PhDs from the University of Chicago." Fama then introduced Booth to John A. McQuown, the head of investments at Wells Fargo, who hired Booth in 1971.[xxi]

While studying under Fama, Booth met another promising MBA student, Rex Sinquefield. Sinquefield was also a student of Fama's, graduated with an MBA from the University of Chicago in 1972, and took a position at American National Bank of Chicago. In 1973, Sinquefield launched the first passively managed index fund applying many of the academic lessons of efficient markets and portfolio construction. Meanwhile, Booth and McQuown maintain they were the first ones to launch a passively managed index fund while at Wells Fargo in 1973. So, who launched it first?—Fama says it was a tie.[xxii] In 1981, David Booth contacted Fama and indicated he wanted to start his own firm offering small-capitalization-focused investment funds. Why small-cap? There were two reasons: first, Booth believed institutional investors were underexposed to these securities; second, having read Rolf Banz's paper demonstrating that small stocks tend to outperform larger stocks, Booth believed he could harvest the small-cap equity risk premium for his investors. Fama agreed to work with Booth as a consultant, Rex Sinquefield also agreed to join the start-up, and several other Chicago Business School professors (many of whom later were awarded the Nobel Prize in economics) joined as fund board members, and in 1981 Dimensional launched its first fund.[xxiii]

Dimensional relocated from Brooklyn, NY, and Chicago, IL, to Santa Monica, CA, in 1985, and for the first eight years the firm focused solely on institutional investors. Marketing was through word of mouth and within eight years they amassed $5.2 billion in assets. In 1989, Booth and Sinquefield agreed to open Dimensional products to retail investors if they purchased the funds through financial advisors. However, Dimensional didn't want advisors who would position a Dimensional fund as the "next big thing." Rather, Dimensional wanted to work with like-minded advisors who agreed with Dimensional's philosophy of market efficiency, invested with long-term views, and primarily utilized low-cost products. Gaining approval to sell Dimensional products was a lengthy process; advisors first attended a Dimensional conference where Dimensional employees explained how the firm operated, and then prospective advisors hosted Dimensional directors at their office and explained to the Dimensional employee what the advisor's investment philosophy and business model was. If an advisor successfully completed this due diligence, he or she could begin incorporating Dimensional funds into his or her client portfolios. To remain in good standing, on a monthly or quarterly basis, a Dimensional manager would facilitate a meeting between advisors who sold Dimensional products and every other year there was a two-day Dimensional event.[xxiv]

Despite the hurdles presented by their application and approval process, Dimensional continued to attract assets and by 1998 the firm managed $28 billion.[xxv] In fact, its close fraternity of advisors who adhere to Dimensional's philosophy has become a tremendous asset to the firm; Dimensional credits their advisors with keeping client assets deployed in 2008 and 2009, with Dimensional funds experiencing inflows both years.[xxvi] Assets under management (AUM) surpassed $153 billion in 2007 and reached $582 billion as of June 30, 2018.[xxvii] According to their website, 73% of Dimensional products have outperformed their benchmark for the 15-year period that ended 6/30/18, while only 14% of equity and fixed income funds that were around at the start of 2003 beat their Morningstar category index over the same 15-year period.[xxviii]

Around the same time that Dimensional was opening its funds to retail investors, another student who would alter the investment management landscape began studying at the University of Chicago. Cliff Asness, like David Booth, was a doctoral student and became one of Fama's research assistants after his first year at the University of Chicago. Prior to completing his doctoral program, Asness took a summer position building quantitative models at Goldman Sachs Asset Management (GSAM). Asness continued working for GSAM prior to completing his doctoral program and he composed his dissertation in the evenings. In a 2015 interview,[xxix] Asness described a conversation he had with doctoral advisor, Fama. "With that said, one of the scariest moments . . . was telling him I wanted to write a dissertation on price momentum. I swear to God, I mumbled the second part, 'and I find it works really well.'

To his credit, Fama immediately said, 'If it's in the data, write the paper.' "

Asness received his PhD in 1994, accepted an offer to remain with GSAM, and was tasked by GSAM to start a new quant group. Asness recruited two Chicago classmates, John Liew and Bob Krail, to join him. The group was given seed capital to begin applying their quantitative models, which combined the value and momentum factors (among others) to identify rich and cheap stocks. Their Global Alpha Fund began with $10 million, grew to $100 million following strong returns and additional Goldman partner contributions, after which it was opened to external investors. By 1997, after several lights-out years of returns, assets had grown to $7 billion.

Around that time, David Kabiller, a client-facing representative at GSAM who regularly interfaced with Asness's team, floated an idea to Asness, Liew, and Krail: leave GSAM to start their own hedge fund. While they would leave behind the benefits of a large organization with brand recognition, a large sales force, $7 billion in assets, and a compensation package that would have been the envy of young PhDs everywhere, they thought they could do better. In 1998, the three

GSAM quants, along with Kabiller, launched Applied Quantitative Research (AQR). The team raised approximately $1 billion in the first several months, making it the second-largest hedge fund start-up behind Long-Term Capital Management. Unfortunately, their timing couldn't have been worse; the value factor materially underperformed as technology stocks soared in 1999. In the first 20 months, the fund's AUM declined from $1 billion to $400 million, and the fund nearly collapsed. Asness and his team held true to their investing style and from 2000 to 2002, the fund produced exceptional returns.[xxx] Since then, AQR has launched more than 40 strategies ranging from equities, fixed income, alternatives (such as risk parity, long/short, diversified arbitrage), has grown to over 900 professionals, of which 73 hold PhDs, and manages $226 billion in assets as of June 30, 2018.[xxxi] In July 2018, the *Financial Times* called AQR a "hedge fund killer" in light of its strong performance and low fees.[xxxii]

In 2002, as AQR was emerging from its difficult start, Rob Arnott founded Research Affiliates in Newport Beach, CA. Tangentially, in 2003, Cliff Asness and Rob Arnott published a paper in the *Financial Analysts Journal*— "Surprise! Higher Dividends = Higher Earnings Growth." This paper states: "historical evidence strongly suggests that expected future earnings growth is fastest when current payout ratios are high and slowest when payout ratios are low." Their findings challenge anecdotal evidence that high-growth companies have low-dividend payout ratios, and therefore a low-dividend payout ratio is indicative of elevated future earnings growth. Asness and Arnott's findings also provide another rationale for investing in high-dividend-paying securities.[xxxiii]

Unlike most of this chapter's protagonists, Arnott does not have an MBA or PhD from the University of Chicago; however, he is still well-known and respected within academia. Arnott has been published over 100 times in journals including *The Journal of Portfolio Management, Harvard Business Review*, and *Financial Analysts Journal*, where he served as editor in chief from 2002 through 2006. In an interview with *The Wall Street Journal*, Vanguard Group founder John C. Bogle called Arnott "a brilliant academic" and "the greatest marketer I've ever met." He went on to say, "I wish I was as sure of anything as he is of everything."[xxxiv] Prior to founding Research Affiliates, Arnott was the chairman of First Quadrant and was an equity strategist at Salomon Brothers. Three years after founding Research Affiliates, Rob Arnott, Jason Hsu, and Philip Moore published *Fundamental Indexation*, which demonstrated that equity indices in which the constituent weightings are based on book value, revenue, dividends, and other metrics rather than the traditional market capitalization, outperformed the S&P 500 from 1962–2004.[xxxv] These findings laid the foundation for the Research Affiliates' Fundamental Index (RAFI) series of funds, which were launched in 2005. Research Affiliates doesn't manage money directly; rather, it designs products for other large managers including Charles Schwab, PIMCO, and Invesco. As of June 30, 2018, $197 billion in assets were managed using Research Affiliates' strategies.[xxxvi]

In 2015, as assets in U.S. Smart Beta exchange-traded funds (ETFs) reached $450 billion,[xxxvii] BlackRock hired Columbia Business School professor Andrew Ang to lead their factor-based strategies group. The previous year, Ang published a book on factor investing titled *Asset Management: A Systematic Approach to Factor Investing*. In the book's preface, Ang compares building an optimal portfolio to healthy eating, stating, "Just as eating right requires us to look through food labels to underlying nutrients, factor investing requires us to look through asset class labels to underlying factor risks."[xxxviii] As of June 30, 2018, BlackRock managed $210 billion in factor-based strategies across several asset classes.[xxxix] Meanwhile, other large managers have continued to add talent either organically or through the acquisition of smaller factor-based investors. In March 2014, Legg Mason acquired QS Investors, a quantitative, customized solutions and quantitative equities manager. At the time, QS Investors managed $4.1 billion,[xl] which has grown to $13.9 billion as of March 31, 2018.[xli] In September 2017, Invesco purchased Guggenheim's ETF business, adding $36.7 billion in AUM to its product offering and becoming the second-largest smart beta ETF manager, behind BlackRock.[xlii]

Academics Pondering: Why Do Factors and Factor Returns Exist at All?

The mere existence of statistical significance isn't necessarily all that an academic or discerning practitioner needs to conclude that a risk factor is *real* or will persist into the future. Type 1 statistical errors, in which an analyst falsely rejects the null hypothesis, increase in likelihood as a dataset is analyzed on ever-increasing dimensions. Said another way, while financial literature accepts momentum, size, value, and many more as factors that have explanatory power, there exists the possibility—however slim—that these factors simply *appear* to have explanatory power by chance because the thousands of other dimensions on which stock returns were measured did not show statistical significance and therefore were not highlighted in literature. Furthermore, it is possible that factors, once exposed in financial literature and exploited by practitioners, will no longer have explanatory power since market efficiency dictates that prices will incorporate all available information.

So, what do academics think drive factor returns, and why might they be persistent? There are currently two lines of reasoning. The first is that certain stocks have risk characteristics that cannot be eliminated through diversification and therefore factor returns represent systematic risks for which the security holder is compensated. For example, with respect to the size factor, Chan and Chen (1991) note that smaller firms are more likely to "have lost market value owing to poor performance, they are inefficient producers, and they are likely to have high financial leverage and cash flow problems . . . they are more sensitive to changes in the economy and they are less likely to survive adverse economic conditions."[xliii] Liu (2006) argues that some factor returns, such as the size and value factor, can be attributed to security liquidity.[xliv] Separately, Zhang (2006) postulates that the momentum factor can be attributed to *information uncertainty*, or "ambiguity with respect to the implications of new information for a firm's value, which potentially stems from two sources: the volatility of a firm's underlying fundamentals and poor information."[xlv]

The second line of reasoning as to why these factors exist is that investors continue to make systematic errors. These systematic errors might be driven by the *behavioral biases* discussed in detail in Chapter 11. However, while there is a growing body of literature describing behavioral biases, analysis directly linking these biases to excess stock returns is limited. Alternatively, systematic errors might be driven by regulatory constraints or motives of market participants that conflict with maximizing risk-adjusted returns. Baker et al. (2011) analyzes the low-volatility factor, whereby stocks with low-equity betas and low volatility generally outperform higher beta, higher volatility stocks on a risk-adjusted basis. They suggest this phenomenon is persistent because "sophisticated investors are, to a large extent, sidelined by their mandates to maximize active returns subject to benchmark tracking error."[xlvi] In other words, equity managers are evaluated against a fixed benchmark; holding low-beta stocks is a good way to ensure that the portfolio will underperform vis-à-vis its benchmark in a bull market, making it unappealing even if its addition will contribute to the portfolio outperforming on a beta- or risk-adjusted basis. Thus, professional equity investors avoid low-beta stocks even if they have high-alpha potential. Another systematic error identified in the literature is *herding*. Jean-Claude Trichet, former president of the European Central Bank, commented in 2001: "Some operators [fund managers] have come to the conclusion that it is better to be wrong along with everybody else, rather than take the risk of being right, or wrong, alone."[xlvii] Dasgupta, Prat, and Verardo (2011) show that this institutional herding, under certain circumstances, can cause short-term price momentum.[xlviii]

Practitioners Pondering: Does Factor Timing Add Value?

Many portfolio managers represent that they can add value for clients by employing some sort of timing, whether that be dialing up or down risk, allocating between different asset classes, or rotating between sectors. While the

benefit to investors of market timing is questionable, market timing nevertheless remains at the bedrock of outlook, positioning, and attribution discussions.
So a natural question, or extension of a market timing discussion is: can a portfolio manager time factors? Asked another way, can a portfolio manager add
value by increasing or decreasing exposure to one or more factors, such as value,
dividend, or momentum, based upon a predetermined framework or metric for
evaluating relative factor attractiveness? This question is likely the most fiercely
debated topic within factor investing—and the jury is still out.

In one camp is Cliff Asness, co-founder of AQR, who strongly believes that
the answer is *not really*. Specifically, if an investor is already diversified across
numerous factors, timing them doesn't improve investor returns. In Asness et
al. (2017), he writes, "Value timing of factors is highly correlated to the value
factor itself. This is both intuitively quite obvious and empirically strongly confirmed. Thus, while value timing of a factor may boost the performance of a
single-factor strategy, especially a negatively correlated factor like momentum,
it is of little added benefit to a diversified portfolio that already includes a strategic allocation to value as it may result in a larger bet on value than intended
and weaken performance due to forgone diversification."[xlix] In other words, in
practice, when one or more factors appears "cheap" on some historic or relative
metric, the value factor also typically appears cheap. So, if the value factor is
already included in a factor portfolio, timing factor exposures will not generate
incremental returns.

In the other camp is Rob Arnott, founder of Research Affiliates, who strongly
believes that the answer is *yes*, one can add value by timing factor exposures. In
Arnott et al. (2016c), the Research Affiliates team ran the following test: "Consider an investor who, in the beginning of each year, selects three strategies or
factors with the least expensive (cheapest) valuations relative to their own history available to that point . . . An investor in the three cheapest smart beta
strategies would have outperformed an investor in the equally weighted strategy
by about 0.5%. This may not seem a large margin, but over the 39-and-a-half-
year period an investor holding the three cheapest smart beta strategies would
have been 108% richer than an investor holding the cap-weighted market . . . By
contrast, the investor holding the equally weighted strategy would have been
75% richer than an investor in the cap-weighted market."[l]

In March 2017, Asness took direct aim at Arnott in an online AQR Perspective.[li] In it he wrote: "In multiple online white papers, Arnott and co-authors
present evidence in support of contrarian factor timing based on a plethora
of mostly inapplicable, exaggerated, and poorly designed tests that also flout
research norms. For (non-exhaustive) example, they use long-horizon regres-
sions for factors with too much turnover to make them applicable (among other
things, please, please, please stop making 5-year forecasts for momentum!).

They also have apples-to-oranges comparisons, with the most egregious being a comparison of contrarian factor timing based on a composite of valuation indicators, using up to date prices, to a simple book-to-price value factor using lagged prices." Asness goes on to state that the researchers at Research Affiliates are "living in your own universe." To our knowledge, Arnott never directly responded to several of Asness's assertions regarding timing. However, the following month in a Bloomberg interview, Arnott stated that he believes Asness is "insufficiently skeptical about the pervasiveness of data-mining and its impact even in the factors he uses."[lii] Asness responded in another AQR Perspective[liii] "What Rob is doing here is the time honored strategy of the best defense is a good offense combined with the old adage about pounding the table when you've got nothing." Ouch.

In perhaps a third camp is Andrew Ang, head of BlackRock's Factor-Based Strategies Group, who believes you can time factors by incorporating business cycle data. In a BlackRock white paper, Ang et al. (2017)[liv] state that "during economic troughs, value has tended to underperform because these companies have relatively inflexible capital structures (Berk, Green, and Naik 1999), but minimum volatility strategies have generally outperformed due to their risk mitigation properties (Ang et al. 2006). As the economy improves, momentum strategies have tended to do well. More defensive quality strategies, as well as minimum volatility strategies, have generally come into favor at the top of the economic cycle as the pace of economic growth slows and the probability of a recession increases." So, unlike Arnott and Asness, who attempt to measure whether factor timing is possible based upon factor valuations, Ang's approach is to first identify the broader macroeconomic business cycle, and then conditional on where the economy is in that cycle (expansion, slowdown, contraction, and recovery), gain exposure to targeted factors. Ang explains, "The signal with the best predictive results comes from positioning across the business cycle. An important result is that reliance on only one predictor—like valuation indicators as in Arnott (2016)—leads to significantly inferior results than combinations of several signals." This approach does come with one obvious caveat—in order to time factors, one needs to be able to correctly identify the current economic regime, which may only be apparent in hindsight.[7]

---

[7] Much of the factor-timing debate prior to 2018 revolved around valuation-based indicators. More recent research has turned to other indications (such as momentum). Specifically, can managers add value by purchasing factors that exhibit *momentum*? Said another way, practitioners are evaluating whether a factor that has recently generated positive return is more likely to continue to do so than other factors. But the bottom line is always the same: any timing must compensate for the resulting lack of diversification implied by a tilt toward or away from any factor. As stated previously, the jury is still out as to whether or not factor timing adds value.

SMART BETA INDUSTRY REVIEW

Smart beta is a term that is generally used to describe low-fee, highly transparent products that utilize quantitative screens to identify securities with targeted factors. In other words, smart beta is a term to describe the product, factor-investing describes the process, and factors are the targeted sources of risk premium. Rob Arnott, in a 2018 interview, said that London-based consulting firm Towers Watson in 2007 coined the phrase *smart beta* after speaking with him on the benefits of fundamental (and not market capitalization) index construction. Today, a product benchmarked against a fundamental index and not a market capitalization index, is also classified as a smart beta product even if the product doesn't target specific factors, per se. Fundamental indexes, unlike market capitalization indexes, are constructed utilizing security-level components. For example, assume company A has a market capitalization of $10 billion and a dividend of $500 million while company B has a market capitalization of $10 billion and a dividend of $250 million. In a typical market capitalization index, companies A and B would have the same proportional representation in an index. However, in a fundamental index that is constructed based on dividend yield, company A would have a representation twice that of company B. In practice, most fundamental indices have a value-factor tilt, as these indices are generally rotating out of securities that have experienced price appreciation. Ironically, Arnott disagrees with today's use of the term smart beta to describe products that are based on fundamental indexes. "There's nothing about factor tilts that make them smart beta under the original definition, but I've lost that fight. The marketplace now says factor strategies or smart beta. I disagree, but I don't define the semantics of our industry."[lv]

With respect to the construction of smart beta portfolios (including portfolios benchmarked against fundamental indexes), portfolio managers rely on financial models to identify and invest in securities that have desired attributes. These screens are rules-based and generally do not necessitate additional company-level due diligence, meaning analysts construct portfolios based on models that do not involve a qualitative assessment of each investment opportunity. Owing to the methodology of screening for investments with predetermined characteristics, smart beta products have both *active* and *passive* elements. As such, these products generally have lower fees than traditional, actively managed portfolios but have higher fees than passively managed portfolios. Finally, a typical objective of the smart beta manager is to outperform (either in absolute or risk-adjusted terms) the equivalent market capitalization weighted index from which the securities in the smart beta portfolio were sourced. This objective is accomplished by gaining exposure to various risk premiums inherent to any number of factors. So, despite Arnott's more nuanced description of smart beta, most market participants today utilize the phrases "smart beta," "factor strategies," and "fundamental indexing" interchangeably.

Smart Beta and ETFs

While smart beta portfolios can be managed in traditional open-end or closed-end mutual funds, there are three reasons most retail smart beta funds utilize ETF vehicles. First, as discussed in Chapter 2, ETFs have become an increasingly popular vehicle for retail investors due to their favorable tax treatment and potential for higher after-tax returns. Through their utilization of a middleman called an authorized participant (AP) and system of creating and retiring shares, ETFs have few taxable events and generally lower transaction costs than open-end mutual funds. Additionally, because ETFs do not need to maintain a cash balance to cover possible fund outflows, retail investors may benefit from the avoidance of a *cash drag*.

Second, from the fund manager's perspective, the ETF structure is operationally efficient because the fund only interacts with a small group of APs, which are responsible for most of the securities trading. As a result, a fund manager does not need to employ a small army of traders and the staff that is associated with processing and settling trades. Rather, the fund manager may focus most of his or her resources on managing portfolios and refining factor exposures. This operational efficiency allows fund managers to operate more cheaply, which is partly passed on to investors in the form of lower fund expenses.

Finally, ETFs are the primary vehicle for smart beta products—partly by chance. The first ETF was launched in 1993, one year after Fama and French at the University of Chicago published their seminal paper *The Cross-Section of Expected Stock Returns*, and only four years after Dimensional opened its funds to retail investors. So, both ETFs and smart beta investing got their start around the same time—it was only natural that the novel and innovative factor-investing methodology gravitated toward the novel and innovative investment vehicle. Annual issuance of new ETF shares has steadily grown from $88 billion in 2008 to $272 billion in 2016, while ETF assets have grown from $496 billion to $2.46 trillion over the same period.[lvi] Meanwhile, as shown in Figure 10.3, smart beta products have grown to nearly $800 billion and constitute approximately 27% of the U.S. ETF marketplace, as of February 2019.[lvii]

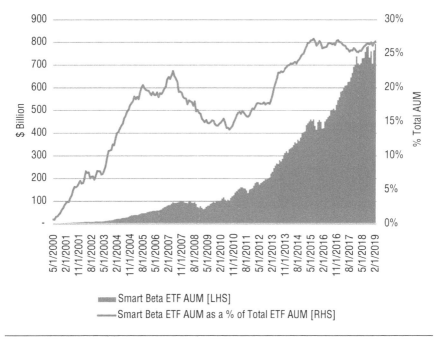

Figure 10.3 United States smart beta ETF assets and percentage of the ETF universe. *Source*: Morningstar

Smart Beta Products and Their Factors

As of December 31, 2018, according to Morningstar data[lviii] approximately 73% of all smart beta ETF assets fell into one of three categories when categorized by their secondary attribute, or their targeted factor exposure. These categories are:

- *Value*: 53 products (7.6% fund offerings), $176.9 billion assets (25.1% assets)
- *Growth*: 40 products (5.8% fund offerings), $168.8 billion assets (23.9% assets)
- *Dividend*: 141 products (20.3% fund offerings), $166.6 billion assets (23.6% assets)

Other common smart beta products include: multi-factor, risk-oriented (i.e., low-volatility), fundamentals (constituents are weighted based on fundamentals like sales or earnings), and momentum. Interestingly, even though many managers categorize stocks as either a *growth* or a *value* (meaning these indices are mirror images), the similar size of these products ($176.9 billion vs $168.6 billion) suggests retail investors seem willing to simultaneously invest, perhaps unknowingly, in two offsetting factors. For example, the Financial Times Stock

Exchange (FTSE) Index produces the Russell 1000 index, Russell 1000 Value, and Russell 1000 Growth indices. To do this, FTSE assigns a composite value score (CVS) to each stock in each index; this score represents the degree to which each stock is a growth or a value stock based on three independent metrics. So, a stock may be 20% value and 80% growth, and therefore would have a 20% weight in the Russell 1000 Value index and an 80% weight in the Russell 1000 Growth index.[lix] The reason this is highlighted is that the relative returns of these indices are additive. That is to say, an investor who has purchased two smart beta products with a 50% weight to the Russell 1000 Value indexed product and a 50% weight to the Russell 1000 Growth indexed product will generate a nearly identical gross of fee return as another investor who simply purchased a Russell 1000 indexed ETF.

Meanwhile, high-dividend smart beta products have experienced several tailwinds with respect to flows into these products since the 2008 global financial crisis. In 2013 the J.P. Morgan U.S. Equity Group made the case that high-dividend-paying stocks are, and will continue to be for years, an appropriate investment for yield-seeking investors who can assume equity market risk.[lx] They provided four reasons: First, high dividend stocks generally outperform their lower- or no-dividend-paying peers (see Figure 10.2). The authors postulate that a commitment to dividends may indicate that the business, industry, or management team is in a strong position and committed to generating shareholder value. Second, qualified dividends are taxed at the long-term capital gains rate and not ordinary income. Third, retiring baby boomers will generate an increase in demand for cash flow and high-dividend stocks, which may provide price support for these securities. Finally, for the first time since the early 1960s, the S&P 500 dividend yield exceeded the dividend yield on the 10-year U.S. Treasury, which significantly increases the relative attractiveness of dividend paying stocks vis-à-vis U.S. Treasury Bonds. For all these reasons, high-dividend smart beta products are one of the most popular products as measured by the number of ETFs and AUM.

Smart Beta Fees

As mentioned previously, because of the rules-based methodology associated with constructing smart beta portfolios, fund managers do not require teams of analysts to conduct company-level due diligence. So, the fund manager's personnel cost to manage smart beta portfolios is lower than that of a traditional active manager whose analysts conduct extensive bottom-up stock-specific analysis. As a result, smart beta managers typically charge lower management fees than their traditional active management counterparts. Conversely, smart beta fund managers have processes that are more complicated and data-driven than typical passive mandates. For example, whereas passive funds are generally constructed by sampling a traditional market-cap-weighted benchmark, smart beta products generally have an additional step of first creating an internal benchmark with targeted factor characteristics. Once this internal benchmark is created, smart beta managers then take the next step of creating a portfolio, often via sampling. Because of the resources required to complete this additional step, smart beta management fees are typically higher than those of a passive portfolio, as shown in Table 10.3.

Smart Beta Product Returns and Criticisms

So, how have smart beta products performed? That depends on who you ask, how you measure performance, which products you evaluate, and over what period you evaluate performance. In other words—results are mixed. Philips et al. (2015)[lxi] argue that "smart beta performance is not produced by capturing market inefficiency related to security-level mispricings, which would be the case if such strategies better tracked a security's intrinsic value. Rather, the historical outperformance relative to cap-weighted benchmarks can be traced to systematic size and value exposures that have demonstrated identifiable historical performance characteristics." Said another way, the authors (all of whom worked at passive-investing behemoth Vanguard) suggest that the smart beta products simply have value and small-cap biases, and after attributing for these tilts, the smart beta products do not outperform their market-cap counterparts. However, do these findings really suggest smart beta products aren't superior

Table 10.3 Average management fees by Morningstar category

Morningstar Category	Average Management Fees		
	Active	Smart Beta	Passive
U.S. Fund Large Blend	0.63	0.24	0.14
U.S. Fund Mid-Cap Growth	0.78	0.55	0.12
U.S. Fund Small Blend	0.80	0.18	0.19
U.S. Fund Small Growth	0.81	0.45	0.30
U.S. Fund Foreign Large Blend	0.69	0.17	0.18
U.S. Fund Foreign Small/Mid Blend	0.91	0.39	0.15
U.S. Fund Diversified Emerging Mkts	0.98	0.23	0.22
U.S. Fund Global Real Estate	0.84	0.39	0.25
Simple Average	**0.81**	**0.33**	**0.19**

Source: Morningstar Direct and Pacific Life. As of June 2018.

in producing risk-adjusted returns vis-à-vis market-cap-weighted benchmarks? Most smart beta managers don't claim to capture mispricings, but rather systematic risks or characteristics (such as yield, value, momentum, quality, etc.). Of note, at the time this report was written, Vanguard didn't have smart beta ETFs; but, they did have ETFs that had value or small-cap tilts. Since then, Vanguard may have had a modest change of heart as they seeded six factor-based ETF strategies in February 2018.[lxii]

UBS took a more direct approach when attempting to determine how smart beta ETFs had performed versus traditional market-capitalization-weighted benchmarks. To do this, their research team sourced performance data for almost 400 smart beta ETFs and compared the smart beta ETF returns to their corresponding S&P or MSCI indices. The team then distributed their findings in a May 2017 research report.[lxiii] In short, a substantial number of smart beta funds underperformed their equivalent market-capitalization indices—in both absolute and risk-adjusted returns. However, does this mean smart beta products are inferior to market-capitalization-weighted passive funds, or are the results of this study merely a reflection of the period over which the funds were evaluated? We know from Figure 10.2 that in the five-year period that ended December 2018, the size and value factors generated negative risk premiums, which may explain why many smart beta products underperformed their market-capitalization benchmarks. Conversely, over the past 15 years, dividend, size, and low-volatility factors all generated positive risk premiums. Therefore, wouldn't we expect smart beta products (if they existed back then) to have outperformed the market-capitalization benchmarks? Quite possibly. In short, more time is required to draw a definitive conclusion if smart beta products truly are a superior investment option to passively managed products. Separately, Vanguard founder Jack Bogle (may he rest in peace) delivered a similar scathing assessment of smart beta products, and fundamentally weighted indices in particular, in a 2016 Morningstar[lxiv] interview when he stated:

"There are only two funds that have been doing that for any period of time; one is Rob Arnott's fund, I think it's called RAFI 1000 and the other is Jeremy Siegel's fund called WisdomTree . . . and they have had respectively, 10 years and 9 years to prove themselves. They have not done so. It's on the record. The RAFI 1000 has done a little bit better than the S&P but at a higher risk and therefore, as it turns out in the data, has a lower Sharpe Ratio, a lower risk-adjusted return than the S&P 500. The WisdomTree is just the opposite. It has a lower return but a lower risk—but again a lower Sharpe Ratio. So the index has provided a better risk-adjusted return than either of those two forays into smart beta.

And as Bill Sharpe says, it's an interesting point, think about it this way: if smart beta is winning, dumb beta is losing by the exact same amount and there is no way around this in the marketplace . . . Not everybody can win. . . . we're unlike Wobegon, where all the children are above average. We all are average before cost and that's the methodology of the index fund. It gives you the average market return and takes five basis points out and it is the winning strategy unequivocally."

He's got a point. As of August 2018, the FTSE RAFI Developed 1000 Index 10-year annualized return and volatility were +7.32% and 18.18%, while its market capitalization equivalent benchmark, the FTSE Developed Index, 10-year annualized return and volatility were +7.74% and 15.97%.[lxv] Additionally, the RAFI fundamentally weighted index underperformed the FTSE index in seven of 10 calendar years ending in 2017. With respect to WisdomTree, it's difficult to evaluate Bogle's assertion. In 2006, WisdomTree launched twenty ETFs, all of which were "fundamentally-weighted dividend funds."[lxvi] To evaluate Bogle's statement, we'll focus on the five products that WisdomTree classified as either "total market" or "broad market" capitalization at the time of product launch. The results as of June 30, 2018, are shown in Table 10.4.

In short, over the past 12 years three have underperformed, one has closed, and one has outperformed its market-capitalization-weighted benchmark. Not a great track record, as Bogle correctly pointed out. However, do these results mean that smart beta—or more specifically in this case fundamentally weighted indexes—are inferior to market-capitalization-weighted indexes? Given these results, one cannot say that fundamentally weighted benchmarks are superior, but like any analysis of smart beta products, the results are highly time-period specific and the sample size is small. As a result, we cannot conclude that smart beta products in general, or fundamentally weighted benchmarks in particular, are inferior. However, we are confident that our readers will continue to hear market practitioners taking sides on the debate, and as they do, they will continue talking their own book.[8]

---

[8] *Talking your own book* is an expression that indicates a person or entity is publicly encouraging others to purchase (or sell) what that person or entity already owns (or doesn't own). The expression originates from a trader promoting line items in their 'book of trade.' This 'book' is the accounting of all stocks, bonds, or derivatives a trader currently owns or is short. By 'talking their book' the trader is encouraging others to purchase or sell the same securities, which is beneficial to the trader as the price of their 'book' will likely increase as a result. More recently, the expression *talking your own book* has extended to an investment manager promoting their strategy or products. Because of this promotion, an investment manager may benefit from both inflows into their products or other investment managers purchasing the same securities.

Table 10.4 Select performance of WisdomTree products

Fund Name	Ticker	Market Capitalization	Region	Benchmark	Since Fund Inception Return	Benchmark Return	Excess Return
WisdomTree Total Dividend Fund	DTD	Total Market	Domestic	Russell 3000 Index	8.07%	9.02%	−0.95%
WisdomTree International Equity Fund	DWM	Total Market	International	MSCI EAFE Index	4.13%	3.86%	0.27%
WisdomTree Europe Total Dividend Fund	DEB	Broad Market	Europe	Fund liquidated	N/A	N/A	N/A
WisdomTree Japan Total Dividend Fund	DXJ	Broad Market	Japan	MSCI Japan/MSCI Japan Local Currency Spliced Index	3.66%	4.22%	−0.56%
WisdomTree Pacific ex-Japan Dividend Fund	AXJL	Broad Market	Pacific	MSCI Pacific exJapan/MSCI AC Asia Pacific exJapan Spliced Index	6.56%	7.13%	−0.57%

Source: WisdomTree quarterly factsheets (June 16, 2006 to June 30, 2018). Returns are NAV returns.

Institutional Adoption

In addition to retail investors gravitating toward smart beta products, and despite a lack of convincing empirical evidence that these products have recently added value versus traditional market-capitalization-weighted benchmarks, institutional investors are also embracing smart beta and factor-investing strategies. Beginning in 2014, FTSE Russell (a global index provider) began surveying hundreds of institutional investors on their utilization of smart beta products and began producing an annual report with their findings.[lxvii] These reports show that institutional investors continue to adopt smart beta products by adding them to the institutional investors' platforms. For example, in 2017, 46% of respondents stated that they have at least one smart beta allocation, up from 26% in 2015. Additionally, more than 50% of the medium-sized ($1–$10 billion) and large ($10 billion or more) institutional investors already have at least one smart beta allocation. The most popular reasons that institutional investors either have or are considering smart beta investments are: risk reduction, return enhancement, improved diversification, and cost savings. Additionally, in 2017, 70% of those surveyed indicated that they are either using or evaluating smart beta strategies for strategic (long-term) use. This suggests smart beta is not a fad and will likely occupy a place in institutional portfolios for the foreseeable future. Finally, the most common smart beta strategy that institutions are utilizing are multi-factor strategies. We interpret this to be a tacit admission that institutions do not believe they can (or should) attempt to time factor risk premium; so, a prudent approach is to diversify and gain exposure to a basket of factors simultaneously. Interestingly, the low-volatility smart beta strategy is the second-most popular product. Why are low-volatility strategies so popular? We're not sure. This factor did outperform other factors in 2008, and it has generated a positive risk premium for the five-year period ending in 2018. However, over long horizons, such as 10- and 15-year periods, the size, dividend, and quality factors have all outperformed the low-quality factor.

SUMMARY AND INVESTMENT IMPLICATIONS

Summary

On the heels of decades of academic research, factor-investing, fundamental indexing, and smart beta products continue to gain broad acceptance among both retail and institutional investors. And for good reason: these products are lower-fee than traditional active (stock picking) portfolios, and they come with a growing library of academic literature that adds credibility to the factor-investing process. Owing in part to these two reasons, flows have followed.

There is around $800 billion in U.S. smart beta ETFs alone, while a majority of surveyed institutional investors now either have or are considering adding one or more smart beta products to their platforms. Early advocates of factor investing, including AQR and Dimensional (both of whom have deep roots at the University of Chicago), have established themselves as industry leaders, while several other firms including Research Affiliates, BlackRock, WisdomTree, and Invesco have built upon their success and now offer a wide range of products to both institutional and retail investors.

But, like anything that seems too good to be true, it may be. So, before replacing either passively or actively managed stock-picking portfolios with smart beta products, investors should first understand the risks and potential shortfalls associated with factor-investing. To name a few: the performance of smart beta and fundamental indexed products has been mixed. Many of these products have not added value over 3-, 5-, and 10-year periods that ended in April 2017 versus traditional market-capitalization-weighted indexes according to UBS.[lxviii] Additionally, many factors have recently performed poorly; the size and value factors that were considered reliable sources of risk premium (until recently) have generally detracted from performance over the five-year period that ended in 2018. But not to worry, according to many academics, because factors generate positive premiums over much longer periods (10 to 20 years); so, 5 or 10 years of a negative factor premium does not mean that an allocation to this factor won't add value over an even longer term. How long? Tough to say. Fortunately, factors are generally uncorrelated, so many managers diversify their factor exposures in an attempt to outperform a traditional market-capitalization-weighted index. So, can managers time factors? Depends on who you ask. Asness says, "Generally no"—Arnott says, "Yes"—and Ang says, "Yes, but you need to first correctly identify the economic regime."

One final concern with factor investing is that there is a nonzero possibility that all the factor research, which relies heavily on statistical analysis, is flawed due to unintentional data mining or model overfitting. Bem (2011) controversially challenged the mathematical foundation upon which much academic research is built when he released the results of years of field study. Using generally accepted methods for data collection and analysis, Bem demonstrated with statistical significance that extrasensory perception is real after conducting nine time-reversing experiments.[lxix] Later that year, professors at the Wharton School and Haas School of Business demonstrated that using seemingly innocuous data analysis procedures, they could generate a false-positive result (at 95% confidence) 60.7% of the time, with a random data set.[lxx] Campbell Harvey, Yan Liu, and Heqing Zhu, who identified 315 factors found in academic literature, stated that they believe that "most claimed research findings in financial economics are likely false." They go on to advocate that academics and practitioners alike utilize a t-statistic of 3.0 and not 2.0, essentially raising the bar and reducing the likelihood that a factor is deemed statistically significant and not a chance occurrence.[lxxi] Robert Novy-Marx (2016) highlighted that smart beta strategies, or multi-signal strategies (like those that weight stocks based on a fundamental weight), are likely built on questionable statistical analysis caused by overfitting. To highlight this point, Novy-Marx started with a stock dataset and random signals, and then used standard statistical tools to develop statistically significant multi-signal strategies. However, "by construction, these signals have no real power and cannot predict performance out-of-sample."[lxxii] So, is all this factor research, upon which factor investing and smart beta products are based, just a product of statistical false-positive results? Probably not, since the biggest, most established factors were ascertained decades ago (and thus have decades of out-of-sample evidence) and have numerous economic theories to explain their existence. But, it does give investors reason to critically evaluate new products and processes based on limited research or empirical data.

Investment Implications

- Factor investing has gained popularity in part because it offers investors an intelligible process for outperforming a market-capitalization-weighted portfolio, and factor investing offers a compelling story as to why this approach will add value into the future. Specifically, there is a growing body of academic research that factors exist and will reward investors with positive risk premiums. Additionally, academics and practitioners alike believe many factor premiums will continue to be positive due to a premium attributed to either systematic risks (undiversifiable risks) or systematic errors (like behavioral biases or structural market inefficiencies). If you believe this, then migrating some of your passive portfolio to factor-based investing is appropriate.
- However, it's important to realize that factor-based portfolio management does not guarantee superior performance. There is additional marginal risk to factor investing, and someone who utilizes this approach must be prepared to underperform market-capitalization-weighted indices for long stretches (possibly five or more years).
- In general, one shouldn't attempt to time factor exposure. Those who attempt to do this have not been wildly successful. But if you do attempt to time factor exposure (a "sin" according to Cliff Asness), only sin a little—not a lot.
- When evaluating factor portfolios, be prepared to critically evaluate any back test that demonstrates superior investment performance. Statistical tools, when applied incorrectly, can demonstrate statistical significance

for almost anything. Even reasonably applied sampling methods can occasionally yield wild results (such as demonstrating extrasensory perception is real). Otherwise, if it seems too good to be true, it probably is, and it's best to wait until there are years of empirical data to better validate a process or product.

CITATIONS

i. Wiggins, Richard. (February 13, 2018). "Smart Beta Is Making this Strategist Sick." Institutional Investor. https://www.institutional investor.com/article/b16x0v5q14ky2k/smartbeta-is-making-this -strategist-sick.

ii. Connor, Gregory. (May/June 1995). "The Three Types of Factor Models: A Comparison of Their Explanatory Power." *Financial Analysts Journal.* Vol. 51. No. 3. pp. 42–46.

iii. Harvey, Campbell, Yan Liu, and Heqing Zhu. (2016). ". . . and the Cross-Section of Expected Returns." Review of Financial Studies. Vol. 29(1). pp. 5–68.

iv. Bender, Jennifer, Remy Briand, Dimitris Melas, and Raman Aylur Subramanian. (December 2013). "Foundations of Factor Investing." MSCI Research Insight. Exhibit 1.

v. Melas, D., R. Briand, and R. Urwin. (2011). "Harvesting Risk Premia with Strategy Indices—From Today's Alpha to Tomorrow's Beta." MSCI Research Insight.

vi. Markowitz, H.M. (March 1952). "Portfolio Selection." *The Journal of Finance.* 7(1). pp. 77–91. doi:10.2307/2975974.

vii. Sharpe, William F. (1964). "Capital asset prices: A theory of market equilibrium under conditions of risk." *Journal of Finance.* 19(3). 425–442.

viii. Lintner, John. (1965). "The valuation of risk assets and the selection of risky investments in stock portfolios and capital budgets." *Review of Economics and Statistics.* 47(1). pp. 13–37.

ix. Mossin, Jan. (1966). "Equilibrium in a Capital Asset Market." *Econometrica.* 34 (4): pp. 768–783.

x. Markowitz, Harry M. (December 7, 1990). "Foundations of Portfolio Theory." Nobel Lecture. Baruch College. The City University of New York, NY.

xi. Black, F., M. Jensen, and M. S. Scholes. (1972). "The Capital Asset Pricing Model: Some Empirical Findings." In: Jensen, M. (ed.). *Studies in the Theory of Capital Markets*, Praeger Publishers, New York, NY. pp. 79–124.

xii. Ross, Stephen A. (December 1976). "The arbitrage theory of capital asset pricing." *Journal of Economic Theory*. Elsevier, Vol. 13(3). pp. 341–360.

xiii. Chen, Nai-Fu, Richard Roll, and Stephen Ross. (1986). "Economic Forces and the Stock Market." *The Journal of Business*. 59. pp. 383–403. 10.1086/296344.

xiv. Basu, S. (June 1977). "Investment performance of common stocks in relation to their price-earnings ratios: A test of the efficient market hypothesis." *Journal of Finance*. pp. 663–682.

xv. Banz, Rolf W. (1981). "The relationship between return and market value of common stocks." *Journal of Financial Economics*. 9. pp. 3–18. 10.1016/0304-405X(81)90018-0.

xvi. Fama, E.F. and K.R. French. (1992). "The cross-section of expected stock returns." *Journal of Finance*. 47, 2. pp. 427–465.

xvii. Jegadeesh, Narasimhan and Sheridan Titman. (March 1993). "Returns to Buying Winners and Selling Losers: Implications for Stock Market Efficiency." *Journal of Finance*, American Finance Association, Vol. 48(1). pp. 65–91.

xviii. Carhart, M.M. (1997). "On Persistence in Mutual Fund Performance." *The Journal of Finance*. 52. pp. 57–82. doi:10.1111/j.1540-6261.1997.tb03808.x. JSTOR 2329556.

xix. Fama, Eugene F. and Kenneth R. French. (September 2014). "A Five-Factor Asset Pricing Model." Fama-Miller Working Paper. Available at SSRN: https://ssrn.com/abstract=2287202 or http://dx.doi.org/10.2139/ssrn.2287202.

xx. Morse, Libby. (November 6, 2008). "The True Believer: David Booth, '71, proves his Chicago smarts by refusing to out-think the market." *Chicago GSB Magazine*. www.chicagobooth.edu. University of Chicago Booth School of Business.

xxi. Houlihan, Patricia. (November 6, 2008). "The Mentor: In his own words, Eugene Fama talks about the power of markets and friendship." *Chicago GSB Magazine*. www.chicagobooth.edu. University of Chicago Booth School of Business.

xxii. Cooperman, Jeannette. (June 23, 2009). "The Return of the King." https://www.stlmag.com/The-Return-of-the-King/.

xxiii. Sumo, Vanessa. (November 6, 2008). "The Science: A deep appreciation for markets and scientific research are the foundations of Dimensional Fund Advisors' success." *Chicago GSB Magazine*. www.chicagobooth.edu. University of Chicago Booth School of Business.

xxiv. Goodman, Beverly. (January 4, 2014). "A Different Dimension." *Barron's*.

xxv. Lewis, Michael. (December 2007). "The Evolution of an Investor." *Portfolio Magazine.*

xxvi. Goodman, Beverly. (January 4, 2014). "A Different Dimension." *Barron's.*

xxvii. https://us.dimensional.com/about-us/our-company (page visited 8/5/2018).

xxviii. https://us.dimensional.com/ (page visited 8/5/2018).

xxix. Conversations with Tyler. (November 18, 2015). Cliff Asness on Marvel vs. DC and Why Never to Share a Gym with Cirque du Soleil (Ep. 5—Live at Mason). Mercatus Center Podcast.

xxx. Cohan, William D. (March 29, 2011). "Man vs. Machine on Wall Street: How Computers Beat the Market." *The Atlantic.*

xxxi. https://www.aqr.com/About-Us/OurFirm#firmfacts.

xxxii. Wigglesworth, Robin. (July 23, 2018). "The hedge fund killer." *Financial Times.*

xxxiii. Arnott, Robert D. and Clifford S. Asness. (January–February 2003). "Surprise! Higher Dividends = Higher Earnings Growth." *Financial Analysts Journal."*

xxxiv. Kuriloff, Aaron. (April 28, 2017). "Rob Arnott, 'Godfather of Smart Beta,' Tells Investors: You're Doing It Wrong." *The Wall Street Journal.*

xxxv. Arnott, Robert D., Jason C. Hsu, and Philip Moore. (March/April 2005). Fundamental Indexation. *Financial Analysts Journal.* Vol. 61. No. 2. pp. 83–99. Available at SSRN. https://ssrn.com/abstract=604842 or http://dx.doi.org/10.2139/ssrn.604842.

xxxvi. https://www.researchaffiliates.com/en_us/about-us.html.

xxxvii. Morningstar Manager Research. (September 2017). "A Global Guide to Strategic-Beta Exchange-Traded Products." www.morningstar .com.

xxxviii. Ang, Andrew. (2014). *Asset Management: A Systematic Approach to Factor Investing.* Oxford University Press, New York, NY. p. x.

xxxix. https://www.blackrock.com/institutions/en-us/strategies/factor-based -investing.

xl. https://www.qsinvestors.com/press-release/legg-mason-announces -acquisition-of-qs-investors.

xli. Form 10-K. Commission File Number 1-8529. Legg Mason Inc. p. 6.

xlii. Diamond, Randy. (September 28, 2017). "Invesco's acquisition of Guggenheim's ETF business enhances smart beta offerings." *Pensions & Investments.*

xliii. Chan, K. C. and Nai-fu Chen. (1991). "Structural and return characteristics of small and large firms." *Journal of Finance.* 46: pp. 1467–84.

xliv. Liu, W. (2006). "A liquidity-augmented capital asset pricing model." *Journal of Financial Economics.* 82(3). pp. 631–671.

xlv. Zhang, X. F. (2006). "Information uncertainty and stock returns." *Journal of Finance.* 61(1). pp. 15–136.

xlvi. Baker, Malcolm, Brendan Bradley, and Jeffrey Wurgler. (2011). "Benchmarks as Limits to Arbitrage: Understanding the Low-Volatility Anomaly." *Financial Analyst Journal.* Vol. 67, No. 1. pp. 40–54.

xlvii. Jean-Claude Trichet, then Governor of the Banque de France. (June 15, 2001). Keynote speech delivered at the Fifth European Financial Markets Convention, Paris. "Preserving Financial Stability in an Increasingly Globalized World."

xlviii. Dasgupta, Amil, Andrea Prat, and Michela Verardo. (2011). "The price impact of institutional herding." *Review of Financial Studies.* 24 (3). pp. 892–925.

xlix. Asness, Clifford S., Swati Chandra, Antti Ilmanen, and Ronen Israel. (March 7, 2017). "Contrarian Factor Timing Is Deceptively Difficult." *Journal of Portfolio Management*, Special Edition. Available at SSRN: https://ssrn.com/abstract=2928945.

l. Arnott, R., N. Beck, and V. Kalesnik. (2016c). "Timing Smart Beta Strategies? Of Course! Buy Low, Sell High!" Research Affiliates.

li. Asness, Cliff. (March 15, 2017). "Factor Timing Is Hard." *AQR Perspectives.* https://www.aqr.com/Insights/Perspectives/Factor-Timing -is-Hard.

lii. Coy, Peter. (April 6, 2017). "Investors Always Think They're Getting Ripped Off. Here's Why They're Right." *Bloomberg Businessweek.*

liii. Asness, Cliff. (April 12, 2017). "Lies, Damned Lies, and Data Mining." *AQR Perspectives.*

liv. Hodges, Philip, Ked Hogan, Justin R. Peterson, and Andrew Ang. (Fall 2017). "Factor Timing with Cross-Sectional and Time-Series Predictors." *The Journal of Portfolio Management Fall 2017.* 44(1). pp. 30–43; doi: https://doi.org/10.3905/jpm.2017.44.1.030.

lv. Carlson, Debbie. (May 10, 2018). "Smart Beta vs. Factor Funds: What's the Difference?" www.etf.com.

lvi. 2017 *Investment Company Institute Fact Book.* pp. 59, 67.

lvii. Morningstar Manager Research. (March 2019). "A Global Guide to Strategic-Beta Exchange-Traded Products." Exhibits 2 and 4.

lviii. ———. (March 2019). "A Global Guide to Strategic-Beta Exchange-Traded Products." Exhibit 6. www.morningstar.com.

lix. FTSE Russell. (August 2018). Russell U.S. Equity Indexes Construction and Methodology, v3.5.

lx.   Hart, Clare and Mariana Connolly. (April 2013). "Dividends for the long term." J. P. Morgan Investment Insights.

lxi.   Philips, Christopher B., Donald G. Bennyhoff, Francis M. Kinniry Jr., Todd Schlanger, and Paul Chin. (August 2015). "An evaluation of smart beta and other rules-based active strategies." Vanguard Research.

lxii.   https://advisors.vanguard.com/iwe/pdf/FAETFTRI.pdf.

lxiii.   Perlman, David. (May 24, 2017). "Exchange-traded funds: Smart beta performance monitor." UBS.

lxiv.   Morningstar News Team. (May 9, 2016). Bogle: Smart Beta Does Not Deliver Better Returns.

lxv.   https://www.researchaffiliates.com/en_us/strategies/performance .html.

lxvi.   Press Release. (June 13, 2006). "WisdomTree Investments Announces Launch of First Family of Fundamentally-Weighted Dividend ETFs."

lxvii.   FTSE Russell. (2017). Smart beta: 2017 global survey findings from asset owners.

lxviii.   Perlman, David. (May 24, 2017). "Exchange-traded funds: Smart beta performance monitor." UBS.

lxix.   Bem, D.J. (March 2011). "Feeling the future: Experimental evidence for anomalous retroactive influences on cognition and affect." (PDF). *Journal of Personality and Social Psychology*. 100(3). 407–25. doi:10.1037/a0021524. PMID 21280961.

lxx.   Simmons, J.P., L.D. Nelson, and U. Simonsohn. (2011). "False-positive psychology: undisclosed flexibility in data collection and analysis allows presenting anything as significant." *Psychol. Sci.* 22. pp. 1359–1366.

lxxi.   Harvey, Campbell, Yan Liu, and Heqing Zhu. (2016). ". . . and the Cross-Section of Expected Returns." *Review of Financial Studies*, Vol. 29(1). pp. 5–68.

lxxii.   Novy-Marx, Robert. (July 2015). Backtesting Strategies Based on Multiple Signals. NBER Working Paper No. w21329. Available at SSRN: https://ssrn.com/abstract=2629935.

11

BEHAVIORAL FINANCE

In March 2015, roughly four years after my disastrous London Interbank Offered Rate (LIBOR)-history e-mail, I found myself pondering Fed policy and eager to express a nonconsensus view to my colleagues. If you remember from this book's preface, my LIBOR e-mail earned me the ire of Bill Gross who publicly chastised me for failing to include clear and concise investment implications. Fortunately, while investment implications needed to be included in such notes, there was considerable latitude for thought piece composition, content, and convention. So, while on vacation, and after showing a draft version of the following e-mail to a small group of colleagues, I forwarded it to the entirety of the firm's traders, analysts, and portfolio managers:

== Subject: Thoughts on Dots ==

Investment Implication: I continue to believe that front-end duration is relatively safe. Look to add on weakness.

The Catch: Yesterday I spent the day at the Houston Rodeo, spending time with my family and following the market while the kids were entertained by bee hives and the like.

Oddly, I seemed to fit right in. I'm not from Houston—my wife is. Being as this was my second time at the rodeo, I dressed appropriately: boots (3rd time wearing/birthday gift), tucked-in plaid shirt (I own but one), and a John Deere hat (I borrowed it from my father-in-law). Before the rodeo began, I even stood and removed my hat while 71k people thanked Jesus for peacefully assembling and prayed for the safety of the bull-riders. In fact, if I didn't speak, nobody would have assumed I am a city-slicker, born and raised in a left-coast blue state.

I was like a Fed dot. Unassuming, fitting in, and relaying little information. In fact, the casual observer would have been better served assuming I know nothing of livestock, roping, and mutton busting.

The Dots: No doubt today's dots were dovish. The median dot changes from the previous release were:

- 2015: −0.50% to 0.625%
- 2016: −0.625% to 1.875%
- 2017: −0.50% to 3.125%

This seemed to come as a surprise. But should it be? [names removed]'s charts demonstrate the Fed consistently over-estimates the forward path of the Fed Funds rate. And why is that?

I postulate the Fed is suffering from four, and possibly more, behavioral biases:

- *Optimism bias*: a bias that causes a person to believe that they are less at risk of experiencing a negative event compared to others.

  FOMC thought: Sure, Japan has been stuck at ~0% since the 1990s, but we're going to achieve liftoff where they couldn't.

- *Anchoring bias*: a bias that describes the common human tendency to rely too heavily on the first piece of information offered (the "anchor") when making decisions.

  FOMC thought: Neutral is 4%, maybe a little less. Let me figure out a way that we'll get there in the 3-year window over which this questionnaire covers.

- *Bandwagon effect*: the probability of individual adoption increasing with respect to the proportion who have already done so.

  FOMC thought: Everybody else seems to assume there'll be ~300bps+ of hiking between now and the end of 2017—I'll put down something similar.

- *Conservatism (Bayesian) bias*: A bias whereby a person with an opinion changes that opinion in an orderly manner as information arrives, but in an insufficient amount as would be indicated given Bayes' Theorem.

  FOMC thought: We've been overly optimistic in the past with respect to the path of future fed hikes, but this time we're going to be spot on, now that more time has passed and we've revised lower our expectations for the path of rates.

The Implication: When the market and the Fed contradict, be inclined to believe the market and not the Fed. Fed officials would like nothing more than to raise rates to a neutral level. This would be a huge victory years after the global financial crisis. Officials are forecasting what they want owing to at least four cognitive biases. The market, on the other hand, is agnostic with respect to whether or not the Fed can declare a victory, and is less subject to behavioral biases (although, it is certainly not immune).

== E-mail End ==

The response to the note was quite positive—around ten people e-mailed me to say I was wrong! Within hours, I was invited to present to the firm's investment committee when I returned. The one-day discussion spilled into a second day, during which time I took the side that the Federal Open Market Committee (FOMC) would fail to reach a policy rate of 1.875% by December 2016 and one-year Treasury bills were cheap. At the time, the market implied one-year rate in one-year's time (or, what the market implied the one-year Treasury bill would be in March 2016), was 0.98%.

I was right, and in March 2016 (one year after I had sent my note), the one-year T-bill rate was 0.63% (0.35% lower than the market implied rate the prior year). Additionally, the FOMC midpoint for the policy rate in December 2016 was 0.625%, or −1.25% lower than the FOMC forecasted in March 2015. As Figure 11.1 shows, the downward trajectory in each of the year-end FOMC policy rate forecasts demonstrates that between Q1 2014 and Q4 2017 the FOMC consistently overestimated the year-end federal funds effective rate.[i] This is a bit surprising since the members of the FOMC are some of the most highly educated and informed economists, and they are the ones who set the rate!

While the thrust of the two-day investment committee debate centered around the economic outlook and the mechanics of normalizing rates with over $2 trillion in excess reserves (see Chapter 4), my assertion that the members of the FOMC suffered from behavioral biases was at the core of the investment thesis. And while it is impossible to state with certainty that this was the case, the failure of the FOMC forecasts suggests this thesis was at least partially right. So, what are behavioral biases, and how could some of the most brilliant economists fall victim to them in such a public manner? I'll tackle those questions here.

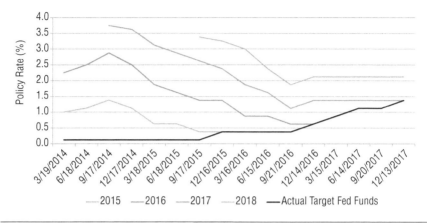

Figure 11.1   FOMC forecasts of the year-end effective federal funds rate.[1]
Source: Bloomberg, Federal Reserve Bank of St. Louis

BRIEF HISTORY OF THE BEHAVIORAL ECONOMICS FIELD OF STUDY

In the 1960s and 1970s, what we now know as *behavioral economics* was largely relegated to cognitive psychology, which is the study of how mental processes affect behavior. Specifically, cognitive psychology studied how people's minds filter and process information, how the mind determines what to filter out, and how that impacts people's reactions to stimulus. Adding to this body of work in 1974, Daniel Kahneman and Amos Tversky, professors of psychology at the University of British Columbia and Stanford University, respectively, published *Judgment under Uncertainty: Heuristics and Biases*. Kahneman and Tversky introduced the idea that people regularly "rely on a limited number of heuristic principals that reduce the complex tasks of assessing probabilities," and while these heuristics are useful "they sometimes lead to severe and systematic errors." A heuristic is a *cognitive shortcut* or *rule of thumb* that allows people

---

[1] This chart is a time series of the median quarterly prediction by the FOMC for the expected federal funds rate (the policy rate set by the FOMC) on the final trading date of each year. Each quarter since January 2012, the FOMC has released a *dot plot* that shows each policymaker's individual forecast of the policy rate at specific year-ends. There are nineteen dots (the seven members of the Federal Reserve board of governors and the twelve presidents of each of the Federal Reserve Banks). The dots are anonymous so they can't be attributed to any specific member. In addition to providing year-end forecasts, the dot plot includes each individual FOMC member's evaluation of the *long-term* or *neutral* policy rate.

to make quick decisions without a formalized process of assessing a situation by assigning probabilities to a series of outcomes. Some examples of these systematic errors included being influenced by a starting point, such as estimating the product of $8 \times 7 \times 6 \times 5 \times 4 \times 3 \times 2 \times 1$ versus $1 \times 2 \times 3 \times 4 \times 5 \times 6 \times 7 \times 8$. Another example is relying on similarities between groups to determine relative probabilities.[ii] While the examples given in this paper were interesting and they clearly laid the foundation for behavioral economics, few economists paid much attention to the anomalies highlighted by Kahneman and Tversky.

This changed five years later when Kahneman and Tversky published *Prospect Theory: An Analysis of Decision under Risk* (1979). In this seminal paper, Kahneman and Tversky offered a descriptive model they called *prospect theory*, which stood in contrast to *utility theory*.[iii] Utility theory was widely accepted until that time, and the prevailing economic thought was that people were purely rational and made choices that optimized their ability to achieve their self-interests. The belief in the perfectly rational individual is also known as *the economic man (econ)*, an expression that can be traced back to 1890.[iv] However, Kahneman and Tversky called into question the purely rational nature of human decision making while putting forward a new model, one that suggested that people were not perfectly rational when presented with uncertainty. Instead, prospect theory stated that while people select options in an attempt to maximize their utility, the estimation of that utility is impacted by seemingly irrational biases. For example, people's utility declines more by a loss than by an equivalent gain, as shown in Figure 11.2. So people are more likely to select options that minimize losses—even if those options don't maximize overall gain. Additionally, people dislike uncertainty so are more likely to select options with certainty than options that will yield higher probability-adjusted outcomes but are uncertain.

The 1979 paper, *Prospect Theory: An Analysis of Decision under Risk*, included surveys of students and faculty who were asked questions like: Which of the following would you prefer: (A) a 50% chance to win $1,000 and a 50% chance to win nothing or (B) $450 outright? If people were purely rational, then they would select the highest probability-adjusted outcome. In this case, people would consistently select option A. However, in practice, people often select option B, and in doing so, demonstrate they have a greater aversion to loss than attraction to gain (loss aversion). Additionally, the authors further demonstrate through surveys that people may overstate the utility gained or lost from a low-probability gain or loss. The willingness of people to pay to avoid a large loss, even if the likelihood of that loss was exceptionally low, seemed irrational. However, people's strong aversion to loss provided the rationale for why people spend so much money to purchase insurance at a price that exceeds the expected actuarial cost.

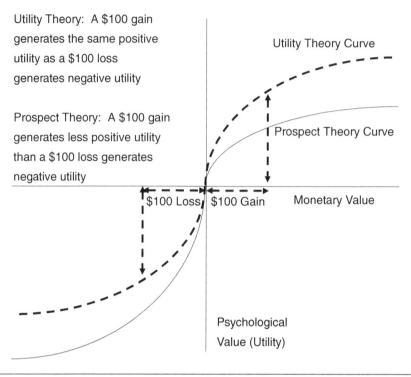

Figure 11.2   Utility theory and prospect theory curves

At the time, both the applicability of and data to support the prospect theory were limited. However, there was a growing body of interesting anecdotal evidence that highlighted investor irrationality. One such example was in 1968 when General Public Utilities Corp. (GPU) proposed to substitute three quarterly cash dividends for stock dividends (investors would still receive at least one annual cash dividend). Investors who wanted the cash dividend could sell the shares back to the company with minimal brokerage fees. The proposal was rational and in line with the objective of profit maximization: both investors and the company would save on taxes. Additionally, investors who wanted cash dividends could still receive them, and investors who had elected to reinvest their dividends would see no change. However, despite the benefits to shareholders that this plan would generate, the reaction among shareholders was decidedly negative. The price of the company's stock fell and Mr. Kuhn, president of GPU, began receiving mail from displeased shareholders. One note called him a *hypocritical ass* while another suggested that he seek psychiatric care.[v] Under pressure from shareholders, the company relented and scrapped the proposal.[vi] Other interesting examples of individuals behaving in a seemingly irrational manner were highlighted by Thaler and Shefrin (1981). While Kahneman and Tversky's paper focused on seemingly irrational decisions made by people due to a potential loss aversion, Thaler and Shefrin's work demonstrated that people seem to act irrational because of difficulties with self-control. Examples that were cited include the popularity of Christmas clubs, which involve investors depositing money each week and only withdrawing the cash on December 1. The savings plan pays no interest, and the participants willingly forgo the opportunity to withdraw the money before December 1. A purely rational individual would put the money in an interest-bearing savings account that provides daily liquidity. So, people who participated in these clubs were not acting like an *econ*. Another cited example was passbook loans, whereby somebody with $5,000 in a savings account (then paying 5% interest), could take a 9% loan with the cash as collateral. People who participated would have been better served simply withdrawing their cash at a 5% opportunity cost than a 4% (9% − 5%) realized interest expense.[vii] These examples, and many more, continued to suggest utility theory was either incorrect or incomplete.

Not everybody was convinced that this growing body of examples of people acting irrationally was evidence that the utility theory was in anyway challenged. In 1986, Nobel economist Merton Miller took a direct shot at the budding economic study of behavioral finance when he published *Behavior Rationality in Finance: The Case of Dividends*. The paper discussed *dividend anomalies* in which companies fail to maximize shareholder value by paying dividends (as opposed to retaining earnings). As highlighted in Shefrin and Statman (1984), due to higher taxes on dividends than on capital gains, investors would be better off if companies retained earnings and didn't pay dividends. But, investors consistently reward companies that pay high dividends and balk when dividends are reduced. They even demanded that GPU continue to pay its dividends and forgo its more tax-efficient plan of dividend distribution. Professor Miller attributed the dividend anomaly to a variety of idiosyncrasies, including individual-specific tax considerations or corporate treasurers who fail to focus their time on tax efficiency because they have more pressing concerns. Additionally, Miller argued that the anomaly "aggregates to be less anomalous than conventional handwringing might suggest." Miller concluded by stating that "rationality-based market equilibrium models in finance in general and of dividends in particular are alive and well . . . The framework is not so weighed down with anomalies that a complete reconstruction (on behavioral/cognitive or other lines) is either needed or likely to occur in the near future. The fact that we shy away from all of these stories in building our models is not because the stories are uninteresting but because they may be too interesting and thereby distract us from the pervasive market forces that should be our principal concern."[viii] Ouch. According to Robert Shiller, years later when both Merton Miller and Richard Thaler were on faculty at the University of Chicago, Miller would not even make eye contact with Thaler when passing in the hallway.[ix]

Despite the criticism from his colleagues, in 2003, Kahneman published a now heavily cited article titled *Maps of Bounded Rationality: Psychology for Behavioral Economics*. Kahneman directly responds to Miller's and others' criticisms of behavioral economics in the beginning of his paper when he states, "Economists often criticize psychological research for its propensity to generate lists of errors and biases, and for its failure to offer a coherent alternative to the rational-agent model. This complaint is only partly justified: psychological theories of intuitive thinking cannot match the elegance and precision of formal normative models of belief and choice, but this is just another way of saying that rational models are psychologically unrealistic. Furthermore, the alternative to simple and precise models is not chaos. Psychology offers integrative concepts and mid-level generalizations, which gain credibility from their ability to explain ostensibly different phenomena in diverse domains."[x]

The following year, in a 26-chapter roundtable series, 18 authors contributed to and published *Advances in Behavioral Economics* (2004). In the first chapter, Colin Camerer and George Loewenstein strike a conciliatory tone when they state, "[behavioral economics] does not imply a wholesale rejection of the neoclassical approach to economics based on utility maximization, equilibrium, and efficiency . . . Most of the papers modify one or two assumptions in standard theory in the direction of greater psychological realism. Often these departures are not radical at all because they relax simplifying assumptions that are not central to the economic approach. For example, there is nothing in the core neoclassical theory that specifies people should not care about fairness, that they should weight risky outcomes in a linear fashion, or that they must discount the future exponentially at a constant rate. Other assumptions simply acknowledge human limits on computational power, willpower, and self-interest."[xi]

In 2017, University of Chicago Professor Richard Thaler was awarded the Nobel Prize in Economics, making him the sixth adherent to behavioral economics to win the prize (the others are George Akerlof, Robert Fogel, Daniel Kahneman, Elinor Ostrom, and Robert Shiller). Speaking at a Dimensional Fund Advisors institutional investors conference in 2018, University of Chicago Professor Eugene Fama, who had won the Nobel Prize in Economics in 2013, described how excited he was for his colleague. According to Fama, he went to Thaler's office, congratulated him, and explained, "Well Richard, I'm now the most important person in behavioral finance."

"Why's that?" Thaler asked.

"Because without me, you'd have nobody to criticize!"

Current Theory of the Causes of Behavioral Biases

While the cause of behavioral biases is still a topic of debate, cognitive scientists have largely coalesced around the theory that these biases are an unfortunate result of human's two modes of thinking. These modes of thinking are intuitive (system one) and reflective (system two). The theory that we have these two systems are often described as *dual processes* and was first developed in the 1970s.[xii] Evans et al. (2010) in their book *Thinking Twice: Two Minds in One Brain*, describe the two systems in this way: "The intuitive mind is old (system one), evolved early, and shares many of its features with animal cognition. It is the source of emotion and intuitions, and reflects both the habits acquired in our lifetime and the adaptive behaviors evolved by ancient ancestors. The reflective mind (system two), by contrast, is recently evolved and distinctively human: It enables us to think in abstract and hypothetical ways about the world around us and to calculate the future consequences of our actions."[xiii]

The source of behavioral biases can be attributed to system one creating an overly simplified narrative and suppressing alternative stories or activating system two. System one uses rules of thumb, oversimplifies complex situations, and enables people to rapidly respond to a stimulus and decide on a course of action. This is extremely helpful, but its existence means that we are prone to systematic errors. Unfortunately, an insidious feature of these cognitive shortcomings is that we are generally unaware of their existence. Fortunately, much research has been done in the past 40 years identifying some of the most common biases that people exhibit, which, at the least, has made it marginally easier to identify when someone else is exhibiting a behavioral bias. So what are the most common behavioral biases? I'll cover those here.

Biases and Nudges

In 2008, Richard Thaler and Cass Sunstein published *Nudge: Improving Decisions about Health, Wealth, and Happiness*, bringing behavioral economics to the masses.[xiv] In this book, Thaler and Sunstein summarize over thirty years of academic research concerning people's heuristics, biases, and human irrationality. Most important, Thaler and Sunstein offer dozens of policy prescriptions, or *nudges*, that have the potential to do everything from increasing our savings, to improving our investment decisions, to making healthier choices, and to producing a cleaner environment. Thaler and Sunstein begin by covering eight well-documented behavioral biases, including: loss aversion, anchoring bias, availability, optimism and overconfidence, representativeness, status quo bias, framing, and herd mentality.

Loss Aversion

This is the tendency for people to place a greater emphasis on avoiding losses than acquiring equivalent gains.[xv] Loss aversion was the first behavior that was highlighted by Kahneman and Tversky in 1984, and in 1992 they set out to quantify the degree to which people place a greater value on avoiding losses than acquiring gains. The result is that people place roughly a 2.25× value on avoiding loss than acquiring the equivalent gain. With this in mind, it makes sense that a person would buy insurance in which the cost is 2 times the expected payout, conditional on a disaster (fire, car wreck, flood, etc.). The estimate of 2.25× was measured using a variety of experiments. If given a mug with your college insignia on it, at what price would you sell it to the person next to you? The result: about 2× the cost that person is willing to pay for it. If we agree that you give me $100 if we flip a coin and it's heads, how much do I have to give you if we flip a coin and it's tails? The result: about $200. Because of this bias, people typically overpay for insurance to avoid a significant loss, and people don't transact (willingly incur a loss) when it might be beneficial for them to do so.[xvi]

Anchoring Bias

A trait whereby people rely too heavily on a single piece of information or a starting input, even if that starting input is of dubious relevance. For example, the list price of a house or car is its anchor, and the final sale price is usually close to the initial figure. However, even when an anchor is uninformed or random, it will still exert a material influence on an outcome. To highlight this phenomenon, Thaler and Sunstein use an example where they asked their students to first write down the last three digits of their phone number, add two hundred, and then write down the year that Atilla the Hun invaded Europe. While the correct answer (411 AD) has no correlation to students' phone numbers, students who started with *high* phone numbers consistently guessed a later date by 200 years than students who started with *low* phone numbers.[xvii] Anchoring high is also a technique used in negotiating: the initial offer for a person's salary, the price of a company, or the settlement of a lawsuit is a critical figure that tilts the final agreed-upon figure. For this reason, the person who begins the negotiation is advised to lead with a high figure, or just low enough so their counterpart does not balk.

Availability

A trait whereby people assess the frequency or probability of an event or item by the ease with which instances of occurrences can be recalled or imagined. This bias was first highlighted by Tversky and Kahneman (1974), who concluded, "this valuable estimation procedure results in systematic errors."[xviii] In practice, this means that having personally experienced a hurricane, earthquake, or car accident (or knowing someone who has) biases our view to believe the likelihood of such an event occurring is higher than it is. Similarly, frequent reports in the news (such as violent crimes) may also bias us to believe that personally experiencing such an event is more likely than it is. Additionally, the ease with which a person can *imagine* an event occurring may lead us to overestimate the likelihood that something might occur. For example, if a person was considering going on an expedition to a previously uncharted territory, if that person can easily imagine a wide variety of worst-case scenarios, they may assign an incorrectly high probability of harm or believe the expedition to be more dangerous than it is.

Optimism and Overconfidence

Optimism and overconfidence are traits whereby people assign a higher likelihood of success (or lower likelihood of failure) than is appropriate given the empirical data. In *Nudge*, Thaler notes that prior to the start of each managerial decision-making course, students fill out an anonymous survey on the course website. One question is: "In which decile do you expect to fall in the distribution of grades in this class?" Only 10% of the class can land in the top decile, and 50% must fall in the bottom half. But, less than 5% of students expect to perform in the bottom half, and more than half of the students expect to perform in the top two deciles. Other examples of the overconfidence bias are well-known and easy to understand. Most people think they are above-average drivers. Newlyweds generally think they will stay married forever, even when the divorce rate is 50%. In short, overconfidence can lead to risk taking (starting a business, getting married, smoking, drinking), when if we had properly assessed the likelihood of all given outcomes, we may have made different choices.

Representativeness

In their 1972 paper, Tversky and Kahneman define representativeness as: "the degree to which [an event] (i) is similar in essential characteristics to its parent population, and (ii) reflects the salient features of the process by which it is generated."[xix] That's a little confusing, so Thaler and Sunstein define it as a *similarity heuristic*. Specifically, this is a measurable tendency for people to look at something with characteristics, and organize it with other items that have similar characteristics. For example, imagine you were asked, what does Tom study in college? And then you were given this description: *Tom is of high intelligence, although lacking in true creativity. He has a need for order and clarity, and for neat and tidy systems in which every detail finds its appropriate place.* You may think Tom studies science, technology, engineering, or mathematics (STEM), and that he does not study the humanities—and you'd probably be right. So, *representativeness* makes it easier for us to categorize and classify. But, it has a negative component as well—it leads not only to stereotyping, but it also causes people to see patterns in randomness. This is a particularly dangerous cognitive bias for traders, portfolio managers, and the investors who hire traders and portfolio managers, as highlighted in Nassim Taleb's *Fooled by Randomness.* The random nature of economic events can cause financial models to be errant, as examined by Taleb: "Trading on economic variables that have worked in the past may have been merely coincidental, or, perhaps even worse, that economic analysis was fit to past events to mask the random element in it. Consider that of all possible economic theories available, one can find a plausible one that explains the past, or a portion of it." As a result, traders and investment professionals, and the people with whom they invest, are often fooled into thinking that past performance can be repeated and are shocked to learn during a major correction that their skilled managers were merely the lucky ones.[xx]

Status Quo Bias

This is the measurable tendency of people to stay with a current status, state of affair, or default setting, whatever that may be. William Samuelson and Richard Zeckhauser (1988) highlighted this heuristic initially through collecting survey data that showed that when presented with various options, whatever option was designated as the current selection was disproportionately selected by the survey takers.[xxi] However, we don't need surveys to recognize this bias all around us: school children tend to sit in the same seats every day, temple and churchgoers do the same every Saturday and Sunday, and shoppers regularly buy the same items every week. There is a rationale to doing this—switching may not bring any benefits and may incur some cost. But, staying with the status quo or the default setting may not always be ideal, rational, or even beneficial. Consider investing in a 401k: Thaler and Sunstein highlight that a vast majority of people simply maintain their employer's default setting (i.e., they don't make any selection). What if the default employee setting is 1% of their gross income invested in a money market account. Consider now if the default setting is 1% of the employee's gross income, stepping up by 1% each year (until 20% of gross income), is invested in a target date fund that matches the employees expected retirement date. Clearly, if the employee does not opt out of the default setting, the latter option will lead to a significantly higher amount of savings at retirement. For this reason, Thaler and Sunstein suggest employers should select default options that invests in target date funds (or similar investments) with corresponding investment rates that step up each year. It's a nudge, and it leads to better outcomes not despite, but because of, people's status quo bias.

Framing

This is a cognitive bias in which people react to or select a choice depending on how it is presented, such as a loss or gain. This was first highlighted by Tversky and Kahneman (1981) in what is now referred to as the *Asian Disease Problem*.[xxii] In the survey, people were asked to select one of two medical policy options aimed at combating a hypothetical deadly disease from Asia. When the options were presented to participants in terms of likelihood and number of lives saved, people selected one option; however, when the same options were presented to participants in terms of the likelihood and number of lives lost, people overwhelmingly selected the other option. In practice, this suggests that a doctor may unknowingly influence the decision of their patient by framing a medical choice as: "this procedure will save your life 90% of the time," and not "this procedure will lead to your death 10% of the time." Marketers are aware of this bias and may induce a desired response by framing something in terms of a penalty for failing to act as opposed to a reward for acting. For example, if a participant fails to register for an event by a deadline they will incur a penalty, as opposed to framing the same item that if a participant registers for an event prior to a deadline they will receive a discount.[xxiii]

Herd Mentality

This is the cognitive bias whereby people are influenced by and are more likely to adopt the behaviors of their peers. As a parent, this cognitive bias concerns me more than any other. Even without a scientifically based study, we intuitively know that kids are more likely to use recreational drugs if their friends do. Studies have also shown college roommates impact each other's grades (strong performers tend to bring up their roommates' GPA and vice-versa), roommates positively impact the likelihood they join fraternities or sororities, and roommates are five times more likely to join the same fraternity or sorority, *cetaris paribus*. This holds true even if roommates are randomly assigned, as was the case in a Dartmouth study from 2001.[xxiv] Even mass suicides can be partially attributed to the herd mentality; the mass suicides of the Heaven's Gate cult in San Diego and the People's Temple in Jonestown are two tragic examples.

Heuristics, Heuristics, and More Heuristics

Unfortunately, in recent years there has been an explosion of identifiable biases that are worth keeping in mind. In 2015, *Business Insider* collected and published 58 known biases that range from the obvious to the absurd.[xxv] Some of these biases include:

1. The *illusion of control*—or the ability of people to overestimate their ability to control an event. So, when you walked to the kitchen to get a beer, the Rams scored a touchdown. Naturally, you should go to the kitchen and get another beer to help the Rams score again.
2. The *ostrich effect*—or the tendency for people to avoid getting bad news by burying their head in the sand. I typically don't check my Schwab account when the market is lower. Why would I?
3. *Planning fallacy*—or the tendency to underestimate how much time it will take to complete a task. Anybody who starts projects and struggles to complete them because they've run out of time may appreciate the knowledge that a heuristic is to blame.
4. *Survivorship bias*—or the error of focusing on survivors to estimate risk and return. Entrepreneurs who start their business by thinking that they may be starting the next Apple or Amazon might be shocked to learn that as many as 80% of businesses fail within the first eighteen months of their founding.[xxvi]

BEHAVIORAL BIAS CASE STUDIES

It is easy to imagine ourselves engaging in irrational behavior with hindsight, but it is exceptionally difficult to identify heuristics as they are occurring. Naturally, we all think we are acting rationally when we make choices, and only with time does it become apparent that we may have selected a suboptimal course of action. But, what about experts? Do doctors, lawyers, and investment management professionals occasionally exhibit heuristics? Of course! After all, even the best in their professions are mere humans. While we would expect the investment professionals with the most impressive track records to have overcome their heuristics, there are a few examples of this industry's best and brightest falling into mental traps that led to both suboptimal choices and poor investment performance. I'll highlight two with the hope that future investors may be better able to spot these heuristics before these biases lead to financial loss.

Case Study 1: Bill Ackman—The Herbalife Short

On Wednesday, December 19, 2012, CNBC announced that storied activist investor, William (Bill) Ackman had shorted Herbalife due to his belief that Herbalife was a *pyramid scheme*. Following the news, shares of Herbalife fell $5.16 (or 12.14%) to close at $37.34 a share. The following day, Ackman presented his investment thesis for three hours at a special Sohn Conference event in Midtown Manhattan. During the event, he went through a 342-slide presentation that was then publicly released; it provided a price target of $0 a share, set up a website (www.factsaboutherbalife.com), and announced that all profits he made of the short would be donated to the Pershing Square Foundation (his charity). During and after his presentation, the stock fell another $3.64 (or 9.75%) to close at $33.70 a share.[xxvii]

Bill Ackman is the founder and manager of Pershing Square, a hedge fund that takes large concentrated positions in publicly traded U.S. equities. Until that time, its returns were stellar. From 2004 (its founding) through 2011, the Pershing Square gross-of-fee returns were +28.3% annualized while the returns of the S&P 500 were +3.6% annualized during the same period. Additionally, in 2008, Pershing square was down only 11.6% (gross of fees) while the S&P 500 was down 37.0%. By 2011, after seven years at the helm of Pershing Square, Ackman had racked up several high-profile victories for his investors. In 2005, Pershing Square pressured the management of Wendy's to spin off its Tim Hortons donut chain, which went public in 2006. In 2008, Ackman purchased General Growth Properties, a mall-based real estate investment trust as it teetered on the brink of bankruptcy. In 2010, General Growth Properties exited bankruptcy protection with Pershing Squire as a major stakeholder.[xxviii] In a 2011 Bloomberg interview, Ackman boasted that his investment in General Growth Properties "turned $60 million into $1.6 billion."[xxix]

Fast forward to December 2012 and Ackman announced he had taken a major short in Herbalife. Ackman's thesis could be summarized as follows:

- The Federal Trade Commission (FTC) defines a company as a pyramid scheme if "participants obtain their monetary benefits primarily from recruitment rather than the sale of goods and services to consumers."[xxx]
- At Herbalife "the recruiting rewards earned by distributors vastly exceed their retail profits."[xxxi]
- Therefore, Herbalife fits the FTC legal definition of a pyramid scheme and will be closed by U.S. regulators.
- To add insult to injury, Ackman also claimed Herbalife's products are overpriced, very few employees make the income marketed to them, and the firm has numerous questionable accounting practices.

It was a powerful message coming from a highly respected investor. But, not everybody was convinced. Herbalife stock bottomed on December 24 at $26.06 a share, down 38.6% in only five days. Then the stock began to rally. By January 15, it had risen to $46.19, +8.7% *higher* than when Ackman announced his short and +77.2% higher than the bottom from December 24 (Ackman's weighted-average short price was $48 per share). Someone was clearly taking the other side of the trade. Rumors swirled that one of those investors was Carl Icahn, and on January 25 any doubt was dispelled in a memorable expletive-laden 30-minute live dual interview on CNBC. Carl Icahn is the founder and manager of Icahn Enterprises, an American conglomerate with large stakes in various industries and companies. Icahn, like Ackman, sits at the helm of a large hedge fund that gives him the ability to take concentrated positions in companies and extract value on behalf of his investors. Icahn earned a reputation as being a corporate raider in 1985 when he purchased more than 20% of TWA airline stock, took the company private in 1988, and sold the airline's London routes in 1991. He resigned as chairman of TWA in 1993 and upon his exit, he signed what became known as the *Karabu ticket agreement*, which allowed him to buy any ticket that connected through St. Louis for 55 cents on the dollar and resell them; this cost TWA around $100 million per year.[xxxii]

Prior to the live interview and battle over Herbalife, Carl Icahn and Bill Ackman already had some history. In 2003, Ackman was in the process of shutting down his first hedge fund, was under investigation by the SEC (he was later exonerated), and needed a buyer for Hallwood Realty (one of his large positions). He sold his position to Icahn and hammered out an agreement that the two would split any profit on returns above 10% should Icahn sell his shares within three years. In 2004, Hallwood was acquired by another company in an all-cash deal for $137.91 a share, a significant premium to the $80 per share Icahn had paid Ackman. Ackman contended that the buyout and conversion of shares to cash constituted a sale of shares—Icahn disagreed, and a lawsuit ensued (Ackman eventually won). Fast forward to the live dual interview on CNBC, and Icahn used this as a public stage, not to pitch Herbalife, but to discredit Ackman. "Ackman is a liar . . . Ackman does pump and dump and has one of the worst reputations on Wall Street." Ackman countered, describing Icahn as "not an honest guy, not a guy that keeps his word, and that takes advantage of little people." Icahn described Ackman's short as a ploy to improve his 2012 annual return figures and said, "Herbalife will be the mother of all short squeezes." Ackman pointed out that in 2003, Icahn pitched a company that Icahn was short at the Sohn Conference, just as Ackman had done in 2012.[xxxiii]

Meanwhile, the fate of Herbalife and the two men's reputations hung in the balance. Despite the points Ackman presented regarding Herbalife's business model, many investors, other than just Icahn, were skeptical. Herbalife had been in existence for 32 years, a rather long time not to have already been shut down by regulators. In fact, while the FTC clearly warns consumers to stay away from multi-level marketing firms, in a 1979 case, the FTC established that multi-level marketing is not illegal in the United States. In March 1985, the California Department of Health Services filed a lawsuit against Herbalife stating that the company made "untrue or misleading" claims, and two months later Herbalife founder and President Mark Hughes (28 years old at the time) appeared under subpoena before the Senate Permanent Investigations Subcommittee. Senators were concerned that the 1982 *Herbalife Career Book* states that certain herbs used in the products help cure cancer, diabetes, and other diseases, as well as aid in weight loss. Senators also discussed the possibility that one or more deaths had been linked to Herbalife products, while one senator accused Hughes of being a *snake oil* salesman; Hughes disputed these charges but acknowledged that up to 40 percent of Herbalife's customers suffer temporary side effects including constipation, diarrhea, and headaches.[xxxiv] Herbalife avoided being shut down and settled with California the next year. As part of the settlement, Herbalife agreed to a permanent injunction whereby Herbalife was forever restrained from (among other things) representing that the products burn calories, "cleans the system," and are responsible for a variety of other health benefits. Additionally, Herbalife was restrained from making false or misleading representations regarding the money that new participants may earn.[xxxv] Despite these near-death experiences and negative publicity, Herbalife continued to operate and in 2011 earned $412 million.[xxxvi]

Proponents of Herbalife—following the disclosure of Ackman's short—argued that Herbalife had already been subjected to significant public and legal scrutiny and continued to operate successfully. Ackman's claims that the firm was a pyramid had been addressed as early as 1985, and the FTC would have taken action decades earlier if the firm was operating outside the law or had violated the terms of its permanent injunction. After a very public battle in February 2018, Ackman admitted to having exited his short position at Herbalife.[xxxvii] Pershing Square covered its short position at an average price of $92, roughly 92% higher than its weighted average short price of $48. Meanwhile, Icahn told CNBC that his position in Herbalife had netted him more than $1 billion in profits in what had become his largest position. From 2011 to 2017, Herbalife annual sales grew from $3.4 billion to $4.4 billion while earnings dipped from $412 million to $214 million.[xxxviii]

So, what went wrong? Did Ackman, a highly intelligent, reputable, and experienced individual fall victim to any heuristics? I will speculate here (with the benefit of hindsight bias).

Potential Heuristic 1: Representativeness Bias

One of the biases originally identified by Tversky and Kahneman, and later explained by Thaler as a *similarity heuristic*, this bias is the tendency for people to categorize and group items that have similarities. Could Ackman have fallen victim to this bias as well? Consider the similarity between multi-level marketing and a pyramid scheme. In both instances, people can improve their economic status by recruiting others to join in the organization. In both instances, some portion of the income generated by subordinate members of the organization is redistributed to members more senior to them. Additionally, early adopters generally stand to gain the most while late adopters lose the most. In fact, according to a study published by the Consumer Awareness Institute, 99% of people who join a multi-level marketing organization lose money.[xxxix]

Therefore, given all these similarities, a multi-level marketing organization like Herbalife must be a pyramid scheme. Right? Unfortunately for Ackman and his investors, multi-level marketing rests its legal legitimacy on the fact that retail sales are generated whereas pyramid schemes generally lack retail sales. In a 1998 speech to the IMF, FTC former General Counsel Debra Valentine explained that there are two *tell-tale* signs that a product is being used to disguise a pyramid scheme: inventory loading and a lack of retail sales. She explained, "Inventory loading occurs when a company's incentive program forces recruits to buy more products than they could ever sell." Meanwhile, the lack of retail sales means sales are occurring among people within the organization and not to customers.[xl] Unfortunately, not clearly defined is the degree to which inventory loading may occur or the percentage of reported sales is to customers and not other members of the organization. So, with a slightly more liberal read of these *tell-tale signs*, an objective observer may in fact conclude that Herbalife fit the FTC definition of a pyramid scheme. However, Herbalife had grown quite adept to operating in a grey area.

Potential Heuristic 2: Illusion of Control Bias

As mentioned previously, this bias is the tendency of people to overestimate their ability to control an event. In this instance, Ackman never established that the FTC was in the process of shutting down Herbalife; so, we might infer that Ackman assumed that, following his public denunciation of Herbalife, the FTC would begin a legal process that would conclude in the cessation of Herbalife's ability to operate in the United States. Thus, Ackman believed he could sufficiently influence the FTC and control the outcome of his short investment. Rewinding to his interview on CNBC with Andrew Sorkin on December 20, 2012, Sorkin asked Ackman at the end of the interview, "This is somewhat dependent on the FTC taking action. If they don't, what happens?"

Ackman responds, "I think the FTC is going to take a very hard look. But I think most importantly, the new distributor that someone is trying to suck into the scheme will be better informed."

We can all agree that anybody who reviews Ackman's presentation or visits his website will be significantly better informed on Herbalife. But, the link between Herbalife overpromising and under-delivering to its distributors and the FTC shutting down the firm was not established. Ackman needed to have a rock-solid reason to believe that the FTC was on the verge of beginning a process to close Herbalife outside of Ackman's belief that his well-intentioned public denunciation of Herbalife would be the necessary catalyst. While Ackman has significant clout on Wall Street, this did not translate to influence at the FTC. So, he may have fallen victim to illusion-of-control bias.

Potential Heuristic 3: Status Quo Bias

To Ackman's credit, his public denunciation of Herbalife did lead to an FTC lawsuit against Herbalife. The FTC filed charges in a California court that Herbalife, among other things, represented to recruits that they are likely to earn substantial income but that the "Defendants' program does not offer participants a viable retail-based business opportunity."[xli] This complaint was in line with Ackman's thesis, and if true, Herbalife's actions were in direct violation of its permanent injunction as part of its 1986 settlement with the California Department of Health Services. Herbalife once again settled, and in July 2016 the FTC announced that Herbalife had agreed to pay a $200 million fine and restructure its compensation policy.[xlii]

That is why this potential behavioral bias is not that of Ackman, but that of the FTC. By allowing a settlement with Herbalife, could the FTC have fallen victim to a status quo bias? The status quo bias relates to people's inclination to maintain the current state of affairs. While Herbalife had both the willingness and ability to "lawyer up," since this FTC investigation constituted an existential threat, the FTC indicated its willingness to settle with Herbalife by agreeing to let them revise a business practice and pay a hefty fine—a typical FTC investigation outcome. Perhaps if someone at the FTC had as much conviction as Ackman and his team, the FTC would have broken from its status quo bias and shut down Herbalife.

When asked to comment on this chapter, Ackman disagreed with my suggestion that he might have fallen victim to either the representativeness or the illusion-of-control biases. Rather, Ackman suggested that he may have fallen victim to something akin to a *morality bias* which he defined as the bias of assuming the regulatory bodies in the United States would act in the best interest of its citizens. He has a point. According to FTC Chairwoman Edith Ramirez, who stated at a press conference following the FTC settlement with Herbalife, "The dream portrayed by Herbalife and reinforced in these and other testimonials was an illusion. The vast majority of Herbalife distributors found that they could make little or no money selling Herbalife products." When pressed during the Q&A regarding the FTC's assessment of whether Herbalife constituted a pyramid scheme, she reiterated that the FTC complaint did not allege Herbalife was a pyramid scheme and that (my emphasis) "they [Herbalife] were *not* determined *not* to have been a pyramid [scheme]."[xliii] Also of note was the absence of an investigation by California Attorney General Kamala Harris. In 1986,

California had imposed a consent decree on Herbalife stating that it may not make misleading statements; so, it was within Harris's authority to investigate if Herbalife had violated its previous settlement with the California Department of Health Services. Harris did not explain why, despite requests from her office to begin an investigation, she declined to do so. Furthermore, according to Yahoo News, three weeks after receiving a memo from prosecutors in the San Diego office requesting resources to investigate Herbalife, Harris received the first of three donations to her U.S. Senate Campaign from Heather Podesta, whose law firm was later hired by Herbalife.[xliv]

"We underestimated Herbalife's ability to manage politics and PR," Ackman acknowledged when we spoke.

Case Study 2: Bill Miller—The Bear Stearns (and Other Financials) Long

On June 22, 2007, Bear Stearns announced it would lend up to $3.2 billion to one of its collapsing hedge funds, the High-Grade Structured Credit Strategies Fund, which was heavily leveraged and invested in asset backed securities. This fund, along with a similar Bear Stearns fund, had recently experienced significant losses, client redemption requests, and margin calls that the fund was unable to meet.[xlv] One week prior to this announcement, Bear executives met with about a dozen banks, all of whom had lent to Bear's funds, and asked for a 60-day moratorium on margin calls. The situation was familiar but the roles were different; in 1998, sixteen financial institutions met at the New York Federal Reserve and each contributed to the bailout of Long-Term Capital Management (LTCM). Bear Stearns did not contribute, whereas most banks contributed $300 million worth of capital apiece;[xlvi] other bank executives were livid. Now, Bear executives were asking for the same financial institutions to lend a hand and avoid a forced unwind of the hedge funds. Bear's counterparts balked (karma) and began seizing collateral and auctioning its holdings. Bear executives panicked. In addition to the embarrassment of a forced unwind of its funds, a disorderly fire-sale of assets risked unsettling the broader mortgage-backed securities market, which might generate losses on positions that Bear Stearns owned on its own balance sheet. So, viewing the extension of a massive $3.2 billion loan as the best of bad options, Bear departed from years of company policy and invested significant capital to prevent a disorderly unwind of the funds.[xlvii] Equity investors weren't thrilled by Bear Sterns' support of its failing hedge fund; Bear Stearns closed June 22, 2007, at $143.75—down 16.8% from its all-time high.

Losses in the hedge fund positions mounted as the housing market weakened and mortgage loan delinquencies rose, and on July 31, 2007, the two funds filed for Chapter 15 bankruptcy protection; lawsuits were filed against Bear Stearns the next day. On August 3, Bear Stearns held an investor call during which their CEO James Cayne opened by stating that the firm was "taking the situation seriously" before turning the call over to another executive. Later in the call an analyst asked a question to Mr. Cayne, to which the response was silence. Mr. Cayne had left the room—he later returned, but the awkward silence left hundreds of participants believing that Cayne had disengaged altogether.[xlviii] Bear Stearns troubles continued as third quarter earnings fell 61% to $171.3 million from $438 million the prior quarter, largely because of a $200 million loss attributed to the failure of the two hedge funds. Criticism of Cayne continued with *The Wall Street Journal* reporting in November that Mr. Cayne had spent 10 of 21 workdays in July out of the office playing at a bridge tournament or golfing. January 7, James Cayne stepped down as CEO and was replaced by Alan Schwartz the following day.[xlix] Bear Stearns closed at $71.01, down 58.9% in the prior 12 months and down 50.6% since the announcement of their fund bailout.

Bear Stearns troubles continued and came to a head on Thursday, March 13. Rumors swirled that Bear Stearns was heavily exposed to toxic mortgage-backed securities, resulting in a modern-day run on the bank. Clients and other dealers, whom provided Bear Stearns with (largely) short-term financing, stopped rolling their financing, creating a dramatic cash-outflow as Bear Stearns was required to return cash to lenders. Cash reserves fell to $3 billion from $10 billion only one day after CEO Alan Schwartz stated on CNBC that the firm had ample liquidity.[l] In reality, without an immediate cash infusion, Bear would need to file for bankruptcy protection. In the early-morning hours of March 14, Fed Board members authorized an emergency $30 billion loan to be provided through J.P. Morgan. Just before the market opened, Bear and J.P. Morgan released similar statements and the stock opened higher.[li]

Enter Bill Miller, Legg Mason's star portfolio manager of the $16.5 billion Legg Mason Value Trust, a mutual fund that had outperformed the broad market every year from 1991 to 2005—a streak unmatched by any competing mutual fund.[lii] Miller was known as a *value* investor who often drifted outside of the traditional value universe of stocks—at times taking large positions in stocks including AOL, Amazon, and Dell Computer. But, whether the stock was a value or a growth play, Miller's strategy was generally the same: lowest average cost wins. In a 2003 interview with *Fortune Magazine*, he described his penchant for buying securities that had fallen out of favor. He closed the interview by explaining: "A lot of people look to hit singles and sacrifice bunts and make small returns. But statistically, you are far better off with huge gains because you are going to make mistakes. And if you are playing small ball and you make a few mistakes, you can't recover."[liii] In 1999, Miller was named Morningstar Fund Manager of the decade.

A flailing Bear Stearns was just the type of situation Miller loved—a big name, which had fallen out of favor, that now offered him the opportunity to buy it at a bargain price. In the third quarter 2007, around the time the two Bear Stearns hedge funds were unwinding, Miller began buying. In the fourth quarter, he added to his financial stock holdings by taking positions in Merrill Lynch & Co., Washington Mutual, Wachovia, and Freddie Mac. He also added homebuilders to his portfolio. Fast forward to March 14, 2008, the day Bear Stearns announced that J.P. Morgan would provide financing to Bear Stearns; Bill Miller was scheduled to speak at a conference in New York opposite Steve Eisman, portfolio manager at FrontPoint. In a scene depicted in *The Big Short* (with names changed to Bob Miller versus Mark Baum), Bill Miller disclosed that he had just purchased more Bear Stearns stock.[liv] Despite the initial pop in investor confidence following that morning's announced agreement with J.P. Morgan, Bear Stearns stock plummeted to $30.85, down 82.1% from its high and 56.6% since Schwartz became CEO three months prior.

The initial term of the $30 billion loan to Bear Stearns was 28 days, enough time, executives reckoned, as was needed for Bear Stearns to either find a buyer or secure financing elsewhere. But, after watching Bear Stearns stock plummet throughout the day, Treasury Secretary Henry Paulson decided that the short-term financing would be inadequate. Instead, he called Bear Stearns CEO Alan Schwartz that evening to inform him that he had the weekend to sell the company. By Sunday morning, J.P. Morgan was prepared to make an offer to buy Bear Stearns for $4 a share, conditional on a $30 billion limited-recourse loan from the Federal Reserve whereby the Federal Reserve would be responsible for losses exceeding $1 billion. Secretary Paulson said $4 was too high, and the offer was reduced to $2 a share. At 7:00 p.m., Sunday evening, the Bear Stearns board accepted the offer. Following a class action lawsuit, the sale price was eventually revised to $10 a share.[lv]

Despite the massive loss he had taken on a stock he had just championed—the troubles for Bill Miller were just beginning. In 2008, as housing prices fell and mortgage delinquencies rose, both asset backed securities and the financial institutions tied to them plummeted. The companies that Miller had snapped up as seemingly bargain prices, ceased to exist:

- Freddie Mac was placed under a conservatorship, giving management control to the Federal Housing Finance Agency, on September 8, 2008.[lvi] The stock traded down to around $1, down from the mid-$60s the prior year.
- Merrill Lynch was purchased by Bank of America on September 14, 2008, for about $29 a share, down 61% from its September 2007 price.[lvii]
- Washington Mutual was seized by the United States Office of Thrift Supervision and placed into receivership with the Federal Deposit

Insurance Corporation (FDIC) on September 26, 2008. The stock was immediately delisted after trading over $30 a share the prior year.[lvii]

- Wachovia was purchased by Wells Fargo for about $7 a share on October 3, 2008. The stock had traded as high as $40 earlier in 2008.[lix]

"Every decision to buy anything has been wrong," Miller lamented in an interview with *The Wall Street Journal* in late 2008. "The thing I didn't do, from day one, was properly assess the severity of this liquidity crisis," he admitted.

By the end of 2008, his Value Trust fund had assets of $4.3 billion, down from $21.5 billion at its peak in 2007. The fund underperformed the S&P 500 by losing around 20% that year, wiping away Value Trust's years of market-beating performance. The fund fell to among the worst-performing in its class for the previous one-, three-, five- and 10-year periods by the end of 2008, according to Morningstar and *The Wall Street Journal*.[lx] The Value Trust fund rebounded strongly in 2009, outperforming the S&P 500 by +14%, and in 2012, Miller handed over control of the Legg Mason Management Value Trust (now called the ClearBridge Value Trust) to another portfolio manager after exactly 30 years at the helm.[lxi]

Despite Value Trust's underperformance in 2008, Miller still has an exceptionally impressive 30-year record, and in 2015, one of Miller's colleagues attempted to set the record straight when she wrote *A Look at Bill's Record*. Specifically, she highlighted that during his 30 years of managing the strategy, Value Trust gained +12.39% net of fees, outperforming the S&P 500 by 130 basis points (bps) per year, which is a cumulative 41% outperformance.[lxii] In August 2016, Bill Miller purchased Legg's interest in an advisory business named LMM, in which Miller and Legg had jointly owned and managed several products including the Legg Mason Opportunity Trust (now rebranded the Miller Opportunity Trust) and the Miller Income Opportunity Trust. In recent years Miller has once again posted exceptional returns; in the 10-year period that ended 3/9/2019, his Miller Opportunity Trust (Class I) outperformed the S&P 500 by 515 bps annualized, placing it among the top 1% of U.S. equity funds according to Morningstar.[lxiii]

So, what went wrong in 2008 with his purchase of Bear Stearns and other financials? Did Miller, like Ackman, fall victim to any heuristics? Again, I will speculate here.

Potential Heuristic 1: Overconfidence Bias

This is the bias where a person's subjective confidence in their assessment is greater than the objective accuracy of their assessment. There was good reason for Miller to be confident in himself. A 15-year streak beating the market and a *Morningstar Manager of the Decade* award to boot was an awesome accomplishment. Also, self-confidence was a critical component of his success up until 2008; purchasing companies that were widely panned by other asset managers takes a high degree of intestinal fortitude. It's okay being wrong when everybody makes the same mistake, but it's a potential career killer when you're wrong while going against the grain. Miller made his career going against the grain. But, if Miller had any self-doubt associated with his assessment of financials and homebuilders in 2008, he didn't show it. He doubled and then quadrupled down as financials and homebuilders continued to freefall. It's possible that he was overconfident in 2008, which blinded him from the possibility that some of the largest banks were truly on the brink of collapse.

Potential Heuristic 2: Confirmation Bias

This is the tendency for people to interpret new information as confirmation of their existing belief. In the days leading up to the Bear Stearns fire sale to J.P. Morgan, there was no shortage of news that could have led one to believe Bear Stearns was stable and its stock was likely to rebound; Bear's CEO was on CNBC reassuring investors it was solvent and had ample liquidity. The following day it received a $30 billion loan from J.P. Morgan. Taken together, these announcements might make a reasonable person rest easy that Bear was in fine shape. Following Bear Stern's failure, there were other reasons to think financials and the broader economy still would be fine. For example, in May 2008, the Federal Reserve released its minutes from its April 29–30 meeting, in which it stated, "The staff projection pointed to a contraction of real gross domestic product (GDP) in the first half of 2008 followed by a modest rise in the second half of this year, aided in part by the fiscal stimulus package. The forecast showed real GDP expanding at a rate somewhat above its potential in 2009."[lxiv] Miller clearly wasn't the only one to get things wrong at that time. So, it is possible that each time a stock dropped in value, while a headline appeared optimistic, this served to only confirm Miller's belief that his strategy of investing in flailing financials was prudent and would soon yield outsized returns.

Potential Heuristic 3: Conservatism Bias

This is the bias where a person may have a tendency to revise their belief by an insufficient degree as new information is presented. So, if Miller believed in late 2007 that the financial and housing sectors were prime for a rebound, he updated his outlook too slowly, as banks failed and home prices plummeted. As a result, he held on to his positions and his initial thesis for far too long. Miller may have been particularly prone to this; in a 2006 interview he described his willingness to continue to buy a stock as it fell, stating "Someone once asked me how I knew when we were wrong to do that. When we can no longer get a quote, was my answer."[lxv] He was true to his word.

ADDRESSING BEHAVIORAL BIASES

Once we acknowledge the existence of behavioral biases, the next question is: "What should be done about it?" Assuming the source of systematic errors of judgment can be traced to dual modes of human thinking and an overreliance on our intuitive (system one) process, it's highly unlikely that humans will ever jettison our primary form of cognition to avoid heuristics altogether. So, we are relegated to recognizing our limitations and attempting to systematically address them. Assuming the objective is to ensure that *others* are more likely to make selections that are in their best interest, a regularly advanced solution to behavioral biases is the utilization of *choice architecture*. Should the objective be to improve our *own* decision-making process, the solution involves what I will refer to as *decision discipline*.

Choice Architecture

Thaler and Sunstein (2008) coined the phrase choice architecture to reflect the notion that the person who structures the way in which choices are presented influences the outcome of a choice, just as a person who designs a building influences how its inhabitants work, communicate, and interact with their surroundings. Johnson et al. (2013) contributed to this study by collecting and summarizing dozens of examples in which choice architecture has been used to optimize outcomes.[lxvi] An early example of choice architecture (before it was labeled as such) is highlighted by Madrian and Shea (2001) when studying the savings behavior of a large company 401(k) plan. In this study, employees exhibited a strong *status quo bias*, in that they maintained the default setting of their 401(k) plan. The study followed a large company that made a subtle but material change to its 401(k) plan: prior to April 1998, all employees with more than one year of tenure could enroll in the retirement plan; however, to participate, the employee must enroll him or herself and select the contribution amount. After April 1, 1998, all employees when hired were automatically enrolled in the 401(k) plan with a default 3% contribution rate. The default investment was a money market fund. The study compared (among other things) the participation rate of the group hired just before and just after the 401(k) defaulted to automatic enrollment. Of the cohort that was automatically enrolled, 86% of employees continued to participate in the 401(k) plan after one year (only 14% of employees opted out). Conversely, of the cohort that was not automatically enrolled in the year prior to the change in the plan, 49% of employees had opted in to the 401(k) plan. Thus, the *default* selection increased the 401(k) participation rate by 37% (86% − 49%)! However, of those participants who were "opted-in" to the 401(k) plan, 71% maintained the money market fund selection and did not choose to invest a (potentially) more appropriate mix of investments such as stock and bond mutual funds.[lxvii] This study, along with several others that followed, were highlighted by those that drafted and voted in favor of the Pension Protection Act (PPA) of 2006. This Act gave employers the authority to automatically enroll employees in 401(k) plans without their consent (i.e., the default is employees may opt in). Additionally, the PPA established Qualified Default Investment Alternatives (QDIA), which protect employers from liability should employees be automatically enrolled and later experience investment losses.[lxviii] Target date funds (see Chapter 2) are one of the qualified options. As a result of the PPA, by 2017 the number of plan sponsors with auto-enrollment increased from 23% in 2004[lxix] to 71% in 2017[lxx] while 85% of new participants defaulted into target date funds.[lxxi]

Thanks to the recognition of a status quo bias heuristic, along with the clever utilization of choice architecture, we can expect Americans to continue to save more of their earnings into target date funds for decades. The benefits will likely be immense over time. Additionally, the utilization of choice architecture in conjunction with a status quo bias has been used in several other areas to great effect. Johnson and Goldstein (2003) show that in Austria, Belgium, France, and several other EU countries, over 98% of the population has agreed to be organ donors. However, in Denmark, the Netherlands, the UK, and Germany, between 4% and 27% of citizens have agreed to be organ donors. The difference? In the former countries, citizens have to opt out to be an organ donor, whereas in the latter citizens have to opt in to be an organ donor.[lxxii] Separately, choice architecture may positively influence the choices we make with respect to our diet; Fox et al. (2005) show that the order in which you present a menu of options, and the way in which options are grouped, can impact people's selection of those items.[lxxiii] Meanwhile, Thorndike et al. (2014) show that labeling food with red (unhealthy), yellow (moderately healthy), and green (healthy) labels materially increases the consumption of healthy foods and reduces the consumption of unhealthy foods.[lxxiv] Therefore, the designer of a cafeteria can increase the consumption of healthy food simply by placing healthy items first and labeling them as healthy. Choice architecture can also help people manage their personal finances. Soll et al. (2011) show that individuals fail to estimate credit card payback periods as a function of monthly payments. However, this problem has been largely alleviated due to the information that is now provided on monthly statements following the passage of the Credit Card Act of 2009.[lxxv]

The aforementioned examples are just a few of the multitude of benefits that choice architecture may yield. However, what should we as humans (and not econs) do if the objective is not to nudge *others* to make optimal choices, but rather ensure that *we* make optimal choices? What rules should we follow to ensure that we address our own shortcomings? Here are a few recommendations for both the professional and nonprofessional investor.

Decision Discipline: Questions for Others

Decision discipline is the term I will use to describe an ongoing process of identifying and addressing personal heuristics while making investment decisions. This discipline includes the acknowledgment of biases, asking questions designed to tease out these biases, continually reviewing options in a rational framework, establishing rules and guidelines, and relentlessly sticking to our rules. While "forewarned is forearmed" is fair for most situations, heuristics are particularly difficult to identify and address due to these biases being innate and oftentimes subconscious. So, simply acknowledging that they exist may be insufficient to address them. With this in mind, in 2011, Daniel Kahneman, Dan Lovallo, and Olivier Sibony published "Before You Make That Big Decision."[lxxvi] In this piece, the authors recommended that managers pose 12 questions prior to making a decision that has material organizational impacts. These questions are:

1. *Self-interest bias check*: Is there any reason to suspect the people who are making the recommendation of biases based on self-interest, overconfidence, or attachment to past experiences?
2. *Affect bias check*: Have the people making the recommendation fallen in love with it?
3. *Groupthink bias check*: Was there groupthink or were there dissenting opinions within the decision-making team?
4. *Saliency bias check*: Could the diagnosis be overly influenced by an analogy to a memorable success?
5. *Confirmation bias check*: Are credible alternatives included along with the recommendation?
6. *Availability bias check*: If you had to make this decision again in a year's time, what information would you want, and can you get more of it now?
7. *Anchoring bias check*: Do you know where the numbers came from? Can there be unsubstantiated numbers, extrapolation from history, or a motivation to use a certain anchor?
8. *Halo effect bias check*: Is the team assuming that a person, organization, or approach that is successful in one area will be just as successful in another?
9. *Sunk cost fallacy check*: Are the recommenders overly attached to a history of past decisions?
10. *Overconfidence, planning fallacy, and optimistic biases check*: Is the base case overly optimistic?
11. *Disaster neglect bias check*: Is the worst case bad enough?
12. *Loss aversion bias check*: Is the recommending team overly cautious?

These are excellent questions that managers should regularly ask. But, what if we are not relying on someone else to provide us with a recommendation, and the objective is to manage our own finances? In this instance, I recommend following the upcoming common sense steps prior to making a financial commitment.

Decision Discipline: Questions for Ourselves

1. *What is my willingness and ability to assume risk?* Only if the person has both the willingness and ability to assume risk should a person choose to invest primarily in a risky asset or project.
2. *What is my objective, and is this objective reasonable?* Objectives that are too aggressive can lead to excessive risk taking, while objectives that are too timid may lead to forgoing opportunities that have an appealing risk/return profile.
3. *Am I sufficiently diversified?* Maintaining diversification across asset classes can eliminate idiosyncratic risk.
4. *Am I trying to time the market?* The data show that strong returns are concentrated in short windows, and frequently entering and exiting the market (in addition to incurring transaction expenses and taxes) increases the probability of missing periods of strong performance.[lxxvii] However, if you insist on timing the market, heed Warren Buffett's recommendation from his 2004 Annual Shareholder letter: "And if they insist on trying to time their participation in equities, they should try to be fearful when others are greedy—and greedy only when others are fearful."[lxxviii]
5. *Am I overconfident in my ability to trade equities?* Brad Barber and Terrance Odean (2000) demonstrated *trading is hazardous to your wealth.* After accounting for the types of stock portfolios held by individuals, individuals' portfolios underperformed the equity market by 3.7% annually.[lxxix]
6. *Am I minimizing expenses?* A growing body of academic research (Wermers 2000 and Fama 2010) has shown that active equity managers rarely outperform their benchmarks after fees.[lxxx,lxxxi] So, invest primarily in low-fee passive funds unless you have high conviction that a fund manager can and will outperform its benchmark by an amount more than its fees.
7. *What are the tax consequences of my actions?* Be mindful of taxes and maximize the use of qualified tax-deferred accounts such as a 401k, IRA, Roth IRA, 529, or other tax-free or tax-deferred accounts. If investments are held in taxable accounts, hold securities or funds (like

equity ETFs) that have few taxable events. Bonds, bond funds, and bond ETFs are most appropriate for a qualified account. See Chapter 2 for more details on investment vehicles.

8. *Has my portfolio drifted away from my target?* Rebalance at least annually if warranted. See Chapter 6 for more details on rebalancing strategies.

9. *Are my portfolio managers any good?* Utilize investment managers and invest in funds that have long track records and generally high (3+) Morningstar ratings. While a five-star Morningstar Fund is not significantly more likely to outperform a one-star Morningstar Fund, a five-star Morningstar Fund is significantly less likely than a one-star fund to close and unwind (which is generally not ideal for a retail investor).

10. *Am I staying true to the aforementioned steps?* Hopefully the utility of asking ourselves these questions is self-evident.

SUMMARY AND INVESTMENT IMPLICATIONS

Summary

Experts in cogitative psychology currently theorize that people utilize two models of thinking: an intuitive system and a reflective system. The intuitive system is almost always engaged, constantly produces a representation of the world around us, and allows us to walk, brush our teeth, and eat our breakfast. The reflective system is less often engaged and is activated when we need to deduce, learn, and problem solve. Owing to our intuitive system, we utilize rules of thumb and mental shortcuts (heuristics) that make us prone to systematic errors and make seemingly irrational choices. This irrationality poses a problem for economic utility theory, which states that people are rational and make choices that are in their self-interest. Daniel Kahneman and Amos Tversky (1979) were the first to introduce the concept of prospect theory. This theory states that while people select options that they think will maximize their utility, sometimes people do not properly assess a distribution of outcomes, occasionally select incorrectly, and may act seemingly irrationally.

Since this paper has been published, there has been a dramatic growth in this field of study that has since been labeled either behavioral finance or behavioral economics. In the past 40 years, scientists and economists have identified dozens of heuristics. Some of the more commonly cited heuristics include: the anchoring bias (an initial point has an outsized impact on an outcome), the loss aversion bias (people experience more negative utility from a loss than positive utility from an equivalent gain), and the status quo bias (people generally stick with the status quo even if it's not in their best interest to do so).

While students of behavioral finance have the advantage of knowing heuristics exist, it is still exceptionally difficult to spot oneself employing a heuristic and engaging in irrational behavior. Even some of the most highly educated and well-respected market practitioners may have suffered from these biases at various points in their careers. My short list of examples includes:

1. Bill Ackman and his Herbalife short (representativeness and illusion of control biases)
2. Bill Miller and his purchase of Bear Sterns (overconfidence, confirmation, and conservatism biases)
3. The FOMC and their failure to forecast their own policy rate (optimism, anchoring, bandwagon, and conservatism biases).

With respect to asking the question: "What should be done about these biases?" There are two approaches. The first approach is to embrace heuristics (in others) when attempting to generate a specific outcome. For example, choice architecture utilizes people's status quo or default bias to increase the likelihood that they utilize a 401(k) savings plan or elect to be organ donors. The second approach to address heuristics to which we fall victim is to engage our reflective system to a greater degree than would normally occur. To achieve this, Daniel Kahneman, Dan Lovallo, and Olivier Sibony (2011) have produced a list of questions they recommend that managers ask themselves (and others) when evaluating a recommendation or considering something transformational to an organization. These questions are designed to tease out biases that might not initially be obvious to the evaluator. With respect to managing personal or professional finances, I've put together a list of suggestions that I believe will benefit my readers should they adhere to these do's and don'ts.

Investment Implications

- The existence of behavioral biases has the potential to create investment opportunities for investors who are less prone to the same biases. For example, the FOMC's propensity to overestimate the forward path of its own policy rate between Q1 2014 and Q4 2017 created an opportunity to discerning fixed income investors. Ackman's Herbalife short created an opportunity for Icahn. Finally, the existence of *factors* and success of *factor investing* may also be partially attributed to the existence of heuristics.
- The existence of behavioral biases makes even the most intelligent, experienced, and educated portfolio managers, traders, and analysts prone to mistakes. Therefore, we must evaluate each trade idea on its own merit to ensure that the idea doesn't contain one or more inherent biases. If an idea has been influenced by a heuristic, we should reevaluate the idea and potentially reject it altogether.

- We should critically evaluate managers and not rely on reputation or past performance to decide if the manager will continue to post strong numbers. It is possible that a manager's inclinations, which may have been successful in the past, will lead that person to make errant choices going forward. If we feel strongly that a manager is suffering from one or more heuristics, we should use that opportunity to reevaluate the manager to decide if an investment with that manager remains prudent.
- Due diligence, planning, and execution, whether it involves personal finance, professional asset management, or manager evaluation, can benefit from a checklist. Additionally, the utilization of weekly, monthly, and quarterly reviews offers us heuristic-prone humans the greatest probability of ensuring that we don't make irrational choices.

CITATIONS

i. Economic projections of Federal Reserve Board members and Federal Reserve Bank presidents under their individual assessments of projected appropriate monetary policy. Figure 2. FOMC participants' assessments of appropriate monetary policy: Midpoint of the target range or target level for the federal funds rate. Each quarterly report from 3/19/14 through 12/13/17. https://www.federalreserve.gov/monetarypolicy/fomccalendars.htm.

ii. Tversky, Amos and Daniel Kahneman. (September 27, 1974). "Judgment under Uncertainty: Heuristics and Biases." *Science*. New Series. Vol. 185, No. 4157. pp. 1124–1131.

iii. Kahneman, Daniel and Amos Tversky. (1979). "Prospect Theory: An Analysis of Decision under Risk." *Econometrica*. 47(2). p. 263. doi:10.2307/1914185. ISSN 0012-9682.

iv. Persky, Joseph. (Spring 1995). "Retrospectives: The Ethology of Homo Economicus." *The Journal of Economic Perspectives*. Vol. 9, No. 2. pp. 221–231.

v. Shfrin, Hersh M. and Meir Statman. (1984). "Explaining Investor Preference for Cash Dividends." *Journal of Financial Economics*. 13. pp. 253–282. North-Holland.

vi. G.P.U. to Continue Its Dividend Policy. (April 7, 1968). *New York Times*.

vii. Thaler, R. and H. Shefrin. (1981). An economic theory of self-control, *Journal of Political Economy*. 89. pp. 392–410.

viii. Miller, Merton H. (October 1986). "The Behavioral Foundations of Economic Theory." *The Journal of Business*, Vol. 59, No. 4, Part 2. pp. S451–S468.

ix. Shiller, Robert. (October 11, 2017). "Thaler's Nobel Boosts Behavioral Economics." *Barrons.*

x. Kahneman, Daniel. (December 2003). "Maps of Bounded Rationality: Psychology for Behavioral Economics." *The American Economic Review.* Vol. 93, No. 5. pp. 1449–1475.

xi. Camerer, Colin F., George Loewenstein, and Matthew Rabin. (eds.). (2004). "Advances in Behavioral Economics (The Roundtable Series in Behavioral Economics)." Russell Sage Foundation. New York, NY. pp. 4–5.

xii. Evans, J. St. B. T. and K. Frankish. (eds.). (2009). *In Two Minds: Dual Processes and Beyond.* New York, NY: Oxford University Press.

xiii. Evans, J. St. B. T. (2010). *Thinking twice: Two minds in one brain.* New York, NY: Oxford University Press.

xiv. Sunstein, Cass R. and Richard H. Thaler. (2008). *Nudge: Improving Decisions About Health, Wealth, and Happiness.* New York, NY: Penguin Group.

xv. Kahneman, Daniel and Amos Tversky. (1984). "Choices, Values and Frames." *American Psychologist* 39. pp. 341–350.

xvi. Tversky, Amos and Daniel Kahneman. (1992). "Advances in Prospect Theory: Cumulative Representation of Uncertainty." *Journal of Risk and Uncertainty.* 5. pp. 297–323.

xvii. Sunstein, Cass R. and Richard H. Thaler. (2008). *Nudge: Improving Decisions About Health, Wealth, and Happiness.* New York, NY: Penguin Group. pp. 23–24.

xviii. Tversky, Amos and Daniel Kahneman. (September 1974). "Judgment under Uncertainty: Heuristics and Biases." *Science.* 185(4157). pp. 1124–31.

xix. Kahneman, Daniel and Amos Tversky. (1972). "Subjective probability: A judgment of representativeness." (PDF). Cognitive Psychology. 3(3). pp. 430–454. doi:10.1016/0010-0285(72)90016-3.

xx. Taleb, Nassim Nicholas. (2004). *Fooled by Randomness.* New York, NY: Random House. p. 91.

xxi. Samuelson, William and Richard Zeckhauser. (March 1988). "Status Quo Bias in Decision Making." *Journal of Risk and Uncertainty.* 1(1). pp. 7–59.

xxii. Tversky, A. and D. Kahneman. (1981). "The framing of decisions and the psychology of choice." *Science.* 211. pp. 453–458.

xxiii. Gächter, S., H. Orzen, E. Renner, and C. Stamer. (2009). "Are experimental economists prone to framing effects? A natural field experiment". *Journal of Economic Behavior & Organization.* 70(3). pp. 443–46. doi:10.1016/j.jebo.2007.11.003.

xxiv. Sacerdote, Bruce. (May 2001). "Peer Effects with Random Assignment: Result for Dartmouth Roommates." *The Quarterly Journal of Economics.*

xxv. Lubin, Gus and Shana Lebowitz. (October 29, 2015). "58 cognitive biases that screw up everything we do." *Business Insider.*

xxvi. Wagner, Eric T. (September 12, 2013). "Five Reasons 8 Out of 10 Businesses Fail." Forbes.com.

xxvii. La Roche, Julia. (December 20, 2012). "We Have Never Seen Anything Like Bill Ackman's Dizzying Takedown of Herbalife." *Business Insider.*

xxviii. De La Merced, Michal J. (April 16, 2009). "General Growth Properties Files for Bankruptcy." *The New York Times.*

xxix. Leaonard, Devin. (February 10, 2011). Bill Ackman's Soft Power. *Bloomberg Businessweek.*

xxx. Vander Nat, P.J. and W.W. Keep. (2002). "Marketing Fraud: An Approach for Differentiating Multilevel Marketing from Pyramid Schemes." *Journal of Public Policy & Marketing.* 21(1). pp. 139–151. https://doi.org/10.1509/jppm.21.1.139.17603.

xxxi. Pershing Square Capital Management, L.P. (December 2012). "Who wants to be a Millionaire?" p. 154.

xxxii. Grant, Elaine X. (October 2005). "TWA—Death of A Legend." *St. Louis Magazine.* Archived from the original on 11-21-2008.

xxxiii. Fast Money Halftime. (January 25, 2013). CNBC.

xxxiv. Bud Newman. (May 15, 1985). "Herbalife chief under fire in hearing." UPI.

xxxv. Permanent Injunction against Herbalife (1986). SUPERIOR COURT OF THE STATE OF CALIFORNIA: COUNTY OF SANTA CRUZ. No 92767.

xxxvi. 2011 Herbalife Annual Report.

xxxvii. La Monica, Paul R. (March 1, 2018). "Bill Ackman's Herbalife disaster is finally over." CNN Money.

xxxviii. 2017 Herbalife Annual Report.

xxxix. Taylor, Jon M. (2011). "The Case (for and) against Multi-level Marketing." Consumer Awareness Institute. FTC website.

xl. Pyramid Schemes. (May 13, 1998). Debra A. Valentine, Former General Counsel. International Monetary Funds Seminar on Current Legal Issues Affecting Central Banks.

xli. Case No. 2:16-cv-05217. COMPLAINT FOR PERMANENT INJUNCTION AND OTHER EQUITABLE RELIEF. Federal Trade Commission, Plaintiff, v. Herbalife International of America, Inc.

xlii. Press Release. (July 15, 2016). Herbalife Will Restructure Its Multi-level Marketing Operations and Pay $200 Million for Consumer Redress to Settle FTC Charges." www.ftc.gov.

xliii. Federal Trade Commission: Herbalife Press Conference. (July 15, 2016). https://www.ftc.gov/system/files/documents/videos/ftc-press -conference-herbalife/ftc_press_conference_on_herbalife_settlement _7-15-16_-_transcript.pdf.

xliv. Nazaryan, Alexander. (March 18, 2019). "Why did Kamala Harris let Herbalife off the hook?" Yahoo News.

xlv. Kelly, Kate and Serena Ng. (June 23, 2007). "Bear Stearns Bails Out Fund With Big Loan." *The Wall Street Journal.*

xlvi. Lowenstein, R. and Long-Term Capital Management (Firm). (2000). *When Genius Failed: The Rise and Fall of Long-Term Capital Management.* New York, NY: Random House. p. 207.

xlvii. Creswell, Julie and Vikas Bajaj. (June 23, 2007). "$3.2 Billion Move by Bear Stearns to Rescue Fund." *The New York Times.*

xlviii. Kelly, Kate. (November 1, 2007). "Bear CEO's Handling of Crisis Raises Issues." *The Wall Street Journal.*

xlix. Gasparino, Charles. (January 7, 2008). "Bear Stearns Chief James Cayne to Step Down." CNBC.

l. Reuters Staff. (March 17, 2008). "Chronology—A Dozen Key Dates in the Demise of Bear Stearns."

li. Kelly, Kate. (May 9, 2009). "Inside the Fall of Bear Stearns." *The Wall Street Journal.*

lii. Lauricella, Tom. (December 10, 2008). "The Stock Picker's Defeat." *The Wall Street Journal.*

liii. Rynecki, David and Bill Miller. (September 15, 2003). "How to Profit from Falling Prices." *Fortune Magazine.*

liv. Lauricella, Tom. (December 10, 2008). "The Stock Picker's Defeat." *The Wall Street Journal.*

lv. Ryback, William. "Case Study on Bear Stearns." Toronto Centre. p. 13.

lvi. Hagerty, James R., Ruth Simon, and Damian Paletta. (September 8, 2008). "U.S. Seizes Mortgage Giants." *Wall Street Journal.*

lvii. Rusli, Evelyn. (September 15, 2008). "The Universal Appeal of BofA." *Forbes.*

lviii. "Washington Mutual, Inc. Files Chapter 11 Case" (September 26, 2008). (Press release). Washington Mutual, Inc. Retrieved 09-27-2008—via Business Wire.

lix. Enrich, David and Dan Fitzpatrick. (October 4, 2008). "Wachovia Chooses Wells Fargo, Spurns Citi." *Wall Street Journal.*

lx. Lauricella, Tom. (December 10, 2008). "The Stock Picker's Defeat." *The Wall Street Journal.*

lxi. Leong, Richard and Ross Kerber. (August 11, 2016). "Legg Mason's Bill Miller leaves firm amid faded glory." *Reuters.*

lxii. McLemore, Samantha. (September 25, 2015). "A Look at Bill's Record." White Paper. https://millervalue.com/a-look-at-bills-record/.

lxiii. 2019 Miller Value Partners, LLC.

lxiv. Federal Reserve. (May 21, 2008). Minutes.

lxv. Editor. (January 27, 2006). "Bill Miller's Secrets to Success." Gurufocus .com.

lxvi. Johnson, Eric J., Suzzane Shu, Benedict G.C. Dellaert, Craig R. Fox, Daniel G. Goldstein, Gerald Haeubl, Richard P. Larrick, John W. Payne, Ellen Peters, David Schkade, Brian Wansink, and Elke U. Weber. (June 11, 2013). Beyond Nudges: Tools of a Choice Architecture. (2012). Marketing Letters. Vol. 23: pp. 487–504. University of Alberta School of Business Research Paper No. 2013-739; Columbia Business School Research Paper No. 13-61. Available at SSRN: https://ssrn.com/abstract=2277968.

lxvii. Madrian, Brigitte C. and Dennis F. Shea. (November 4, 2001). "The Power of Suggestion: Inertia In 401(k) Participation and Savings Behavior." *Quarterly Journal of Economics.* Vol. 116. pp. 1149–1187.

lxviii. PENSION PROTECTION ACT OF 2006. 109th Congress Public Law 280. From the U.S. Government Printing Office. DOCID: f:publ280.109.

lxix. Deloitte Consulting LLP's Annual 401(k) Benchmarking Survey 2005/2006 Edition, Exhibit 15.

lxx. 2018 Defined Contribution Trends Survey. Callan Institute. p. 2.

lxxi. ———. Callan Institute. p. 24.

lxxii. Johnson, E.J. and D.G. Goldstein. (2003). "Do defaults save lives?" *Science.* 302. pp. 1338–1339.

lxxiii. Fox, C.R., R.K. Ratner, and D. Lieb. (2005). "How subjective grouping of options influences choice and allocation: Diversification bias and the phenomenon of partition dependence." *Journal of Experimental Psychology.* General, 134. pp. 538–551.

lxxiv. Thorndike, Anne, Jason, M. Riis, Lillian M. Sonnenberg, and Douglas Levy. (2014). Traffic-Light Labels and Choice Architecture Promoting Healthy Food Choices. *American Journal of Preventive Medicine.* 46. pp. 143–9. 10.1016/j.amepre.2013.10.002.

lxxv. Soll, Jack, Ralph Keeney, and Richard Larrick. (2011). Consumer Misunderstanding of Credit Card Use, Payments, and Debt: Causes and Solutions. *Journal of Public Policy & Marketing.* 32. 10.1509/jppm.11.061.

lxxvi. Kahneman, Daniel, Dan Lovallo, and Olivier Sibony. (June 2011). "Before you make that big decision." *Harvard Business Review.* Vol. 89(6). pp. 50–60.

lxxvii. Charles Schwab. Schwab Center for Financial Research. (2017). www.julyservices.com.

lxxviii. Buffett, Warren. 2004 Annual Shareholder Letter.

lxxix. Barber, Brad and Terrance Odean. (April 2000). "Trading Is Hazardous to Your Wealth: The Common Stock Investment Performance of Individual Investors." *The Journal of Finance.* Vol. LV, No. 2.

lxxx. Wermers, Russ. (August 2000). "Mutual Fund Performance: An Empirical Decomposition into Stock-Picking Talent, Style, Transactions Costs, and Expenses." *Journal of Finance.* Vol. 55, No. 4. pp. 1655–1703.

lxxxi. Fama, Eugene and Kenneth French. (October 2010). "Luck versus Skill in the Cross-Section of Mutual Fund Returns." *Journal of Finance.* Vol. 65, No. 5.

INDEX

Note: Page numbers followed by a "t" indicate tables and "n" indicates the entry is in a footnote on that page.